Creating The Future You

BRAD GARNER
Indiana Wesleyan University

CATHERINE A. SANDERSON
Amherst College

WILEY

Copyright © 2025 by John Wiley & Sons. All rights reserved, including rights for text and data mining and training of artificial intelligence technologies or similar technologies.

Published by John Wiley & Sons, Inc., Hoboken, New Jersey.

Published simultaneously in Canada.

No part of this publication may be reproduced, stored in a retrieval system, or transmitted in any form or by any means, electronic, mechanical, photocopying, recording, scanning, or otherwise, except as permitted under Section 107 or 108 of the 1976 United States Copyright Act, without either the prior written permission of the Publisher, or authorization through payment of the appropriate per-copy fee to the Copyright Clearance Center, Inc., 222 Rosewood Drive, Danvers, MA 01923, (978) 750-8400, fax (978) 750-4470, or on the web at www.copyright.com. Requests to the Publisher for permission should be addressed to the Permissions Department, John Wiley & Sons, Inc., 111 River Street, Hoboken, NJ 07030, (201) 748-6011, fax (201) 748-6008, or online at http://www.wiley.com/go/permission.

The manufacturer's authorized representative according to the EU General Product Safety Regulation is Wiley-VCH GmbH, Boschstr. 12, 69469 Weinheim, Germany, e-mail: Product_Safety@wiley.com.

Trademarks: Wiley and the Wiley logo are trademarks or registered trademarks of John Wiley & Sons, Inc. and/or its affiliates in the United States and other countries and may not be used without written permission. All other trademarks are the property of their respective owners. John Wiley & Sons, Inc. is not associated with any product or vendor mentioned in this book.

Limit of Liability/Disclaimer of Warranty: While the publisher and author have used their best efforts in preparing this book, they make no representations or warranties with respect to the accuracy or completeness of the contents of this book and specifically disclaim any implied warranties of merchantability or fitness for a particular purpose. No warranty may be created or extended by sales representatives or written sales materials. The advice and strategies contained herein may not be suitable for your situation. You should consult with a professional where appropriate. Further, readers should be aware that websites listed in this work may have changed or disappeared between when this work was written and when it is read. Neither the publisher nor authors shall be liable for any loss of profit or any other commercial damages, including but not limited to special, incidental, consequential, or other damages.

For general information on our other products and services or for technical support, please contact our Customer Care Department within the United States at (800) 762-2974, outside the United States at (317) 572-3993 or fax (317) 572-4002.

Wiley also publishes its books in a variety of electronic formats. Some content that appears in print may not be available in electronic formats. For more information about Wiley products, visit our web site at www.wiley.com.

Library of Congress Cataloging-in-Publication Data

Names: Garner, Brad, author. | Sanderson, Catherine Ashley, 1968- author.
Title: Creating the future you / Brad Garner, Catherine A. Sanderson.
Description: Hoboken, New Jersey : Wiley, [2025] | Includes bibliographical references and index.
Identifiers: LCCN 2024034933 (print) | LCCN 2024034934 (ebook) |
  ISBN 9781119899198 (paperback) | ISBN 9781119899136 (adobe pdf) |
  ISBN 9781119899112 (epub)
Subjects: LCSH: College freshmen. | College student orientation.
Classification: LCC LB14.7 .G384 2025 (print) | LCC LB14.7 (ebook) | DDC
  378.1/98--dc23/eng/20240821
LC record available at https://lccn.loc.gov/2024034933
LC ebook record available at https://lccn.loc.gov/2024034934

Cover image: © Lightspring/Shutterstock
Cover design: Wiley

SKY10098933_030425

Dedicated to today's college students. Our hopes for you include enriched lives, encouraging and rewarding relationships, and the inspiration to pursue and accomplish big dreams.

Brief Contents

ABOUT THE AUTHORS ix
PREFACE x
ACKNOWLEDGMENTS xii

PART 1 Envision: Knowing the Destination 1
  1 Keys to Success: Meaning and Motivation 3
  2 Plan for Success! 23

INFOGRAPHICS
  Time Management
  Reading
  Note Taking
  Studying Well

PART 2 Pursue: Getting the Most from Yourself 51
  3 Take Care of Your Body 53
  4 Build and Maintain Relationships 81
  5 Learn Your Way 103
  6 The Power of Emotional Intelligence 125
  7 Engage with Digital Technology 147

INFOGRAPHICS
  Test Taking
  Writing
  Presentations
  Financial Wellness

PART 3 Persist: Rising Above the Challenges 173
  8 Take Advantage of Every Opportunity 175
  9 Embrace Diversity, Equity, and Inclusion 193
  10 Find Your Happiness 227

REFERENCES R-1
SUBJECT INDEX SI-1

Contents

ABOUT THE AUTHORS   ix
PREFACE   x
ACKNOWLEDGMENTS   xii

PART 1   Envision: Knowing the Destination   1

1   Keys to Success: Meaning and Motivation   3

Envision, Pursue, and Persist: Ang Lee   4
Module 1.1   Exploring Our Meaning in Life   4
   What Is a Good Life?   4
   Perspectives on Life's Meaning   5
Module 1.2   Ikigai: A Way to Visualize Meaning in Life   7
   The Elements of Ikigai   7
   Ikigai and the Future You   8
Module 1.3   Motivation: Leveraging Belief and Desire   11
   Self-Efficacy: Believing in Yourself   11
   A Desire to Achieve   14
Module 1.4   Focus and Balance   16
   Where Do You Focus?   16
   Seeking Balance   18
Think Ahead: Career and Lifelong Applications   19
Take Some Action: Here and Now   20
Chapter Summary   21
Key Terms   21
Resources   22
References   22

2   Plan for Success!   23

Envision, Pursue, and Persist: Ingvar Kamprad   24
Module 2.1   The Unique Nature of Your Story   24
   Where You've Come From   24
   Where You're Going   24
Module 2.2   Navigating Higher Education   27
   Colleges and Universities   27
   Pathways to a Degree: Degree Requirements   28
   College Credits and Grade Point Average (GPA)   31
Module 2.3   Getting from Here to There with Help Along the Way   37
   Material Resources   37
   Academic Resources   38
   Well-Being Resources   40
Module 2.4   The Devil Is in the Details   43
   This Is Not 13th Grade   43
   Setting Yourself Up for Success   44
Think Ahead: Career and Lifelong Applications   46
Take Some Action: Here and Now   47
Chapter Summary   48
Key Terms   48
Resources   49
References   49

INFOGRAPHICS
Time Management
Reading
Note Taking
Studying Well

PART 2   Pursue: Getting the Most from Yourself   51

3   Take Care of Your Body   53

Envision, Pursue, and Persist: LeBron James   54
Module 3.1   Defining Healthy Behaviors   54
   Fuel Your Body   54
   Exercise Regularly   59
   Get Enough Sleep   60
Module 3.2   Avoiding Substance Abuse   63
   Alcohol and Other Substances   63
   Drug Addiction and Its Prevention and Treatment   68
Module 3.3   Managing Healthy Sexual Behavior   71
   Choosing Abstinence   71
   Preventing Unwanted Pregnancy   71
   Avoiding Sexually Transmitted Infections   72
   Understanding Sexual Assault   74
Think Ahead: Career and Lifelong Applications   76
Take Some Action: Here and Now   77
Chapter Summary   78
Key Terms   79
Resources   79
References   79

CONTENTS

4 Build and Maintain Relationships 81

Envision, Pursue, and Persist: Ruth Bader Ginsburg 82
Module 4.1 Building and Maintaining Connections 82
- Managing Different Relationships 82
- Building New Relationships 85

Module 4.2 Communicating Well 87
- Types of Communication 88
- Common Problems in Communication 89
- Strategies for Effective Communication 90

Module 4.3 Managing Conflict 93
- Common Causes of Conflict 93
- Benefits of Conflict 94
- Skills for Resolving Conflicts 96

Think Ahead: Career and Lifelong Applications 98
Take Some Action: Here and Now 100
Chapter Summary 100
Key Terms 101
Resources 101
References 101

5 Learn Your Way 103

Envision, Pursue, and Persist: Amy Cuddy 104
Module 5.1 Understanding Learning 104
- Models of Learning 104
- Learning Styles 106
- Using Learning Styles to Maximize Success 111

Module 5.2 Defining Multiple Intelligences 112
- Types of Intelligence 113
- Evaluating Multiple Intelligences 116

Module 5.3 Understanding Mindset 116
- Types of Mindsets 117
- Mindset Matters 118
- Changing Your Mindset 120

Think Ahead: Career and Lifelong Applications 121
Take Some Action: Here and Now 123
Chapter Summary 123
Key Terms 124
Resources 124
References 124

6 The Power of Emotional Intelligence 125

Envision, Pursue, and Persist: Oprah Winfrey 126
Module 6.1 Understanding Emotional Intelligence 126
- Components of Emotional Intelligence 126
- The Role of Empathy 128
- Strategies for Increasing Emotional Intelligence 130

Module 6.2 Understanding Grit 131
- Components of Grit 132
- How Grit Predicts Success 133
- Strategies for Increasing Grit 134

Module 6.3 Understanding Resilience 136
- The Value of Resilience 136
- The Upside of Adversity 137
- Strategies for Building Resilience 138

Think Ahead: Career and Lifelong Applications 143
Take Some Action: Here and Now 144
Chapter Summary 144
Key Terms 145
Resources 145
References 145

7 Engage with Digital Technology 147

Envision, Pursue, and Persist: Paul Otlet 148
Module 7.1 Living in a Digital World 149
- Technology: Love It or Leave It? 149
- Bridging the Digital Divide 152

Module 7.2 Technology in Higher Education 154
- Campus- and Course-Based Resources 154
- Evaluating Digital Content in an Information-Rich Environment 157

Module 7.3 Leaving a Credible Digital Footprint 164
- Long-Term Impact 164
- Safety and Security 165
- Your Image on Social Media 165

Think Ahead: Career and Lifelong Applications 167
Take Some Action: Here and Now 169
Chapter Summary 169
Key Terms 170
Resources 170
References 171

INFOGRAPHICS
Test Taking
Writing
Presentations
Financial Wellness

PART 3 Persist: Rising Above the Challenges 173

8 Take Advantage of Every Opportunity 175

Envision, Pursue, and Persist: Curtis Jackson/50 Cent 176
Module 8.1 Looking to the Future 176
- The Nature of Employment in the 21st Century 177

What Do Graduate Schools Look for from College Graduates? **179**

Module 8.2 **Opportunities to Build Your Skills and Employability Quotient** **179**
    Activities On and Off Campus **179**
    Find a Mentor **182**
    Engage with Faculty in Research **185**

Module 8.3 **Opportunities to Market Your Skills** **185**
    Use Your LinkedIn Profile as a Networking Tool **187**
    Keep Updating Your Résumé **188**

Think Ahead: Career and Lifelong Applications **190**
Take Some Action: Here and Now **191**
Chapter Summary **191**
Key Terms **191**
Resources **192**
References **192**

9 Embrace Diversity, Equity, and Inclusion **193**

Envision, Pursue, and Persist: Sarah McBride **194**

Module 9.1 **Our Multiple Identities: The Many Ways That We Are Different** **195**
    Ability **196**
    Age **199**
    Ethnicity **201**
    Gender **202**
    Race **204**
    Religion **205**
    Sexual Orientation **207**
    Socioeconomic Status **209**

Module 9.2 **The Types and Impacts of Identities** **211**
    Privileged Identities **212**
    Targeted Identities **213**

Module 9.3 **Diversity As a Weapon and a Tool** **215**
    Diversity As a Weapon **215**
    Diversity As a Tool **219**

Think Ahead: Career and Lifelong Applications **222**
Take Some Action: Here and Now **223**
Chapter Summary **224**
Key Terms **224**
Resources **225**
References **225**

10 Find Your Happiness **227**

Envision, Pursue, and Persist: Tony Hsieh **228**

Module 10.1 **Predicting Happiness** **228**
    Benefits of Happiness **228**
    Understanding Happiness **229**
    Myths about Happiness **231**

Module 10.2 **Understanding Stress** **233**
    Sources and Types of Stress **233**
    Effects of Stress **234**
    Strategies for Managing Stress **237**

Module 10.3 **Increasing Happiness** **241**
    Change Your Thoughts **242**
    Change Your Behavior **245**

Think Ahead: Career and Lifelong Applications **246**
Take Some Action: Here and Now **248**
Chapter Summary **248**
Key Terms **249**
Resources **249**
References **249**

REFERENCES **R-1**
SUBJECT INDEX **SI-1**

About the Authors

BRAD GARNER serves as Digital Learning Scholar in Residence on the Academic Innovation Team at Indiana Wesleyan University. Brad has been actively involved for several years in directing and teaching the first-year seminar on his campus. Prior to moving into higher education, his career was focused on program and faculty development in K–12 public school settings where he worked as a classroom teacher, school psychologist, and administrator.

Garner is a frequent presenter at global conferences and campus-based workshops. He has authored several publications, including *Teaching in the First-Year Seminar* (2012), *Creating Digital Citizens* (2017), *Digital Content Curation* (2019), and *Inclusive Hospitality in Online Learning* (2023). Garner also writes an electronic newsletter, *The Toolbox*, for the National Resource Center for the First-Year Experience and Students in Transition at the University of South Carolina.

In the past, Garner worked with groups of teachers and parents in Bosnia as part of an Educational Leadership Institute designed to empower them to be change agents in their own communities and schools. For the past fifteen years, he has done volunteer teaching at Indiana's largest maximum-security prison, and he currently leads an IWU initiative to offer college credit courses in Indiana prisons. He also serves as the cohost for the *Digital2Learn* podcast.

Photo by Jo Chattman

CATHERINE A. SANDERSON is the Poler Family Professor of Psychology at Amherst College. She received a bachelor's degree in psychology, with a specialization in health and development, from Stanford University, and received master's and doctoral degrees in psychology from Princeton University.

Her research has received grant funding from the National Science Foundation and the National Institute of Health. Professor Sanderson has published over twenty-five journal articles and four college textbooks, including *Psychology in Action, Real World Psychology,* and *Psychological Science,* which she coauthors with Karen R. Huffman. She has also published two trade books, *The Positive Shift: Mastering Mindset to Improve Happiness, Health, and Longevity* and *Why We Act: Turning Bystanders into Moral Rebels.*

Professor Sanderson regularly speaks for public and corporate audiences on topics like the science of happiness, the power of emotional intelligence, the art of aging well, and the psychology of courage and inaction. These talks have been featured in numerous mainstream media outlets, including the *Washington Post*, the *Boston Globe*, *USA Today*, *The Atlantic*, CNN, and *CBS Sunday Morning with Jane Pauley*. Catherine's work on integrating DEI into the Introduction to Psychology course has been presented at national conferences and featured in the APA's Introductory Psychology Initiative Course Design Institute.

In 2012, she was named one of the country's top 300 professors by the *Princeton Review*.

Preface

Every student's journey through college is a unique and personal experience. They have chosen to attend the same institution as peers who come to that institution from a variety of geographic locations and socioeconomic backgrounds, varied perspectives on social issues, and differing levels of academic ability, each with their own set of hopes and dreams for the future.

In the transition from secondary to higher education, students tend to focus on themselves and their need to know more about who they are and where they are headed. This can be true even of students starting college after having graduated from high school several years earlier. *Creating The Future You* acknowledges that experience, along with its challenges and opportunities. The program gives first-year college students an engaging, appealing, and encouraging introduction to higher education with a focus on mindset and taking ownership of their college experience, and it provides them tools to help them succeed in college and beyond.

The topics selected and the manner in which they are examined continually take students from their current or prospective role as students to the options they will have upon graduation and entry into the job market:

- Identifying their passions
- Planning for success
- Taking care of themselves
- Building and maintaining relationships
- Understanding the power of emotional intelligence
- Learning their way
- Engaging with digital technology
- Taking advantage of available opportunities
- Embracing diversity
- Finding their happiness

Engaging students in learning and conversations about these issues greatly increases their opportunities for success. *Creating The Future You* provides a format for students to gain information on each topic, assess their own levels of performance, and engage in meaningful conversations with each other, with their professors and other members of their campus community, and with other important figures in their lives. We underscore the reality that adopting the right mindset, doing well in their courses, and establishing solid personal habits are key elements in students' success through and after college. This theme is more than just a chapter on "career development"; it is a continuous theme of students' lives, the college experience, and the goal of "creating the future you."

It is worth noting that this text also helps students consider the path of their lives after graduation. Although success in college is of utmost importance, students will eventually be leaving that world to get on with the rest of their lives. *Creating The Future You* helps students bridge the gap between what they are learning and experiencing in college and the knowledge, skills, and dispositions that will contribute to their success in life.

Our student-centric approach fosters success through a concise, highly personalized, and multimedia format with abundant opportunities for self-assessment, personal reflection, discussion, and taking action. After beginning with the profile of an individual who embodies our subtitle—*Envision, Pursue, Persist,* each of the ten short chapters blends reading, video content, and interactive learning activities, and while *Creating The Future You* includes quizzes and test questions, every chapter compels students to demonstrate progress and mastery through engagement that goes far beyond traditional quizzing and testing.

In addition to being more concise than many titles available for the college success or first-year experience course, *Creating The Future You* uses lively Infographics, complemented by video content and practical activities, to present information and invite conversation on some of the basic skills that contribute to success in college (i.e., reading, writing, time management, note taking, study skills, test taking, making presentations, financial wellness) but whose coverage students—and instructors—often find less than engaging in traditional textbooks.

Features

Readings and video presentations are just the beginning from which students then personalize their experience through engagement with interactive self-assessments and personal reflection activities and commit to action steps in identified areas of concern (e.g., mindset, diversity, relationships, technology). Program features include the following:

- **Modular Organization:** Each chapter is presented in a series of modules, each with a terminal learning objective, and within each module, every major section heading corresponds to an enabling learning objective. This modular organization is intended, in part, to accommodate college success or first-year experience courses that integrate a text with locally developed campus-specific content.

- **Self-Assessments:** *Test Yourself* self-assessments throughout each chapter are adapted from vetted, third-party sources to help students evaluate their current thinking, behaviors, and skills related to a topic of discussion within a chapter module. Each provides students with guidance on how to interpret their results.

- **Personal Reflections:** *Think Deeper* activities use specific questions to prompt students to apply what they have learned in the chapter reading in journal-type commentary on current practices and future directions in their own, unique endeavor to create their future selves.
- **Interactive Tools for Practical Application:** *Make It Personal* activities provide students with simple frameworks for personally applying what they are learning in practical and concrete ways.
- **Discussion Prompts:** Following each major chapter section, these are set up with the flexibility to be real-time in the classroom or asynchronous in an online environment.
- **Career and Lifelong Applications:** One important way to build relevance into course-based readings and learning experiences is to make frequent and ongoing references to how this content applies to the college experience *and beyond*, culminating in each chapter's ***Think Ahead: Career and Lifelong Applications*** feature. Following a brief, illustrated reading about post-college applications, a video-driven *What Would You Do?* activity asks students to put what they have learned in the chapter to use in sharing advice with a recent college graduate seeking help with an everyday or workplace situation. Chapter 1 introduces readers to the diverse cast of characters from whom they will hear throughout the text.
- **Action Steps and Responsibility Taking:** Knowing what to do is the first step; making the commitment to pursue specific courses of action is quite another. Each chapter's ***Take Some Action: Here and Now*** feature provides a framework for students' commitment to determined courses of action after reflecting on their personal outcomes from the chapter's *Test Yourself, Make It Personal,* and *Think Deeper* activities.
- **References and Resources:** At the end of each chapter, students will find references for articles and other sources the chapter draws upon as well as links to additional online resources.

Among resources provided for instructors are an *Instructor's Manual* with chapter outlines, lecture notes, suggestions for in-class activities and curated web links; *Lecture Presentation* slides that are easily customizable; and a *Test Bank* in formats suited for pen-and-paper use or for easy deployment in popular learning-management systems.

An Interactive, Multimedia Learning Experience

This textbook includes access to an interactive, multimedia e-text. Icons throughout the print book signal corresponding digital content in the e-text.

Video: A variety of appealing video content complements the text to engage students more deeply with the reading and topics explored, and the wide range of people and perspectives reflected in the video content helps *all* students develop a sense of belonging and appreciation of diversity.

- **Video introductions:** Presented by Catherine Sanderson and produced by Brad Garner, these videos provide a lively introduction to the chapter's main topics and questions.
- **Reading Companion Videos:** Each of these short videos introduces a specific topic, corresponding to one of a module's enabling learning objectives, drawing students into the reading, self-assessments, and personal reflections. Each of the text's eight infographics on essential skills also comes to life in a dynamic video presentation.
- **What Would You Do? Videos:** In these short videos, members of a diverse cast of characters, all fairly recent college graduates, share an everyday or workplace dilemma and ask readers' advice on how to handle the situation.

Interactive Self-Assessments: Easy-to-use interactive versions of the abundant *Test Yourself* self-assessments tabulate students' results automatically, letting the student focus on the interpretation of those results or download a copy of the self-assessment for pen-and-paper use.

Download Documents & Templates: The text's many *Think Deeper* question sets for self-reflection and *Make It Personal* frameworks for personal application are downloadable from the e-text, facilitating students' keeping a personal companion file to review in the chapter's culminating *Take Some Action: Here and Now* activity.

Interactive Figures, Charts, & Tables: Interactive figures and tables throughout the text engage students and facilitate study. Even some of the simplest figures are interactive, encouraging online readers to stop and absorb the information they contain before scrolling on through the reading.

Interactive Self-Scoring Quizzes: Appearing with each module's *Review, Discuss, and Apply* questions in the e-text, students will find a short self-scoring review quiz, and a self-scoring *Practice Quiz* appears with each chapter's *Summary*.

Many programs traditionally available for the first-year seminar or college success course focus on the institution of higher education and the behaviors students must demonstrate to navigate their way through it successfully. *Creating The Future You* focuses, instead, on students envisioning their future, developing the mindset to pursue that future, and owning and leveraging their college experience in their persistence toward achieving it.

Acknowledgments

We and our colleagues at Wiley are deeply indebted to the many of you who reviewed early samples of *Creating The Future You* and provided invaluable feedback. We also are indebted to many others whose interest and engagement in sessions presented at events like the FYE and Students in Transition conferences have fueled our dedication to bringing this book forward. Our sincerest thanks go to the following:

Nicole Albert, *South Dakota State University*
Hanna Andrews, *University of Nevada, Las Vegas*
Tricia Armstrong, *Valparaiso University*
Galina Bennett, *Jackson State University*
Antoine Carson, *Pellissippi State Community College*
Larissa Ciuca, *University of Pittsburgh*
Sandy Collazos De Kijanka, *University of Nevada, Las Vegas*
Kindra Conley, *Mott Community College*
Demetra Dantzler, *Delgado Community College*
Amy Davis, *Pima Community College*
Trakenya Dobbins, *University of Arkansas at Little Rock*
Michael Donnelly, *Lone Star College*
Kyle Ellis, *University of Mississippi*
Heidi Ellis, *Western New England University*
Rebecca Faircloth, *Riverside City College*
Theresa Garren-Grubbs, *South Dakota State University*
Deborah Gilmore, *Temple College*
Amy Ginck, *Messiah University*
Kathy Hacker, *Maricopa Community Colleges*
Tyler C. Hanna, *Saginaw Valley State University*
Sheryl Hartman, *Miami Dade College*
Amy E. Humphrey, *Walters State Community College*
Rainie Ingram, *Weber State University*
LaQuinta L. Jackson, *Pellissippi State Community College*
Greg Jones, *Lone Star College*
Lois Kahl, *Suffolk Community College*
Jeffrey Kaplan, *University of Central Florida, Orlando*
Maureen Keller, *Ivy Tech Community College*
Danielle Kellum, *The University of Southern Mississippi*
Glenn Kepic, *University of Florida*
Stacy Kirch, *Orange Coast College*
Kade Kittley, *Amarillo College*
Sandra Lancaster, *KCTCS–Bluegrass Community and Technical College*

Thomas Largent, *Jackson College*
Nicole Lewis, *Houston Community College*
Holly Lincoln, *Jefferson College*
James Lohrey, *Shippensburg University*
Kerry Mcshane-Moley, *Cape Fear Community College*
Venetia Miller, *Jackson State University*
Aubrey Moncrieffe, *CT State Community College Housatonic*
Patti Morton Gibbs, *North Central Texas College*
Liz Moseley, *Cleveland State Community College*
Christine Murphy, *Colorado Mesa University*
Bryant Nall, *Houston Community College*
Bao-Chi Nguyen, *Mount San Antonio College*
Leslie E. Nichols, *KCTCS–Southeast Kentucky Community and Technical College*
David R. Peck, *Brigham Young University–Idaho*
Jennifer Perkins, *Central Piedmont Community College*
Sarah Pettus-Wakefield, *North Central Texas College*
Keith Proctor, *Brigham Young University*
Michele Pullen, *KCTCS–Jefferson Community and Technical College*
Melissa Quinby, *Bowdoin College*
Ashley Raburn, *Cleveland State Community College*
Marci Reiter, *Cleveland State Community College*
Keith Rocci, *Pima Community College*
Steven Rodriguez, *Northwest Vista College*
James Rubin, *Paradise Valley Community College*
Felicia Russell, *Jackson State University*
Linda Slomin, *Rowan College of South Jersey*
Brynn Smith, *Evergreen State College*
Lamonte Stamps, *University of San Francisco*
Anglea M. Swim, *KCTCS–Somerset Community College*
Avery D. Swinson, *Walters State Community College*
Kim Toby, *KCTCS–Somerset Community College*
Staci Tyler, *Weatherford College*
Jennifer Verive, *Western Nevada College*
Jared Vidal, *Orange Coast College*
Gina Wellman, *Post University*
Amber Whisenhunt, *Northeastern State University*
Fallon Willoughby, *KCTCS–Southcentral Kentucky Community and Technical College*
Mary Elizabeth Yancosek Gamble, *Fairmont State University*

PART 1

Envision
Knowing the Destination

What do you envision for the future as you begin your college career . . . and beyond? An essential part of attending college is sharpening your focus on what you want to be doing and accomplishing. That outcome does not arrive magically. It requires that you become keenly aware of who you are—gifts, talents, abilities, preferences, mindset, and the possibilities for the future, academic major, career, relationships, and personal priorities. Planning for the now and the then will require that you consistently reflect on who you are, what is happening now, and where you are heading. To accomplish these outcomes and to help you remain aware of your progress, we have included several features, including the *Test Yourself* self-assessments, *Think Deeper* personal reflections, and *Make It Personal* frameworks throughout the text. At the end of each chapter, you will be prompted to reflect on your results and responses in these features and commit to take action toward creating the future you.

1 Keys to Success: Meaning and Motivation   3

2 Plan for Success!   23

INFOGRAPHICS

Time Management

Reading

Note Taking

Studying Well

CHAPTER 1

Keys to Success: Meaning and Motivation

Author's Introduction

"Whatever we are, whatever we make of ourselves, is all we will ever have—and that, in its profound simplicity, is the meaning of life."

—Philip Appleman, American poet

CHAPTER OUTLINE	LEARNING OBJECTIVES
Envision, Pursue, and Persist: Ang Lee	
Module 1.1 Exploring Our Meaning in Life What Is a Good Life? Perspectives on Life's Meaning *Think Deeper: What Is Your Pattern of Thinking?* *Test Yourself: What Is Meaning in Life to You?* *Think Deeper: Your Meaning in Life*	**LO 1.1** To articulate the varied perspectives on the meaning of life
Module 1.2 Ikigai: A Way to Visualize Meaning in Life The Elements of Ikigai Ikigai and the Future You *Think Deeper: Ikigai* *Make It Personal: Alignments with Your Major*	**LO 1.2** To describe and apply the elements of ikigai, including mission, passion, vocation, and profession
Module 1.3 Motivation: Leveraging Belief and Desire Self-Efficacy: Believing in Yourself *Test Yourself: What Is Your Level of Self-Efficacy?* *Think Deeper: Self-Efficacy: How Are You Doing?* A Desire to Achieve *Think Deeper: Where Do You Look for Encouragement?* *Make It Personal: What Moves You Forward?*	**LO 1.3** To examine the influence of self-efficacy and motivation on personal performance
Module 1.4 Focus and Balance Where Do You Focus? *Test Yourself: Past, Present, Future: Where Do You Focus?* *Think Deeper: Focus* Seeking a Balance *Think Deeper: Résumé and Eulogy Virtues*	**LO 1.4** To reflect on where you focus your energy—the past, the present, or the future—and how you find a sense of balance
Think Ahead: Career and Lifelong Applications	
Take Some Action: Here and Now	
Chapter Summary Key Terms Resources References	

3

Envision, Pursue, and Persist | Ang Lee

Ang Lee was born in a village in Taiwan. His parents emphasized the importance of receiving a good education, and his father was the principal of Lee's high school. Lee failed the Joint University Entrance Examination twice and was forced to enter a three-year program at the National Taiwan University of Arts, studying drama and the arts. Lee reported that seeing the Ingmar Bergan film *The Virgin Spring* was a significant turning point in his life.

After completing his mandatory military service in China, he moved to the United States and enrolled at the University of Illinois, where he received a degree in theater. He then enrolled at the Tisch School of the Arts at New York University and completed a master's degree in film production. While in graduate school, Ang Lee won awards for his abilities as a film director.

After graduation, Lee had difficulty getting a start in the movie business. He was unemployed for six years and stayed at home as a full-time house husband. This was a difficult time for Lee, but he continued to foster his dream of directing motion pictures. Lee was invited to return to Taiwan, and there he gained significant experience directing the film *Eat Drink Man Woman*. Ang Lee's award-winning direction provided him many new opportunities.

Over his career, Lee directed several films that received Academy Award nominations and wins, including *The Wedding Banquet; Sense and Sensibility; Crouching Tiger, Hidden Dragon;* and *The Life of Pi*. In total, Lee's films have received thirty-eight Academy Award nominations (with twelve wins), forty-eight British Academy Film Award nominations (with fourteen wins), and twenty-three Golden Globe Award nominations (with nine wins).

Ang Lee discovered his passion in life and continuously worked to improve his skills and proficiency as a director. Even during challenging periods when he could not find work in the film industry, he persisted in developing ideas and concepts that were later incorporated into his films.

Module 1.1 | Exploring Our Meaning in Life

LO 1.1.1 To reflect on what constitutes a "good life"

LO 1.1.2 To identify personal practices related to a cognitive, motivational, or affective approach to define meaning in life

---

Think of people you know who you would describe as having lived a "good life". What types of criteria might be used to make those selections? Could a good life be based on specific accomplishments, the nature of your relationship with that person, or their consistently good life choices and demonstrations of good character? Or are there other things you might consider? Second, what would those people say about themselves or the idea that you think of them as people who demonstrate a high-quality life?

What Is a Good Life?

The dimensions of what constitutes a good life have been part of an ongoing discussion by philosophers, psychologists, sociologists, and theologians for the past 2,000 years. Those conversations have often been centered around a series of questions:

- Why am I here?
- What is the purpose of my life?
- What should I be accomplishing in the time that I have available?
- Am I making good choices?
- What is meaningful and valuable in life?

Our search for answers to these questions often continues across the entire span of our lives. It is interesting and intellectually challenging, yes, but usually not that helpful, as we often infuse meaning into the choices that we make and the goals that we pursue. Positive psychologist Michael Steger and his colleagues have suggested that there is a significant difference between discussions about the meaning *of* life as opposed to meaning *in* life. They argue that the **meaning of life** tends to focus on larger, more abstract questions like those listed above. Contrast that, however, with **meaning in life**. This phrase is more personal and relates to how each of us experiences and defines the purpose of what we do each day and what we hope to accomplish throughout our lives. We all want to feel and believe that our lives count for something. That "something" could be measured in accomplishments, our influence in the lives of others, the nature of our relationships, and countless other personal ways. Ultimately, we each have an opportunity to shape and define the dimensions of meaning in our lives.

Perspectives on Life's Meaning

 VIDEO CONTENT

In researching this topic, Steger and his colleagues have also proposed that there are three primary lenses through which each of us might examine the role of meaning in our lives:

1. **A cognitive perspective**—A process through which we try to analyze and make sense of our lives. Beyond the trivial or momentary times of challenge, we might ask, "How am I doing overall?" In a sense, we are taking an inventory of what we do every day and the level at which these activities contribute to the big picture of what we have defined as meaningful. This is a valuable process as it provides a kind of accountability check on how we achieve the goals we have set for ourselves.

2. **A motivational perspective**—This involves the degree to which we pursue and achieve worthwhile goals by asking, "What are the internal and external factors that are spurring me forward to accomplish those things that are important to me?" In other words, "What gets me going and keeps me pursuing the things that I think are most important?" (We will examine the role of motivation later in this chapter.)

3. **An affective perspective**—This vantage point focuses on our sense (or lack) of satisfaction and fulfillment in life by asking, "How do the overall events of my life make me feel?" All of us, of course, experience ongoing ups and downs throughout our lives. This feature is more related to our overall feelings about the path and focus of what we are doing and where we are going (e.g., satisfaction, fulfillment, enjoyment).

Think Deeper | What is Your Pattern of Thinking?

When you think about the future, do you do the following?

- Inventory what you do daily and how those actions contribute to your goals (cognitive).
- Reflect on what it will take to be motivated enough to accomplish your goals (motivational).
- Think about how you feel about your progress toward achieving your goals (affective).
- Use a combination of these approaches.

 DOWNLOAD DOCUMENTS & TEMPLATES

Being a college student requires a heavy commitment of time, energy, and financial resources. The goal is to graduate, but you are likely to have specific goals, outcomes, and dreams you wish to pursue and achieve. These could include a career in your chosen field, a promotion at a current job, increased opportunities, and setting an example for family members, among others. Whatever these reasons may be, they are personal and essential to you. Steger and his colleagues created the Meaning in Life Questionnaire (MLQ) based on their research on life questions and their meaning. The questionnaire provides insights into two related areas:

1. The degree to which you might have already defined what you believe to be your meaning in life. This is your "presence" score or the current level of meaning in your life.
2. The degree to which you may be in the process of searching for your true meaning in life. This is your "search" score and it corresponds to the level at which you still search for meaning in life.

Test Yourself | What Is Meaning in Life to You?

Use this adaptation of the Meaning in Life Questionnaire by Steger and his colleagues to assess the extent to which you may have already defined your meaning in life and the extent to which you are still working on it. As you take the survey below, pay particular attention to the language used around defining meaning in life (e.g., mission, purpose, meaningful, significant, satisfying).

Respond to each of the following statements as truthfully and accurately as you can using the following scale:

Absolutely Untrue 1	Mostly Untrue 2	Somewhat Untrue 3	Can't Say True/False 4	Somewhat True 5	Mostly True 6	Absolutely True 7

Remember that these are very subjective questions and that there are no right or wrong answers!

1. I understand my life's meaning.
2. I am looking for something that makes my life feel meaningful.
3. I am always looking to find my life's purpose.
4. My life has a clear sense of purpose.
5. I have a good sense of what makes my life meaningful.
6. I have discovered a satisfying life purpose.
7. I am always searching for something that makes my life feel significant.
8. I am seeking a purpose or mission for my life.
9. My life has no clear purpose.
10. I am searching for meaning in my life.

Your *presence* score is determined by subtracting item 9 from item 8 and adding your ratings for items 1, 4, 5, and 6. Your *search* score is determined by adding your scores for items 2, 3, 7, 8, and 10.

Steger, M. F., Frazier, P., Oishi, S., & Kaler, M. (2006). The meaning in life questionnaire: Assessing the presence of and search for meaning in life. *Journal of Counseling Psychology, 53*, 80–93.

To interpret these results, Steger (2006) provided the following explanation:

If you scored above 24 on presence and above 24 on search, you feel your life has a valued meaning and purpose, yet you are still openly exploring that meaning or purpose. Life's meaning is an ever-unfolding and ever-deepening process for you. You are more drawn to the question, "What can my life mean?" than to any single answer.

If you scored above 24 on presence and below 24 on search, you feel your life has a valued meaning and purpose and you are not actively exploring that meaning or seeking meaning in your life. One might say that you are satisfied that you've grasped what makes your life meaningful, why you're here, and what you want to do with your life.

If you scored below 24 on presence and above 24 on search, you probably do not feel your life has a valued meaning and purpose, and you are actively searching for something or someone that will give your life meaning or purpose. You may feel lost in life, and this idea may cause you distress.

If you scored below 24 on presence and below 24 on search, you probably do not feel your life has a valued meaning and purpose and are not actively exploring or seeking meaning in your life. Overall, you probably don't find the idea of thinking about your life's meaning very interesting or important.

> **Think Deeper** | Your Meaning in Life
>
> Reflect on your results from the Meaning in Life Questionnaire by considering the following questions:
>
> 1. Are the results of this survey compatible with what you know about yourself? In other words, is the designation of "presence" or "search" descriptive of your current status in relation to meaning in life?
> 2. What steps could you take to strengthen or identify your meaning in life?
> 3. Who are the people in your life with whom you could have a conversation about the questionnaire and its results?

Review, Discuss, and Apply

Discussion Questions

1. Who are people you know who are living what you would define as a "good life"?
2. What characteristics of their lives lead you to choose them for this designation?
3. Looking forward, what criteria will you use to assess the overall quality of your life?

Module 1.2 | Ikigai: A Way to Visualize Meaning in Life

LO 1.2.1 To understand the elements of ikigai: passion, mission, profession, and vocation

LO 1.2.2 To reflect on ikigai from a personal perspective

As we have described, researchers and theorists have, for many years, worked tirelessly to create an understanding of meaning in life. Looking back in history, however, one of the more understandable and valuable ways of thinking about this topic comes from the eighth century in Japan, where the concept of **ikigai** (生き甲斐) was created. Ikigai combines two Japanese words that can be translated to mean "the thing that you live for" or "a reason to enjoy life." It is, in many ways, a state of mind that reflects a positive and happy approach to living. In the book *Ikigai: The Japanese Secret to a Long and Happy Life* (2017), Héctor García and Francesc Miralles observed: "Our ikigai is different for all of us, but one thing we have in common is that we are all searching for meaning."

The Elements of Ikigai

CNN reported that the island of Okinawa is often referred to as the "village of longevity" because residents there have the highest life expectancy rate in the world. This fact can be linked to several factors, but a common adherence to the principles of ikigai as a way of viewing one's passion, mission, profession, and vocation are included. The elements of ikigai, and their interrelationships, are illustrated in **Figure 1.1**.

FIGURE 1.1 The four overlapping circles of ikigai.

As you can see, ikigai includes four main aspects of our lives that interact with one another in various ways. These include the following:

1. Things you love to do
2. Things you can do that the world needs
3. Things for which you can be paid
4. Things you are good at doing

These four elements interact and help define several aspects of our lives, including mission, passion, profession, and vocation. The core of ikigai is the place where all of these elements intersect. The goal is to reach a place in our lives where we are doing things we love to do that meet a need of the world, for which we can be paid, and that we are good at doing. In the blog *Better Humans*, Melody Wilding made the following observations about the journey toward ikigai:

- **It's challenging.** Your *ikigai* should lead to mastery and growth.
- **It's your choice.** You feel a certain degree of autonomy and freedom in pursuing your *ikigai*.
- **It involves a commitment of time and belief**, perhaps to a particular cause, skill, trade, or group of people.
- **It boosts your well-being.** *Ikigai* is associated with positive relationships and good health. It gives you more energy than it takes away.

Ikigai and the Future You

As we examine the intersectional elements of ikigai in further detail, think about what defines—or how you want to define—*your* mission and passions and how your mission and passions align with the profession you envision for yourself.

Passion Ikigai conceptualizes **passion** as the intersection of the things that we love to do, which, coincidentally, we are also very good at doing. Examples of passion-related activities could include the following:

- Someone who enjoys and is skilled at sports and participates in various community recreation leagues
- Someone who loves to read and voraciously goes through one or two books per week
- An individual who is a skilled mechanic and spends weekends restoring an antique car

Passion is taking what you love to do and seeking places to engage in that activity. That will often also involve connecting with like-minded people who share your passions and interests.

When engaging in an activity that we love and are good at, we often lose track of time and block out everything around us because we are so involved. Psychologist Mihaly Csikszentmihalyi articulated these experiences as being in a state of **flow**. In his book *Flow: The Psychology of Optimal Experience*, he summarized the level at which we can pursue these experiences:

> **Contrary to what we usually believe, moments like these, the best moments in our lives, are not the passive, receptive, relaxing times—although such experiences can also be enjoyable, if we have worked hard to attain them. The best moments usually occur when a person's body or mind is stretched to its limits in a voluntary effort to accomplish something difficult and worthwhile. Optimal experience is thus something that we make happen. (p. 3)**

This description demonstrates that vision, and the state of flow, are things to be pursued, so they do not occur accidentally. They require intentional action. Hopefully, you can identify activities like these to include as regular events in your life schedule. Even now, while you are in college, you can intentionally find ways to seek out activities that you enjoy and are also good at. These activities often provide a break from the focus and energy needed to complete your assigned schoolwork.

Mission

According to ikigai, **mission** is evident in our lives when we are doing those things that we love while, at the same time, meeting a need of the world. The concept of a "need of the world" can include a variety of initiatives ranging from those in your local community to other countries and from mentoring an individual to leading an organization or initiative and many actions between and beyond these needs. The primary focus is on serving others. An old Chinese proverb captures the spirit of mission: "If you want happiness for an hour, take a nap. If you want happiness for a day, go fishing. If you want happiness for a year, inherit a fortune. If you want happiness for a lifetime, help somebody." Think about the things you love to do (outside of what you do for work) that may also serve others. Examples of mission-related activity could include the following:

- A man who loves to cook and volunteers to prepare meals at a local rescue mission
- A woman who enjoys singing and spends time at a nursing home sharing songs with the residents
- A parent who loves to spend time playing with children and provides babysitting for a single mom while she is at work

Proclaiming a personal mission, or even putting those words in writing as a mission statement, is one thing. Living out that mission, day by day, and taking on the inconvenient choice of meeting a need of the world is an entirely different matter. The exciting thing, however, is that if we genuinely do something we love (e.g., cooking, singing, playing with children) and meet a need of the world, it's a win-win!

As you think about your current academic program and the career you envision after you graduate, it is also worthwhile to consider how you might invest your skills and knowledge to benefit others.

Profession

According to ikigai, our **profession** is doing something we are good at and getting paid for it. This element of ikigai is a little different to think about. Hopefully, the career you choose will allow you to do what you are good at daily (and get paid for it). That's what we all hope and strive for. At the same time, we can all think of people we know who are miserable during the work week and dread the beginning of every work week. Some of the data follow:

- *Forbes* magazine reported in 2013 that work is a source of frustration for approximately 90 percent of the workforce.
- Gallup reports that 87 percent of employees are emotionally disconnected from their jobs.
- Just as important as either of these two statistics are the reasons people hate their jobs. Commonly stated reasons include dissatisfaction, complicated relationships, boredom, and bosses who do not appreciate their value. These reasons are mainly personal (i.e., how I feel about things and what I need) and interpersonal (i.e., how I get along with coworkers and supervisors).

Consider this caveat. What if you find a job where you get to do things that align with your knowledge and skills but you also are miserable every day? The reasons for being miserable could be a lack of challenge, limited opportunities for growth and advancement, or a supervisor who makes the workplace uncomfortable. Notice that we have not mentioned salary as a variable in this discussion about job dissatisfaction. There are certainly people who are underpaid for the work they do and find it challenging to earn what they need to survive. Concerning job satisfaction, however, although people often point to being underpaid as their primary complaint, their real concerns are more likely related to interpersonal relationships or the details of their work situation.

How do these factors relate to our conversation about profession? The answer is straightforward. We all spend a significant portion of our adult lives working. Estimates are that we will spend roughly 90,000 hours working throughout our lives. It is critically important, therefore, to find ways to secure employment that matches our unique skill sets (or the things we are good at) and a work environment that includes the other variables important to our well-being in the workplace. Now is an excellent time to begin thinking about the factors that you believe are most important in defining an optimal work environment. This list can serve as a tool for evaluating employment opportunities coming your way soon.

Vocation Finally, our vocation, as differentiated from our profession, consists of those things we do that can meet a need of the world and for which we are also being paid. This element requires some unpacking. Your first response may be, "The career I am considering doesn't fit into the category of meeting a need of the world." Typical vocations that we might think of in this category could include a teacher, nurse, pastor, or social worker. These, of course, would easily qualify as roles that meet a need of the world. As with our earlier conversation about the world's needs, however, it is essential to expand our thinking. Regardless of the career you choose, with a limited number of exceptions, you will interact with a wide variety of people daily, including coworkers, supervisors, and customers. Consider that all these people have needs, challenges, and concerns in their daily lives. Regardless of the role, career, or job description that you carry, you can play a role in supporting and encouraging others in your workplace. Even in the narrowest sense, that is meeting a need of the world.

Think Deeper | Ikigai

Perhaps you began thinking about ikigai concerning your future as you read about it. Was pinpointing a particular mission, passion, profession, or vocation difficult? The good news is that you don't have to! This exercise will help you identify various good possibilities.

As you look ahead, what are some possibilities for pursuing ikigai? Using a graphic like the one here, identify the following:

- What you love to do
- What the world needs
- What you are good at doing
- What you (could) get paid for doing

Now, fill in the intersections between the various pairs of elements to identify possible options for your passion, mission, profession, and vocation. Share and discuss your results with a friend when you have filled in the spaces in this diagram.

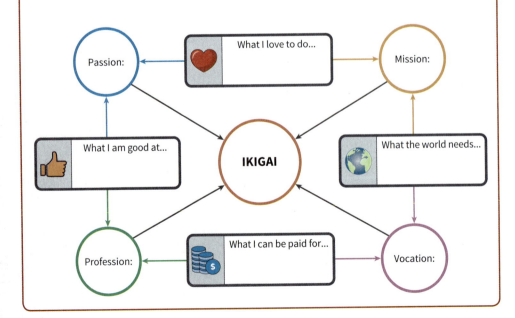

> **Make It Personal** | Alignments with Your Major
>
> Given the results of your ikigai, consider how your academic major relates to the components of this process.
>
> My academic major: _____
>
> How does this choice connect with each of the following?
>
> - What you love to do: _____
> - What the world needs: _____
> - What you are good at doing: _____
> - What you (could) get paid for doing: _____
>
> What conclusions have you drawn from this analysis?

Did you identify things you love to do or are very good at doing and for which you might be paid or meet a need in the world? Take a moment to celebrate that discovery!

Review, Discuss, and Apply — INTERACTIVE SELF-SCORING QUIZZES

Discussion Questions

1. When you think about your future and where you are headed, do you reflect more on pursuing a mission, a passion, a vocation, or a profession?
2. Which of these aspects of ikigai is most important to you?
    a. What you love to do
    b. What you are good at doing
    c. What you get paid for doing
    d. What the world needs

Module 1.3 Motivation: Leveraging Belief and Desire

LO 1.3.1 To reflect on the level at which you believe that you have the skills and abilities to accomplish your goals

LO 1.3.2 To identify evidence that you are motivated to succeed in college

How would you respond if asked whether you were motivated to succeed and do well in pursuit of your meaning in life? Knowing the destination is one (critically important) thing. However, traveling to your chosen destination and sustaining that effort are equally important endeavors. Let's look at some of the elements and thought processes that impact achieving those outcomes that contribute to our meaning in life. We will do this by examining two key elements: self-efficacy and motivation.

Self-Efficacy: Believing in Yourself

The origin of **self-efficacy** is attributed to psychologist Albert Bandura from Stanford University. As part of social learning theory, he defined self-efficacy as "how well one can execute courses of action required to deal with prospective situations." More basically, it is the level

at which someone believes they can accomplish the tasks before them. This can be evidenced in several ways:

- A woman who graduates from college and takes a high-level job with tremendous demands. Amid this challenging opportunity, she believes in her ability to be successful.
- Because of an injury, an athlete who is told that she will not be able to compete for one year doubles her efforts and workout schedule.
- A person who has been in a series of unsuccessful relationships continues seeking new ones with a positive and hopeful attitude.
- Presented with a requirement to pass a professional licensure examination that has been reported to be extremely difficult to pass on the first attempt, a man doubles his efforts to be successful. He believes in his ability to master this content!

You can probably think of people you know who exemplify self-efficacy based on their belief in themselves, their choices, and their commitment to overcoming any challenges they may face. This may also be a pattern of behavior that you observe in yourself. It is easy to see the value of self-efficacy as a tool that contributes to accomplishing personal goals and dreams. Indeed, we all would choose to be up to life's challenges and move forward, find solutions, and persist even in the most difficult situations. Or maybe you think, "I would like to have more self-efficacy as I face life's challenges."

Positive psychology trainer Miriam Akhtar quoted the advice of Mahatma Gandhi that captures the importance of self-efficacy in our lives: "Your beliefs become your thoughts. Your thoughts become your words. Your words become your actions. Your actions become your habits. Your habits become your values. Your values become your destiny." As a person with an extraordinary level of self-efficacy, Gandhi observed that it all begins with our beliefs. Akhtar summarized the four sources of efficacious ideas as initially identified by Albert Bandura, and a fifth source was added by psychologist James Maddux:

1. **Mastery experiences**—As we learn and grow, there are times when we demonstrate mastery in performing specific tasks. The old expression "Success breeds success" applies here. When we are successful, particularly in studies that we find challenging, our self-efficacy is enhanced by performing those tasks. Related to this process is resilience—the ability to bounce back and continue moving forward when we face challenges.

2. **Vicarious experiences**—These are times when we observe people and the behavior of the people around us. If we observe people we consider to be like us succeeding in their pursuit of accomplishment and success, we are more likely to believe we can achieve success. This dimension speaks to the value of engaging with role models who exemplify the kinds of things that we value and would like to accomplish.

3. **Social persuasion**—Some individuals are influential in our lives, including parents, coaches, mentors, teachers, pastors, or others with whom we interact regularly. A word of encouragement from someone in these influential roles can tremendously influence the levels at which we sustain our efforts in pursuit of our goals.

4. **Emotional and physiological states**—How we feel at various times may impact our level of self-efficacy. If we are depressed, anxious, or tense, it may be challenging to muster feelings of self-efficacy. On the other hand, if we are energized, enthusiastic, and hopeful, we are more likely to take risks and attempt challenging tasks.

5. **Imaginal experiences**—James Maddux added to Albert Bandura's original list of elements that can impact self-efficacy by describing imaginal experiences. These are times when we visualize the possibilities of success in an upcoming activity. In a sense, we are imagining the steps necessary to realize a positive outcome. Although taking the next step and putting those visions into action is essential, positive imaginal experiences are a factor in enhancing expectations for success and actual performance levels.

There will undoubtedly be moments when you, as a college student, doubt your ability to conquer the academic challenges you face. At these moments, believing in yourself and being aware of what you have accomplished in the past and your capabilities for success are vital. The following *Test Yourself* personal assessment will help you evaluate your self-efficacy.

People with high levels of self-efficacy manage to solve complex problems, find the means and ways, stick to their aims, accomplish their goals, deal efficiently with unexpected events, handle unforeseen situations, invest the necessary effort, remain calm when facing difficulties, and rely on their coping abilities. They also can usually think of and find several solutions to problems, and they handle whatever comes their way.

Test Yourself | What Is Your Level of Self-Efficacy?

Ralf Schwarzer and Matthias Jerusalem have created a self-efficacy scale to help individuals examine the level at which this mindset is present. As you read through the list, observe the words chosen to describe patterns of high self-efficacy (e.g., manage to solve difficult problems, find the means, stick to my aims).

Review each statement below using the scale given. Then add up your ratings for the ten statements. Scores can range from 10–40. Higher scores indicate higher levels of self-efficacy.

Not at All True 1	Hardly True 2	Moderately True 3	Exactly True 4

1. I can always manage to solve difficult problems if I try hard enough.
2. If someone opposes me, I can find the means and ways to get what I want.
3. It is easy for me to stick to my aims and accomplish my goals.
4. I am confident that I could deal efficiently with unexpected events.
5. Thanks to my resourcefulness, I know how to handle unforeseen situations.
6. I can solve most problems if I invest the necessary effort.
7. I can remain calm when facing difficulties because I can rely on my coping abilities.
8. When I am confronted with a problem, I can usually find several solutions.
9. If I am in trouble, I can usually think of a solution.
10. I can usually handle whatever comes my way.

Schwarzer, R., & Jerusalem, M. (1995). General Self-Efficacy Scale. In J. Weinman, S. Wright, & M. Johnston (Eds.), *Measures in health psychology: A user's portfolio. Causal and control beliefs* (35–37). Windsor: NFER-NELSON.

Think Deeper | Self-Efficacy: How Are You Doing?

How well did your survey results in *Test Yourself: What Is Your Level of Self-Efficacy?* align with what you know about yourself? As an extension of your survey results, have a conversation with someone who knows you well and ask them to share how they view your level of self-efficacy and to provide specific examples.

What were the biggest surprises from that conversation? Believing in yourself and what you might be able to accomplish will be an important factor in shaping your future. Below you will find some strategies for expanding your self-efficacy.

For all of us, there are probably areas of our lives where we experience a high degree of self-efficacy and others where we might struggle. On the website Thrive Global, Kayla Matthews recommended six activities to consider:

1. **Accomplish small tasks**—There is sometimes a tendency to focus only on the *big* accomplishments of life (e.g., getting a raise, winning an award, becoming a valedictorian). In each of these examples, there are much smaller, necessary, incremental components like working hard, focusing on daily outcomes and achievements, and studying consistently that must come first. It is rarely possible to achieve *big* accomplishments without daily attention to the small details. Your path to earning your college degree will be paved with small achievements like completing a difficult assignment, learning a new skill, and passing a challenging examination—small tasks leading to a significant accomplishment.

2. **Learn from the successes of others**—How have others been successful in achieving their goals? Looking to others in similar pursuits and situations helps us identify the practices that lead to success. They can provide tips about how they reached their achievements.

3. **Shape your goals**—It is crucial to have long-range goals. At the same time, intermediate steps contribute to reaching those goals (e.g., finishing my degree, getting the necessary certifications, internships, and finding employment in my field). Without achieving those short-term outcomes, the path to our long-range goals is more difficult or impossible.

4. **Create a positive physical space**—Find a place and take the time to reflect on your progress, habits that may need to be changed or created, and the types of resources that will contribute to success. This time of reflection focuses on things done well that are worthy of celebration as well as those things that need modification.

5. **Clear out negative thoughts**—No one is perfect and neither is the path to success.

6. **Look for role models**—They are out there! These people have been on the same path that you are traveling. Learn from their successes and challenges.

People with self-efficacy are not successful all of the time. What makes them different is the ability to face challenges, quickly learn from their successes and failures, maintain faith in their abilities, upgrade their skills when needed, and, most important, maintain their focus on the goals and outcomes they have defined for themselves while overcoming the obstacles they may find in their path.

A Desire to Achieve

It is essential to have definite goals related to defining your meaning in life and a belief system that confirms your capability to be successful. Along with these critical ingredients for success, however, is the level at which we have the desire and passion to achieve our stated goals. Leadership guru John C. Maxwell observed, "Words might tell a story, but actions tell the truth."

Motivation has been defined in a variety of ways. According to psychologist Jeffrey Nevid, motivation refers to

> ...factors that activate, direct, and sustain goal-directed behavior....Motives are the 'whys' of behavior—the needs or wants that drive behavior and explain what we do. We don't actually observe a motive; rather, we infer that one exists based on the behavior we observe. (2013, p. 288)

This definition acknowledges three essential elements of motivation that have a direct connection to you as a college student:

1. **The presence of a goal**—By taking this course and reading this textbook, you have declared that one of your key goals is to earn a college degree. That is an achievable goal.
2. **Factors influencing movement toward the goal**—Events and circumstances that challenge your progress. Focus your energy on those circumstances and resources that move you past any obstacles.
3. **The fact that motivation is inferred by the progress shown in striving to reach the goal**—This progress includes attending class, reading your textbooks, studying for and passing examinations, and completing your courses individually. These actions demonstrate your motivation.

Extrinsic and Intrinsic Motivation

There are two primary categories of motivation: extrinsic and intrinsic. **Extrinsic motivation** is rewards-driven and relies on incentives like praise, fame, recognition, salary increases, or promotions. In relying on extrinsic motivators, we become dependent on the judgments and evaluations of others. In some ways, relying on extrinsic motivations gives away the level at which we maintain accountability and responsibility for our actions. We depend on others to determine whether we have succeeded. Granted, we always keep an eye on the expectations of teachers, employers, and others who are important to us in some way, and we enjoy their kind words and affirmations. At the same time, we cannot always rely on those who are available to reinforce us at the level we need to sustain our efforts.

Intrinsic motivation relies on internal rewards. Choices are made based on personal goals, assessments of one's performance, and an inner drive to do better, improve performance, and succeed. People who have intrinsic motivation are not immune to the influence of extrinsic motivators like rewards and incentives but primarily rely on their own internally established rewards to keep them moving forward. These include a sense of accomplishment, personal satisfaction, curiosity and intellectual stimulation, enjoyment, and a sense of passion toward issues of concern. See Figure 1.2 for a summary of extrinsic versus intrinsic motivation.

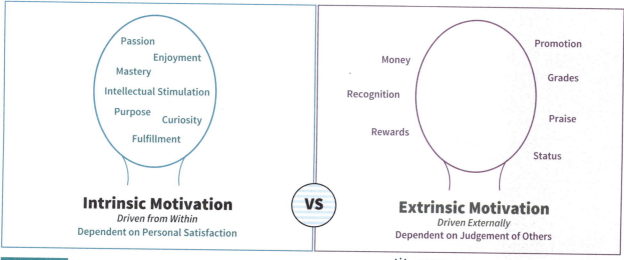

FIGURE 1.2 The differences between intrinsic and extrinsic motivation. INTERACTIVE FIGURES, CHARTS, & TABLES

DOWNLOAD
DOCUMENTS & TEMPLATES

Make It Personal | What Moves You Forward?

Think back to some of the most memorable accomplishments of your life (so far, as there will be many great accomplishments to come). What was your primary motivation? Was it something inside that moved you to compete and achieve? Or was it because others in your life were encouraging and praising you for what you were doing? Of course, it could also be a combination of both sources of motivation.

Now think about your decision to attend college. What will be your sources of motivation to excel and accomplish what you have set out to do?

DOWNLOAD
DOCUMENTS & TEMPLATES

Think Deeper | Where Do You Look for Encouragement?

Think briefly about your life's sources of encouragement and rewards and reflect on the following questions:

1. How do you respond when you do not receive the level of external affirmation (e.g., praise, commendations, words of encouragement) that you might need at any given time?
2. Does this situation tend to discourage you from trying harder, or do you just move on using your internal motivations?
3. What do you routinely do to celebrate your accomplishments and success?

Module 1.4 | Focus and Balance

LO 1.4.1 To reflect on where you focus your energy—the past, the present, or the future

LO 1.4.2 To examine the level at which you are living with a balance of time and energy among academic studies, current employment, clubs and other activities, and time with friends and family

Are there events from the past that you just keep thinking about? Do you find yourself thinking often about what's next after college? How will you balance being a college student with being a member of a family? With being a friend? Perhaps with being an employee? Now that we have examined meaning in life and motivation, let's take a look at *focus* and *balance*.

Where Do You Focus?

VIDEO CONTENT

As we will reinforce throughout this text, life is a journey. Along the way, there are points in our lives where we know exactly where we are headed and how to get there. Sometimes, however, the destination may seem unclear, and we must decide which path to take. Think for a minute about a typical day in your life. Where do you focus your energy?

- **Do you focus on the past?**—Like those words we find in a rearview mirror, "Objects in Mirror Are Closer Than They Appear," our history can sometimes impact the present. Opportunities missed, lost relationships, personal pain and circumstances, and bad decisions can haunt and distract us. Do you find yourself thinking about those events from the past that could have turned out differently?
- **Do you focus on the future?**—It will be so great when I get "there," wherever there might be: a new job, that dream home, an upcoming vacation trip, a new and exciting relationship, or finishing college and walking across that stage to receive your diploma. Do you often daydream about how great your planned future will be when you get there?
- **Do you live in the moment?**—I've got it right now and will make the best of it! Spur-of-the-moment decisions, going with the flow, and taking the good with the bad: Are these

the types of thoughts that you regularly have, not being held back by the past, not looking to the future, but living for now?

Which of these options is most like you? It is proposed that the best approach may be one that takes advantage of lessons that can be learned from all three vantage points:

- Things happen throughout our lives—some good, some bad, and some ugly. All these experiences help make us the person we are right now.
- Looking to the past, we can learn from our experiences (e.g., "I will never do that again"). These lessons can be valuable as we move forward.
- It is good to be aware of those objects in the rearview mirror, but not to the extent that they become a burden that slows us down as we move through life.
- Looking to the future, it is good to have goals, dreams, and aspirations about what we want to accomplish throughout our lifetime.
- Finally, we can spend so much time thinking about the past or focusing on what might happen in the future that we become oblivious to daily life experiences.

The best-case scenario is one where we learn from the past, have plans for the future, and still have time to focus on the events of our lives.

Test Yourself | Past, Present, Future: Where Do You Focus?

Here is a fun little activity to help examine where you focus—on the past, present, or future. Psychologist Frederick Koenig (1979) created the Three Circles test to determine where people focus—on their past, in the present, or to the future.

Directions

On a blank sheet of paper, draw three circles. The circles represent the past, the present, and the future. You can organize them any way that you wish. When you have finished drawing the circles, label them Past, Present, and Future.

Interpretation

The relative size of the circles and their placement/interrelationships are a guide to how you view the past, present, and future. Here are some of the possible conclusions that can be made from your drawing of the three circles (from Corry, 2018; and Dworken, 1985):

- If your circles are separated (i.e., not overlapping), then you might tend to view the past, present, and future as unrelated.
- If your circles are overlapping, then you might tend to view the past, present, and future as a continuous, interrelated process. So, what was done in the past impacts the present and the future.
- If the circles are roughly the same size, this suggests a flexible approach to the future.
- On the other hand, if the circles are varying in size, the largest (or smallest) are representative of a greater or lesser emphasis on that time frame.
- If the past is the largest, your family and background are important to you.
- If the present is the largest, you tend to lead a busy life.
- If the future is the largest, you tend to be optimistic
- If the past is the smallest, there is a tendency to think of yourself as a self-made person.
- If the present is the smallest, you tend to be an inquisitive and thought-oriented person.

As an additional step, share your circles with a friend or classmate, describing your circles and what they signify to you. Where do you focus?

Koenig, F. (1979). Future orientation and external locus of control. *Psychological Reports*, *44*(3), 957–958. https://doi.org/10.2466/pr0.1979.44.3.957

Think Deeper | Focus

 DOWNLOAD DOCUMENTS & TEMPLATES

Given the information above, where do you focus? Consider the following questions to guide your reflection in this area:

1. When you focus on the past, are your thoughts mostly about positive or negative events?
2. When you focus on the future, how optimistic are you about what you can accomplish?
3. You may want to discuss this topic with people who know you well. Ask them for some feedback on where they see you focusing your time, energy, and resources.

Seeking Balance

Don't doubt it: your decision to pursue a college degree will be a life changer. Your priorities may be temporarily rearranged as you seek to maintain current responsibilities like a job, family, and as a parent, church member, or softball coach with your new responsibilities as a student. David Brooks describes one way of thinking about this dilemma in the book *The Road to Character*. He suggests we have two types of virtues, **résumé virtues**, and **eulogy virtues**. Résumé virtues are related to the skills, training, and experience you bring to your employment. These may include degrees, certifications, publications, and other job-related accomplishments. Eulogy virtues are things you would like people to say about you at your funeral. These might include reflections on your character, your virtues as a friend, or anecdotes about your kindness and empathy for others. Brooks argued that we all spend a great deal of time polishing up our résumé virtues as we strive to get ahead and be successful on the job. Conversely, he suggested we spend less time than we should or could working on enhancing our eulogy virtues.

An example of seeking a balance can be observed in the 1993 film *My Life*, starring Michael Keaton and Nicole Kidman. In this film, Michael Keaton portrays a career-driven public relations executive named Robert Jones. He has directed all his time and energy toward becoming the world's best, most successful public relations executive. This path forced Jones to neglect other aspects of his life, like his relationships with friends and family. In one part of the film, Jones commissions the creation of a documentary about himself. He has an opportunity to see firsthand what his employees think of him. The conclusion is that they don't know him as a natural person but rather as a task-oriented, driven-to-succeed employer. This lesson becomes even more stark when Jones discovers that he has terminal cancer. This news arrives about the same time he and his wife find out she is pregnant with their first child, a son. Given the reality of his mortality and the news that he has only months to live, Jones creates a different video that he can leave for his unborn son after his death. This video features a variety of conversations that he will never be able to have with his son as he grows up: things like how to change a tire, stories about his boyhood home, and reading a story together. This poignant film reminds us that we are all mortal beings and never know how much time we have to accomplish our goals and dreams. It also calls us to consider how we might continually evaluate how well we balance our energies about work, leisure, friends, and family.

Think Deeper | Résumé and Eulogy Virtues

Think of someone you know who exemplifies pursuing résumé virtues by striving to enhance their accomplishments. With that as a focus, consider the following:

1. What are some of the common patterns of behavior that you can observe in that individual?
2. How well are they balancing their relationships with friends and family?
3. How would you assess their level of happiness with their life in general?

Now think of someone you know who exemplifies the pursuit of eulogy virtues through their interest in others, empathy, character, and kindness. With that as a focus, consider the following:

1. What are some common patterns of behavior that you can observe in that individual?
2. How well are they balancing their relationships with friends and family?
3. How would you assess their level of happiness with their life in general?

What would you say about your tendencies to pursue and value résumé virtues and eulogy virtues?

Module 1.4 Focus and Balance 19

Review, Discuss, and Apply

 INTERACTIVE SELF-SCORING QUIZZES

Discussion Questions

1. How does focusing on past events impact what you are doing now or will do in the future?
2. How does a total focus on the future contribute or detract from what needs to be done in the short term to reach your desired destination?
3. When things don't go as well as you would like, what strategies do you use to motivate yourself to get up and move forward?
4. How much should we rely on the positive comments and praise of others as a source of motivation? What is the downside of relying too heavily on extrinsic motivation?

We all have a personal story. We would like to introduce you to some of our friends, who, much like you, are on the journey of crafting their lives. At the end of each chapter, you will be asked to think ahead to career and lifelong applications of what you have learned. Then, two of these people will share personal dilemmas with you and ask for your advice. Let's get to know them first.

 VIDEO CONTENT

ANG
- Studied Journalism
- Working as a Writer and Activist

Watch Ang's video.

IMANI
- Studied Black History
- Working and Exploring Careers

Watch Imani's video.

AIDEN
- Studied Business
- Works at Family's Hardware Store

Watch Aiden's video.

OLIVIA
- Studied Marketing Communication
- Works in Website Development

Watch Olivia's video.

DEWAYNE
- Studied Music Production
- Working at a Small Record Label

Watch Dewayne's video.

ISABELA
- Studied Child Development
- Runs her own preschool

Watch Isabella's video.

WILLIAM
- Studied Computer Science
- Considering Graduate School

Watch William's video.

JULIA
- Studied Nursing
- Working and Considering Further Education

Watch Julia's video.

Think Ahead | Career and Lifelong Applications

Your most immediate goal could be to earn a college degree. Subsequently, you will have a purpose of seeking employment in a field aligned with your skills, passions, and interests. It does not stop there. You will have many opportunities throughout your life to create new goals that describe your plans. As you think ahead about this reality, consider the following:

Meaning in life can be a tricky concept. We all want to accomplish things and create evidence that our lives matter. Sometimes this leads to comparing our accomplishments to those of others in our lives (e.g., friends, family, members of our graduating class). We are all different. Remember that your path through life will be different from all others.

emiliegerard/Adobe Stock

Although résumé virtues document what you have learned and accomplished, having eulogy virtues will help you engage with coworkers and be viewed as a team member. These virtues are often overlooked when thinking about career advancements. In addition to the things you are working on to include on your résumé, what are you doing to enhance the kind of friend you are, along with your kindness and empathy for others?

It is sometimes tempting to focus all our energies on that new career or subsequent promotion. These goals are essential. At the same time, it is vital to maintain a connection with family and friends.

What Would You Do?

In this chapter, Imani and Ang need your advice.

VIDEO CONTENT

IMANI

Imani is struggling to decide between two job offers, both of which have pros and cons.

Watch Imani's video: **Multiple Job Offers**

ANG

Ang wants your advice to help him, in turn, give good advice to one of his co-workers.

Watch Ang's video: **Loving the Work**

What would you tell Imani? What would you tell Ang?

Take Some Action | Here and Now

DOWNLOAD DOCUMENTS & TEMPLATES

We all have strengths and weaknesses when it comes to meaning and motivation. Awareness of those strengths and weaknesses is key to success in college, the workplace, and life.

Review your outcomes on the Test Yourself assessments and your responses to the Think Deeper questions throughout this chapter. Reflect on your results and reactions, and then answer these questions:

1. What are your strengths concerning meaning and motivation?

   How will you put those strengths to work for you toward a successful college experience?

   How will sharpening those strengths in college help you be successful in the workplace?

2. What aspects of meaning and motivation do you want to use to improve your strengths?

3. Review the suggested action steps in that area and choose two or three of those to commit to here and now, and for each, say how taking that step will help you succeed in college and beyond.

   Share your responses to these questions with a friend, classmate, or family member.

Chapter Summary

Module 1.1 Exploring Our Meaning in Life

- The phrase *meaning in life* relates to how we experience and define the purpose of what we do each day and what we hope to accomplish throughout our lives. We perceive meaning in our lives through cognitive (what we think), motivational (what drives us), and affective (how we feel) lenses, and we each have an opportunity to shape the dimensions of meaning in our lives.
- You have the goal of graduating and earning your college degree in common with your fellow students. At the same time, you have specific goals, wishes, and dreams that are personal and essential to you.

Module 1.2 Ikigai: A Way to Visualize Meaning in Life

- The concept of Ikigai combines two Japanese words equivalent in meaning to "that which you live for" or "a reason to enjoy life" and offers a way of thinking about meaning in our lives. It conceptualizes *passion* as the intersection of what we love, or love to do, with what we are good at doing; *mission* as the intersection of what we love, or love to do and what the world needs; *profession* as the intersection of what we are good at doing and what we can be paid for doing; and *vocation* as the intersection of what we can be paid for doing and what the world needs.
- The core of ikigai is the place where all of these elements intersect and achieving it is your choice. It is challenging and it involves a commitment of time and belief, but it is also rewarding and leads to positive relationships and better health and well-being.

Module 1.3 Motivation: Leveraging Belief and Desire

- Psychologist Albert Bandura described *self-efficacy* as "how well one can execute courses of action required to deal with prospective situations." It refers to belief in one's self and one's ability to accomplish that tasks one is faced with and achieve one's goals.
- We develop self-efficacy through *mastery experiences* (times when we demonstrate success in completing specific tasks), *vicarious experiences* (times when we see people we think are like us demonstrate success in completing specific tasks), *social persuasion* (encouragement from influential people in our lives), *emotional and physiological states*, which may have negative or positive effects on our sense of self-efficacy, and *imaginal experiences* (visualizing success and the steps required to achieve it).
- Along with self-efficacy, we must have motivation to pursue our goals and take specific actions toward achieving them. Motivation can be *extrinsic*, based on incentives and rewards, or *intrinsic*, based on our own internal desire and drive and internal rewards like enjoyment and intellectual fulfillment.

Module 1.4 Where Do You Focus?

- Our past, our present, and our future can each be a helpful lens through which to focus on examining our sense of meaning in life. Our past, with both its successes and its failures, makes us who we are in the now and offers valuable lessons learned. Focusing on the present gives us an opportunity to take stock of how we're going and what is giving meaning to our lives. And having goals, dreams, and aspirations for the future gives us direction and motivation to achieve success and fulfillment.
- In his book, *The Road to Character*, author David Brooks describes *résumé virtues*, related to the skills, training, and experience you bring to your employment, and *eulogy virtues*, or things you would want people to say about you at your funeral. You might think of résumé virtues as what you can do as measured in degrees, certifications, promotions, and other job-related accomplishments, and eulogy virtues as who you are as measured in reflections on your character, your virtues as a friend, or anecdotes about your kindness and empathy for others. Too often we are focused on developing our résumé virtues. It is important to balance that focus with a focus on developing our eulogy virtues.
- You are now moving toward the completion of your college degree. That will be a great accomplishment. Remember, however, that this achievement does not mark the end of your learning. This will necessarily need to continue throughout the remainder of your life. Embrace the need to be a lifelong learner.

INTERACTIVE SELF-SCORING QUIZZES
Chapter 1 Practice Quiz

Key Terms

Eulogy virtues Things that we would like people to say about us at our funeral. These might include reflections on our character, the kind of friend that we were, and our kindness and empathy.

Extrinsic motivation Rewards-driven motivation that relies on incentives like praise, fame, recognition, salary increases, or promotions

Flow According to Mihaly Csikszentmihalyi, a state in which we are so involved in an activity that we lose track of time and block out everything around us

Ikigai A Japanese term that can be translated to mean "the thing that you live for" or "a reason to enjoy life." Ikigai is, in many ways, a state of mind that reflects a positive and happy approach to living.

Intrinsic motivation Motivation based on internal rewards. Choices are made based on personal goals, assessments of one's performance, and an inner drive to do better, improve performance, and succeed.

Mastery experiences Experiences in which we demonstrate mastery in performing specific tasks

Meaning in life Meaning focusing on how we experience and define the purpose of what we do each day and what we hope to accomplish throughout our lives; a more personal measure than *meaning of life*

Meaning of life An exploration of essential questions about life, such as "Why are we here?" and "What is meaningful and valuable in life?"

Mission The element of ikigai that involves doing the things we love to do while meeting a need of the world

Passion The element of ikigai that involves doing the things we love to do and are also very good at doing

Profession The element of ikigai that involves doing something we are good at and that we also get paid for doing

Résumé virtues The skills, training, and experience we bring to our employment

Self-efficacy The level at which we believe we can accomplish the tasks before us

Vicarious experiences Experiences in which we observe the people around us and their behavior

Vocation The element of ikigai that involves things we do that meet a need of the world and for which we are also being paid

Resources

Brooks, D. (2015, April 11). The moral bucket list. *The New York Times.* Retrieved from https://www.nytimes.com/2015/04/12/opinion/sunday/david-brooks-the-moral-bucket-list.html.

Emotional intelligence at work. Retrieved January 16, 2024, from http://www.emotionalintelligenceatwork.com/this-website/

General self-efficacy scale (GSE). Retrieved January 16, 2024, from http://userpage.fu-berlin.de/~health/selfscal.htm

Khosrowshahi, C. N. (2019, July 1). What is self-efficacy, and how can it help you succeed at work? Retrieved from https://thriveglobal.com/stories/self-efficacy-confidence-improve-performance-work-how-to-tips/

Kowalski, K. `Ikigai: The Japanese secret to a long and happy life' by Héctor García and Francesc Miralles (book summary). Retrieved January 16, 2024, from https://www.sloww.co/ikigai-book/

Steger, M. S. *Meaning in life questionnaire.* Retrieved January 16, 2024, http://www.michaelfsteger.com/?page_id=13

References

Akhtar, M. (2017, April 8). What is self-efficacy? Bandura's four sources of efficacy beliefs. Retrieved from http://positivepsychology.org.uk/self-efficacy-definition bandura-meaning/

Bandura, A. (1982). Self-efficacy mechanism in human agency. *American Psychologist, 37*(2), 122–147. doi:10.1037/0003-066X.37.2.122

Brooks, D. (2016). *The road to character.* London: Penguin Books.

Corry, P. (2018, November 15). *Focus is about past, present and future.* Medium. https://medium.com/serious-scrum/focus-is-about-past-present-and-future-d43583793012

Csikszentmihalyi, M. (2009). *Flow: the psychology of optimal experience.* Harper Row.

Dworken, A. (1985, February 6). The three-circle test. *Washington Post.* https://www.washingtonpost.com/archive/lifestyle/wellness/1985/02/06/the-three-circle-test/e959299f-5640-4e17-bc0e-98e61ae18c2d/

García, H., & Miralles, F. (2017). *Ikigai: The Japanese secret to a long and happy life.* Penguin Books.

Koenig, F. (1979). Future orientation and external locus of control. *Psychological Reports, 44*(3), 957–958. https://doi.org/10.2466/pr0.1979.44.3.957

Martela, F., & Steger, M. F. (2016) The three meanings of meaning in life: Distinguishing coherence, purpose, and significance, *The Journal of Positive Psychology, 11*(5), 531–545. DOI: 10.1080/17439760.2015.1137623

Nevid, J. S. (2013). *An introduction to psychology.* Wadsworth, Cengage Learning.

Rubin, B. J. (Director). (1993). *My Life* [Motion picture]. Columbia Pictures.

Schwarzer, R., & Jerusalem, M. (1995). General Self-Efficacy Scale. In J. Weinman, S. Wright, & M. Johnston, *Measures in health psychology: A user's portfolio. Causal and control beliefs* (35–37). NFER-NELSON.

Steger, M. F., Frazier, P., Oishi, S., & Kaler, M. (2006). The meaning in life questionnaire: Assessing the presence of and search for meaning in life. *Journal of Counseling Psychology, 53,* 80–93.

CHAPTER 2

Andrii/Adobe stock

Plan for Success!

VIDEO CONTENT
Author's Introduction

"The backbone of success is hard work, determination, good planning, and perseverance."
—Mia Hamm, soccer player, two-time Olympic gold medalist, two-time FIFA Women's World Cup champion

CHAPTER OUTLINE	LEARNING OBJECTIVES
Envision, Pursue, and Persist: Ingvar Kamprad	
Module 2.1 The Unique Nature of Your Story Where You've Come From *Make It Personal: Creating a Life Map* Where You're Going *Think Deeper: Starting Your New Chapter*	**LO 2.1** To analyze the unique and personal characteristics of your life story
Module 2.2 Navigating Higher Education Colleges and Universities Pathways to a Degree: Degree Requirements *Think Deeper: Your Major* College Credits and Grade Point Average (GPA) *Make It Personal: Other Interests* *Make It Personal: Do Any of These Apply?* *Test Yourself: Are You Confident for the Journey?*	**LO 2.2** To understand the institution of higher education
Module 2.3 Getting from Here to There with Help Along the Way Material Resources *Make It Personal: I Found It!* Academic Resources Well-Being Resources *Make It Personal: Which Services Are for You?* *Test Yourself: Do You Recognize That You Need Help and Then Act?*	**LO 2.3** To consider the abundance of campus-based resources designed to assist you in earning your degree
Module 2.4 The Devil Is in the Details *Think Deeper: What Kind of Learner Are You?* This Is Not 13th Grade Setting Yourself Up for Success *Test Yourself: Do You Know Yourself?*	**LO 2.4** To understand the differences between learning in high school and learning in college
Think Ahead: Career Applications Take Some Action: Here and Now	
Chapter Summary Key Terms Resources References	

Envision, Pursue, and Persist | Ingvar Kamprad

Have you ever heard of Ingvar Kamprad? Probably not, but you have undoubtedly heard of the chain of IKEA stores he started. Kamprad was born in Småland, Sweden. By age five, he was selling matches in his neighborhood. He quickly figured out that he could buy matches in bulk from Stockholm and then sell them locally at a higher price. Kamprad rapidly expanded his business by using his bicycle to reach new customers and then extended his inventory to include fish, Christmas tree decorations, seeds, ballpoint pens, and pencils.

At seventeen, Kamprad began IKEA and named it from his initials, plus the name of the family farm at Elmtaryd and the village of Agunnaryd where he was raised. Kamprad started out by selling his Uncle Ernst's kitchen table replicas and then expanded to include other furniture forms. Kamprad was listed as the eighth-richest person in the world when he died in 2018 with a net worth of $58.7 billion. This man had a plan, even from a very young age. Consider some of his observations:

- "Happiness is not reaching your goal. Happiness is being on the way."
- "Time is your most important resource. You can do so much in ten minutes. Ten minutes; once gone, is gone for good."
- "Simplicity and common sense should characterize planning and strategic direction."

Imagine what each of us could achieve if we approached our lives with the discipline and perspective held by Ingvar Kamprad. An article by Tom Popomaronis published in *Inc.* magazine shortly after Kamprad's death highlighted three lessons that can be learned from his life:

- "Think outside the box (literally)": IKEA is a company that breaks the mold. An example was the creation of the "flat-pack" strategy that dramatically reduced the costs of shipping and handling.
- "'Obstacle': It was just a word," Popomaronis observed. "He understood that our only limitations are the ones we set up in our own minds and that there was no such thing as a barrier. Perseverance and resilience became the lifeblood of this pioneering entrepreneur."
- "In entrepreneurship, age is irrelevant." Until his death at ninety-one, Kamprad was active, motivated, and engaged. He continued his lifelong pattern of creative thinking and leadership.

Ingvar Kamprad's zest for life and spirit of accomplishment can be an encouragement to all of us. You are encouraged to approach your college career with the same commitment. With this mindset, you can achieve great things in college and perhaps have a lifetime of adventure.

Like this snapshot of Ingvar Kamprad's life, we begin by thinking about our unique stories. From there, we will examine how to get the most out of your college education while remaining agile and open to new opportunities. That all begins with having a plan and working it day by day. We hope to start equipping you with those skills in this chapter.

Module 2.1 The Unique Nature of Your Story

LO 2.1.1 To analyze the unique and personal characteristics of your life story up to the present day

LO 2.1.2 To visualize milestones in your life story from now forward

Where You've Come From

VIDEO CONTENT

As we have suggested, you have a unique collection of gifts, talents, and abilities. Beyond that, you have had a variety of experiences, both positive and challenging, that are woven together to define the person you are today. Celebrate that uniqueness. What you bring to your college experience differs from every other student sitting beside you in class. The challenge ahead is to leverage the collection of traits and experiences that are uniquely you into a plan for success in college and beyond as you move toward your chosen career.

Where You're Going

VIDEO CONTENT

Many chapters of your life story have already been written. Some have been joyous; others are challenging and complex. But here is the excellent news: Many chapters are yet to be written, and you control the keyboard (or pen, if you want to go old school). The chapter you are about to begin is about your college career. Let's start writing that chapter.

Think Deeper | Starting Your New Chapter

Before we move any further, take a few minutes to think about two critical aspects of your success as a college student and this newest chapter in your life:

1. As you begin your pursuit of a college degree, what are the goals and dreams that you are pursuing?
2. Who can serve as a source of encouragement, advice, wisdom, and honest feedback?

Write down your answers to these crucial questions. Refer to them often as you proceed through your college program. Remembering these two answers will help keep you focused, on track, and encouraged as you progress.

Review, Discuss, and Apply

Discussion Questions

1. What are you most proud of in your life story to date?
2. What do you most look forward to in the future?
3. How does college contribute to what you have in mind for your future?

Make It Personal | Creating a Life Map

This activity visually depicts the most important and transformative events in your life.

1. First, list ten of your life's most meaningful events (e.g., achievements, family events, first date, first car, surgeries, travel, disappointing or tragic events).
2. Now rate each event on a 1–10 scale where 1 is an event that was extremely challenging, difficult, and painful, and 10 is an event that was amazing, happy, and joyful. Use 2 through 9 to designate the level at which the events fall between these extremes.

Top Ten Most Influential Events in My Life	Rating

26 CHAPTER 2 Plan for Success!

3. When you have rated these items, place them on a timeline like the one below. Be creative and employ images to illustrate your choices.

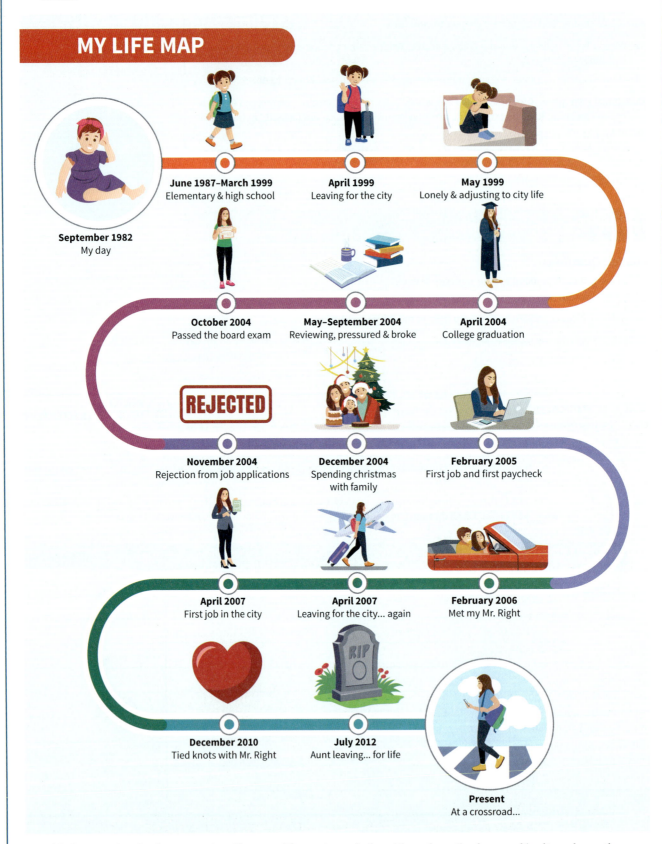

4. This document is a visual representation of how your life experiences, both positive and negative, have combined to make you the person you are today. You are unique. Embrace your story!

Module 2.2 Navigating Higher Education

LO 2.2.1 To understand the organizational structure of colleges and universities

LO 2.2.2 To explore the necessary ingredients of a college degree

LO 2.2.3 To understand credits and grade point average (GPA)

You have gone through the admissions process, secured the necessary funding for your current courses, and now find yourself ready to begin pursuing your goal of a college degree. You will find higher education is a unique place. Specific terms, procedures, and customs will be critical to your success as a student. To help you understand the landscape of higher education, let's examine some basics that will contribute to your success as a college student.

Colleges and Universities

It is common in the United States to designate institutions of higher education either as colleges or universities. Oddly, however, in conversations, these two are often lumped together and referred to as "colleges" (e.g., "Hey, where are you going to college?"). Colleges and universities can be publicly or privately funded. Governments do not operate private institutions, which are sometimes affiliated with religious denominations or have a unique focus (e.g., historically Black colleges and universities, liberal arts colleges, professional colleges, tribal colleges, and women's colleges).

Colleges are typically smaller in size than universities, most in the range of 1,000 to 2,500 students, with lower faculty–student ratios. They may offer associate's degrees, bachelor's degrees, or both. Schools that identify as being **liberal arts colleges** offer students coursework across a wide range of topics in the humanities, arts, sciences, and social sciences with a focus on critical thinking, writing, and an integrated approach to learning. Other designations include **community colleges**, which generally offer associate's degrees, often with a vocational or technical focus, and technical colleges.

Some schools identified as colleges commonly have open enrollment and offer certificates, diplomas, and associate's degrees across various disciplines, or the curriculum may focus on credits and skills as preparation for transfer to a four-year college or university. Two-year colleges sometimes have formal agreements with four-year programs on a "2+2" program where you can earn a bachelor's degree with two years of community college, followed by two years of study at a university. Many colleges also typically offer workforce training and skills training for enrolled students. Across the United States, there are 1,462 community colleges. Of these, 1,047 are public institutions and 415 are private. The National Center for Educational Statistics reported that in 2019, nearly six million students were enrolled in public and private two-year colleges.

Universities are institutions of higher education that focus on baccalaureate degrees in various academic disciplines, along with graduate and professional degrees in academic or professional fields. The modern university has its roots in the medieval universities in Europe. The word *university* is derived from the Latin *universitas magistrorum et scholarium*, which can be interpreted to mean a community of teachers and scholars. In the fall of 2017, the National Center for Educational Statistics reported that the United States has 4,298 four-year institutions. Of those, 1,626 were publicly funded, 1,687 were private and nonprofit, and 985 were for-profit. There were roughly 17 million students enrolled in undergraduate programs and another 3 million in graduate programs.

Colleges and universities must operate under specific standards to ensure that high-quality programs are taught by qualified faculty. These accrediting bodies are both regional (e.g., New England Association of Schools and Colleges), national (e.g., Accrediting Commission of Career Schools and Colleges), and disciplinary (e.g., Commission on Collegiate Nursing Education). Colleges and universities must also meet standards issued by the United States Department of Education.

Organization: Schools and Departments Colleges and universities are often divided into several academic departments, schools, or faculties. So, for example, a school of business within a college or university might be subdivided into various departments like business administration, leadership, marketing, accounting, finance, nonprofit, and non-governmental organization studies. These departments relate directly to the overall mission of the school of business, and assigned faculty would be responsible for teaching courses in these varied academic majors. Depending on the size of the college or university, schools and departments could be organized and interrelated in countless ways. It is helpful for you as a student to be aware of where your chosen major fits within the overall organization of your particular institution.

Faculty Faculty in higher education may teach on a full-time or an adjunct basis. In either case, it is typically necessary for faculty members to have at least a master's degree in their academic discipline, with preference given to those who hold a doctorate in their area of specialty. Additionally, preference can be given to individuals with educational or work experiences in the field in which they will be teaching. In addition to teaching, many faculty are actively involved in research to expand the available knowledge in their academic disciplines. This activity and their involvement in university committees are vital in determining their academic rank (e.g., instructor, assistant professor, associate professor, full professor). It is customary to refer to those with a doctorate by the appropriate title (i.e., Dr. _____) and to refer to others who are professors with the appropriate title (i.e., Professor _____).

Faculty typically have established office hours for meeting with students. Know when your faculty are available and whether you need to make an appointment or can simply drop in for a conversation.

Pathways to a Degree: Degree Requirements

VIDEO CONTENT

Typically, an associate's degree requires that students complete sixty semester hours distributed across needed courses in the major area of study, **general education courses**, and **elective courses**. This translates into two years when taking fifteen credit hours per semester. A bachelor's degree requires that students complete a similar collection of courses totaling 120 semester hours (i.e., fifteen credit hours per semester over eight semesters). As we specify below, in addition to accumulating a required number of hours, students must ensure that these are distributed according to college and university policies.

For various reasons (e.g., illness, changing majors, family issues, changes in employment conditions), completing a degree on a typical two-year or four-year schedule is not always possible. Approximately 13 percent of students enrolled in two-year colleges complete their programs within two years; by the same token, about 36 percent of students enrolled in four-year colleges complete their programs within four years. Do not be discouraged by these figures. The most important thing is to finish and earn your degree, while taking into consideration other demands like having a full-time job or a family.

College Catalogs Colleges and universities publish an annual catalog approved by faculty groups and their boards of trustees or other governing bodies. These catalogs describe the following:

- History of the institution
- Mission and vision of the institution
- Board of trustees, university officials, and governance
- Accreditations
- Description of governance
- Requirements for all academic programs, degrees, and certifications the institution offers
- Course descriptions
- Student life services
- Disability services
- General regulations, procedures, and expectations

Nuthawut/Adobe Stock

Your school's catalog is a significant resource for you as a student and is typically available on your school's website. The catalog that is available the year you enroll will generally define the expectations you need to meet to complete your degree program.

Academic Majors and Minors As you begin your journey through higher education, it is necessary and helpful to declare an **academic major**—the field of study on which you choose to focus. Within that major are required courses related directly to your chosen field. For example, here is a sample of courses that could be required for an associate-level program in business administration:

- Introduction to Business (3 credit hours)
- Business Ethics (3 credit hours)
- Business Leadership (3 credit hours)
- Introduction to Accounting (3 credit hours)
- Legal Issues in Business (3 credit hours)
- Human Resources (3 credit hours)
- Project Management (3 credit hours)
- Accounting for Business (3 credit hours)
- Principles of Entrepreneurship (3 credit hours)
- Business Information Systems (3 credit hours)
- Principles of Marketing (3 credit hours)

Students completing this course collection will have accrued thirty-three credit hours specifically related to business administration.

In a four-year bachelor's degree program, some students also pursue an **academic minor**, which is often related to their major. For example, a business student might also take required courses to document studies in a related area like leadership, information technology, management, or marketing. In a two-year associate-level program, it would be more common to collect elective courses in the same manner.

When entering higher education, you will be asked to declare a major area of study. Research indicates that these decisions are often made based on prospective financial rewards (i.e., "I can make a lot of money doing that job!"), job availability, and interest. Those may all be valid reasons for selecting an academic major. At the same time, however, roughly one-third of students in higher education change their academic major at least once within three years of their initial enrollment. Reasons often cited for changing majors included underestimating the difficulty of the subject matter, a general lack of understanding of what was involved in the selected major, not being encouraged to explore other majors, positive experiences with other possible areas of study, and boredom. Changing your major should not be viewed as a bad decision. It may mean that you will be adding additional required courses to your schedule (for your new major). Quite often, however, courses that were required in your previous major can be redefined as electives in your new chosen field. These types of details can be discussed in a conversation with your advisor.

It is, of course, essential to think carefully before choosing or changing an academic major. At the same time, pursuing a degree, a major field of study, and a career that matches your goals, dreams, and talents are equally important. If you find yourself thinking about changing your major, make sure that you consult with advisors, faculty members, and other knowledgeable people to gain some feedback on what you are considering as your next steps.

Think Deeper | Your Major

Reflect on the academic major that you have chosen. Consider the following questions:

1. What were the factors that led you to choose this academic major?
2. What types of strengths and talents match this academic major, and what do you anticipate will be your future career field?
3. How has your experience in taking coursework related to your chosen academic major matched up with your expectations?

General Education The United Nations Educational, Scientific and Cultural Organization (UNESCO) defines general education as the following:

> Education that is designed to develop learners' general knowledge, skills, competencies, and literacy and numeracy skills, often to prepare students for more advanced education programmes at the same or higher ISCED [International Standard Classification of Education] levels and to lay the foundation for lifelong learning. General education programmes are typically school- or college-based. General education includes educational programmes that are designed to prepare students for entry into vocational education, but that do not prepare for employment in a particular occupation or trade or class of occupations or trades, nor lead directly to labour market relevant qualification.

In both two- and four-year programs, colleges and universities require their students to complete general education courses that apply to all offered academic majors. In a two-year associate level program, students might be required to complete the following courses:

- Introduction to Human Communication (3 credit hours)
- English Composition (3 credit hours)
- Technical Writing (3 credit hours)
- Modern Concepts in Mathematics (3 credit hours)
- Critical Thinking (3 credit hours)

The logic is that effective communication skills, the ability to communicate in writing, basic mathematics, and critical thinking apply to whatever students choose to study or pursue as a career. In four-year bachelor's degree programs, this collection of courses might be expanded to include courses related to the following subject areas:

- English composition
- Mathematics (e.g., algebra, calculus, statistics, quantitative analysis)
- Natural sciences (e.g., chemistry, biology, anatomy, environment science)
- Social sciences (e.g., psychology, sociology, history, government, economics)
- Humanities (e.g., art, music, philosophy, literature, religion, languages)
- Diversity (e.g., global diversity, world religions)

The combination of courses taken in an associate or bachelor's degree program of general education is always specified in the catalog of your college or university.

It is common for college students to complain about required general education classes, preferring to focus their energies on coursework in their major area of study. In his 2019 book *Range: Why Generalists Triumph in a Specialized World*, David Epstein describes the research of Todd Rose and Ogi Ogas regarding people who became successful but seemed to take a strange path to get there. Here are some of the stories from their research:

- Phil Knight, the founder of Nike, reported that he had visions of becoming a professional athlete. He found, however, that he did not have the skills to make that happen. So, instead, he simply made it his business to stay involved with sports. He had a coach named Bill Bowerman who liked to tinker around with athletic shoes. These two founded the company, which was recently valued at 32.4 billion dollars.
- Charles Darwin, best known for his theory of evolution, started out studying medicine in response to a goal that his father had for him. He decided medicine was not for him and began studying at Christ's College Cambridge to become an Anglican parson. Later, he took an unpaid position as a naturalist on the HMS Beagle. It was on this voyage that he began to conceptualize his theory of evolution.
- After graduating from Harvard Medical School and then practicing medicine for several years, Michael Crichton became disgruntled with that career. He became a writer. His books, which parlayed his medical and scientific knowledge, became wildly successful. His novel *Jurassic Park* and the television program *ER* (which landed a record 124 Emmy nominations) are examples of his work.

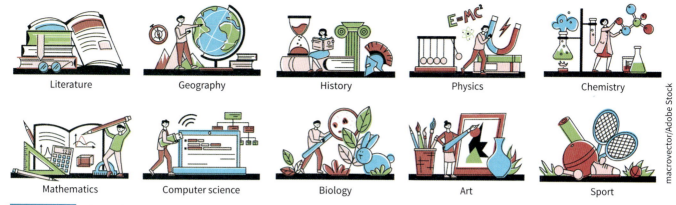

FIGURE 2.1 The varied fields of study included in general education.

These individuals found themselves in situations they had not predicted. In each case, the career path they had visualized for themselves did not meet their needs. Instead of being paralyzed, they planned out an alternative path. Epstein described these people as follows:

> They focused on, 'Here's who I am at the moment, here are my motivations, here's what I've found I like to do, here's what I'd like to learn, and here are the opportunities. Which of these is the best match right now? And maybe a year from now I'll switch because I'll find something better' (p. 154).

Do you ever feel that way? The author suggests that we should endeavor to learn about everything we can in life, well beyond just achieving a narrow band of being an expert on one topic. Equipped with those skills, we can be better equipped to adapt to situations that may arise. As you approach your general education courses (**Figure 2.1**), learn all you can and widen your range of understanding beyond your chosen academic field of study. (See also **Chapter 8**, where we talk further about taking advantage of every possible learning opportunity during your college career.)

Elective Courses   Beyond courses required for an academic major or minor, as well as general education, most academic programs include a provision for elective courses. In a two-year business administration program, students might choose to complete elective courses around management, marketing, or entrepreneurship. The same principle applies to a four-year program as the collection of electives may accumulate to meet the requirements for an academic minor. Elective courses will give you choices about what courses are included in your academic program. You can accumulate elective credits as part of your **degree requirements**. This is an excellent opportunity to explore topics of interest or courses from other academic majors that might supplement the knowledge you are gaining.

Make It Personal | Other Interests   ⬇ DOWNLOAD DOCUMENTS & TEMPLATES

What three topic areas outside your academic major would you like to explore through elective courses?

1. _____
2. _____
3. _____

College Credits and Grade Point Average (GPA)

The unit of measuring progress in higher education is the **credit hour**. When courses are created, developers assess the knowledge, skills, and dispositions required in that course and how long it will take students to demonstrate those proficiencies by specifying how many credit hours can be earned. The United States Department of Education has determined that a three-credit-hour course, for example, includes three contact hours per week in a classroom or lab over a fifteen-week semester, along with six hours of work per week outside the classroom, for a total of 135 total hours of engagement. Students taking twelve semester hours translates into twelve hours per week in a classroom along with thirty-six hours of assigned academic engagement outside the classroom. This definition spells out the expectation that taking a full load of courses in higher education is equivalent to having full-time employment. Fulfilling those hours will require that you be focused and disciplined.

Dual and Advanced Placement Credits

It is becoming increasingly common for high school graduates to begin their careers in higher education with an accumulation of dual and advanced placement credits. Dual credits can be earned in two ways:

1. Credits are earned by taking a high school class from an appropriately qualified teacher who has earned a specified number of graduate hours in their subject area, which is also identified as being equivalent to a college credit. Courses are typically approved by the state department of education and may be the result of a partnership between a school corporation and a higher education institution. These course credits are often available at a discounted rate.
2. Students leave their high school during the day to take classes on a college or university campus. When the course is completed, they have earned college and high school graduation credit for that course.

Recent data indicates that roughly 30 percent of the students currently enrolled in community colleges are high school students taking **dual credit courses**. The prevalence of this practice has grown dramatically in the past ten years.

Advanced placement credits are earned in high school courses with college curricula and examinations. After completing an advanced placement (AP) course, students take an examination administered by the College Board to determine whether they can receive college credit. In 2014, over four million students took AP examinations in various content areas, including calculus, chemistry, Chinese language, environmental science, physics, statistics, United States history, and world history.

Prior Life Experience Credits

Many colleges and universities will grant college credit for work experience or related training provided by employers. Quite often, to earn these credits, students are required to submit a written portfolio or evidence of the training received through an employer. Examples of activities that might be considered for **prior life experience credits** include industry-based training, professional development activities, private study documented by a portfolio, and work or volunteer experiences.

Commonly, colleges and universities will provide a summary of the requirements for the portfolio required to substantiate student learning at a level that warrants the awarding of college credit. Quite often, the portfolio is constructed in such a way as to demonstrate connections between the prior learning experience (e.g., employment experiences and roles, volunteer experiences and roles, international travel/residency) and the learning outcomes in a specific course. See **Figure 2.2** for a sample rubric from Zane State College used to assess requests for portfolio-based credit.

Although in many ways this process is more straightforward and generally less expensive than enrolling in a semester-based course, students are required to submit artifacts that describe the relevant experiences, demonstrate the types of learning that occurred, provide evidence of knowledge, and document mastery, along with a reflection on what has been learned Occasionally, there is also a requirement that students make direct connections between their prior learning experiences and the specific course learning outcomes.

Most colleges and universities have defined limits on the number of credits that can be earned or waived through prior life experience programs. Students are often required to pay for these credits at a discounted level.

ZANE STATE COLLEGE

RUBRIC FOR PORTFOLIO BASED CREDIT

Student:		Student ID:	Course ID & Title for Assessment:		
Assessed by:		Date:	Assessor's Signature:		
Assessment Ratings	**0** Does not meet expectations	**1** Partially meets expectations	**2** Meets expectations	**3** Exceeds expectations	**Score**
Sources of Learning *Experiences relevant to learning outcomes*	Documentation and description of learning experiences related to course learning outcomes are **lacking or substantially inadequate**	Documentation and description of learning experiences related to course learning outcomes are **not effectively or completely presented**	Documentation and description of learning experiences related to course learning outcomes are **appropriate and effectively presented**	Documentation and description of learning experiences related to course learning outcomes **exceed expectations**	
Demonstration of Learning *Artifacts*	The portfolio's materials and artifacts are **not appropriate and/or adequate**, and are not supported by the presentation	The portfolio materials and artifacts are **not fully supported** by or connected to the course's learning outcomes	The portfolio includes **appropriate** artifacts that support the demonstration of learning outcomes	The presentation of artifacts is **convincing**, with **strong support** for the course's learning outcomes	
Evidence of Learning *Competencies*	The portfolio shows **little or no evidence** of learning tied to sound educational theory	The portfolio documents some, but **not sufficient**, learning tied to sound educational theory (or grounded in appropriate academic frameworks)	The portfolio **adequately** documents learning tied to sound educational theory (or grounded in appropriate academic frameworks)	The portfolio provides **clear evidence** of learning tied to sound educational theory (or grounded in appropriate academic frameworks)	
Mastering Knowledge & Skills *Application of Learning*	The portfolio provides **little evidence** of the student's ability to use knowledge and skills for the course's learning outcomes in practice	The portfolio demonstrates the student's ability to use the knowledge and skills for the course learning outcomes in practice is **limited**	The portfolio documents the **acquisition** of knowledge and skills for the course learning outcomes, with **some ability** to apply them in practice	The portfolio demonstrates the student has **mastered** the knowledge and skills for the course learning outcomes and can **apply them in practice**	
Reflection on Learning *Aligned with course learning outcomes*	The portfolio provides **little or no evidence of reflection** to increase learning aligned with the course learning outcomes for which credit is being sought	The portfolio provides **inadequate evidence of reflection** to increase learning aligned with the course learning outcomes for which credit is being sought	The portfolio provides **evidence of reflection** to increase learning aligned with the course learning outcomes for which credit is being sought	The portfolio shows that the student has reflected with **substantial depth** upon how the prior learning experience is aligned to the course learning outcomes for which credit is being sought	
Presentation *Completeness and quality of the portfolio presentation*	Assembly instructions have **not been followed** with critical portfolio elements **not** included; the quality of written, visual and/or digital presentation **does not meet postsecondary standards**	**Most of the expected elements** are included; the quality of written, visual and/or digital presentation does not meet postsecondary standards with **too many errors** in spelling, grammar and punctuation	The portfolio is **well organized** with all critical elements included; the quality of written, visual and/or digital the presentation is **competent** with minor errors in spelling, grammar and punctuation	The portfolio is **well organized** with all critical elements included; learning is **well-documented** with writing and production skills that **exceed** those of most college students	
Overall Assessment	*The recommended cut score for a successful (i.e., passing) portfolio is **12**, with a score of at least 1 in each of the six assessment criteria.*			**TOTAL:**	

ATTACH LEARNING OUTCOMES FROM COURSE SYLLABUS

FIGURE 2.2 A rubric for completion of a course-based portfolio.

Micro-Credentials In the digital world in which we live, the newest kids on the block are **micro-credentials**. These often come in **digital badges** that can be earned by completing a course or demonstrating and documenting a particular set of competencies. This practice is more prevalent in business and industry than in higher education, but that reality changes quickly, as noted in the following:

- In business and industry, IBM was one of the first companies to create and deliver a collection of digital badges. On the IBM website, there is a quote reflecting the value and need for digital badges: "I had a tough time finding a job as my computer skills were considered out of date, and the IBM badges were the perfect way to show employers that I could easily get back up to speed and learn new skills." This example illustrates that those badges focusing on specific skills, with documented learning offered by a reputable provider, are becoming increasingly common in the marketplace.

- With increasing regularity, colleges and universities are accepting digital badges to demonstrate the outcomes associated with coursework.

- Another common source of learning is **massive open online courses (MOOCs)**. These courses are easily accessible and are offered from some of the most prestigious universities in the world. Although they have demonstrated massive enrollments, there has been a correspondingly low level of completion. Badge-bearing MOOCs can be accessed through Coursera, edX, Udemy, FutureLearn, Khan Academy, and Udacity.

- Colleges and universities will likely begin to use digital badging to document student learning and achievements. For example, the University of Notre Dame has developed an extensive collection of badges students can earn. Examples include library research and information literacy, media skills, civic engagement, peer advisor leadership, and professional readiness. As can be seen, these are not directly related to courses in which students would enroll and complete. Instead, they verify competencies a student demonstrates and that can later be used to enhance one's résumé.

- Another aspect of digital badging is the level at which badges are "stackable." This becomes a benefit like prior learning credits. Soon, it will be possible to stack together a collection of digital badges and present that collection to a college or university for consideration in awarding credit. Digital badging and stackability will play a vital role in the future of higher education.

College Level Exam Program (CLEP) The **College Level Exam Program (CLEP)** is a group of standardized assessments overseen by the College Board. Passing a CLEP exam, based on previous knowledge and experience, is another way to earn college credit. The College Board reported that approximately 2,900 colleges and universities accept the CLEP as a means to waive course requirements and provide credit. CLEP exams are available on a variety of topics in business, composition and literature, foreign languages, history and social sciences, and science and mathematics.

This may be an excellent option if you think you can "test out" of one or more courses by passing a CLEP exam. To help you in making this decision, there are practice examinations available on a variety of websites. If you can pass a CLEP exam, you earn credit for coursework and move one step closer to your degree.

Transfer Credit Hours It has become increasingly common for students to begin their college experience at one institution and then **transfer credit hours** to one or more other colleges before completing their degrees. Colleges and universities are increasingly interested in attracting and enrolling transfer students in the competitive higher education market. Each school has a policy on the number of credits that can be transferred and may require that specific courses can be taken only at their institution.

Roughly one-third of transfer students are community college students moving on to a four-year school. Other common reasons for transferring include sports, military, moving away, corporate transfers, enrollment in summer courses, switching majors, and moving back home. Transfer students need to work with their receiving school to maximize the number of credits transferred from their previously attended schools. When transferring courses from one institution to another, credits are typically transferred without including the grade received in the course. In other words, transfer credits do not contribute to (or detract from) your **grade point average** at the new school.

This is another area of higher education that is changing rapidly. Websites and formal organizations focus exclusively on determining which courses at one institution can potentially be matched for transfer (or trade-off) for credit at another college or university.

Make It Personal | Do Any of These Apply?   ⬇ DOWNLOAD DOCUMENTS & TEMPLATES

You will want to maximize any credits you can apply to your degree. Think about these options. Do any of these apply to you?

_____ Dual and advanced placement credits

_____ Prior life experience credits

_____ Micro-credentials

_____ College Level Exam Program (CLEP)

_____ Transfer credit hours

Grade Point Average (GPA)

In colleges and universities in the United States, students typically receive grades of A, B, C, D, and F. These grades are converted into number equivalents: $A = 4$, $B = 3$, $C = 2$, $D = 1$, and $F = 0$. The grade received and the number of credit hours for individual courses are multiplied and averaged throughout a student's enrollment. Colleges and universities establish the GPA required for graduation. In addition, it is common for unique programs to establish a GPA appropriate to individual areas of study.

Research has shown that the average GPA among college students is currently 3.15 (out of 4.0). The GPA you earn while in college will not only determine whether you can graduate but will also impact future options for enrollment, like moving to a four-year school or attending graduate school.

Review, Discuss, and Apply    INTERACTIVE SELF-SCORING QUIZZES

Discussion Questions

1. When you think about your strengths and challenges in learning, what types of resources will be most helpful in promoting your success as a student?

2. What are your personal expectations related to a desired grade point average at the end of your first year of college?

Test Yourself | Are You Confident for the Journey?

INTERACTIVE SELF-ASSESSMENTS

In Chapter 1, we examined the role of self-efficacy in pursuit of our goals and dreams. We have now also reviewed some of the unique organizational features of higher education. Let's take a few minutes to explore your level of confidence for this journey

1. How confident are you that you can complete all the work that is assigned in your college courses?

Extremely Confident	Quite Confident	Somewhat Confident	Slightly Confident	Not at All Confident
☐	☐	☐	☐	☐

2. How equipped are you to wrestle with complicated course content, philosophies, and concepts?

Extremely Confident	Quite Confident	Somewhat Confident	Slightly Confident	Not at All Confident
☐	☐	☐	☐	☐

3. How confident are you that you can put in the effort to be successful in college?

Extremely Confident	Quite Confident	Somewhat Confident	Slightly Confident	Not at All Confident
☐	☐	☐	☐	☐

4. How confident are you in understanding the policies and procedures that guide the operation of your college/university?

Extremely Confident	Quite Confident	Somewhat Confident	Slightly Confident	Not at All Confident
☐	☐	☐	☐	☐

5. I know I can stick to my aims and accomplish my goals in my field of study.

Extremely Confident	Quite Confident	Somewhat Confident	Slightly Confident	Not at All Confident
☐	☐	☐	☐	☐

6. The motto "If other people can, I can too" applies to me when it comes to my field of study.

Extremely Confident	Quite Confident	Somewhat Confident	Slightly Confident	Not at All Confident
☐	☐	☐	☐	☐

The level at which you believe in yourself is a key element in your success as a student.
- About which aspects of your role as a college student are you most confident?
- About which aspects of your role as a college student are you most concerned?

Adapted from University of London, Centre for Higher Education Research and Scholarship. (n.d.). Educational self-efficacy scale. Imperial College London. https://www.imperial.ac.uk/educationresearch/evaluation/what-can-i-evaluate/self-efficacy/tools-for-assessing-self-efficacy/educational-self-efficacy-scale/ and van Zyl, L. E., Klibert, J., Shankland, R., See-To, E. W., & Rothmann, S. (2022). The general academic self-efficacy scale: Psychometric properties, longitudinal invariance, and criterion validity. *Journal of Psychoeducational Assessment, 40*(6), 777–789. https://doi.org/10.1177/07342829221097174

Module 2.3 Getting from Here to There with Help Along the Way

LO 2.3.1 To evaluate material resources that may be available to students

LO 2.3.2 To identify one's need for academic support and the academic resources that may be available to students

LO 2.3.3 To describe the types of well-being resources that may be available to students

---

Colleges and universities have a vested interest in your success as a learner. For this reason, they have created various resources designed to assist you in your progress toward graduation. It is in your best interest as a student to take advantage of these resources when needed during your time in higher education.

Material Resources

Your commitment to success in college is essential to achieving your goals. At the same time, however, there will be times when you need answers and assistance. Your campus financial aid office, university website, and library are great places to get the answers and support that you need. Remember, these resources are offered by your school for this purpose. No question is too silly or frivolous if it is preventing you from your success in college.

Financial Aid Financial aid can be a tricky business. Whether you are attending college using funds from a personal or federal loan, specific conditions must be met during your time in college and beyond. The personnel in your institution's financial aid office on your campus are experts on the nuances of obtaining financial aid. If you have any questions like those below, make sure to stop by your campus financial aid office to get the answers you need.

The website SavingforCollege.com has identified ten pivotal questions that students should be asking about their financial aid:

1. What's the actual cost of attending school here (i.e., some schools will discount the "sticker" price for tuition)?
2. What are your financial aid deadlines, and when will we hear back after filing the Free Application for Federal Student Aid (FAFSA)?
3. What is the appeal process if we don't get enough financial aid?
4. How do I receive financial aid from my school (i.e., what is the schedule for disbursing funds)?
5. What is the average debt of your school's graduates?
6. What are the part-time employment opportunities on campus?
7. How will scholarships impact my financial aid?
8. Do you engage in front-loading of grants (i.e., giving the grants up front versus intermingling them across multiple years)?
9. Does the college meet my total demonstrated financial need (i.e., this may vary depending on how much the school wants to enroll you as a student based on your grades, test scores, etc.)?
10. How might studying abroad impact my financial aid package?

For most of us, applying for financial aid is a new or uncommon experience. Being aware of these questions will give you great places to start conversations with those in your school's financial aid office who are there to help you.

Online Resources on Your School's Website   Every college or university has a robust online presence to assist prospective and enrolled students. It is worth your time to become familiar with these resources.

> **Make It Personal** | **I Found It!**   ⬇ DOWNLOAD DOCUMENTS & TEMPLATES
>
> Go to your college or university website and locate the following information:
>
> _____ Requirements for your academic major and minor (if applicable)
>
> _____ Calendar for the upcoming semester
>
> _____ Graduation requirements
>
> _____ How to request a transcript
>
> _____ FAFSA deadlines
>
> _____ Tuition due dates
>
> _____ Campus map
>
> _____ Student clubs and organizations
>
> _____ Location of your school's career development services
>
> _____ Procedures for completing a CLEP exam
>
> _____ Electronic databases available through the college library
>
> _____ The website and office location of your faculty advisor

Library Resources   College libraries offer a rich collection of services. These go well beyond the collection of books that you may find on the shelves. The librarians who work in your school's library are there to help you locate and use various tools for your course-related research. In addition to what you might find on the physical shelves of your library (e.g., books, videos, newspapers, journals), colleges and universities may also have other essential resources (e.g., media tools, printers, copiers, equipment for loan, software, study rooms). Colleges and universities are increasingly aware of the need to provide digital resources to assist students in their learning. These often include the following:

- Research assistance from librarians
- Onsite collections of books, journals, videos, and other resources
- Searchable electronic journal databases
- eBooks
- Writing tools
- Reference citation resources
- Interlibrary loan resources

Take the time to visit your campus library, talk with the librarians, and familiarize yourself with what they can do to help you learn and succeed.

Academic Resources

It is quite common to find yourself a bit overwhelmed as you begin to take college courses. The pace and complexity of course readings and assignments can quickly become overwhelming. It is wise to be aware of your campus academic resources that are available to help you create a plan for success. The people who work in these offices are there for the sole purpose of helping you.

Here are some examples of academic resources:

- Tutoring
- Accommodations for students with disabilities
- Workshops and seminars on effective learning practices
- Assistance for students on academic probation
- Peer tutoring
- Study skills assistance
- Online learning tools
- Academic assessments
- Assistive technology

It is always better to get help when you need it. Take advantage of the academic support available on your campus.

Academic and Student Advising

Every college campus has individuals assigned to advise students on their academic programs. It is quite common for faculty members to fill this role for the students enrolled in their academic majors. Or there may be individuals on your campus who perform this task full-time. Regardless of the model used, there is someone assigned to serve in the capacity of your advisor. These **academic advisors** can be of help to you in several areas, including the following:

- Choosing academic majors and minors
- Discussing the requirements of academic majors and minors
- Guiding and assisting students in planning a schedule and recommending courses (both for individual semesters and throughout a degree program)
- Tracking student advancement and offering guidance and direction when challenges arise
- Helping students to identify necessary institutional resources that promote learning and success
- Assisting students in understanding institutional policies and procedures

As a student, you must make connections with your advisor. Advisors can be a valuable part of your success in higher education. Do you know the name of your advisor and where their office is located? Make it a point to get acquainted and view your advisor as an important academic resource. Their knowledge of academic requirements and opportunities can be invaluable.

Tutoring Resources and Academic Support

As noted earlier, as part of your academic program, you will take courses specific to your academic major, general education courses, and elective courses. Sometimes you are confronted with a course or an assignment that presents a significant challenge. When this occurs, don't delay. Make an appointment with tutoring resources on your campus.

The University of Wisconsin website has offered seven common myths regarding campus tutoring and academic support:

1. **Tutoring replaces independent study time**—It should be viewed as a supplement or add-on to your regular studying routine.
2. **Tutoring is only for struggling students**—Tutoring can help a student who moves from struggling in a course to passing a course and from just passing a course to achieving excellence.
3. **I don't need to prepare for my tutoring session**—The better you are equipped with questions and identified areas of challenge, the more your tutor can focus on providing the support you need.

4. **Tutoring is equal to spoon-fed answers**—The tutor's role is to help you become a better learner with an improved understanding of the course content.
5. **I don't have time for tutoring**—Trying to master content that you find confusing can be incredibly misleading and time-consuming. Take advantage of expert help, save time, and walk away with a better understanding of what you need to learn.
6. **Tutoring is the only type of learning resource**—This resource can also help you organize your research, find needed learning tools, and connect you with other campus-based resources.
7. **I can't afford tutoring**—These services are typically free to enrolled students on the campuses of most colleges and universities.

Writing Center

One of college students' most significant challenges is transitioning to college-level writing assignments. Writing assignments in college are typically more complex and held to a higher standard of writing quality. Your campus writing center staff can help you polish up your written work and enhance your chances for a good grade on that research project. Writing centers typically offer a variety of services, including the following:

- One-on-one writing consultations
- Online and face-to-face services
- English language learning
- Assistance with grammar, formatting, and referencing
- Writing workshops
- Grammar-checking software
- Recommended online writing websites for assistance

Well-Being Resources

To be successful in college, you will want to be at your best physically, spiritually, and emotionally. Making an adjustment to the social and academic world of college can be demanding when you are faced with so many new people, opportunities, and challenges. If you find yourself struggling, it is better to seek assistance rather than trying to resolve these challenges by yourself.

Health Center

Most colleges and universities have a campus health center to provide ambulatory health care for sick and injured students. Possibilities include the following:

- Allergy shots, immunizations, and vaccinations
- Evaluation and management of acute health problems
- TB tests
- Blood draws
- HIV/sexually transmitted infection (STI) testing
- International travel vaccines
- Wellness programs
- Monitoring of ongoing health concerns
- Prescriptions if the condition warrants

For certain services, there may be a fee or a requirement to have current health insurance. In any event, it is helpful to make yourself aware of the resources your campus health center provides.

Counseling Center

Most colleges and universities offer enrolled students campus counseling and mental health services. Possibilities include the following:

- Mental health and life concern consultations
- Evaluation and management of acute health problems
- Individual and small-group counseling
- Emergency services
- Workshops on varied topics related to mental health
- Support and assistance related to drug and alcohol issues
- Body image, eating, and exercise concerns

As with the campus health center there may be a fee or a requirement to have current health insurance.

Religious and Spiritual Services

Most colleges and universities host various services, often sponsored by external sources, focusing on religious and spiritual resources for students from multiple faith traditions and denominations. These services also often include resources to connect students with faith-related groups in the surrounding community.

Career Services

One of the outcomes that all college students hope to achieve is employment after graduation. Colleges and universities typically have an office of career services to assist you. These professionals have unique skills and expertise in a variety of areas that are critical to finding that perfect job and other post-graduation options:

- Career assessments
- Getting referrals to employers
- Information about career fairs
- Résumé and cover letter writing
- Preparation for job interviews
- Networking
- Volunteer opportunities
- Internships
- Assistance in choosing and applying for graduate programs

It is also worth noting that colleges and universities are now required to report the number of graduates who were placed into employment in their field of study or who advance in jobs related to their field of study while they are in attendance or after they have graduated. This information is available on your school's website.

Make It Personal | **Which Services Are for You?**

As you think about your strengths and weaknesses as a learner and your college adjustment, which campus-based services should you explore in this first semester?

_____ Tutoring resources/academic support

_____ Library resources

_____ Career services

_____ Writing center

_____ Academic support services

_____ Health center

_____ Counseling center

_____ Religious and spiritual services

DOWNLOAD DOCUMENTS & TEMPLATES

Test Yourself | Do You Recognize That You Need Help and Then Act?

INTERACTIVE SELF-ASSESSMENTS

Seeking help is a choice. Consider these scenarios as an indication of your willingness to seek assistance from others:

Scenario	I identify completely with the statement	I identify with the statement	I identify partially with the statement	I do not identify with the statement
If, for whatever reason, I were to have prolonged difficulty walking, I would do whatever possible to avoid asking help from anyone.	☐	☐	☐	☐
When something breaks down in my home, I usually persist in trying to fix it myself, even when it is difficult and I am wasting time and money.	☐	☐	☐	☐
I believe that a time of mourning for a loved one would be a time when I would need other people.	☐	☐	☐	☐
If I had a chronic illness, such as diabetes, I would seek out persons who could offer me guidance in addition to the medical treatment.	☐	☐	☐	☐
I would be embarrassed to admit to my professor that I do not understand the course content.	☐	☐	☐	☐
I would rather struggle alone, even for a long time, rather than ask for help.	☐	☐	☐	☐
When I see someone express their need for help, I view that as a sign of weakness.	☐	☐	☐	☐
Adversity is part of learning, and I would rather suffer alone than seek help.	☐	☐	☐	☐
My success in college is dependent on my ability to achieve on my own.	☐	☐	☐	☐

Consider the pattern of your responses. Are you a person who is likely to seek assistance and help when needed, or will you travel on alone trying to figure out a solution to what is confronting you? Discuss your results with a friend or classmate.

Adapted from Cohen, B.-Z. (1999) Measuring the willingness to seek help. *Journal of Social Service Research, 26*(1), 67–82. https://doi.org/10.1300/jo79v26n01_04

Review, Discuss, and Apply

Discussion Questions

1. What is your greatest fear about beginning your college career?
2. As you think about the ways that you react to new situations, what is the greatest challenge that you will face? Which campus office(s) can be of help with that challenge?

Module 2.4 | The Devil Is in the Details

LO 2.4.1 To understand the differences between learning in high school and learning in college

LO 2.4.2 To design action steps that will promote opportunities for success and ease the transition into college

---

Most students enter college with a healthy sense of fear of the unknown as well as an understanding that "I can handle this!" College is markedly different from high school in several ways. One that is very important is the level of personal responsibility you must take for your own success. Let's start by contrasting, in general terms, high school and college experiences. Then, let's examine some strategies for easing the transition and setting yourself up to succeed.

This Is Not 13th Grade

Just as you likely had different teachers for different subjects in high school and had to get used to their varied styles, you will have a variety of professors and instructors, each with their own style and approach. Beyond that, similarities are few and difference abound:

- In high school, most of the work was done in class. In college, most of the work is done outside of class.
- In high school, your class attendance was carefully monitored by your teachers. Although some professors take attendance in college, you are generally on your own to make decisions about class attendance.
- In high school, you attended classes six hours a day. You will be in class twelve to fifteen hours per week in college. This reality creates an abundance of free time. Thinking to yourself, "I've got lots of time; I will study later," can get you in big trouble.
- In high school, your classes generally included twenty to twenty-five students. You may be in a lecture hall with two hundred or more students in college.
- In high school, numerous data points like quizzes and daily homework determined your final grades in the courses you were taking. In college, you may only have one or two tests, a research paper, and a presentation over a semester that will determine your grade in a course.
- In high school, the content was delivered in small chunks, requiring minimal reading and studying. The volume and pace of what you must learn increase dramatically in college.
- In high school, you often had time in class to get assistance from the teacher on things you did not understand. In college, finding your own sources of help on things you do not understand is often necessary.
- In high school, you were given careful directions on completing assignments and reminders of when assignments were due. In college, you assume responsibility to complete assignments in a timely manner.

Think Deeper | What Kind of Learner Are You?

Think back for a minute over your career as a learner through elementary, middle, and high school, and reflect on the following questions:

1. How would you describe yourself as a learner?
2. What did you do well during your career as a learner?
3. What are some things that you would do differently to enhance your pattern of learning?

Setting Yourself Up for Success

Being successful in college requires attention to these differences and details, not occasionally, but every day. Here are ten tips to keep on your radar as you engage with the daily routines that lead to success:

1. **Read the syllabus**—In every course you take, the faculty have developed a syllabus. This is a valuable resource for your learning and success. At the beginning of each semester, take a few minutes to review the syllabus and acquaint yourself with the details of what lies ahead:

   - A general course description
   - Course learning outcomes (i.e., what you are expected to learn in this course)
   - Required and optional textbook(s)
   - How to contact your professor/office hour times
   - A schedule of topics, reading assignments, and assessments
   - How your final grade will be determined.

   Here's a thought: Transcribe the due dates for all your assignments for all your courses onto a single calendar. This will help you keep track of every assignment.

2. **Attend class**—As a student, you are paying for the lectures and other resources that comprise the courses that you are taking. But as we learn very quickly in college, it is easy to decide to skip classes. A recent study at Harvard, where the annual tuition is north of $78,000 per year, revealed that as many as 60 percent of enrolled students are AWOL for any given lecture. The reasons that students gave for cutting class included hanging out with friends (37 percent), being too tired (32 percent), engaging in various recreational activities (17 percent), studying for another class (11 percent), and facing bad weather conditions (3 percent). Make an early commitment to yourself to attend class and take full advantage of what is offered and what you are paying for through your tuition. Attending class connects you with your classmates, the professor, and the content being taught.

3. **Sit in the T-zone**—When you walk into a classroom, where are you inclined to sit? Generally, most people look for a seat near the back of the room or within striking distance of an electrical outlet. Beginning with the research of Adams and Biddle in the 1970s, ongoing research has identified a T-zone or action zone where the best students tend to locate themselves (**Figure 2.3**). Sitting in this zone tends to provide better connections with the professor and enhances your likelihood of paying attention to classroom activities.

4. **Read every day**—There are many estimates about the average number of pages college students must read each week. Consider, however, that if you take five courses, and each professor assigns forty pages of reading per week, you are responsible for reading and digesting roughly two hundred pages of content in any given week. Additionally, it is essential to remember that college textbooks offer more complex coverage than high school textbooks. This means that reading in college will require more sustained attention to the details of what is being read. If you want a better chance of retaining the content you are reading, the best advice is to schedule a time every day to engage with assigned textbooks and other reading assignments. Some specific tips for effective reading practices have been included in infographic format in the appendix of this text.

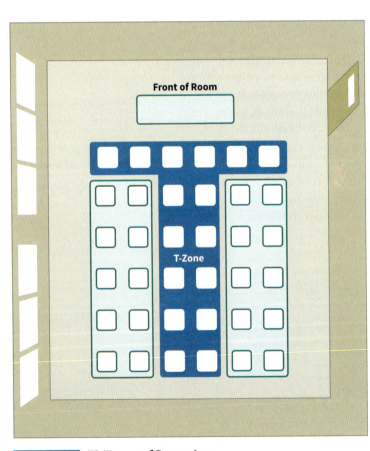

FIGURE 2.3 **T-Zone of Learning.**

5. **Get to know your professors**—Part of the learning experience available to you in higher education is to learn from individuals who are experts in their academic disciplines. This provides the opportunity to learn not only in the classroom but in other ways as well. Quite often, faculty will partner with students on research projects. Make an effort to become acquainted with your professors.

6. **Take notes**—Sitting in class, it is easy to think, "I'll remember that." Typically, we don't. Find a strategy for recording the key talking points from class lectures and activities. (Some specific tips for effective reading practices have been included in infographic format in the appendix of this text.)

7. **Don't get behind**—Once a semester starts, it can be a blur. You will be confronted with new classes, routines, and many assignments when classes begin. In semesters that last fourteen to sixteen weeks, it can be easy to fall behind in completing assigned reading and other course-related assignments.

8. **Do your learning by spaced practice**—Students sometimes have a tendency to wait until the last minute and cram for their examinations. This is based on the belief that we can look through our textbook, review class notes and PowerPoint slides, and remember the content when we sit down to take a quiz or test. Research has shown that one of the best practices in learning is to spread your learning out over a series of study sessions. So instead of feverishly studying for six hours the night before the big test, you will be further ahead by spacing out your reviews of course content into eight sessions of forty-five minutes each. In each of these shorter sessions, you can quickly review what you previously learned and then add some new content. The amount of time spent studying is the same. Still, the results will be dramatically different, with greater levels of recall and an understanding of the big picture of the material being learned.

9. **Ask questions**—You have heard it said that there is no such thing as a dumb question. In class, students are often reluctant to ask a question for fear of what others may think. The reality, however, is that most often, when someone asks a question in class, others have the same question or concern. Take the initiative and find out the answers to questions you may have about course content. Here is another small secret to consider—faculty appreciate it when students ask questions to help clarify the content being learned.

10. **Join a study group**—One of the best ways to learn is through conversation with others. Brain research has revealed that discussing and processing content increase the likelihood that the material will be retained in your long-term memory. As you begin a new course, look for classmates you can meet with regularly to review the week's materials.

Test Yourself | Do You Know Yourself?

INTERACTIVE SELF-ASSESSMENTS

How complex will these tasks be for you based on what you know about yourself and your approach to learning? Rate each task on a 1–10 scale where 1 is extremely easy, and 10 is extremely difficult.

Read the syllabus.	
Attend class.	
Sit in the T-zone.	
Read every day.	
Get to know your professors.	
Take notes.	
Don't get behind.	
Do your learning in chunks.	
Ask questions.	
Join a study group.	

Each of these activities can contribute to your success. Strongly commit to these practices, regardless of how difficult you find them to perform, with a personal commitment as you begin each semester.

A score of 10 means you have nothing to worry about; academic success is in the bag for you. A score of 100 means you might want to think about whether you're ready for college-level academic work. Like virtually all your peers, your score is likely somewhere in between 10 and 100.

Review, Discuss, and Apply

 INTERACTIVE SELF-SCORING QUIZZES

Discussion Questions

1. What are three areas of challenges in relation to academic learning that will need special attention and a level of commitment as you start college?
2. What is your typical way of responding when you find yourself experiencing a life challenge (e.g., call or text someone, sit back and figure it out for yourself, google possible solutions)?

Think Ahead | Career and Lifelong Applications

Entering college is a lot like starting a new job. You are entering into a world where you are not completely aware of the expectations, customs, and rituals. You will figure that out, but as we have said multiple times (and you are probably tired of hearing it), please be willing to ask those who are in the know for assistance and clarification. This experience is good practice for times in the future when you might move to a new city where you don't know anyone, start a new job, or transfer to a new job. On such occasions, you will need to quickly figure out your issues of concern and map out a course of action.

In college, as we have described, there are people on campus who are ready and willing to help you and answer your questions. The same will be true in the workplace when you find yourself having questions about work responsibilities, vacations, health insurance, retirement, and so forth. There is never an expectation that you will know all about these items when you start a new job. But as questions arise, you will need to find someone who can answer your questions. Your time in college is a great opportunity to begin practicing those skills.

You have a unique story unlike anyone on the planet. That reality also opens the door for you to explore a variety of career and lifelong opportunities. As you proceed through your college experience, continually ask yourself whether the path you are following maximizes your unique gifts, talents, and capabilities. This may require that you change your plans and your academic major. That decision is quite common among college students. It is better to make that choice than to feel that you are locked into a career that will not bring you happiness and personal satisfaction.

Gajus/Adobe Stock

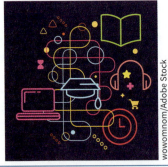
wowomnom/Adobe Stock

Higher education has its own unique set of rules, expectations, and rituals. In some ways, it is a world unlike any other. Within each college and university are unique sets of policies and procedures that guide the courses you will take, financial aid rules, and the kinds of support available. These policies and procedures are designed to help you be successful. As you move on with your life, this reality will continue, as there are rules and policies for your place of employment, buying a car or a home, paying your taxes, and countless other responsibilities that you will face.

There is good news! In college and throughout your life, there will be questions that you do not feel equipped to answer. Whenever you enter a new situation, like that first job after college, begin to observe and identify the people who can be sources of information and available to answer your questions.

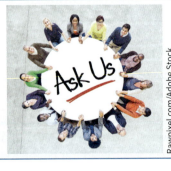
Rawpixel.com/Adobe Stock

Module 2.4 The Devil Is in the Details   47

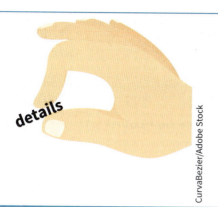

Success in life is largely a matter of attending to the details. In college, your personal life, and work career, attending to even the smallest details will enhance your opportunities

Develop your skills in seeking out the details you need for success in life and in work. Details may include deadlines for completing tasks, formats for required tasks, forms and procedures, and approvals.

What Would You Do?

In this chapter, Julia and Isabela need your advice.

VIDEO CONTENT

ISABELA

Isabela is thinking about going back to school and expanding her pre-school to another location and needs someone to bounce ideas off of.

Watch Isabela's video: **Feedback Needed**

JULIA

Julia is thinking about the next stage in her career but is having trouble coming up with a plan.

Watch Julia's video: **Too Many Options**

What would you tell Julia? What would you tell Isabela?

Take Some Action | Here and Now

DOWNLOAD DOCUMENTS & TEMPLATES

We all have strengths and weaknesses when preparing for the next major evolution in our lives, like starting college. Awareness of those strengths and weaknesses is crucial to success in college, the workplace, and life.

Review your outcomes on the *Test Yourself* assessments throughout this chapter and your responses to the *Think Deeper* questions. Reflect on your results and reactions and then answer these questions:

1. What are your strengths in knowing what you want from your college experience? How will you put those strengths to work for you toward succeeding? How will sharpening those strengths in college help you be successful in the workplace?

2. In what aspects of college preparedness do you want to improve your strengths?

3. Review the suggested action steps in that area and choose two or three of those to commit to here and now, and for each, say how taking that step will help you succeed in college and beyond.

Share your responses to these questions with a friend, classmate, or family member.

Chapter Summary

Chapter 2 Practice Quiz

Success in the world of higher education requires that you understand how things work and how to leverage the available tools and resources that will enhance your probability of success. Equipped with this information, you can maximize your abilities as you prepare for the future you have envisioned for yourself.

Module 2.1 The Unique Nature of Your Story

- You have a unique story. Entering higher education, embrace your story and understand how you got here and where you are headed.
- Never forget the degree to which your story is personal to you. Your successes and challenges have made you the person you are today.
- Attending college and pursuing your degree make up the next chapter in your story.
- Remember, several chapters of your life story have already been written. At the same time, there are many chapters yet to write, and you control the keyboard.

Module 2.2 Navigating Higher Education

- As you approach the higher education experience, you need to understand how higher education works and how it may differ from your previous learning experiences.
- Higher education has a unique set of terms and concepts used to describe how colleges and universities are organized.

Module 2.3 Getting from Here to There with Help Along the Way

- Consider which services are available on your campus and how they might contribute to your success.
- Arm yourself with knowledge and information about possible ways to use previous experiences and courses taken to reduce the number of credit hours needed for graduation. These primarily include prior learning credits, transfer credits, and CLEP exams.
- On every campus, various resources are designed and available to promote your success as a learner. Take full advantage of these resources.

Module 2.4 The Devil Is in the Details

- There will be many details to attend to during your college experience. Keeping track of these requirements across the courses you take each semester will significantly influence your opportunities for success.
- These details include reading the syllabus, attending class, sitting in the T-zone, reading daily, getting to know your professors, taking notes, not getting behind, learning in chunks, and joining a study group.

Key Terms

Academic advisor   A faculty member or professional staff member assigned to guide students in course selection, university matriculation requirements, campus resources, and other variables related to college success

Academic major   The academic discipline to which an undergraduate student formally commits

Academic minor   An academic discipline to which an undergraduate student formally commits that is secondary to the student's academic major

Advanced placement credits   Courses taken in high school that also provide college credit. Advanced placement credits are often based on performance on a standardized examination.

Colleges   Institutions of higher learning, often referring to community colleges, technical schools, and liberal arts colleges

College Level Exam Program (CLEP)   A program that provides tests students can take to earn college credit instead of taking a course.

Community colleges   Institutions of higher education where students typically take two years to complete courses of study that usually have a vocational or technical focus

Credit hour   The unit of measuring educational credit, usually based on the number of classroom hours per week throughout a term

Degree requirements   The number and type of credit hours required by a college or university for a student to qualify for a specific degree

Digital badges   Virtual awards offered by colleges, universities, and other organizations to signify learning and accomplishment in specified areas of study

Dual credit courses   Courses offered in high school settings, taught by a teacher who also meets college/university requirements as a faculty member, where students earn high school and college credit

Elective courses   Courses offered outside the requirements of the academic major that also count for graduation. Students can choose elective courses based on personal interest.

Financial aid   Money used to pay college tuition that comes from grants, work-study, loans, and scholarships

General education courses   Core courses required for graduation of all students, regardless of their academic major, typically focusing on the arts and humanities, social sciences, natural sciences, mathematics, and sometimes a foreign language

Grade point average (GPA)   The sum of grades earned in all courses divided by the number of credit hours they represent

Liberal arts college   A four-year undergraduate institution that offers a broad approach by focusing on the arts, sciences, natural sciences, humanities, and social sciences

Massive open online course (MOOC)   Free, flexible online courses, available for credit or awarded micro-credentials

Micro-credentials   Short, competency-based courses for demonstrating designated accomplishments or test scores. Some colleges and universities offer credit for "stacked" combinations of micro-credentials.

Prior life experience credits College credit offered for documented life experiences, typically outside the classroom, including work, volunteer experiences, workplace training, military training and service, independent study, professional certifications, and civic activities

Transfer credit hours Credits earned at one college or university that can be used to meet the requirements of a degree or diploma at a different college or university

Universities Institutions of higher learning that are authorized to award undergraduate, graduate, and professional academic degrees

Resources

Earn college credit with CLEP. Retrieved January 17, 2024, from https://clep.collegeboard.org/

Federal student aid website. Retrieved January 17, 2024, from https://studentaid.gov/

How to prepare for college: Paying for college. Retrieved January 15, 2024, from http://www.act.org/content/act/en/students-and-parents/college-planning-articles.html

Institute for career research. Retrieved January 17, 2024, from http://www.careers-internet.org/

Morris, R. (2018, January 10). 25 Most useful websites and apps for college students that will make you smarter and more productive. Retrieved from https://www.lifehack.org/articles/productivity/25-most-useful-websites-and-apps-for-college-students-that-will-make-you-smarter-and-more-productive.html

References

Adams, R., & Biddle, B. (1970). *Realities of teaching*. Holt Rinehart & Winston.

Cohen, B.-Z. (1999). Measuring the willingness to seek help. *Journal of Social Service Research*, *26*(1), 67–82. https://doi.org/10.1300/j079v26n01_04

Digital Badging in the MOOC Space. (n.d.). https://er.educause.edu/articles/2016/11/digital-badging-in-the-mooc-space Dispelling 7 myths about college tutoring. (2017, October 24). https://parent.wisc.edu/news/dispelling-7-myths-about-college-tutoring/

Epstein, D. (2019). Range: *Why Generalists Triumph in a Specialized World*. New York: Riverhead Books.

General education (2019, September 12). UNESCO Institute for Statistics. http://uis.unesco.org/en/glossary-term/general-education

Hall-Ellis, S. D. (2016). Stackable micro-credentials – a framework for the future. *The Bottom Line: Managing Library Finances*, *29*(4), 233–236. https://doi.org/10.1108/BL-02-2016-0006.

LaMagna, M. (2017). Placing digital badges and microcredentials in context. *Journal of Electronic Resources Librarianship*, *29*(4), 206–210. DOI: 10.1080/1941126X.2017.1378538

Petrone, P. (2019). The Skills Companies Need Most in 2019 – And How to Learn Them. https://learning.linkedin.com/blog/top-skills/the-skills-companies-need-most-in-2019—and-how-to-learn-them

Popomaronis, T. (2018, January 31). 3 Unforgettable life lessons learned from the iconic IKEA founder. https://www.inc.com/tom-popomaronis/3-unforgettable-life-lessons-learned-from-iconic-ikea-founder.html

University of London, Centre for Higher Education Research and Scholarship. (n.d.). Educational self-efficacy scale. Imperial College London. https://www.imperial.ac.uk/education-research/evaluation/what-can-i-evaluate/self-efficacy/tools-for-assessing-self-efficacy/educational-self-efficacy-scale/

van Zyl, L. E., Klibert, J., Shankland, R., See-To, E. W., & Rothmann, S. (2022). The general academic self-efficacy scale: Psychometric properties, longitudinal invariance, and criterion validity. *Journal of Psychoeducational Assessment*, *40*(6), 777–789. https://doi.org/10.1177/07342829221097174

Time Management

1. Create a Routine.

Unlike in high school or at a job, no one is monitoring you. This can make it easy to procrastinate and waste time. Find a routine that works for you. Maybe it's studying after class and before you go to your job or to the gym. Maybe it's going to the library after dinner to prepare for class the next day. Stick to the routine that works for you.

2. Know Yourself.

What time of day you feel most alert? Do you need a quiet environment to focus? This self-knowledge will help you plan your classes and study time. If you have trouble getting up early, don't sign up for 8 am classes. If you get distracted by noise, don't study in a loud coffee shop. If it's hard for you to focus while hungry, have a snack, like a granola bar, before class or before studying.

3. Keep a Calendar.

Keep a detailed calendar on your phone or laptop (class time, extracurricular activities, work schedules, social events, and study time). Input deadlines and enable reminders and notifications. This will help you think about projects, exams, or papers ahead of time. Include other commitments you have, such as exercising, sports practice, or grocery shopping.

4. Make Use of Small Blocks of Time.

For instance, if you have 30 minutes between class and your job, read a chapter, take a practice quiz, or start your homework assignment. You could read for class while on the treadmill or taking the bus. You could use a phone application to review flashcards while waiting for a meeting to start.

5. Create a To Do List.

Successful students keep ongoing to do lists, on paper or on their phones or laptops, to which they add tasks. They also note how much time they expect each task will take. It's also a good idea to prioritize tasks based on when they are due: High priority tasks are due in the next 24 hours, medium priority tasks in the next few days, and low priority tasks in the next week or so. Review your list every day and delete or cross off items as you complete them, which confirms your accomplishment and feels great!

6. Divide Large Tasks into Smaller Ones.

For example, you could start a big paper by researching your topic and identifying the sources you want to consult. You could also create an outline to determine the sources that will help you for each part of the paper. Making incremental progress on a large task reduces anxiety. The next time you work on the paper, it will seem less daunting because you'll have work already done.

7. Stop Procrastinating.

It's always better to start—and finish—early. This way, when unexpected things, such as getting sick or wanting to see that new movie with friends, come up, you will still be on top of your academics. Getting ahead on assignments feels great and gives you free time. It also reduces stress later in the semester when deadlines pile up.

8. Get Help When You Need It.

If you feel overwhelmed, reach out for help. Ask family members, friends, or roommates for a hand. They can't study or write a paper for you, but they can help in other ways like bringing you a snack while you study or doing your chores for a few days. This can give you time to focus on academics. Your academic advisor or counseling center are good resources if you have trouble managing time.

READING

01 Make a plan.

In many courses, faculty will assign textbook readings. You should have a plan for engaging with these readings so you can process, remember, and use what you have read. Just saying you read assigned chapters is insufficient.

02 Preview the assignment.

Before you read assigned chapters, get an overview of the content. Look for the following:
- Headings and sub-headings.
- Bold or italicized text.
- Vocabulary terms.
- Review and discussion questions
- Chapter summaries

Being aware of these components should give you context for what you are reading.

03 Read out loud.

Evidence suggests you pay more attention when you read out loud. You can also better remember what you read.

04 Note questions about what you are reading.

As you read, list your questions about chapter content. If you are reading an eBook, you may be able to add your questions in comment boxes next to the relevant text. Answering these questions may require delving deeper into concepts you have learned.

05 Highlight.

Highlight text sections that seem most important. On an eBook, use the built-in highlighter. Highlights provide a path you can follow when reviewing and recalling the content.

06 Make flashcards.

Flashcards are a great way to quiz yourself on chapter content. Various websites and phone apps provide quick and easy methods of creating flashcards. Your eBook may also allow you to make flashcards. In addition to reviewing your flashcards on a device, print them to review off-line.

07 Discuss what you have read.

To determine whether chapter content is embedded in your long-term memory, discuss the chapter with a classmate. Ask each other questions or take turns summarizing portions of the text. This process, called *self-explanation*, is a powerful learning tool.

08 Reread and Reflect.

Reading a chapter once may make you feel like you have completed your assignment. However, you should always reread a chapter's key portions to ensure you have mastered the content.

The more time you think about, and reflect upon, the chapter, the more likely you will be to remember and recall that information later.

Note Taking

01 READ BEFORE CLASS.

Do assigned reading and homework before class. If you understand a topic's basics, you can determine the lecture's important points and take good notes. If you only do some of the assigned reading, skim the whole selection.

02 SHOW UP.

Many students feel it's fine to occasionally skip class. But missing class impairs your ability to do well. You must be in class to take good notes. A friend's notes are a poor substitute. By missing class, you will miss the chance to ask questions about the material or hear questions other students asked. If you have an emergency, you may have to miss class. But you should never miss class for a reason like sleeping through your alarm, feeling hungover, or staying home during rainy weather.

03 SIT IN THE FIRST ROW.

Sitting in the back makes it harder to take good notes. Less prepared students often hide by sitting there. They are more likely to be playing games on their phones, or even, sleeping and that can be distracting. Sitting in the front means you avoid distractions and have the best view of the slides or of the material on the board, so it's easier to take notes. Your instructor can see you if you raise your hand. Your professor will also recognize you are a student who cares, which can pay off.

04 BE PREPARED.

Come to class prepared with what you need to take good notes like pens or pencils, a notebook, highlighters, or a calculator—if necessary. Being prepared also means being alert. If permitted, bring your water bottle or your insulated coffee mug. Eat a snack before class so you aren't hungry.

05 HANDWRITE; DON'T TYPE.

Research studies show that students who hand-write process information at a deeper level than those who type. This makes it easier to remember the information later, leading to better test scores. Taking notes by hand also gives you flexibility so you can ensure you capture key class material. You can make outlines, draw graphs, create mind maps, or write in paragraphs. Students who take notes on laptops tend to pay less attention to class material. They may check emails, play games, or complete different assignments. This multi-tasking makes it harder to take good notes. If you need to use a laptop to take notes, turn off your email or message notifications and close applications aside from your word processor.

06 THINK WHILE YOU WRITE.

Good note taking involves thinking about what the instructor says and writing down key points, not each word. Pay attention to the professor's cues. If the instructor writes something on the board or repeats a point several times, the instructor probably considers that material important. If you notice a cue, circle, star, or underline the corresponding information in your notes so you remember to study it well.

07 ASK QUESTIONS.

During class, ask questions if you don't understand something. Many college students worry about feeling dumb for asking questions, so they don't ask. But if you don't understand something, many of your classmates also don't understand that same concept. Your classmates, and your instructor, will appreciate your asking questions. If you are unable to ask questions during class, you should ask your professor later. Jot down your questions so you remember them. Ask questions while they're fresh in your mind, after class, via email, or at office hours.

08 STAY ORGANIZED.

Use different notebooks—or, at least, different sections of a notebook—for each course. Start each lecture's notes, with a date, on a new page. If possible, organize each class's notes with headings and subheadings. You can then connect the notes to other material, such as course readings. Leave space between sections for future information, like your instructor's responses to questions.

09 REVIEW YOUR NOTES.

Read through your notes within 24 hours of taking them. This review will help you process and retain the material. You can also identify missing or unclear points. To test your understanding, summarize the lecture using your own words.

Studying Well

01 Take Good Notes.
Taking great notes can cut your study time in half. Good notes will help you prepare better for exams. They will also help you write stronger papers. Good notes focus on a lecture's, or a book's key points, not on everything in that lecture or book. Remember to take notes on key points of videos and online presentations, too.

02 Find Your Zone.
Figure out where you study best. Some students study best in a quiet room at the library. Others in a noisy coffee shop. Some students like to study with friends. Others prefer studying alone. Studying in different locations can help you connect material to a place. For example, you might study for your math test in the library but review your history notes in your dorm room. On an exam, you can then recall the information more easily.

Also, figure out when you study best. Think about the time during which you are most alert and plan your work blocks accordingly.

03 Use Flashcards.
Many students find it helpful to use flashcards with key terms and concepts. Flashcards force you to focus on the essential facts and details, and you can use them to test yourself on what you know.

04 Get—and Stay—Organized.
Before you study, organize your materials. These materials could include your notes, textbook, or other readings you have highlighted and annotated. Additional materials could include sticky notes or flashcards.

05 Find Your Method.
Find the approach that helps you master material. Do you prefer to review material on a laptop or a tablet, or do you prefer to review material in print? Do you learn information better from reading a textbook or by talking with classmates?

06 Form a Study Group.
Studying in a group can pay off. Group members can divide the work so each person focuses on a section of material. Each person can then present their material to the other group members. Research shows you learn things at a deeper level when you have to present or teach that material.

07 Stay Focused.
It can be hard to focus when you are working online. You may be tempted to look up the score of the game or check your social media accounts. Email and instant-message alerts may divert your attention. Reducing distractions, is, therefore essential to good studying. Silence your phone and turn off email and other application notifications on your computer.

08 Stop Multi-Tasking.
It's impossible for the brain to focus on two things at the same time. Instead of multi-tasking, focus on doing one thing at a time and doing it well. If you have a paper due tomorrow for one class and an exam that afternoon for another class, finish the paper first, then study for the exam. This approach will take you less time; plus, you'll do better on both.

09 Build in Breaks.
Studying is most effective when you can concentrate on the material. That's why it's important to take breaks to rest your mind. This strategy helps you stay energized and focused on what you are studying. Studying one thing for too long can make it harder to remember information.

You can also use scheduled breaks as a reward. Set a timer on your phone to study for an hour, and then, take 10 minutes to do something fun: Check out your friends' social media posts, eat a snack, or walk around campus.

10 See Your Instructor.
Guess who writes and grades the exam? The instructor or their teaching assistant (TA). So, seeing your instructor or their TA early and often is a good idea. You can see them to ask questions about course material you didn't understand. You can ask them about the questions they will ask on an exam or how best to prepare. An instructor might even say, "Oh, that's not going to be on the test," or "I'd focus more on this."

11 Start Early.
Leaving your studying to the last minute makes it harder to retain information. You often miss important details, costing you points on the exam. Cramming also increases anxiety, which can disrupt test performance.

Instead of cramming a day or two before the test—or even worse, pulling an all-nighter—study every day for smaller blocks of time. This strategy is known as *spaced repetition*, or *distributed practice*.

12 Test Yourself.
One of the best ways to prepare for a test is to figure out what you know and don't know. Your textbooks and online course materials often include practice test or quizzes. Use them. Some instructors give students access to old exams as practice tests. Even if you can't see an old test, ask about the questions to expect. Will there be multiple-choice questions, short-answer questions, essay questions, or all three? Will you be asked to define things? Compare and contrast? Explain? Knowing how you will be tested can help you determine the best approach to studying and help you create your own practice tests.

When you try to answer questions you've created or use an available practice quiz, you recognize what you know well and what you don't know. Focus your study time on what you don't know.

13 Take Care of Yourself.
An important part of studying well is being physically and mentally able to focus on the material you need to learn. It's impossible to study effectively if you are sick, exhausted, or anxious.

Therefore, it's important to take care of yourself, especially, during exam period. This means getting enough sleep, eating right, and engaging in regular exercise.

PART 2

Pursue

Getting the Most from Yourself

Success in life, no matter how you might personally define it, is the result of consistent effort. Developing good time management, reading, note taking, and studying skills is important for doing well in your classes, but success also requires that you take good care of yourself physically, mentally, and emotionally. Establishing good habits in these areas will enable you to be ready when opportunities arise. Working to become the best version of yourself is an everyday priority. This may sound challenging, but the good news is that there are some basic things you can do to prepare yourself and keep moving forward to pursue your goals and dreams. Let's get started!

3   Take Care of Your Body   **53**

4   Build and Maintain Relationships   **81**

5   Learn Your Way   **103**

6   The Power of Emotional Intelligence   **125**

7   Engage with Digital Technology   **147**

INFOGRAPHICS

Test Taking

Writing

Presentations

Financial Wellness

CHAPTER 3

Take Care of Your Body

Author's Introduction

"It is health that is real wealth and not a piece of gold and silver."
—Mahatma Gandhi

CHAPTER OUTLINE	LEARNING OUTCOMES
Envision, Pursue, and Persist: LeBron James	
Module 3.1 Defining Healthy Behaviors	**LO 3.1** To make healthy choices regarding eating, exercise, and sleep
Fuel Your Body	
Test Yourself: Do You Engage in Mindful Eating?	
Think Deeper: Making Healthy Food Choices	
Exercise Regularly	
Make It Personal: Making Time for Exercise	
Get Enough Sleep	
Test Yourself: Are You Sleep Deprived?	
Module 3.2 Avoiding Substance Abuse	**LO 3.2** To understand the consequences of substance use and abuse
Alcohol Use and Other Substances	
Test Yourself: Are You at Risk for Alcohol Abuse?	
Drug Addiction and Its Prevention and Treatment	
Make It Personal: Identify Challenging Situations	
Think Deeper: Standing Up to Peer Pressure	
Module 3.3 Managing Healthy Sexual Behavior	**LO 3.3** To develop strategies for maintaining good sexual health
Choosing Abstinence	
Preventing Unwanted Pregnancy	
Avoiding Sexually Transmitted Infections	
Think Deeper: Making Good Sexual Decisions	
Understanding Sexual Assault	
Test Yourself: How Well Do You Understand Sexual Assault?	
Think Ahead: Career and Lifelong Applications	
Take Some Action: Here and Now	
Chapter Summary	
Key Terms	
Resources	
References	

53

Envision, Pursue, and Persist | LeBron James

As a high school student, LeBron James was widely seen as one of the best basketball players in the country. He was the National High School Player of the Year during his junior and senior years. James chose to enter the National Basketball Association (NBA) draft as a high school senior and was selected as the first overall pick in the 2003 NBA draft by the Cleveland Cavaliers.

James has had a highly successful professional career. He has received numerous awards, including the NBA's Most Valuable Player (MVP) (four times), the NBA All-Star Game Kobe Bryant MVP Award (three times), and the NBA's Finals MVP (four times). James is the all-time leading scorer in the history of the NBA. He's also won two Olympic gold medals. Not surprisingly, James is considered one of the greatest basketball players of all time.

James is clearly a very talented and motivated athlete. But he also places a strong focus on health and wellness. This includes paying attention to how much he sleeps. James credits his strong performance with getting at least eight hours of sleep a night as well as taking a nap before every game. As James himself says, "The thing I prioritize above everything else is sleep."

James isn't the only professional athlete who recognizes the link between adequate sleep and athletic success. Numerous professional and college teams have consulted with sleep experts to make sure their athletes are getting enough sleep.

Why is sleep so important for athletic performance? People who are sleep deprived show higher levels of the stress hormone cortisol. Sleep deprivation also leads to lower levels of energy and less focus. This finding helps explain why National Football League (NFL) players who don't get enough sleep score fewer points and experience more injuries.

But it's not only professional athletes who are harmed by not getting adequate amounts of sleep. As you'll learn in this chapter, college students who are sleep deprived have less energy, feel less awake and alert during class, and perform worse on memory tests. They also have lower grades.

This chapter examines how taking care of yourself—including your mind and body—is an essential component of college success. First, you'll learn how to adopt healthy behaviors, including eating nutritious foods, engaging in regular physical activity, and getting enough sleep. The next section describes the very serious—even life-threatening—hazards of substance abuse and strategies for avoiding harmful behaviors. The final section of this chapter will describe strategies for maintaining good sexual health. This includes how to avoid unintended pregnancy and sexually transmitted infections (STIs) as well as how to understand and reduce sexual assault.

Module 3.1 | Defining Healthy Behaviors

LO 3.1.1 To define the components of healthy eating

LO 3.1.2 To examine the value of regular exercise

LO 3.1.3 To review strategies for getting enough sleep

One of the best ways to manage the normal stress of college life is to make sure your body stays healthy. In this section, you'll learn how to adopt healthy behaviors, including eating well, exercising, and getting enough sleep (perhaps the hardest challenge for many college students).

Fuel Your Body

Think about what you've had to eat today. Did you eat a real breakfast—such as cereal with milk—or grab a power bar as you raced out the door to class? Or did you skip breakfast completely? Now, think about what you've eaten—or intend to eat—for lunch. Will you choose a balanced meal or just wait and grab fast food? You may not have thought much about the food choices you've made today. But what you eat—and drink—has a major impact on your ability to stay healthy. Overall, the body needs about forty-five different types of nutrients a day. This is why eating a varied diet full of nutritious foods is really important for maintaining good health.

Why is eating healthy foods so important? Eating the right types of foods provides energy your body needs. For example, your body uses carbohydrates to make the sugar glucose, which is your body's primary source of energy. Glucose allows your brain to concentrate and pay attention. Have you ever skipped breakfast and then had trouble concentrating in class? This difficulty is caused by your body running out of glucose. Having a quick candy bar or soft drink, both of which provide lots of sugar, can give you an instant pick-me-up. But these choices don't have long-term benefits or provide the nutrition you need.

Eating a healthy diet also ensures that your body has essential vitamins and minerals. For example, people who don't eat enough iron can develop anemia, a condition that causes weakness, tiredness, and headaches.

Choosing a Balanced Diet

What is a healthy diet? According to the Dietary Guidelines for Americans, a healthy diet has three distinct features:

1. Emphasizes fruits, vegetables, whole grains, and fat-free or low-fat milk and milk products
2. Includes lean meats, poultry, fish, beans, eggs, and nuts
3. Is low in solid fats (saturated fats and trans fatty acids), cholesterol, salt (sodium), added sugars, and refined grains

According to the Dietary Guidelines for Americans, the healthiest meal plan consists of the following:

- 45 percent to 65 percent of calories as carbohydrates
- 10 percent to 35 percent of calories from protein
- 20 percent to 35 percent of calories from fat

In addition, it is recommended that people eat 7 grams of dietary fiber for every 500 calories they consume each day (**Figure 3.1**).

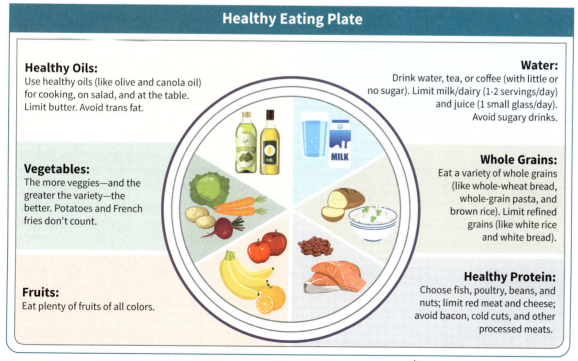

FIGURE 3.1 Recommendations for a balanced diet.

FIGURE 3.2 The *MyPlate* Guide from the USDA Dietary Guidelines for Americans 2020–2025.

Strategies for Making Healthy Food Choices

Making good choices about the types of foods and drinks you consume is an essential part of staying healthy. It helps you make sure your body has the energy and nutrients it needs. It also reduces your chances of gaining weight during the first semester of college. You've probably heard about this tendency (and the so-called freshman fifteen). Here are some strategies for eating right:

- **Choose energy sources wisely**—When people are feeling hungry, they often choose the fastest and easiest way to consume some extra calories to satisfy this need. But all sources of energy are not the same. For example, foods that are high in sugar—such as a soft drink or a candy bar—quickly raise the level of glucose in the body. This provides a fast source of energy. But the body quickly uses up this type of energy, which means you feel hungry again relatively soon. Eating a balanced meal—meaning a meal that contains protein, carbohydrates, and fats—is a better way of getting energy from food.

- **Watch portion size**—Many college students underestimate how much food they eat in a given meal. It's easy to overeat in a campus dining hall when you can eat an unlimited amount. It's also easy to overeat at home, especially if you eat right out of a container or while watching TV. Use **Figure 3.2** to make sure that you are eating the right amount of different types of food.

- **Limit processed foods**—Many types of foods have been cooked, canned, frozen, or prepared in some way that changes the nutrition they provide. This type of processing often results in lower amounts of fiber and other nutrients and higher amounts of added sugar and salt. For example, frozen pizza and microwaveable dinners are heavily processed. Other foods have little or no processing, such as fruits, vegetables, and milk products. Try to choose breakfast cereals that contain little or no added sugar and choose fruits instead of desserts with high levels of added sugar.

- **Limit fats**—Choose leaner cuts of meats, trim away any fat you can see, and for chicken and turkey, remove the skin before eating. Choose low-fat dairy products, such as fat-free or low-fat milk, yogurt, and cheese. Choose healthy fats, such as olive oil, olives, peanut butter, avocados, and nuts.

- **Watch out for stress eating**—Many people eat as a way to help manage how they feel. They may eat when they are bored, angry, or sad. For example, people who are watching sad movies eat substantially more popcorn than those who are watching funny movies. Many college students snack as a way to manage stress. If this is your tendency, choose healthier foods to snack on, such as baby carrots, low-fat popcorn, or fruits. Try to avoid high-fat foods, such as cookies, potato chips, and candy. You can also develop new strategies for managing stress, such as working out, calling a friend, or listening to music.

- **Engage in mindful eating**—Many college students engage in mindless eating, meaning they eat without really paying attention to what they are eating and whether they are hungry. This can lead to unhealthy eating habits. Instead, engage in mindful eating, in which you focus on what you are eating and why. Mindful eating involves paying attention to the taste and smell of food, eating slowly and savoring each bite, and eating until you are satisfied but not overall full. You can test how much you engage in mindful eating using the following *Test Yourself*.

> **Test Yourself** | Do You Engage in Mindful Eating?
>
> These statements will help you assess how much you engage in mindful eating. For each item, answer on a 1 to 4 scale, with 1 = never/rarely, 2 = sometimes, 3 = often, and 4 = usually/always.
>
> 1. When I'm sad, I eat to feel better.
> 2. When I'm feeling stressed, I'll go find something to eat.
> 3. I snack without noticing that I'm eating.
> 4. I have trouble not eating ice cream, cookies, or chips if they're around.
> 5. When I'm eating one of my favorite foods, I don't recognize when I've had enough.
> 6. When I eat at all-you-can-eat buffets, I tend to overeat.
> 7. If there's good food at a party, I'll continue eating even after I'm full.
> 8. If it doesn't cost much more, I get the larger size food or drink regardless of how hungry I feel.
>
> Add up your scores. Higher numbers mean you engage in less mindful eating.
>
> Framson, C., Kristal, A. R., Schenk, J. M., Littman, A. J., Zeliadt, S., & Benitez, D. (2009). Development and validation of the mindful eating questionnaire. *Journal of the American Dietetic Association*, 109(8), 1439–1444. https://doi.org/10.1016/j.jada.2009.05.006

- **Eat a variety of foods**—Try to eat a range of different types of foods, including vegetables, fruits, and whole grains, such as wheat bread, brown rice, and oatmeal. Choose non-meat sources of protein, such as beans and legumes, at least on occasion.
- **Avoid fad diets**—Some college students are tempted to use unhealthy strategies for losing weight. This can include using fad diets that forbid eating entire food groups, such as carbohydrates. It can also include diets in which you consume only one type of food or drink. They can also include so-called juice or soup cleanses in which you consume only one type of food for a period of time. Unfortunately, these types of diets can result in muscle loss and nutritional deficits, which are dangerous to your health. In addition, people almost always quickly regain any weight lost because the habits that led to the initial weight gain persist.
- **Monitor your eating**—If you notice yourself gaining weight, try keeping a list of what and when you eat. This will help you figure out what types of situations lead you to overeat, such as eating potato chips while you study, having a candy bar as a quick pick-me-up snack after class, or drinking alcohol at parties. It's very easy to forget about some of the calories you eat each day, especially if that eating occurs outside of a regular meal.
- **Plan carefully if you follow a vegetarian or vegan diet**—People who avoid eating animal-based foods rely entirely on plant-based sources to meet their protein needs. People who choose these diets need to make sure they are taking in different types of food that can work together to provide what their body needs. They need to consume complementary proteins, or two or more incomplete protein sources that together provide adequate amounts of all the essential amino acids, over the course of the day (see **Table 3.1**).

TABLE 3.1 Pairing Complementary Proteins

Black beans and rice
Pasta and peas
Whole wheat bread and peanut butter
Bean soup and crackers
Tofu or tempeh with brown rice or quinoa
Hummus (chickpeas and tahini) and whole wheat pita bread
Lentils and almonds
Yogurt with sunflower seeds or almonds
Tofu stir-fry with whole-grain noodles and peanuts

- **Drink enough water**—Water is essential for most body functions. It is estimated that everyone should drink six to eight cups of water or other beverages a day to maintain adequate water in the body. Other beverages, such as fruit drinks, sports drinks, and coffee, do provide water. But these choices don't provide the same benefits as pure water alone.
- **Make a plan**—Making healthy food choices can be hard for college students with a busy schedule. It can be hard to find time to shop and prepare healthy foods. Healthy foods can also be more expensive. Plan ahead so that you can make healthy food choices, even with limited time and money. Buy healthy snacks—nuts, popcorn, raisins—and carry those in your backpack. Think about what you will eat before you head into the dining hall. Many websites provide good ideas for meals that are healthy, quick to prepare, and inexpensive.

> **Think Deeper** | Making Healthy Food Choices  DOWNLOAD DOCUMENTS & TEMPLATES
>
> Many college students find it challenging to make healthy food choices. Unhealthy foods, such as fast foods, are readily available and very inexpensive. It can be hard to find time to shop for and cook healthy foods. Many students eat on the run and rush through meals. All of these factors can lead to unhealthy eating habits. The first step in developing healthier habits is to understand your own food choices. Reflect on these questions to learn more about your own eating patterns:
>
> 1. Do you often eat on the run, for example, eating a donut or muffin on your way to class, snacking on a candy bar for an afternoon pick-me-up, or eating fast food for dinner while you study?
> 2. Do you consume large amounts of empty calories in the beverages you choose, for example, alcohol, smoothies, or coffee drinks with cream and sugar?
> 3. Do you eat when feeling sad, stressed, or bored? Do you snack on candy while studying, eat ice cream when feeling lonely, or mindlessly munch on chips while watching television?

Reflecting on situations in the past that prompted unhealthy eating provides insight into the factors that influence your food choices. Once you have an understanding of these situations, you can then make healthier choices in the future. For example, you could bring healthier snacks when you must eat on the run, opt for black coffee instead of a frappe, or go for a walk with a friend or play basketball when feeling lonely. Remember that you control what you eat and drink, and you can choose healthier options anytime.

Be Wary of Eating Disorders   An eating disorder is a serious illness that is associated with serious concerns about your body as well as serious problems in your eating behavior. All types of eating disorders share some common features. But these disorders each have different symptoms:

- People with **anorexia nervosa** attempt to maintain an extremely thin body size, allow only very restricted eating, and have an intense fear of gaining weight. They eat only very small amounts of food. They may also engage in distinct eating rituals as a way of avoiding eating, such as cutting their food into very small pieces or refusing to eat certain types of foods.
- People with **bulimia nervosa** show two distinct types of behavior. One of these is called binge eating, in which enormous quantities of food are consumed. The other is called purging. Purging involves trying to get rid of the calories consumed during the binge, perhaps by vomiting or excessive exercising. These episodes are often triggered by some type of negative emotion, such as anxiety, tension, or tiredness.
- The most common eating disorder is known as **binge eating disorder**. Binge eating disorder consists of frequent episodes of uncontrollable binge eating. People with this disorder typically feel extremely distressed or upset during or after bingeing.

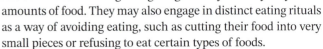
Monthira/Shutterstock

Eating disorders can lead to very serious, and in some cases life-threatening, problems. These problems include anemia (low iron), osteoporosis (thinning of the bones), low blood pressure, infertility, extreme weakness and tiredness, and damage to the stomach and intestines. Most important, people with eating disorders put their own lives at risk. In fact, an estimated 4 percent to 6 percent of people with an eating disorder die as a result of this disorder. Most of the deaths are a result of heart failure, organ failure, or suicide.

People with eating disorders are often very reluctant to seek treatment. They may feel ashamed and embarrassed to admit their behavior and may believe that the disorder will simply go away on its own at some point. They also may be concerned that "fixing" their disorder will lead them to gain weight. But these disorders cause significant psychological—and physical—harm. It is therefore important for people to seek treatment. If you or someone you know struggles with disordered eating, contact the National Association of Anorexia Nervosa and Associated Disorders free hotline at (888) 375-7767 or send an email to hello@anad.org.

Exercise Regularly

Engaging in regular physical activity is a great way to stay healthy and manage stress. People who engage in regular physical activity also experience mental health benefits, including lower levels of depression and anxiety.

What's so beneficial about exercising? Engaging in physical activity causes the brain to release chemicals—endorphins—that make you feel good. Engaging in regular physical activity helps improve thinking, learning, and judgment skills. This can lead to better academic performance. Exercising can also help distract you from problems you are facing and clear your mind from the stress of daily life (**Figure 3.3**).

Strategies for Increasing Exercise Although the health benefits of engaging in regular physical activity are clear, most people spend most of their day engaging in sedentary behavior. This includes driving, sitting at a desk, watching TV or movies, scrolling on social media, or playing video games. If you aren't currently doing any sort of regular exercise, it can seem hard to get started. Here are some easy strategies that you can try:

- **Integrate physical activity into your daily life**—Find ways of adding exercise that match up well with your daily life. Many of these options don't require too much time or money. Most colleges and universities provide free or low-cost opportunities to engage in physical activity. These can include dance and yoga classes, weight rooms, swimming pools, running tracks, and tennis courts. You could join an intramural club or interscholastic sports team offered through your school.
- **Find small blocks of time**—Most people feel that they are too busy to find time to exercise. But everyone can find a few hours each week to exercise. For example, it may also be easier to find three ten-minute periods a day in which you can engage in some type of physical activity than one thirty-minute block of time.

Why Exercise Is Important for Every College Student

Relieves Stress
The best way to relieve stress is by exerting energy into exercise–it's how the body is meant to respond to daily stressors.

Boosts Energy & Mood
Exercise causes a release of your body's feel-good neurotransmitters, also called endorphins. Many studies have shown that exercise can reduce symptoms of depression just as much as antidepressants.

Builds Confidence
Exercise produces endorphins, which make you feel good psychologically. Looking good, feeling strong, and seeing daily physical improvements help to boost one's self-esteem.

Boosts Immune System
College is the ideal environment to get sick. Exercise is vital, as it causes changes in antibodies and white blood cells, which are the body's immune system cells that fight diseases. Spend 30 minutes exercising a day, at least 3-4 days a week.

Increases Focus
Exercise causes the brain to release a chemical called brain-derived neurotrophic factor (BDNF). Only the brain can make BDNF, and only with exercise.

When you exercise and move around, you are using more brain cells. Using more brain cells turns on genes to make more BDNF.

FIGURE 3.3 Benefits of exercise.

- **Take small steps**—Even taking small steps to increase your amount of physical activity can have valuable benefits. Try using stairs instead of an elevator or escalator, walking or biking to school instead of taking the bus or driving, parking farther away from a building, and doing push-ups, sit-ups, or stretches while watching television. These are free and relatively easy ways to increase your activity.
- **Choose activities you enjoy**—It is much easier to stick with an exercise program if you find some types of physical activity that you enjoy doing. For some people, engaging in team sports, such as basketball, soccer, or frisbee, is more fun. Other people prefer to exercise alone and might find swimming, jogging, or weight lifting more enjoyable.
- **Exercise with a friend**—For many people, it's more fun to exercise with someone else, so try to find someone who is interested in engaging in physical activity with you. Do you know someone who might be interested in going for a brisk walk after classes, taking a bike ride on the weekends, or joining a yoga class? It's also harder to make excuses and skip exercising if someone is expecting you to be there.
- **Use technology wisely**—Many college students use technology to help them increase their exercise. Fitness trackers and phone pedometers can encourage you to take more steps each day. This type of technology can help you mark your progress and increase motivation.

Most college students have really busy schedules. This makes it hard to find time to fit in exercise. To help you adopt—and stick with—an exercise routine, complete the following *Make It Personal*:

Make It Personal | Making Time for Exercise  DOWNLOAD DOCUMENTS & TEMPLATES

New Strategy

Identify times in your schedule in which you could exercise. Remember that it may be easier to fit in a few ten- or twenty-minute blocks of exercise than one sixty-minute block.

Consider what types of exercise you enjoy. It's much easier to stick with exercise when you enjoy what you are doing.

List small steps you can take to increase exercise in your daily life.

Identify some type of support for your exercise routine. This could be a friend or some type of technology.

Get Enough Sleep VIDEO CONTENT

How did you feel waking up this morning? Did you feel completely refreshed and rested, ready to face the day? Or did you hit the snooze button a few times before crawling out of bed, drag yourself into the shower to wake up, and find yourself close to nodding off in class?

If you don't get enough sleep, you're not alone. Many college students don't get enough sleep. You can test your own level of sleep deprivation using the following *Test Yourself*.

Failing to get sufficient sleep may not seem like a big deal. But lack of sleep can actually have major consequences for your psychological and physical health. In fact, getting enough sleep is just as important to good health as eating well or exercising. Sleep deprivation can also have other consequences, including hurting your academic performance (**Figure 3.4**).

Module 3.1 Defining Healthy Behaviors 61

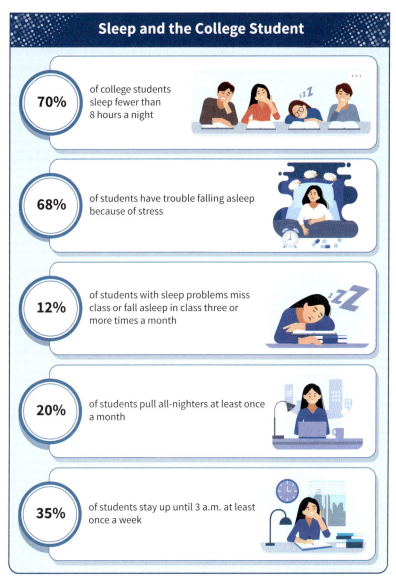

FIGURE 3.4 Sleep deprivation in college students.

INTERACTIVE FIGURES, CHARTS, & TABLES

Test Yourself | Are You Sleep Deprived?

INTERACTIVE SELF-ASSESSMENTS

These statements will help you assess whether you are putting your health at risk by getting too little sleep. If the statement is true for you, answer yes. If the statement is not true for you, answer no.

	I get drowsy during times when sleeping is not allowed.
	I sometimes feel sleepy during the day.
	I sometimes fall asleep when sitting down.
	I frequently doze off during break periods.
	I yawn frequently.
	My sleepiness interferes with my work.
	I feel like I do not get a deep sleep.
	I sometimes wake up suddenly after falling asleep.
	I have trouble sleeping.
	I am still tired after waking up in the morning.

Add up the number of yes answers. The more yes answers you have, the greater is your sleep deprivation.

Kato, T. (2014). Development of the Sleep Quality Questionnaire in healthy adults. *Journal of Health Psychology, 19*(8), 977–986. https://doi.org/10.1177/1359105313482168

The Impact of Too Little Sleep

For many years, scientists believed that sleep was a time in which the body and brain were basically inactive and at rest. However, we now know that essential activities associated with learning, memory, and body repair occur during sleep. In turn, getting too little sleep leads to serious consequences, including the following:

- **Poor academic performance**—Students who get too little sleep often have problems concentrating, paying attention, solving problems, and retaining information. Students who are especially tired may even fall asleep during class. Not surprisingly, having too little sleep leads to lower academic performance. One study found that every day of sleep disturbance a college student experienced in a week increased their risk of dropping out and lowered their GPA.
- **Mood**—People who don't get enough sleep often experience mood problems. They may feel irritable, sad, or short-tempered. Long-term sleep deprivation can increase the risk of developing a mood disorder such as anxiety or depression.
- **Accidents**—People who get too little sleep have reduced muscle coordination, concentration, and reaction time. In turn, sleep-deprived people are at greater risk of having motor vehicle accidents.
- **Negatively impacted athletic performance**—Athletes who don't get enough sleep experience various problems, including reduced coordination, endurance, and reaction time. They are also at increased risk of injury and show a slower rate of recovery from injury. College basketball players who get more sleep show increases in their free-throw and three-point field goal percentages.

Strategies for Getting Enough Sleep

Getting enough sleep is an essential part of staying healthy and making sure you function at your best. Yet many college students do not get the sleep they need. If you're one of these students, here are some strategies you can try:

- **Set (and follow) a schedule**—One of the best ways to make sure you get enough sleep is to set and follow a sleep–wake schedule. This means you go to bed at approximately the same time each night and get up at approximately the same time each morning. Use the same schedule throughout the week—not just Monday through Friday. This type of predictable pattern makes it easier for the body to fall asleep and wake up. Many people get too little sleep during the week and then try to catch up on sleep on the weekends. However, when you sleep in for two or three extra hours on the weekends, your body clock is disrupted, which just makes it more difficult to get up on Monday morning.
- **Nap carefully**—Napping is a better way of catching up on sleep than sleeping in late on the weekends. Napping during the day can help you get some extra sleep without disrupting your regular sleep schedule. Moreover, people who take even a short nap—say for twenty to thirty minutes—feel more alert. They also find it easier to learn new skills and use their memory. They are also more creative. But naps should be short so you don't get too much sleep during the day and then have trouble falling asleep at night.
- **Exercise regularly**—Exercising for as few as twenty to thirty minutes a day can help people get to sleep. However, try to exercise at least five or six hours before you plan to go to sleep. Exercising leads to increases in physiological arousal. This type of stimulation in the evening can make it difficult to fall asleep.
- **Avoid substances that interfere with sleep**—Certain substances—**stimulants**—produce a temporary increase in activity in the body and make it difficult to sleep. Caffeine is one of these substances. You should avoid any food, drink, or substance that contains caffeine, including coffee, chocolate, energy drinks, soft drinks, nonherbal teas, and diet drugs. It's also a good idea to avoid eating large meals or snacks in the late evening. Eating this late can make falling asleep more difficult, especially if the foods cause stomach trouble and heartburn. Similarly, avoid drinking too many liquids in the evening, which may result in frequent bathroom trips throughout the night.

- **Relax before heading to bed**—When they try to fall asleep, some people focus on stressful experiences or worry about upcoming events. Not surprisingly, people who go to sleep feeling stressed, worried, and angry have trouble falling asleep. Instead, practice relaxation techniques before bed to wind down, calm the mind, and prepare for sleep. Some simple relaxation techniques include listening to quiet music, concentrating on relaxing all of the muscles in your body, taking a shower, practicing yoga or gentle stretching, or reading a book or magazine.
- **Control exposure to light**—Minimize time spent in front of a television or computer screen at the end of the evening. Avoid reading from an electronic device that emits extra lighting just before you go to bed. If you do use your phone, tablet, or computer late at night, use a low light setting or blue light filter. Reading a physical book with a bedside lamp exposes your body to less light, which makes it easier to fall asleep.

If you've tried the strategies described above and you are still experiencing difficulty getting to sleep or staying asleep, talk to a doctor. In some cases, sleep disorders may require treatment.

Review, Discuss, and Apply

Discussion Questions

1. What factors make it hard for many college students to eat a healthy diet?
2. Looking forward, what strategies will you try to get more exercise?
3. Which of the findings about the impact of too little sleep do you find most surprising?

Module 3.2 Avoiding Substance Abuse

LO 3.2.1 To examine the consequences of abusing alcohol and other substances

LO 3.2.2 To understand how to prevent and treat drug addiction

Every day, college students face many decisions, including decisions about managing time, preparing for academic challenges, and developing various social relationships. But some of the most important decisions college students make are about whether they engage in behaviors known to be harmful to their health. In this section, you'll learn how binge drinking, tobacco, and illegal drug use can have serious consequences. You'll also learn how to make choices that help you stay healthy.

Alcohol and Other Substances

Many people consume drugs on a regular basis. Taking ibuprofen to relieve a headache, having a beer to relax with friends after work, or drinking caffeine to start the day are examples. For some people, use of these legal drugs never creates a problem and can even lead to beneficial effects.

But in other cases, the use of particular drugs can cause serious problems. The term **substance abuse** describes the use of drugs, including alcohol or illegal drugs, even when such use is leading to negative consequences. These can include getting arrested, losing one's job, or experiencing health problems. People who have a family history of substance abuse are especially at risk of developing these problems.

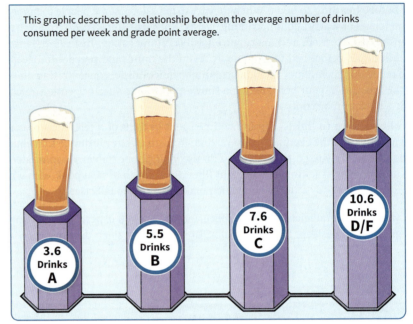

FIGURE 3.5 Alcohol and academic performance.

Alcohol Use At virtually all colleges and universities, alcohol use is pretty common, even though many college students may not be of legal drinking age. In fact, an estimated 80 percent of college students consume alcohol.

Some college students may think of drinking as no big deal. They may even feel proud about how much they drink. But alcohol use can have serious consequences. It may hurt your grades, your athletic performance, and your dating relationships (see **Figure 3.5**).

Do you have a problem with drinking? Take the following *Test Yourself* to find out.

Test Yourself | Are You at Risk for Alcohol Abuse?

These questions will help you assess if you are at risk of abusing alcohol. Answer based on the frequency with which you've experienced each of these problems in the past three months as a result of drinking alcohol. Use the following scale: 1 = never, 2 = yes, but not in the past three months, 3 = 1–2 times, 4 = 3–5 times, 5 = 6–9 times, and 6 = 10 or more times.

1. Feeling sad, blue, or depressed
2. Feeling nervousness or irritability
3. Felt bad about yourself
4. Had problems with appetite or sleeping
5. Engaged in unplanned sexual activity
6. Drove under the influence
7. Did not use protection when engaging in sexual activity
8. Engaged in illegal drug use

Add up your answers to assess your own personal risk of developing problems related to alcohol use. Higher numbers mean you are at greater risk.

Maddock, J. E., Laforge, R. G., Rossi, J. S., & O'Hare, T. (2001). The College Alcohol Problems Scale. *Addictive Behaviors*, 26(3), 385–398. https://doi.org/10.1016/s0306-4603(00)00116-7

Effects of Alcohol

Alcohol is a depressant, which means it slows down the central nervous system. At low levels, alcohol use has relatively minor effects. People who have had a drink may show more lively speech and movement. They may also feel more relaxed and less inhibited.

But higher levels of alcohol use can have more serious effects, including the following:

- Impairments in the ability to plan and use good judgment
- Decreases in reaction time
- Memory loss (e.g., blacking out)
- Slurred speech
- Difficulty walking steadily

One of the most serious effects is that alcohol impacts a person's ability to process information. This means that people who are drinking alcohol are often not very good at thinking about the consequences of their behavior. This is one reason people who have been drinking are more likely to engage in unsafe behaviors, such as driving while drunk.

Other consequences of alcohol use include the following:

- Engaging in risky sexual behaviors, such as unprotected sex and sex with multiple partners, which can result in unintended pregnancy or sexually transmitted infections
- Increased risk of both experiencing and committing sexual assault
- Increased risk of accidents and injuries, including those caused by car accidents, falls, burns, partial drownings, and electrical shocks
- Violent behavior, such as getting into fights

Alcohol use can also lead to significant, and long-term, legal consequences. Driving under the influence (DUI) is the most common criminal offense in the United States. People who receive a DUI face fees and fines, the loss of their driver's license, mandatory community service, higher insurance premiums, and even jail time.

Most seriously, car accidents caused by alcohol use account for 28 percent of all traffic-related deaths in the United States each year. Every day, twenty-nine people die in car accidents that involve a driver who has been drinking. This is one death every fifty minutes.

Alcohol Poisoning

Many college students engage in **binge drinking**, meaning drinking four or more drinks during a single occasion for women and five or more drinks during a single occasion for men. Binge drinking can lead to **alcohol poisoning**. Alcohol poisoning is a medical emergency that is caused when high blood alcohol levels suppress the central nervous system. This can cause loss of consciousness, low blood pressure and body temperature, and difficulty breathing. Extreme levels of alcohol consumption can lead to permanent brain damage and even death.

Signs of alcohol poisoning include the following:

- Mental confusion, stupor, coma, or inability to be roused
- Vomiting
- Seizures
- Slow or irregular breathing
- Hypothermia (low body temperature), bluish skin color, paleness

Given the serious consequences of alcohol poisoning, it is extremely important to know the danger signs (see **Figure 3.6**). You should also seek help immediately by calling 911 if you suspect a person is experiencing alcohol poisoning.

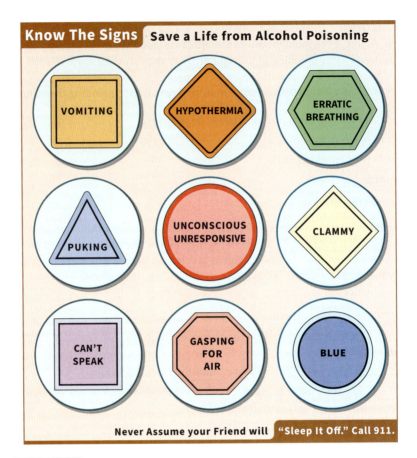

FIGURE 3.6 The signs of alcohol poisoning.

Tobacco Smoking, which causes nearly half a million deaths each year, is the leading cause of preventable mortality in the United States. In fact, more deaths are caused by cigarette smoking than by car accidents, HIV, guns, illegal drug use, and alcohol use combined. Although smoking is most commonly linked with cancer, it can also lead to other major illnesses, such as coronary heart disease, stroke, emphysema, bronchitis, and diabetes.

How exactly does smoking lead to so many negative health consequences? First, nicotine—a chemical found in all tobacco products—increases heart rate and blood pressure. This leads the heart to become overworked. Second, small particles of residue in smoke (tars) cause abnormal growth of cells in the mouth, throat, and lungs. This increases the risk of cancer. Third, consistent exposure to smoke disrupts the lungs' ability to clear out foreign particles. All of these factors contribute to the negative effects of tobacco use on health.

Many college students use other forms of tobacco, such as chewing tobacco, e-cigarettes, and vapes. These alternatives to cigarettes are somewhat safer since they don't produce smoke. But they are by no means harmless. First, these products all contain nicotine, which leads to addiction (and you'll learn more about the hazards of addiction later in this chapter). Second, many people who first use e-cigarettes or vapes later go on to start smoking cigarettes.

Perhaps most important, many college students who occasionally smoke a cigarette at a party, vape, or use e-cigarettes don't see themselves as smokers. They believe that their use of these tobacco products is simply a part of their social scene at college. They also believe that it will be easy to stop this use later on. Unfortunately, nicotine is a powerful drug, and many students find themselves unintentionally dependent on tobacco products for years.

Drugs All drugs share a common feature: They alter mental processes in some way, such by changing awareness, mood, and/or perception. All drugs contain chemicals that change how the brain sends, receives, and processes information. For example, opiates cause the brain to release large amounts of a chemical that leads to very positive feelings.

Use of drugs can have serious, and lasting, side effects (see **Table 3.2**). Short-term effects of drug use include problems with learning, judgment, memory, and decision making. Many drugs also cause unpleasant physical side effects, such as nausea, constipation, vomiting, and convulsions.

Many drugs that lead to serious consequences are illegal. These include cocaine, heroin, and hallucinogens. But other drugs are legal for use if prescribed by a doctor. Some people take these drugs for purposes other than those intended by the prescribing doctor. The most commonly abused prescription medications are opioids, depressants, and stimulants.

TABLE 3.2 Common Types of Drugs

Drug	Side Effects	Long-Term Consequences
Marijuana (weed, pot, Mary Jane, grass)	Distorted perceptions; poor coordination; difficulty with thinking and problem solving; learning and memory problems	Cardiovascular and respiratory problems
Cocaine (blow, coke, crack, candy, rock, snow)	Increases in body temperature, heart rate, and blood pressure; headaches; abdominal pain; nausea; paranoia	Highly addictive; heart attacks, respiratory failure, strokes, and seizures; in rare cases, sudden death during or immediately after first use
Crystal meth (methamphetamine, meth, ice, crank, crystal, speed)	Increased wakefulness; decreased appetite; mood swings; increased blood pressure and body temperature; irregular heart rate; hallucinations, severe anxiety, and paranoia; homicidal and suicidal thoughts	Dependence; tolerance; tooth decay and cracked teeth; malnutrition; skin sores caused by scratching; brain damage; coma; stroke; death
Hallucinogens (LSD, peyote, psilocybin, PCP, and MDMA, ecstasy)	Delusions and hallucinations; increased heart rate and blood pressure; extreme anxiety; profuse sweating; cramping, tremors, and uncoordinated movements; muscle weakness and numbness; sleep disturbances; paranoia	Memory loss; difficulties with speech and thinking; seizures; loss of balance; blurred vision; drops in blood pressure, pulse rate, and respiration; flashbacks
Heroin (black tar, big H, brown sugar)	Feelings of euphoria; dry mouth, nausea, and vomiting; severe itching; difficulty thinking; drowsiness	Highly addictive; cardiovascular problems; spontaneous abortion; death
Club drugs (GHB, Rohypnol, ketamine)	Impaired attention, learning ability, and memory; amnesia, delirium, and hallucinations; sleep disturbances	Dependence; tolerance; impaired motor function; seizures; coma; death
Opioids (hydrocodone, codeine, morphine, oxycodone)	Drowsiness, dizziness, and weakness; nausea and vomiting; impaired coordination; confusion; sweaty and clammy skin; constipation	Dependence; tolerance; slower breathing rates; low blood pressure; and unconsciousness, coma, death (especially when combined with alcohol or other depressants)
Depressants and sedatives (anti-anxiety medications, sleep medications, barbiturates)	Drowsiness and sleepiness; slowed and slurred speech; poor concentration; lack of coordination; confusion; lowered inhibitions	Dependence; tolerance; depression; chronic fatigue; breathing problems; sleep difficulties; coma; death (often by overdose)
Stimulants or amphetamines (ADHD medications, energy pills, weight-loss supplements)	Increased blood pressure and heart rate; decreased quality of sleep; decreased appetite possibly leading to malnutrition; apathy and depression	Dependence; tolerance; feelings of hostility and paranoia; increased body temperature; irregular heartbeat; increased risk of heart attack stroke

Many of the negative consequences of drug use are caused by impairments in judgment and decision making. These include the following:

- Engaging in unsafe sexual behavior, which can result in unplanned pregnancy and sexually transmitted infections
- Contracting an infectious disease, such as HIV or hepatitis, if they share needles to inject drugs with another person
- Driving accidents

The most serious consequence of illegal drug use is a drug overdose. Drug overdoses are caused by taking in more of a drug than the body can effectively process, or break down. For example, narcotics and depressants both slow breathing and heart rate. This can lead someone to become unconscious and even die. Drug overdose is now the second leading cause of accidental death in the United States each year (see **Figure 3.7**). On average, 130 Americans die every day from an opioid overdose.

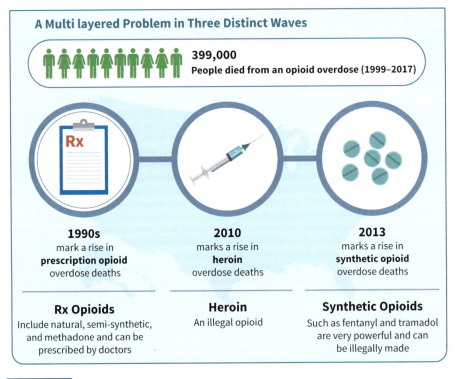

FIGURE 3.7 A rise in overdose deaths in America.

Drug Addiction and Its Prevention and Treatment

No one who starts using drugs plans to become an addict. Unfortunately, many people who use drugs become addicted and spend years trying to break their habit. **Addiction** is a chronic disease in which a person has a physical and/or psychological need to continue taking a given drug, regardless of any harmful or negative consequences that may result.

People who are addicted to a particular drug feel they need that drug to function normally. They may become distressed if they cannot use it. For example, many people who smoke cigarettes will become upset if they are in situations in which smoking is not allowed. People who are addicted to a drug also develop a **tolerance** to a given level of the drug. This means they need to take in even more of the drug to experience the same effects. Moreover, if they try to stop taking the drug, they will experience **withdrawal**, or unpleasant physical side effects. These side effects can include difficulty concentrating, hallucinations, seizures, muscle tremors, and anxiety and depression. These negative feelings make it particularly hard to stop using a drug.

The best way to avoid addiction is to avoid ever using substances that are highly addictive, including tobacco products and drugs. Make a commitment to yourself to not use drugs, and develop strategies for resisting any pressure from friends.

Reducing Substance Use

If you've experienced problems due to substance use, make a plan to reduce your use. It can be hard to reduce, or completely end, the use of particular drugs, but here are some strategies you can try:

- First, think about situations in which you are tempted to use, or abuse, drugs. This could include attending parties, spending time with particular friends, or feeling stressed. Then, try to avoid those situations or people whenever possible.
- Second, come up with new ways to handle situations in which you are tempted to use drugs. Do you smoke when hungry? Try chewing gum instead. Does stress make you crave having a drink? How about going for a walk outside with a friend?
- Third, develop a plan for refusing offers of drugs. You could say that you have work the next morning or need to be able to focus on writing a paper the next day. You could also practice just saying, "No, thank you, I've quit smoking."

Changing patterns of behavior, including substance use and abuse, takes time and effort. But given the serious hazards of addiction, you owe it to yourself to make a plan—and stick with it—to stop using drugs. Complete the following *Make It Personal* to develop a strategy for reducing your own substance use. First, list situations in which you are tempted to use drugs, including specific environments, people, and mood states. Then list new strategies for avoiding or handling those situations.

If you find it too difficult to resist peer pressure to use drugs, it's a good idea to seek professional advice. Talk to a counselor or therapist at your school's health or counseling center.

If you currently use drugs, but are trying to stop, get help: it could literally save your life. Most people with a drug addiction need the help of family, friends, and professionals, such as counselors, to end their dependence on drugs and return to their normal lives.

Make It Personal | Identify Challenging Situations

List Challenging Situations	New Strategy
1.	
2.	
3.	
4.	

DOWNLOAD DOCUMENTS & TEMPLATES

> ### Think Deeper | Standing Up to Peer Pressure
>
> Many college students sometimes experience pressure from friends, roommates, or teammates to use alcohol or other drugs. Understanding this pressure can help you stand up for yourself in these situations. Reflect on these questions to learn more about your own experiences and reactions:
>
> 1. Have you ever used alcohol or another drug due to social pressure from friends? What types of situations have led to this pressure in the past?
> 2. Are there times when you've resisted the pressure to use alcohol or drugs? What strategies did you use?
> 3. What strategy could you try the next time you are pressured to use to make sure you stand up for your own decision?
>
> Reflecting on situations you've experienced in the past can help you plan for future situations. Remember that you get to make your own choices about whether and when you choose to drink alcohol, smoke, and/or use drugs. Don't let other people make that choice for you.

Helping a Friend or Family Member If you know someone who is addicted to drugs, here are some ways you can help that person:

- Express your concern about the person's overall well-being and your willingness to help whenever they are ready to seek help.
- Offer to help the person find someone to talk with about the addiction, or give the person the number of a hotline to call, such as the Substance Abuse and Mental Health Services Administration's free hotline at 1-800-662-HELP (4357).
- Offer to go with the person to a meeting with a counselor or a group, such as Alcoholics Anonymous or Nar-Anon, that provides support to people with an addiction.

It is also important to remember that sometimes people are not ready to accept help, even if they really need it. They must want to break their addiction, and they have to be willing to make an effort to do so. It is not your fault if they are not ready to hear your concerns and take your advice. You may need to be patient and wait for them to admit they have a problem and want help in treating their addiction.

If you are concerned that their behavior is life-threatening, talk to a counselor at your school or call the hotline listed above for advice. In some cases, extreme measures may be needed to get that person the help they need.

Review, Discuss, and Apply

Discussion Questions

1. Why do so many college students drink alcohol and use tobacco products, given their serious negative consequences?
2. What steps can you take to avoid developing an addiction to alcohol, tobacco, or drugs?
3. Why do you think groups, such as Alcoholics Anonymous or Narcotics Anonymous, may be especially helpful for people who want to break an addiction?

Module 3.3 Managing Healthy Sexual Behavior

To develop strategies for maintaining good sexual health

LO 3.3.1 To review the benefits of choosing abstinence

LO 3.3.2 To examine different strategies for preventing unwanted pregnancy

LO 3.3.3 To understand how to avoid sexually transmitted infections

LO 3.3.4 To define different types of sexual violence

For college students who decide to engage in sexual behavior, making the choice to engage in safe sexual behavior is an important part of staying healthy. In this section, you'll learn how to protect yourself from unwanted pregnancy, sexually transmitted infections, and HIV. In the final section, you'll learn factors for protecting yourself against sexual assault.

Choosing Abstinence

Many college students choose not to have sex—that is, they choose to practice **abstinence**. Some students may never have had sex prior to starting college. Other students have previously been sexually active but have made the decision to abstain from sex.

There are many reasons to choose not to engage in sex. These include the following:

- Not feeling ready for a sexual relationship
- Wanting to find the right partner
- Getting over a relationship break-up
- Wanting to avoid pregnancy and STIs
- Following personal, cultural, or religious values
- Choosing to focus on academic, career, or extracurricular activities

If you've made a decision to stay abstinent, feel good about that decision. Don't feel embarrassed about this choice or have sex just to fit in with what other students seem to be doing. Remember that many college students do make a choice to stay abstinent, even if this choice often isn't talked about so much. In fact, students often wrongly believe that their peers are more sexually active than they actually are (see **Figure 3.8**).

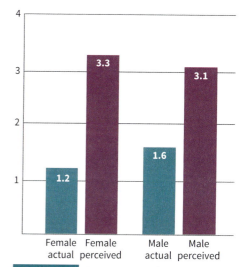

FIGURE 3.8 Average actual number of sex partners versus perceived number of sex partners among college students.

Preventing Unwanted Pregnancy

For college students who want to engage in sexual activity and avoid becoming pregnant or impregnating others, it is really important to use a safe and reliable form of contraception. The following methods are all reversible methods of birth control, meaning you can stop using them when you no longer want to prevent pregnancy. These methods vary considerably in terms of how they are used, whether they need to be prescribed by a doctor, and how effective they are at reducing pregnancy. Many forms of birth control are very effective when used correctly and consistently. However, their failure rate during typical use—meaning what happens in real life situations—is somewhat higher. These methods include the following:

- **Birth control pills**—This method—often called just "the pill"—consists of hormones that prevent ovulation from occurring, meaning a pregnancy can't occur as long as the pills are taken every single day (ideally at the same time of day). Birth control pills require a physical by a doctor and a prescription. This is a highly effective strategies for preventing pregnancy when used consistently; the typical failure rate is 9 percent.

- **Intrauterine device (IUD)**—An IUD is a small device inserted by a medical professional into the uterus. An IUD can stay in place for as long as ten years. This is a highly effective method of preventing pregnancy; the typical failure rate is less than 1 percent.
- **Implants**—The implant is a single, thin rod that is inserted under the skin of a women's upper arm. It releases a hormone that prevents pregnancy. This is a highly effective method of preventing pregnancy; the typical failure rate is less than 1 percent.
- **Injection**—This method—sometimes called "the shot"—involves getting a shot of a hormone in the buttocks or arm every three months from a doctor. The typical use failure rate is 6 percent.
- **Patch**—This method consists of a patch, prescribed by a doctor, that is worn on the lower abdomen, buttocks, or upper body. It releases hormones that prevent pregnancy. A new patch is put on every week for three weeks, and then, in the fourth week, a patch is not worn so that menstruation can occur. The typical failure rate is 9 percent.
- **Ring**—The ring, which is placed inside the vagina, releases hormones to prevent pregnancy. A woman wears the ring consistently for three weeks, removes it during the week she has her period, and then puts in a new ring. The typical failure rate is 9 percent.
- **Diaphragm or cervical cap**—These devices are placed inside the vagina to cover the cervix to block sperm. Prior to having sex, these small cups are filled with spermicide to kill sperm and are inserted into the body. The failure rate for these methods is about 12 percent.
- **Condom**—Condoms keep sperm from being released into a woman's body. Although if used consistently and correctly, condoms are very effective at preventing pregnancy, the typical failure rate is 18 percent.
- **Withdrawal**—This method involves withdrawing the penis from the vagina before ejaculation to prevent pregnancy. The goal of withdrawal is to prevent sperm from entering the vagina. However, this method has some serious drawbacks. It can be hard to have the self-control to withdraw in time. Sperm may also be released even prior to ejaculation. Withdrawal therefore isn't considered an effective method of preventing pregnancy.
- **Natural family planning or fertility awareness**—This method relies on understanding when a woman is fertile during a given month and avoiding having sex during these days (typically around nine or so days a month). This method requires paying close attention to various indicators of fertility, such as body temperature and menstruation, and is easier for women who have a regular menstrual cycle. The typical use failure rate is 24 percent.

In some cases, a woman can use emergency contraception, which is not a method of birth control because it is used after sex has already occurred. **Emergency contraceptive pills** are available over the counter and without a prescription at drugstores and pharmacies in most states. These pills can be taken up to five days after sex, although the sooner they are taken, the more likely they are to stop pregnancy from occurring. Emergency contraception is typically used after no birth control was used or a birth control method failed, such as a condom breaking. Emergency contraception may also be used following cases of rape.

Avoiding Sexually Transmitted Infections

Sexually transmitted infections (STIs) are spread from one person to another through some type of intimate physical contact, such as vaginal, oral, or anal sex. All of these diseases can lead to serious long-term consequences. As shown in **Table 3.3**, many STIs can, if left untreated, lead to infertility. HIV (human immunodeficiency virus) can over time develop into AIDS and lead to death.

TABLE 3.3 Common Sexually Transmitted Infections

Name	Symptoms	Consequences
Chlamydia	Most people have no symptoms, but when symptoms do appear, they include an abnormal discharge from the vagina or penis or a burning sensation when urinating.	Can cause serious, permanent damage to a woman's reproductive system, including infertility and ectopic pregnancy (a pregnancy that occurs outside the womb).
Gonorrhea	Many people have no symptoms at all, but when symptoms do appear, they may include an abnormal discharge from the vagina or penis, a burning sensation when urinating, or vaginal bleeding between periods.	Can cause serious and permanent health problems in both women and men; in women, consequences include infertility, ectopic pregnancy, and long-term pelvic/abdominal pain, and in men, consequences include infertility.
Hepatitis A	Most adults with hepatitis A have symptoms, including fatigue, low appetite, stomach pain, nausea, and jaundice, that usually resolve within two months of infection.	Most people who get hepatitis A feel sick for several weeks, but they usually recover completely and do not have lasting liver damage.
Hepatitis B	Many people who have hepatitis B do not show symptoms. For those who do, symptoms can include fever, fatigue, loss of appetite, nausea, vomiting, abdominal and/or joint pain, dark urine, and jaundice (yellow color in the skin or the eyes).	For some people, hepatitis B is an acute, or short-term, illness, but for others, it can become a long-term, chronic infection that can lead to serious health issues, like cirrhosis or liver cancer.
Genital herpes (caused by the herpes simplex virus, or HSV)	Most people who have genital herpes have no symptoms or have very mild symptoms. Herpes sores usually appear as one or more blisters on or around the genitals, rectum, or mouth. The blisters break and leave painful sores that may take a week or more to heal.	Genital herpes can cause painful genital sores and can be severe in people with suppressed immune systems. If you touch the sores, herpes can be transferred to another part of the body such as the eyes.
Genital warts (caused by the human papilloma virus, or HPV)	Most people with HPV—the most common sexually transmitted infection in the United States—do not know they are infected and never develop symptoms or health problems from it. Some people find out they have HPV when they get genital warts, which usually appear as a small bump or group of bumps in the genital area.	In most cases, HPV goes away on its own and does not cause any problems. But when HPV does not go away, it can cause genital warts and cancer, including cancer of the cervix, vulva, vagina, penis, anus, or throat.
HIV/AIDS (a virus)	Many people with HIV do not know they are infected. Some people may experience a flu-like illness within two to four weeks after infection, but others do not feel sick during this stage. The only way to determine whether you have HIV is to be tested for HIV infection.	HIV attacks the body's immune system, making it harder for the body to fight off infections and some other diseases. People who die of AIDS die of opportunistic infections or cancers that take advantage of a very weak immune system.

STIs are very common, especially among young adults. Nearly 50 percent of the 20 million new cases of STIs each year and about 25 percent of the 40,000 new cases of HIV infections are diagnosed in people who are fourteen to twenty-four years old.

The safest way to protect yourself from acquiring an STI or HIV is to avoid all sexual activity or to be in a long-term mutually monogamous relationship with an uninfected partner. But college students who choose to be sexually active should follow these strategies to reduce their risk:

INTERACTIVE FIGURES, CHARTS, & TABLES

- Use latex condoms correctly every single time you have sex.
- Limit your number of sexual partners.
- Avoid engaging in sexual activity following alcohol or drug use, which can reduce the likelihood of using a condom.
- Get vaccinated for human papillomavirus (HPV), which helps prevent many different kinds of cancer as well as genital warts.
- If you are in a high-risk group for HIV, talk with your doctor or health care provider about PrEP (Pre-Exposure Prophylaxis).
- Get tested every year for STIs, since early diagnosis can reduce the risk of developing long-term consequences such as infertility.

If you are diagnosed with a sexually transmitted infection, notify your sex partners so they can be tested and receive treatment if needed. Conversely, if your sex partner is diagnosed with a disease, you need to be evaluated, tested, and treated.

> **Think Deeper** | Making Good Sexual Decisions
>
> Think about your own feelings about sexual behavior at this point in your life. Then consider the following questions:
>
> 1. What factors in a relationship influence whether you want to engage in sexual behavior?
> 2. How can you communicate to romantic partners your feelings about sexual behavior?
> 3. If you decide to have sex, what strategies can you use to avoid unwanted pregnancy and STIs?
>
> Reflecting on the types of sexual behavior you do—and don't—want can help you stick with your choices. It can also help you better share those choices with dating partners.

Understanding Sexual Assault

People often think about sexual assault as something that occurs between strangers. But in reality, most people who are the victims of sexual assault know the person who hurt them. The term **date rape** describes forced, unwanted sex committed by someone the victim knows. In date rape, a rapist takes advantage of being trusted and alone with the victim. The person may also use alcohol or drugs to reduce the victim's ability to resist sex.

Although more men than women carry out acts of sexual violence, both men and women can be the victims of sexual attacks. In a survey of adults, 10.6 percent of women, and 2.1 percent of men reported that they were forced to have sex at some time in their lives. A survey of college women found that 20 percent to 25 percent reported being raped or experiencing an attempted rape while in college.

Some people continue to have misconceptions about date rape, since it doesn't fit the traditional definition of sexual assault committed by a stranger. For example, they may believe that being in a dating relationship with someone means rape can't occur or that someone who is flirting or has engaged in other forms of sexual activity has already indicated their desire to have sex. They may also believe that people who are sexually assaulted provoked the attack in some way—by drinking too much, using drugs, or dressing in a particular way. However, there is no justification for engaging in sexual activity with someone without their consent. The person who commits this act, not the victim, is entirely to blame.

Check your own knowledge about sexual assault using the *Test Yourself* below.

> **Test Yourself** | How Well Do You Understand Sexual Assault?
>
>
>
> Respond to each of these statements on a 1 to 5 scale where 1 = strongly agree and 5 = strongly disagree.
>
> 1. If someone is raped while they are drunk, they are at least somewhat responsible for letting things get out of control.
> 2. If a person goes to a room alone with someone they meet at a party, it is their own fault if they are raped.
> 3. Individuals don't usually intend to force sex on others, but sometimes they get too sexually carried away.
> 4. If the accused "rapist" doesn't have a weapon, you really can't call it a rape.
> 5. It shouldn't be considered rape if a person is drunk and didn't realize what they were doing.
> 6. If both people are drunk, it can't be rape.
> 7. If someone doesn't physically fight back—even if they protest verbally—it can't be considered rape.
> 8. If a person doesn't say "No," they can't claim rape.
> 9. A lot of times, people who say they were raped agreed to have sex and then regretted it.
> 10. A lot of times, people who say they were raped led the person on and then had regrets.
>
> Add up your scores on these items. The higher your score, the *less* accurate your beliefs are about sexual assault. All of these items are common myths about sexual assault. Learning what sexual assault is—and what it isn't—is really important.
>
> Johnson, N. L., Lipp, N. S., & Stone, H. K. (2023). Initial evaluation of a gender-inclusive version of the Illinois Rape Myth Acceptance Scale. *Psychology of Sexual Orientation and Gender Diversity, 10*(2), 206–216. https://doi.org/10.1037/sgd0000536

It's also important to remember that sexual violence can take many forms. It can include the following:

- Sexual touching (either directly or through a person's clothing)
- Watching someone undress or shower without their knowledge
- Exposing one's genitals
- Verbal or behavioral sexual harassment
- Taking nude photographs of a person
- Exposing someone to pornography

Another type of sexual violence occurs when someone threatens to share intimate images of you online unless you give in to their demands. These demands may involve money, sexual favors, or additional intimate images. This type of blackmail is known as sextortion.

Consequences of Sexual Violence Sexual violence, including date rape, can have lasting and harmful effects. These effects include the following:

- Physical problems, such as bruises, back pain, and headaches
- Unwanted pregnancy
- Sexually transmitted infections (STIs)
- Psychological problems, such as shock, denial, fear, anxiety, shame, guilt, and confusion
- Fear of being alone or going to specific places
- Difficulty trusting other people and having future intimate relationships

Some of these symptoms may disappear or lessen with time. However, some people who have experienced sexual violence have long-term psychological consequences. They are more likely to develop **posttraumatic stress disorder (PTSD)**, a psychological disorder that can include sleep disturbances, flashbacks, and repeated mental replaying of the attack. They may also become depressed, and some may contemplate suicide.

Strategies for Preventing and Treating Sexual Violence You can reduce your risk of becoming a victim of sexual assault, including date rape. Here are some strategies to follow:

- **Stay in public settings**—Unless you really know someone well, stay with friends in a group setting or in a public space. Don't leave a party with someone you don't know well. Leave with a trusted friend and get to a safe place right away. Never go alone to unfamiliar, isolated places with people you do not know well. This includes people you've met on a dating app.
- **Limit alcohol and drug use**—Using alcohol and drugs can impair your ability to sense danger, make good decisions, and clearly communicate your limits regarding sexual activity.
- **Watch your drink**—Do not leave a drink unattended or take a drink from someone you don't know or trust. Certain drugs, called date rape drugs, are used by attackers. When these drugs are slipped into an unsuspecting person's drink, they cause the person to become intoxicated, drowsy, disoriented, and even unconscious, which increases the risk of assault.

If you are sexually assaulted, you have many options about how to respond. You may want to call 911 or the police, go to a hospital, or talk to a friend or family member. You can also contact the National Sexual Assault Hotline at (800)-656-4673, which is free and available 24 hours a day. Many people find it helpful to talk to a specially trained counselor. Although reporting an assault to the police may seem hard to do, remember that sexual assault is a crime and should be immediately reported. Reporting sexual assault to the police may also deter the perpetrator from assaulting someone else.

Review, Discuss, and Apply

INTERACTIVE SELF-SCORING QUIZZES

Discussion Questions

1. Why do college students tend to underestimate how many students have chosen abstinence?
2. What are the advantages—and disadvantages—of different methods for avoiding unplanned pregnancy?
3. Why are STIs so common among young adults?
4. Why do many people hold misperceptions about sexual violence? What factors contribute to these errors?

Think Ahead | Career and Lifelong Applications

Taking care of your body is an essential part of a healthy lifestyle. People who take care of themselves—by eating well, exercising regularly, and getting enough sleep—are more effective in their careers. They also have happier and longer lives. In contrast, people who experience addiction, unplanned pregnancy, and STIs may have more trouble advancing in their careers. These factors may also decrease their psychological and physical well-being. How does taking care of your body improve your work—and personal—lives? Here are some of the advantages:

Increased energy—People who follow a healthy diet, exercise regularly, and get enough sleep have more energy. This increased energy helps them accomplish more at work and experience greater success. They also have more energy for engaging in fun activities with family members and friends.

More alert—People who get adequate sleep, engage in regular physical activity, and avoid substance abuse are more alert. They also have better thinking, learning, and judgment skills. They are better able to concentrate on the task at hand, and therefore perform well at work. They are less at risk of having a car accident that could injure them or others.

Module 3.3 Managing Healthy Sexual Behavior 77

Better stress management—People who engage in regular physical activity and get enough sleep are better at managing stress. This ability helps them succeed when working under pressure and on deadline at their jobs. It also helps them cope with challenges in their personal life, such as conflict with a friend, buying a house, or becoming a parent.

Better health—People who exercise regularly, get enough sleep, and avoid substance abuse experience better physical health. They are less likely to get sick, and they recover faster from illness and injuries. This better overall health means they are less likely to miss work or social events due to illness.

People who prioritize their physical health—including eating healthy foods, engaging in regular exercise, getting enough sleep, and avoiding substance abuse—experience benefits in their personal and professional lives. They have more energy and are more alert. They are more effective at managing stress and experience better health. These benefits help explain why taking care of your body is an essential part of life success.

What Would You Do?

In this chapter, Aiden and Imani need your advice.

VIDEO CONTENT

AIDEN
Aiden is concerned about his somewhat unhealthy lifestyle and wants your advice.

Watch Aiden's video: **Taking Care**

IMANI
Imani is having trouble getting to sleep at night and needs some suggestions.

Watch Imani's video: **Tired All of the Time**

What would you tell Aiden? What would you tell Imani?

Take Some Action | Here and Now

DOWNLOAD DOCUMENTS & TEMPLATES

We all have strengths and weaknesses when it comes to taking care of ourselves physically and being sexually responsible. Being aware of those strengths and weaknesses is key to success in college, in the workplace, and in life.

Review your outcomes on the *Test Yourself* assessments throughout this chapter and your responses to the *Think Deeper* questions. Reflect on your results and responses, and then answer these questions:

1. What are your strengths with respect to taking care of yourself physically? How will you put those strengths to work for you toward succeeding in college? How will sharpening those strengths in college help you succeed in the workplace?

2. How do you want to improve your strengths when it comes to taking care of your body?

3. Review the suggested action steps in that area and choose two or three of those to commit to here and now, and for each, say how taking that action step will help you succeed in college and beyond.

Share and discuss your responses to these questions with a friend, classmate, or family member.

Chapter Summary

Chapter 3 Practice Quiz

Module 3.1 Defining Healthy Behaviors

- What you eat—and drink—has a major impact on your ability to stay healthy. Eating the right types of foods provides energy your body needs and ensures that your body has essential vitamins and minerals. Make healthy eating a priority, including selecting balanced meals with a variety of foods, watching portion size, drinking enough water, limiting processed foods and fats, and avoiding fad diets.

- Engaging in regular physical activity is a great way to stay healthy and manage stress. People who engage in regular physical activity also experience mental health benefits, including lower levels of depression and anxiety. Easy strategies for staying active include integrating exercise into your daily life, using small blocks of time, taking small steps to increase physical activity, choosing activities that you enjoy, and exercising with a friend.

- Many college students don't get enough sleep, which can have major consequences for your psychological and physical health. Sleep deprivation is linked with worse academic performance, mood problems, accidents, and poor athletic performance. Strategies for getting enough sleep include setting (and following) a schedule, limiting naps, exercising, avoiding stimulants, relaxing before heading to bed, and limiting exposure to lights late at night.

Module 3.2 Avoiding Substance Abuse

- Substance abuse describes the use of drugs, including alcohol or illegal drugs, even when such use is leading to negative consequences. All drugs alter mental processes in some way and can have serious and lasting side effects. Although alcohol use is pretty common on many colleges, it can lead to serious negative consequences, including risky sexual behavior, sexual assault, accidents, injuries, violent behavior, and alcohol poisoning. Many college students use cigarettes as well as other tobacco products, such as chewing tobacco, e-cigarettes, and vapes. These products all contain nicotine, which can lead to addiction. Many drugs that lead to serious consequences are illegal, such as cocaine, heroin, and hallucinogens. Other drugs may be legal, but they can be taken for purposes other than those for which they are intended. All types of drug use can have negative consequences, including drug overdoses.

- Many people who use drugs develop an addiction, meaning a physical and/or psychological need to continue taking a given drug. They develop a tolerance to a given level of the drug, meaning they need to take in even more of the drug to experience the same effects, and experience withdrawal, or unpleasant physical side effects, if they try to stop taking the drug. Strategies for reducing substance use include thinking about situations in which you are tempted to use drugs, handling these situations in a new way, and developing a plan for refusing offers of drugs. Strategies for helping someone who is addicted to drugs include expressing concern about their well-being, offering to find someone for them to talk to about their addiction, and going with them to a meeting or counselor for help.

Module 3.3 Managing Healthy Sexual Behavior

- Many college students choose not to have sex, meaning to practice abstinence. There are many reasons to choose not to engage in sex. If you've made a decision to stay abstinent, feel good about that decision. Don't feel embarrassed about this choice or have sex just to fit in with what other students seem to be doing. Many college students do make a choice to stay abstinent, even if this choice often isn't talked about so much.

- For college students who want to engage in sexual activity and avoid becoming pregnant or impregnating others, it is really important to use a safe and reliable form of contraception. Many forms of birth control are very effective when used correctly and consistently. In some cases, a woman can use emergency contraception, which is used after sex has already occurred. Emergency contraceptive pills are available over the counter and without a prescription at drugstores and pharmacies in most states.

- Sexually transmitted infections (STIs) are spread from one person to another through some type of intimate physical contact, such as vaginal, oral, or anal sex. All of these diseases can lead to serious long-term consequences. STIs are very common, especially among young adults. The safest way to protect yourself from acquiring an STI or HIV is to avoid all sexual activity or to be in a long-term mutually monogamous relationship with an uninfected partner. College students who choose to be sexually active should follow strategies to reduce their risk.

- People often think about sexual assault as something that occurs between strangers. But in reality, most people who are the victims of sexual assault know the person who hurt them. The term *date rape* describes forced, unwanted sex committed by someone the victim knows. Anyone can be a victim of sexual violence. Sexual violence can take many forms and can have lasting and harmful effects. Strategies for reducing the risk of becoming a victim of sexual assault include staying in public settings, limiting alcohol and drug use, and watching your drink.

Key Terms

Abstinence The choice not to have sex

Addiction A chronic disease in which a person has a physical and/or psychological need to continue using a given substance, regardless of harmful or negative consequences that may result

Alcohol poisoning A medical emergency that is caused when high blood alcohol levels suppress the central nervous system

Anorexia nervosa An eating disorder in which people attempt to maintain an extremely thin body size, engage only in very restricted eating, and have an intense fear of gaining weight

Binge drinking Drinking four or more drinks during a single occasion for women and five or more drinks during a single occasion for men

Binge eating disorder An eating disorder in which people engage in frequent episodes of uncontrollable binge eating

Bulimia nervosa An eating disorder in which people engage in binge eating (consuming enormous quantities of food are consumed) and purging (trying to get rid of the calories consumed by the binge, such as by vomiting or excessive exercising)

Date rape Forced, unwanted sex committed by someone the victim knows

Emergency contraceptive pills Pills that can be taken up to five days after sex to stop pregnancy from occurring

Posttraumatic stress disorder (PTSD) A long-lasting, trauma- and stressor-related disorder that overwhelms an individual's ability to cope.

Sexually transmitted infections (STIs) Infections spread through some type of intimate physical contact, which can lead to serious long-term consequences

Stimulant A drug that increases overall activity and general responsiveness.

Substance abuse The use of drugs, including alcohol or illegal drugs, even when such use is leading to negative consequences

Tolerance The need to take in even more of a drug to experience the same effects

Withdrawal Unpleasant physical side effects caused by stopping use of a given drug

Resources

American Psychological Association. (2020, March 4). Working out boosts brain health. Retrieved from https://www.apa.org/topics/exercise-fitness/stress

College students: getting enough sleep is vital to academic success. (2017, November 6). Retrieved from https://aasm.org/college-students-getting-enough-sleep-is-vital-to-academic-success/

Drugs, brains, and behavior: The science of addiction. Retrieved January 15, 2024, from https://nida.nih.gov/publications/drugs-brains-behavior-science-addiction/addiction-health.

Editorial staff. (2024, March 6). Ways of helping someone with drug or alcohol addiction. Retrieved from https://drugabuse.com/treatment/how-to-help-a-drug-addict

Glassman, K. Healthy eating 101: How to eat healthy in college. Retrieved January 15, 2024, from https://nutritiouslife.com/eat-empowered/how-to-eat-healthy-in-college/

Harmful and underage college drinking. (2023, December). Retrieved from https://www.niaaa.nih.gov/publications/brochures-and-fact-sheets/college-drinking

Safe sex guide for college students. Retrieved January 15, 2024, from https://www.campusexplorer.com/student-resources/safe-sex-guide-college-students/

Sleeping to succeed. Retrieved January 15, 2024, from https://learningcenter.unc.edu/tips-and-tools/sleeping-to-succeed/

References

Framson, C., Kristal, A. R., Schenk, J. M., Littman, A. J., Zeliadt, S., & Benitez, D. (2009). Development and validation of the mindful eating questionnaire. *Journal of the American Dietetic Association*, *109*(8), 1439–1444. https://doi.org/10.1016/j.jada.2009.05.006

Garcia, L., Pearce, M., Abbas, A., Mok, A., Strain, T., Ali, S., Crippa, A., Dempsey, P. C., Golubic, R., Kelly, P., Laird, Y., McNamara, E., Moore, S., de Sa, T. H., Smith, A. D., Wijndaele, K., Woodcock, J., & Brage, S. (2023). Non-occupational physical activity and risk of cardiovascular disease, cancer and mortality outcomes: A dose-response meta-analysis of large prospective studies. *British Journal of Sports Medicine*, bjsports-2022-105669. Advance online publication. https://doi.org/10.1136/bjsports-2022-105669

Huff, C. (2022). A crisis of campus sexual assault. *Monitor on Psychology*, *53*(3), p. 26.

Johnson, N. L., Lipp, N. S., & Stone, H. K. (2023). Initial evaluation of a gender-inclusive version of the Illinois Rape Myth Acceptance Scale. *Psychology of Sexual Orientation and Gender Diversity*, *10*(2), 206–216. https://doi.org/10.1037/sgd0000536

Kato, T. (2014). Development of the Sleep Quality Questionnaire in healthy adults. *Journal of Health Psychology*, *19*(8), 977–986. https://doi.org/10.1177/1359105313482168

Kivlichan, A. E., Lowe, D. J. E., & George, T. P. (2022, May 25). Substance misuse in college students. *Psychiatric Times*, *39*(5).

Krieger, H., Young, C. M., Anthenien, A. M., & Neighbors, C. (2018). The epidemiology of binge drinking among college-age individuals in the United States. *Alcohol Research: Current Reviews*, *39*(1), 23–30.

Maddock, J. E., Laforge, R. G., Rossi, J. S., & O'Hare, T. (2001). The College Alcohol Problems Scale. *Addictive Behaviors*, *26*(3), 385–398. https://doi.org/10.1016/s0306-4603(00)00116-7

Prather, A. A., Janicki-Deverts, D., Hall, M. H., & Cohen, S. (2015). Behaviorally assessed sleep and susceptibility to the common cold. *Sleep*, *38*(9), 1353–1359. https://doi.org/10.5665/sleep.4968

Prentice, D. A., & Miller, D. T. (1993). Pluralistic ignorance and alcohol use on campus: Some consequences of misperceiving the social norm. *Journal of Personality and Social Psychology*, *64*(2), 243–256. https://doi.org/10.1037/0022-3514.64.2.243

Wilsnack, R. W., Wilsnack, S. C., Gmel, G., & Kantor, L. W. (2018). Gender differences in binge drinking: Prevalence, predictors, and consequences. *Alcohol Research: Current Reviews*, *39*(1), 57–76.

Winerman, L. (2018). Making campuses safer. *APA Monitor*, *49*(9), 45. https://www.apa.org/monitor/2018/10/campuses-safer

CHAPTER 4

Build and Maintain Relationships

VIDEO CONTENT
Author's Introduction

"Life is partly what we make it, and partly what is made by the friends we choose."
—Tennessee Williams

CHAPTER OUTLINE

Envision, Pursue, and Persist: Ruth Bader Ginsburg

Module 4.1 Building and Maintaining Connections
Managing Different Relationships
Think Deeper: Forming Positive Friendships
Building New Relationships
Test Yourself: Are You Lonely?

Module 4.2 Communicating Well
Types of Communication
Common Problems in Communication
Think Deeper: Avoiding Online Communication Problems
Strategies for Effective Communication
Test Yourself: How Assertive Are You?
Make It Personal: Using I-Statements

Module 4.3 Managing Conflict
Common Causes of Conflict
Benefits of Conflict
Test Yourself: How Do You Manage Conflict?
Skills for Resolving Conflict
Make It Personal: Steps for Resolving Conflict
Think Deeper: Solving a Conflict with a Friend

Think Ahead: Career and Lifelong Applications
Take Some Action: Here and Now
Chapter Summary
Key Terms
Resources
References

LEARNING OBJECTIVES

LO 4.1 To understand the value of different types of relationships

LO 4.2 To examine different approaches to communication

LO 4.3 To understand and manage conflict effectively

81

Envision, Pursue, and Persist | Ruth Bader Ginsburg

Steve Petteway/Supreme Court of the United States/Wikimedia Commons

You've undoubtedly heard about the late Supreme Court justice Ruth Bader Ginsburg and her impressive advocacy for gender equality in the law. But what you may know less about is the significant role relationships played in her life.

Ginsburg met her future husband when they were both college students. They had been married for fifty-six years at the time of his death in 2010. What was the secret of their long—and by all accounts happy—marriage?

One factor was almost certainly the couple's decision to share housework and child-raising, and to support each other's goals. (Remember, they were married in the 1960s, when most marriages were much more traditional.)

Another factor may have been the advice Ruth received on her wedding day from her mother-in-law: In a happy marriage, "sometimes, it helps to be a little deaf." Ginsburg joked that the advice also has been relevant to her long career in law. "It was excellent advice for the two law faculties on which I served, the D.C. Circuit and even today at the Supreme Court."

On a professional level, one of Ginsburg's closest friends during much of her time as a Supreme Court justice was her fellow justice Antonin Scalia (until his death in 2016). This friendship is particularly surprising: the two justices were appointed by presidents of different political parties and disagreed on many legal issues. Yet Ginsburg placed a high priority on building professional relationships. They focused on what they had in common. This included growing up near New York City, serving as law professors, and sharing a love of the opera. They spent many New Year's Eves together with their families. "I never heard them talk about anything political or ideological, because there would be no point," said Ginsburg's grandson, Paul Spera.

Ginsburg's approach to managing her relationships, both personal and professional, may help explain her considerable success. She prioritized building close relationships and effectively managed conflict.

This chapter examines how to build and maintain good relationships, which will help you experience success in college and throughout your life. First, you'll learn about how to maintain different types of relationships and how to find and build new relationships. Next, you'll learn about different types of communication, common problems people face in communicating, and strategies for communicating effectively in your personal and professional relationships. The final section of this chapter will describe different approaches for managing conflict and positive approaches you can use to manage conflict.

Module 4.1 Building and Maintaining Connections

LO 4.1.1 To identify common challenges in different types of relationships

LO 4.1.2 To describe strategies for building new relationships

---

Relationships play an important role throughout our lives. They can provide much-needed support, provide considerable happiness, and, sometimes, cause pressure and conflict.

One of the joys—and challenges—of college is managing different types of relationships. This might be especially hard in your first year, when you are also developing skills for managing your academic work. In this section, you'll learn how to manage the different types of relationships you have in college as well as strategies for forming new relationships.

Managing Different Relationships

Most college students have many different types of personal relationships. These relationships can help you grow and develop new perspectives and skills. They sometimes can also involve some challenges.

Roommates Some college students live with roommates, either in a shared room or an apartment. These relationships can play an important role in helping with adjustment to college life. In some cases, roommates may even become lifelong friends.

But adjusting to living with someone can pose challenges. You may hold different attitudes, beliefs, or values than your roommate. You may also have different preferences for your shared living space, such as level of cleanliness, amount of noise, or sleeping patterns. These differences can sometimes create conflict.

Here are some effective strategies for creating a good roommate relationship:

- **Form a roommate contract**—Sit down with your roommate and write out a list of rules with which you both agree; this could include agreements about how often you will clean the room, what time lights should be off and noise limited, and when to have friends over. Developing a set of rules early on can help you avoid problems later. **Figure 4.1** provides a helpful example for setting up such a contract.
- **Have realistic expectations**—Some students arrive at college and believe their roommate will immediately become their best friend; this idealistic expectation puts lots of pressure on the relationship and can set you up for failure. Instead, set reasonable expectations, such as maintaining a friendly relationship and being considerate of each other's needs. Make sure to develop other friendships as well (as you'll learn more about later in this chapter).

Step 1: My Personal Preferences

Fill this out before meeting with your RA and your roommate(s). You should feel comfortable sharing this information in that meeting.

Section 1: At home, I lived:

☐ Alone

☐ With sibling(s)/family member(s)

What I liked most about that living arrangement was: _____

What I liked least about that living arrangement was: _____

Section 2: Guests

You may want to have friends over in your room. It's important to really think about what matters to you when it comes to guests. Please refer to the *Hallways Handbook* for the guest policies in your hall. Guests are to be accompanied by a resident student at all times.

Guests that I anticipate having visit (friends, family members, study partners, etc.): _____

In order for guests not be a problem for me, I will need: _____

For what purposes are you comfortable having Guests?		Visitors Allowed	Overnight Guests	Same Gender Overnight Guests?	Opposite Gender Overnight Guests?
Social	Study	☐ Yes ☐ No	☐ Yes ☐ No	☐ Yes ☐ No	☐ Yes ☐ No
☐ Yes ☐ No ☐ Ask First	☐ Yes ☐ No ☐ Ask First	☐ Ask First	☐ Ask First	☐ Ask First	☐ Ask First

What are my guidelines for how my belongings are used/left while I am away and guests are present? _____

FIGURE 4.1 A sample roommate contract.

- **Address problems**—In some cases, your roommate may do things that irritate you, but not know how you are feeling. This makes it likely that these things will continue. Instead of just ignoring problems, it's better to openly share with your roommate how you are feeling. Perhaps they could make simple changes, if only you would ask. This could include wearing headphones instead of listening to music aloud, keeping their side of the room a bit cleaner, or asking before they borrow your clothes.
- **Solve issues together**—When conflicts arise in a roommate relationship, it's good to discuss strategies for working through them together. Instead of criticizing your roommate for their behavior, focus on how you can work together to resolve problems. It is easier to work through differences if you have a discussion than if one person feels attacked. Can you arrange your schedules so that both of you can have time alone in the room? Can you alternate weekends for hosting friends or throwing parties? Try to use a friendly and approachable tone. Show respect for each other's point of view.
- **Seek help**—If you've tried on your own to raise concerns with your roommate and things aren't getting better, it's a good idea to get some help. Students who are living in dorms typically have resident assistants (RAs) who can help roommates work through conflicts. RAs have received special training on how to resolve common issues, and simply having an outside perspective can be helpful.

In some cases, schools may allow for changing rooms. But this is almost always considered a last resort. It's always better to try working through conflicts with your current roommate first. You may not become best friends, but in many cases it is possible to make bad living situations somewhat better.

Friendships College students spend a considerable amount of time with their friends. In fact, they almost always spend far more time with their friends than actually going to class! Friendships also play an essential role in shaping your college experience.

Given how much time college students spend with their friends, it's important to make sure that your friendships are a positive influence. In healthy friendships, each person recognizes and respects the other's decisions. Friends do not pressure you to do things you don't want to do, ridicule you for the choices you make, or try to change who you are. Choosing friends who share your interests and values can help reduce the pressure to engage in unhealthy behaviors. In fact, friends can influence you in positive ways, such as encouraging good study habits, engaging in regular exercise, or even attending class.

Think Deeper | Forming Positive Friendships  DOWNLOAD DOCUMENTS & TEMPLATES

Think about your different friendships in high school. Then consider the following questions:

1. Which friendships were a positive influence on your life?
2. In what ways did these friendships provide support, encourage healthy behaviors, and make you feel good about yourself?
3. Which approaches could you use in college to find positive friendships?

Reflecting on the types of friendships you have experienced in the past can help you find friends who will have a healthy and positive influence on your college experience.

Romantic Partners Many college students are excited to meet new people and form romantic relationships. But it's important to remember that dating in college can also be challenging.

It can be hard navigating a dating relationship in college while also keeping up with schoolwork and other friendships. Make sure to keep your other responsibilities in mind. Don't let the dating relationship consume all of your time and energy. In healthy relationships, each person maintains their own separate identity, including a focus on their classes, jobs, and activities. They also spend time with friends.

It's also important to make sure that both people in a dating relationship have the same expectations. Is this relationship exclusive or more casual, meaning you can both also see (or hook up with) other people? Talk to your partner to avoid misunderstandings and hurt feelings.

Some college students try to maintain long-distance dating relationships. These relationships have different challenges than relationships in which you can see and interact with the person regularly. Here are some strategies for navigating long-distance relationships:

- Make time to connect, through calling, texting, or emailing. This will help you stay connected even if you can't spend time together in person.
- Plan times for getting together in person. It is easier to manage a long-distance relationship if you know specifically when you can look forward to being together in person.
- Understand that long-distance relationships take work. Maintaining these relationships can be hard, as they require trust, energy, and effort. Make sure that each person is on the same page in terms of their expectations to avoid misunderstandings.

Although some college dating relationships lead eventually to marriage, many do not. If your relationship ends, keep the breakup civil and respectful. Treat your former partner as you would like them to treat you. Do not share private things they told you with others or post mean things about them on social media. Remember that this person played a meaningful role in your life, and you learned some valuable things from that relationship.

Family Members   Family relationships are some of the most important relationships throughout our lives. Many college students find it hard to stay close to family members if they aren't living at home. Here are some strategies you can use to maintain close ties with your family members while in college.

- **Stay in touch**—Even if you are very busy, make time to keep in touch with family members. This could include a weekly call to update them on your life. It could also be brief texts or emails a few times a week to let them know how you are doing. Family members care about you and want to know what is going on with your life.
- **Listen**—Relationships are a two-way street, meaning it's also important for you to learn what's going on with your parents or guardians, siblings, and extended family. Ask questions about what family members are up to so that you also stay in touch with their lives.

It can seem hard to prioritize family relationships while in college. But remember that family members have known you the longest. They will also be with you your entire life. So, take some time to maintain these relationships, even in the midst of your hectic college life.

Building New Relationships

Starting college can be hard, especially for students who are attending a school far from home. **Loneliness,** meaning discomfort or uneasiness caused by feeling emotionally or socially isolated from other people, is very common for many college students. This is especially true in the first few weeks or months. It's very easy to compare the new friendships you are forming with those of your high school friendships, which developed over years. You can test whether you are experiencing loneliness in the following *Test Yourself*.

But here's the good news: there are many steps you can take to meet new people and develop lifelong friendships during college. In fact, it's easier than you think!

Test Yourself | Are You Lonely?

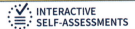
INTERACTIVE SELF-ASSESSMENTS

Respond to the following statements using a 1–4 scale, where 1 = never and 4 = often.

1. I feel in tune with the people around me.
2. I lack companionship.
3. There is no one I can turn to.
4. I do not feel alone.
5. I feel part of a group of friends.
6. I have a lot in common with the people around me.
7. I am no longer close to anyone.
8. My interests and ideas are not shared by those around me.
9. I am an outgoing person.
10. There are people I feel close to.
11. I feel left out.
12. My social relationships are superficial.
13. No one really knows me well.
14. I feel isolated from others.
15. I can find companionship when I want it.
16. There are people who really understand me.
17. I am unhappy being so withdrawn.
18. People are around me but not with me.

First, add up your ratings for the following items: 1, 4, 5, 6, 9, 10, 15, and 16. Then add up your ratings on these items: 2, 3, 7, 8, 11, 12, 13, 14, 17, and 18. Now, subtract your score on the first set of items from your score on the second set of items. Higher scores indicate greater loneliness.

Russell, D., Peplau, L. A., & Cutrona, C. E. (1980). The revised UCLA Loneliness Scale: Concurrent and discriminant validity evidence. *Journal of Personality and Social Psychology, 39*(3), 472–480. https://doi.org/10.1037/0022-3514.39.3.472

Meet New People   All colleges host events at which students can meet new people. This could include social events in the dorm or apartment building, gatherings to learn about different majors, or opportunities to learn about new campus clubs. Go to some of these events and introduce yourself.

You can also meet new people in your classes. This can be a great way to find people with whom to study. People who are taking the same classes may also have similar academic and career interests. This means that you may already have something in common.

Remember that other students are feeling just like you are feeling. They want to meet people and make friends. They will really appreciate your efforts to reach out.

Leave Your Room   If you are living in a dorm or college apartment building, spend time in common spaces, such as a lounge, dining hall, or even laundry room. Many students in a dorm leave their doors open in the first few weeks so that other students will stop by and say "Hi." Introduce yourself to people you meet and be friendly. Ask them where they are from, what classes they are taking, or what they are majoring in. These types of casual encounters can form the basis for longer interactions later on.

Spend time on campus in places where you can meet new people. This could include studying in the college library, attending school sporting events, or working out in the campus gym.

Join Extracurricular Activities   All colleges offer many different types of extracurricular activities, from sports teams to religious groups to community service. Getting involved in some of these activities is a great way to meet people with common interests. You will also see the same people over time. This makes it easier to form and build friendships. Check out the different organizations your college offers on the school website. Then, go to a few meetings to learn about those that interest you.

Some schools have a Greek system, in which students can join a fraternity or sorority. For some students, this can be a great way to build friendships. Talk to older students at your school to figure out if participating in this type of social group is a good fit for you.

Invite People If you meet someone with whom you connect, invite them to do something. This will help you get to know them better and to see if a friendship can form.

Here are some ideas for a casual shared activity:

- Lunch or coffee
- Watching a TV show or movie
- Attending a sporting event, concert, or party
- Going to the gym
- Checking out a campus club or organization
- Studying

Remember that meeting new people is hard for many college students early on. Other people will appreciate an invitation to do something. Spending time with people is also how you will build friendships.

If someone invites you to do something, say yes! Even though you may be focused on staying on top of academic work, make time to form friendships. You can always carve out a bit of time in your day to play pickup basketball, attend a comedy show or campus lecture, or take a study break and have coffee. Meeting new people and doing new things in the first weeks of college can help you figure out what friendships you want to build. This will help you make the most of your college experience.

Review, Discuss, and Apply

Discussion Questions

1. How have your relationships with different people—family members, friends, romantic partners—changed from high school to college?
2. Which of the strategies for building new relationships would you find most helpful? How might different strategies work best for different people?

Module 4.2 Communicating Well

LO 4.2.1 To identify different types of communication

LO 4.2.2 To describe common problems in communication

LO 4.2.3 To review strategies for effective communication

How many times a day do you talk with other people, including your friends, family members, coworkers, and professors? Virtually all college students spent a lot of time communicating with other people. You might talk to your roommates and friends about making plans for the

weekend. You might talk to professors about upcoming assignments. This type of **communication**, meaning exchanging messages, is an important part of our daily lives. In this section, you'll learn about different types of communication as well as common problems in communication. Most important, you'll learn about strategies for communicating more effectively in both your personal and professional relationships.

Types of Communication

Effective communication is perhaps the most important part of a healthy relationship. It is also an essential skill that we use in all types of relationships. This includes our personal relationships with friends and family members and our professional relationships with professors and colleagues.

Communication involves sending some type of message, such as thoughts, ideas, feelings, and/or information, to one or more receivers. This message can be delivered verbally, either in person or over the phone. You might talk with your professor during office hours about a question you have regarding course material. Messages can also be delivered in writing. For example, you could text your friend that you'd like to meet up after class to go to the gym.

Effective communication happens when the receiver understands the message and provides a constructive response. This response communicates that the message was received and understood. The communication process may continue with the further exchange of messages. You might ask your boss if you could switch your work schedule over the next week because you have several big assignments due. Your boss could offer you some different shifts, which you could then accept or turn down.

People send messages using two types of communication: **verbal communication** and **nonverbal communication**.

Verbal Communication
Verbal communication is the use of words to send an oral (spoken) or written message. You use verbal communication all the time in your everyday conversations. This includes through text messages, in-person conversations, phone calls, emails, social media posts, letters, and notes. Telling a roommate you will meet them at the concert at a certain time is a form of verbal communication. So is talking with your brother online.

Nonverbal Communication
Communication involves more than just words (see Figure 4.2). You can also communicate with your face and body. Nonverbal communication involves communicating through facial expressions, body language, gestures, tone and volume of voice, and other signals that do not involve the use of words. Your nonverbal communication shows people whether you are paying attention and are interested in a conversation. These signals are an important part of showing respect for the person communicating with you.

Examples of nonverbal communication include the following:

- Eye contact or lack of eye contact
- Facial expressions, such as smiling, frowning, or eye rolling
- Gestures, such as nodding, shaking the head, or moving the hands
- Posture, such as leaning forward, facing away, or slumping in a chair
- Tone of voice, which can communicate friendliness, doubt, or sarcasm
- Volume of voice, such as loud or soft
- Intonation or pitch of voice, such as high-pitched or low-pitched

Nonverbal communication is possible only if you can see or hear the other person. For example, if you are talking with someone at school or video calling a friend, you can see the other person's facial expressions and hear the person's voice. If you are talking over the phone, you can hear the other person's tone of voice.

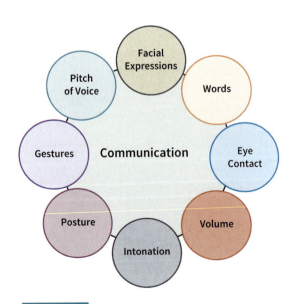

FIGURE 4.2 Elements of communication.

Common Problems in Communication

Communicating effectively is an important part of building and maintaining relationships. But sometimes we have difficulty communicating clearly, which can lead to misunderstandings, confusion, and even conflict.

Cultural Differences in Communication
One factor that influences communication is the culture in which we grow up. The simplest example of how culture impacts communication is the different languages people speak.

Culture also affects how people use and interpret nonverbal communication. For example, in some cultures, making a lot of eye contact with someone when you talk shows respect and attention. In other cultures, direct eye contact is seen as aggressive and insulting. Different cultures also use and interpret facial expressions in different ways. For example, in the United States, smiling is a sign of friendliness. In Japan, smiling at someone you do not know can be seen as inappropriate, especially for women.

Cultures also differ in their expectations about touch. In some cultures, people tend to stand close together when they talk and may touch each other. In other cultures, people stand farther apart and rarely touch someone they do not know well. These differences sometimes make communication between people from different cultures challenging. To navigate these challenges, you can recognize and appreciate that cultures vary in communication and that there is no right or best way to communicate.

The Challenge of Online Communication
Most college students regularly communicate online. Online communication occurs on social media and websites and through any digital device—a phone, computer, laptop, tablet, or gaming system. This type of communication has many advantages. It provides instant feedback, allows for long-distance communication, and gives you time to think of the best response. Unfortunately, online communication can also lead to problems.

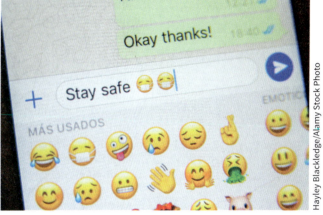

Forms of communication in which you cannot see or hear the other person can present challenges. Have you ever had a miscommunication online because someone wrote a message they intended to be sarcastic, but the other person didn't recognize this intent?

When you are sending an email or a text, the person cannot see your nonverbal cues, such as your tone of voice, facial expression, or gestures. These nonverbal cues help people interpret the message. This is why online messages increase the likelihood of miscommunication and conflict.

Online communication has evolved to incorporate some types of nonverbal communication. This includes emoticons, audio messages, pictures, and fonts (for example, capitalizing or italicizing words). These cues help express tone and intent in the absence of body language and voice.

But even the features that try to make up for the lack of nonverbal communication do not always succeed. One person may use an emoticon to express one emotion, but another person may associate an entirely different meaning to that same symbol.

Fortunately, there are some strategies you can use to avoid misunderstandings and communicate online safely and effectively. These strategies include the following:

- **Be kind and respectful**—Treat people the way you would like to be treated. If someone is rude or aggressive, you can ignore the message or tell the person to stop. If the aggressive behavior continues, block the person or talk to a trusted friend for advice about what to do next.
- **Solve conflicts offline**—If you have a disagreement with someone, approach the person face-to-face. If you cannot talk in person, reach out to the person privately online. Share your feelings and try to work through the conflict together. Do not share this disagreement on social media or in a public way. This will just make the conflict worse.

- **Think before sharing**—Content you share online, even in private emails or messages, can easily become public and spread. Think carefully before you share anything you would not want other people to see. Even if you are sharing private content only with a friend or dating partner, think about what might happen later on if you have conflict or if the relationship ends. Assume everyone will be able to see anything you post online, even if you try to remove what you posted.
- **Keep passwords private**—Create a password that you can remember, but that others cannot guess. Do not share this password with anyone, even with friends or dating partners, and change your password every few months. Sharing a password with a friend can cause issues if that friend pretends to be you, even if it seems like no big deal.

> **Think Deeper** | Avoiding Online Communication Problems
>
> Think about a time when communicating with someone online led to confusion, a misunderstanding, or conflict. Then consider the following questions:
>
> 1. What led to this problem?
> 2. Could this situation have been avoided by communicating in person or on the phone?
> 3. How could you use a different approach in the future to prevent this type of problem from occurring?
>
> Reflecting on the factors that lead to problems with online communication can help you communicate more effectively in the future.

Strategies for Effective Communication

In effective communication, people communicate their thoughts, information, values, and feelings. Many communication techniques encourage effective, open communication. You can use these techniques to communicate with care, consideration, and respect for yourself and others.

Pay Attention and Use Active Listening When someone is talking, fully focus on what that person is saying. Listen to their words and tone of voice to make sure you are understanding the intent of the words.

When listening, also pay attention to a person's body language, not just what the person is saying out loud. Observe the emotions in the person's facial expressions. Is the person feeling sad, anxious, or afraid? Sometimes nonverbal messages tell you even more about people's feelings than what they say directly. This is why paying full attention is so important. Do not check your phone or computer or get distracted by other people or activities in the room.

Good communication requires excellent listening skills, as shown in **Figure 4.3**. When you listen and focus on what another person is saying, you can better understand the person's point of view and show respect.

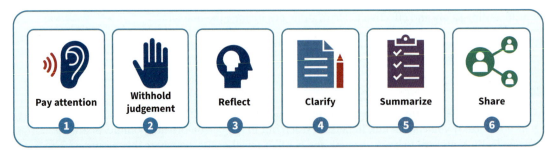

FIGURE 4.3 Active listening skills.

Active listening involves two key steps that put good listening skills to use:

- **Focus your full attention on the person talking**—Make eye contact and face the person talking. Let the person finish what they are saying without interrupting. If you have a question, or need a clarification, wait for a natural pause in the conversation to ask it. Do not think about your response or something else while the person is speaking.
- **Acknowledge and repeat what you heard in your own words**—Give feedback by saying, "Oh, wow" or "Yeah, I know." Ask questions about the message and indicate that you understand the message. You can repeat the message back to the person to show your understanding. This also allows the speaker to clarify any misunderstandings about the message. Reflect the person's feelings back by relating to and acknowledging the person's emotions.

Active listening is a great way to avoid misunderstandings. If you carefully listen to what others say, others will be more likely to do the same for you.

Keep in mind that being a good listener means allowing some periods of silence. People may share because they need to vent. They may not want or need an immediate response or solution. Simply letting people express how they feel can help.

Clearly Express Your Needs and Preferences To communicate effectively, people need to clearly state their wants, needs, opinions, and feelings. Some people assume others should be able to pick up on their subtle hints and know how they are feeling. This is a poor communication strategy. Instead of expecting the other person to be a mind reader, explain what you want the other person to understand.

Be Assertive You have probably noticed that people use different **communication styles**, or ways of expressing their thoughts and feelings. As shown in **Figure 4.4**, four common communication styles are the following:

1. **Passive**—**Passive communication** does not clearly state needs, wants, and feelings. Someone with a passive communication style may seem to say yes to everything, speak very quietly, and let hurt feelings build up. An example of passive communication is agreeing to an activity you do not want to do and thinking that no one cares about your feelings. Another example is not speaking up when someone hurts you.
2. **Aggressive**—**Aggressive communication** makes demands of others and insults others. A person with this communication style expresses needs and feelings disrespectfully. Examples of aggressive communication are interrupting or speaking over others, blaming or attacking others, getting frustrated easily, and speaking loudly.
3. **Passive-aggressive**—**Passive-aggressive communication** also makes demands of or insults others, but it does so by using techniques that do not clearly state needs, wants, and feelings. This communication style can include smiling when you are angry, muttering to yourself, spreading rumors, using sarcasm, denying your feelings, and using sabotage.
4. **Assertive**—**Assertive communication** clearly expresses feelings, needs, and goals in a way that shows respect to the other person. This type of communication values people and seeks clarity. Examples of assertive communication are calmly and truthfully saying, "It hurts when you say stuff like that," "I really miss you and wish we could hang out more often," or "Sure, let's do it."

What's the best style for effective communication? Being assertive. Assertive communication allows you to express how you feel and make yourself

INTERACTIVE FIGURES, CHARTS, & TABLES

	I Win—You Win	I Lose—You Lose
	Assertive	**Passive-aggressive**
	• I care about myself.	• I don't care about myself.
	• I care about you.	• I don't care about you.
	Aggressive	**Passive**
	• I care about myself.	• I don't care about myself.
	• I don't care about you.	• I care about you.
	I Win—You Lose	I Lose—You Win

FIGURE 4.4 Common communication styles.

known. Assertive communication also helps you express yourself respectfully in a way that is understanding of others. Communicating assertively can help you build honest relationships, set healthy boundaries, and defend your decisions and goals.

Do you want to know whether you tend to use assertive communication? Take the following *Test Yourself* to see.

Test Yourself | How Assertive Are You?

Please rate yourself honestly on each of the following items. Use the following scale:

| Never | Occasionally | Sometimes | Often | Always |
1	2	3	4	5
I stand up to my friends if they are doing something I don't feel comfortable doing.				
I'm usually able to tell people how I'm feeling.				
I express my opinions, even if others disagree with me.				
If I don't like the way someone is being treated, I speak up about it.				
I speak up about things I really care about.				
If I disagree with someone, I talk to them about it.				
I speak up when someone is not respecting my personal boundaries, like "no cheating off my homework" or "I don't let friends borrow money."				
If a person has borrowed money (or a game, clothes, or something else of value) and is overdue in returning it, I talk to the person about it.				

Sum up your score on all of these items. Higher scores indicate greater assertiveness. How often do you communicate assertively?

Gaumer Erickson, A. S., Noonan, P. M., Monroe, K., & McCall, Z. (2016). Assertiveness Formative Questionnaire. In P. M. Noonan & A. S. Gaumer Erickson (2017), *The skills that matter: Teaching interpersonal and intrapersonal competencies in any classroom* (pp. 181–182). Thousand Oaks, CA: Corwin.

Use I-Statements Effective communication uses **I-statements** to express thoughts, feelings, and desires. I-statements explain how the speaker thinks or feels without passing judgment on the receiver. An example of an I-statement is "I feel ignored, which makes me worried. Is something wrong?" This is more constructive than a you-statement, which makes assumptions about and blames the other person (for example, "You don't like me anymore"). Using I-statements can help others understand your point of view without making them feel attacked.

How well do you use I-statements? Revise each of the following you-statements to create some type of I-statement:

Make It Personal | Using I-Statements

You-Statement	Revised Wording
You don't value our relationship.	
You keep forgetting when we make plans.	
You ignore me when we hang out with friends.	
You are always late.	
You never do your share of the cleaning.	

Watch Your Nonverbal Communication When communicating, be aware of the nonverbal messages you send. What messages do your facial expressions and body language communicate to others? For example, suppose you are having a conversation with your sister. As she speaks, you look down at your phone and periodically roll your eyes. These signals do not communicate active listening or respect for your sister. Making eye contact, nodding your head, and leaning forward would communicate that you value what she is saying.

Respect Others and Value Diversity People who communicate well respect other people. They recognize that people differ in their backgrounds, experiences, and perspectives. They value this type of **diversity**, which refers to people's differences in many areas, such as race or ethnicity, sex, political ideas, gender identity, sexual orientation, or spiritual beliefs. People who respect other people can get along with people from a variety of backgrounds and benefit from learning different perspectives.

Review, Discuss, and Apply

Discussion Questions

1. Why is paying attention to nonverbal communication so important?
2. How can cultural differences create problems in communicating effectively? What can you do to overcome such challenges?
3. Can you identify people in your life who tend to use different styles of communication, such as passive, aggressive, passive-aggressive, and assertive? How do you feel when talking with people who use these different styles?

Module 4.3 | Managing Conflict

LO 4.3.1 To describe common causes of conflict

LO 4.3.2 To identify benefits of engaging in conflict

LO 4.3.3 To review skills for resolving conflict

The disagreements that occur in relationships are known as **conflict**. Conflict is a normal part of everyday life, even for healthy relationships. In fact, engaging in conflict can have positive outcomes for your and for your relationships. Understanding conflict—including what causes it and how to best resolve it—is important.

Common Causes of Conflict

Many different factors can lead to interpersonal conflicts, meaning conflicts between people or groups of people. The following differences can cause conflicts to occur:

- **Different priorities**—People may prioritize events, situations, and preferences differently. For example, maybe it is important to you that you see your friend every week, but it is equally important to your friend to attend soccer practice. Your friend may therefore not have time to see you every week.
- **Different values**—Family, culture, personal views and opinions, and experiences influence your values—the things that are important to you. For example, maybe your teacher values hard work and is strict with a fellow classmate, but you value your classmate's feelings and disagree with your teacher's approach.
- **Different goals**—People's individual goals can sometimes cause conflict. For example, a goal of your family is to keep you safe, which might clash with your goal to be more independent.

- **Different needs**—People have different needs at different times. For example, maybe you need some time to wind down after school, but your dating partner needs to vent about a fight with a sibling.
- **Misunderstandings**—Misunderstandings are failures in communication that lead to conflict. For example, maybe when you complain about your weekend, your friend thinks you are complaining about your time together. If your friend does not clarify your message, this could lead to hurt feelings and conflict.

What separates healthy conflict from unhealthy conflict is how conflict is resolved. In disagreements of little importance, it may be best to simply accept differences between yourself and another person and agree to respectfully disagree. There is no point in arguing with a friend who does not like your favorite TV show, for example. Other conflicts—for example, you and your sibling disagreeing about which movie to see—are easy to settle with no hurt feelings. Many conflicts, however, are more complicated and too serious to ignore.

Conflicts that are not resolved can lead to serious and lasting consequences. Conflicts that go unresolved for a long time often escalate and can then become major issues. Unresolved conflicts can have negative effects on a person's psychological and emotional well-being. Interpersonal conflict can even impact a person's physical health. Conflict is a type of stress, and people who experience long-term stressors in the form of conflict can develop serious health conditions. (You will learn more about the link between stress and heath in Chapter 10.)

Benefits of Conflict

How often do you have conflict with your sibling, best friend, or dating partner? Did you know that some conflict is actually a good thing? Many people worry that trying to resolve a conflict will destroy a relationship or make the conflict worse. In reality, working through a conflict can strengthen a relationship. When people decide to work together to resolve a conflict, they show their commitment to the relationship. What matters most is how people interact when resolving conflict.

Research by Dr. John Gottman at the University of Washington examined how couples resolve conflict and how their interactions impact happiness. In one study, researchers examined videos of married couples trying to solve a conflict in their relationship. They counted how many different positive and negative interactions the couple had during a fifteen-minute interaction. Positive interactions included behaviors like laughing, teasing, and showing affection. Negative interactions included criticism, anger, and defensiveness. Researchers then contacted these same couples nine years later to see if they were still together.

Couples who stayed together had at least five positive interactions for every one negative interaction when they resolved conflict. This led to a so-called magic ratio of five to one.

What is the key take-home point here? Good relationships involve conflict, but they also involve lots of positive interactions. Even when people are working through a conflict, people in a healthy relationship show positive behaviors toward each other. Conflict is inevitable in a relationship. Conflict is even a sign of a healthy relationship, as long as it is balanced with affection, laughter, and love.

Are you interested in learning how you tend to resolve conflicts in your close relationships? If so, try the following *Test Yourself*.

Test Yourself | How Do You Manage Conflict?

Read each of the following statements, and rate how often you tend to use each approach when facing conflict on a 1–9 scale, with 1 meaning you never do this, and 9 meaning you always do this. Use 2 through 8 to indicate degrees between never and always.

1. When I'm unhappy with my partner, I consider breaking up.
2. When I'm angry at my partner, I talk to him/her about breaking up.
3. When we have serious problems in our relationship, I take action to end the relationship.
4. When I'm irritated with my partner, I think about ending our relationship.
5. When we have problems, I discuss ending our relationship.
6. When things are going really poorly between us, I do things to drive my partner away.
7. When I'm dissatisfied with our relationship, I consider dating other people.
8. When my partner says or does things I don't like, I talk to him/her about what's upsetting me.
9. When my partner and I have problems, I discuss things with him/her.
10. When I am unhappy with my partner, I tell him/her what's bothering me.
11. When things aren't going well between us, I suggest changing things in the relationship in order to solve the problem.
12. When my partner and I are angry with one another, I suggest a compromise solution.
13. When we've had an argument, I work things out with my partner right away.
14. When we have serious problems in our relationship, I consider getting advice from someone else (friends, parents, minister, or counselor).
15. When we have problems in our relationship, I patiently wait for things to improve.
16. When I'm upset about something in our relationship, I wait a while before saying anything to see if things will improve on their own.
17. When my partner hurts me, I say nothing and simply forgive him/her.
18. When my partner and I are angry with each other, I give things some time to cool off on their own rather than take action.
19. When there are things about my partner that I don't like, I accept his/her faults and weaknesses and don't try to change him/her.
20. When my partner is inconsiderate, I give him/her the benefit of the doubt and forget about it.
21. When we have troubles, no matter how bad things get, I am loyal to my partner.
22. When I'm upset with my partner, I sulk rather than confront the issue.
23. When I'm really bothered about something my partner has done, I criticize him/her for things that are unrelated to the real problem.
24. When I'm upset with my partner, I ignore him/her for a while.
25. When I'm really angry, I treat my partner badly (for example, by ignoring him/her or saying cruel things).
26. When we have a problem in our relationship, I ignore the whole thing and forget about it.
27. When I'm angry at my partner, I spend less time with him/her (for example, I spend more time with my friends, watch a lot of television, work longer hours, etc.).
28. When my partner and I have problems, I refuse to talk to him/her about it.

This scale measures four different approaches people commonly use to resolve interpersonal conflicts. Add up your scores on items 1 to 7, then 8 to 14, then 15 to 21, and then 22 to 28. Which of these four scores is the highest? The first seven items measure *exit*, which is a tendency to just leave the relationship. The next seven items measure *voice*, meaning a tendency to work through and resolve conflicts. Items 15 to 21 measure *loyalty*, meaning a tendency to hope that things will get better. The last seven items measure *neglect*, meaning a tendency to ignore the problem and reduce effort to fix the relationship. Can you predict the best approach? It's voice, which gives people a chance to work through problems so that they can get better.

Rusbult, C. E., Martz, J. M., & Agnew, C. R. (1998). The Investment Model Scale: Measuring commitment level, satisfaction level, quality of alternatives, and investment size. *Personal Relationships, 5*(4), 357–391. https://doi.org/10.1111/j.1475-6811.1998.tb00177.x

Skills for Resolving Conflicts

Your interpersonal interactions may be pleasant most of the time, but conflicts are sure to arise. Learning strategies for resolving conflict in productive and positive ways is important because conflict is an inevitable part of life. Settling a conflict requires good communication skills, such as assertive communication and active listening. It also requires negotiation, a process in which people work together to think and talk through a solution to a conflict.

Identify the Cause of the Conflict The first step in resolving a conflict is identifying what is causing the conflict (see **Figure 4.5**). This step can start on an individual level but should eventually involve communication between both people in the conflict. Conflicts continue or grow worse if you do not share your feelings. Instead of trying to pretend you are not upset, plan to talk about the conflict with the other person.

Before setting a time to talk, identify what you think is causing the conflict. Pay attention to your feelings and thoughts to get a clear picture of why the conflict is occurring. Sometimes you may not feel ready to talk directly to the other person in a conflict. In that case, talk to someone else first. Explaining the situation to another friend can help you work out how you feel and what you want. It can also give you a new perspective.

For example, you might feel hurt that your friend forgot it was your birthday. But your friend may have written down the wrong day and didn't realize it. Your friend may also have been dealing with a challenging issue in their own life, which caused them to forget. Understanding the cause of the problem is an important first step in resolving it.

Before starting a discussion with the other person in the conflict, agree with the person on a time and place to discuss the situation. Meet when you both have enough time to focus on the issue. Choose a neutral meeting place away from other people and distractions.

Remember that when two people are in conflict, they often identify the cause differently. Apply effective verbal and nonverbal communication strategies during this stage. Both people

FIGURE 4.5 Three steps to resolving conflict.

must honestly and clearly state the conflict from their perspectives. Sometimes feelings get heated when people are in the middle of a conflict. Intense feelings, such as disappointment and frustration, can make a conflict worse. To avoid this, learn to manage and control your anger. Use assertive I-statements instead of aggressive you-statements and avoid making accusations or name-calling.

Some types of conflict are easier to resolve after time has passed. If you feel too angry or upset to have a productive conversation about a conflict, let the person know you need some time. Walk away and give yourself and the other person a chance to calm down.

Ask for Solutions from Both Parties After discussing the cause of the conflict, brainstorm ways to solve the conflict. Find out what each person wants or needs as a desired outcome to the situation. Keep an open mind about everyone's ideas and do not rule out any suggestions. Be creative. People from both parties should state their ideas firmly, but not demand that the other person agree.

For example, your roommate may have one idea about when it is OK to have friends stay over in your room. You may have a different approach. Listening to both ideas—and even brainstorming about other ideas—can help you explore different options.

People must also listen carefully to what others have to say and recognize and accept the other person's opinions. Sometimes people are so focused on seeing a conflict from their own perspective they have difficulty imagining any other perspective. This makes conflicts harder to resolve. Instead, listen carefully to the other person's proposed solutions and try to understand the person's perspective.

Identify Solutions and Agree on One After discussing all possible solutions, recommend a solution or combination of solutions. Calmly discuss the issue and possible solutions to reach an agreement both people can support. Both parties should be open to suggestions and focus on finding a solution together, not just on meeting their own needs.

During this step, both people agree on a solution. Rarely is there a solution that makes everyone happy. Often, both sides agree to give in a little, or to compromise. Through compromise, each side can reach a solution that is acceptable for everyone involved. Sometimes a compromise is not possible, and the solution involves the two sides simply agreeing to disagree.

For example, your friend may want to spend all day Sunday together doing something such as shopping or watching sports. You have a big paper due on Monday, and you planned to spend most of the day working on that assignment. You could compromise and decide to spend the morning working, but the afternoon hanging out.

DOWNLOAD DOCUMENTS & TEMPLATES

> **Think Deeper** | Solving a Conflict with a Friend
>
> Think about the last time you had a conflict with a friend. Then consider the following questions:
>
> 1. What strategies did you use to try to resolve the conflict?
> 2. Which approaches did you find most effective?
> 3. How could you use a different approach the next time?
>
> Reflecting on the types of approaches you used to work through a conflict is a good idea. It can help you figure out what strategies work well. It can also remind you of other strategies you can use in the future. This type of self-reflection can help you resolve conflicts more effectively.

Think about a recent conflict you've had—or are having—with someone in your life. Then think through each of the steps you could use to resolve it and write down what you could do or say.

Make It Personal | Steps for Resolving Conflict

 DOWNLOAD DOCUMENTS & TEMPLATES

Steps	Your Response
Set up a specific time to discuss the conflict and resolve it.	
Start by saying something positive about the relationship.	
State how you feel using an I-statement.	
Acknowledge your own role in the conflict.	
Seek solutions to the conflict from both parties.	
Agree on a solution that works for both of you.	

Review, Discuss, and Apply

INTERACTIVE SELF-SCORING QUIZZES

Discussion Questions

1. Think about a recent conflict you've experienced in one of your relationships. What do you think was the cause?
2. What surprised you about the benefits of conflict?
3. What factors might influence whether people can successfully agree on a solution to a problem?

Think Ahead | Career and Lifelong Applications

People who can communicate effectively and manage conflict experience better relationships with work colleagues as well as with family members, friends, and romantic partners. They use active listening and pay attention to nonverbal communication. They also use assertive communication. These communication techniques help them clearly express their own views and avoid misunderstandings. When conflicts arise, they use constructive strategies for finding a mutually acceptable solution. Here are some of the ways of communicating well, along with their advantages:

Use active listening—People who use active listening focus their full attention on the person talking and acknowledge and repeat back what they heard in their own words. This approach avoids misunderstandings, which can create conflict in your work life as well as your personal life. People who use active listening have better relationships with family members, friends, and colleagues.

Be assertive—People who use assertive communication clearly express their feelings, needs, and goals in a way that shows respect to the other person. This type of communication allows people to express how they feel and to be respectful of others. This ability helps people have healthy relationships with colleagues in their workplace. It also helps people build good relationships with friends, family members, and romantic partners.

Pay attention to nonverbal communication—People who pay attention to nonverbal messages are aware of the message they send to others as well as the messages they receive. Their focus on facial expressions and body language helps them avoid misunderstandings that can create conflict in their personal and professional relationships.

Resolve conflicts—People who learn strategies for resolving conflicts can work through issues in a productive way. This ability helps them navigate conflicts with supervisors and colleagues. It also helps them work through conflicts with people in their personal lives to reach positive resolutions.

As you can see in these examples, skills in communication and conflict resolution help people succeed in their personal and professional lives. People with skills in these areas are better at working with supervisors and colleagues, which helps them have more productive careers. People who are able to communicate clearly also have better relationships with friends, family members, and romantic partners. Developing these skills is therefore an important strategy for greater success during college and throughout the rest of your life.

What Would You Do?

In this chapter, Olivia and Julia need your advice.

VIDEO CONTENT

JULIA

Julia has just received some news from her boyfriend that feels like it's coming out of the blue.

Watch Julia's video: **Shocked, Hurt, Disappointed**

OLIVIA

Olivia is having a problem getting along with one of her colleagues at work and needs your advice.

Watch Olivia's video: **Responding to Snarky**

What would you tell Olivia? What would you tell Julia?

Take Some Action | Here and Now

DOWNLOAD DOCUMENTS & TEMPLATES

We all have strengths and weaknesses when it comes building and maintaining good relationships with other people. Being aware of those strengths and weaknesses is key to success in college, in the workplace, and in life.

Review your outcomes on the *Test Yourself* assessments throughout this chapter and your responses to the *Think Deeper* questions. Reflect on your results and responses, and then answer these questions:

1. What are your strengths with respect to building and maintaining relationships? How will you put those strengths to work for you toward succeeding in college? How will sharpening those strengths in college help you be successful in the workplace?

2. How do you want to improve your strengths when it comes to building relationships?

3. Review the suggested action steps in that area and choose two or three of those to commit to here and now, and for each, say how taking that action step will help you succeed in college and beyond.

Share and discuss your responses to these questions with a friend, classmate, or family member.

Chapter Summary

INTERACTIVE SELF-SCORING QUIZZES
Chapter 4 Practice Quiz

Module 4.1 Building and Maintaining Connections

- College students have many different types of personal relationships, including relationships with roommates, romantic partners, and family members. Strategies for creating a good roommate relationship include forming a roommate contract, having realistic expectations, addressing problems, solving issues together, and seeking help if necessary. Choose friends who are a positive influence on your life. Work on creating healthy dating relationships by setting realistic expectations and taking steps to maintain long-distance relationships. You can maintain close relationships with family members by staying in touch and listening.

- Many college students work on building new relationships, which can help prevent loneliness. Steps for developing new relationships include making an effort to meet new people, spending time out of your dorm room, joining extracurricular activities, and inviting people to do something with you.

Module 4.2 Communicating Well

- Communication is an important part of our daily lives. Communication involves sending some type of message, such as thoughts, ideas, feelings, and/or information, to one or more receivers. Effective communication happens when the receiver understands the message and provides a constructive response. Verbal communication is the use of words to send an oral (spoken) or written message, which can include in-person conversations, phone calls, emails, text messages, social media posts, letters, and notes. Nonverbal communication involves communicating through facial expressions, body language, gestures, tone and volume of voice, and other signals that do not involve the use of words.

- Problems in communication can lead to misunderstandings, confusion, and even conflict. Cultural differences can lead to problems in communication. Culture impacts the languages people speak, how people use and interpret nonverbal communication, and their expectations about touch. Online communication, which occurs on social media and websites and through digital devices, can also lead to problems. When you are sending an email or a text, the person cannot see your nonverbal cues, which can lead to miscommunication and conflict. Strategies to avoid misunderstandings and communicate online safely and effectively include being kind and respectful, solving conflicts offline, thinking before sharing, and keeping passwords private.

- In effective communication, people communicate their thoughts, information, values, and feelings. Techniques for communicating well include paying attention to what the other person is saying, using active listening, clearly expressing your needs and preferences, being assertive, using I-statements, watching your nonverbal communication, and respecting others and valuing diversity.

Module 4.3 Managing Conflict

- Conflict is a normal part of everyday life, even for healthy relationships. Many different factors can lead to interpersonal conflicts, including different priorities, values, goals, and needs as well as misunderstandings. What separates healthy conflict from unhealthy conflict is how conflict is resolved. Conflicts that are not resolved can lead to serious and lasting consequences.

- Many people worry that trying to resolve a conflict will destroy a relationship or make the conflict worse. In reality, working through a conflict can strengthen a relationship. When people decide to work together to resolve a conflict, they show their commitment to the relationship. What matters most is how people interact when resolving conflict. Even when working through a conflict, people in a healthy relationship show lots of positive behaviors toward each other.

- Learning strategies for resolving conflict in productive and positive ways is important because conflict is an inevitable part of life. First, identify the cause of the conflict. Next, ask for solutions to the conflict from the people or groups involved. Finally, identify potential solutions and try to reach an agreement.

Key Terms

Active listening Act of concentrating on the person talking and acknowledging what one has heard

Aggressive communication Making demands of and insulting others

Assertive communication Clearly stating needs, wants, and feelings

Communication Exchange of messages between people

Communication styles Different ways of expressing thoughts and feelings

Conflict Disagreement or argument that occurs due to misunderstandings or differing priorities, values, goals, or needs

Diversity People's differences in many areas, such as race or ethnicity, sex, political ideas, gender identity, sexual orientation, or spiritual beliefs

I-statements Words that explain how the speaker feels without judging the receiver

Loneliness Discomfort or uneasiness caused by feeling emotionally or socially isolated from other people

Nonverbal communication Use of body language, tone and volume of voice, and other signals to send a message

Passive communication Hiding or not clearly stating needs, wants, and feelings

Passive-aggressive communication Using techniques that do not clearly state needs, wants, and feelings for the purpose of making demands of and insulting others

Verbal communication Use of words, spoken or written, to send a message

Resources

Abrams, Z. (2023, June 1). The science of why friendships keep us healthy. *Monitor on Psychology, 54*(4), 42. Retrieved from https://www.apa.org/monitor/2023/06/cover-story-science-friendship

Bergmann, E. (2018, October 9). Advice from a formerly lonely college student. *The New York Times*. Retrieved from https://www.nytimes.com/2018/10/09/well/family/advice-from-a-formerly-lonely-college-student.html

Cacioppo, J. T., & Patrick, W. (2009). *Loneliness: Human nature and the need for social connection*. W. W. Norton & Co.

Cherry, K. (2023, February 22). Types of nonverbal communication. *Verywell Mind*. Retrieved from https://www.verywellmind.com/types-of-nonverbal-communication-2795397

Franco, M. G. (2022). Platonic: *How the science of attachment can help you make—and keep—friends*. G.P. Putnam's Sons.

Grenny, J., Patterson, K., McMillan, R., Switzler, A., & Gregory, E. (2021). *Crucial conversations: Tools for talking when stakes are high*. McGraw-Hill.

Nichols, M. P., & Strauss, M. B. (2021). *The lost art of listening: How learning to listen can improve relationships* (3rd ed.). Guilford Press.

Paterson, R. J. (2020). *The assertiveness workbook: How to express your ideas and stand up for yourself at work and in relationships*. New Harbinger Publications.

References

DePaulo, B. M., & Friedman, H. S. (1998). Nonverbal communication. In D. T.Gilbert, S. T.Fiske, & G.Lindzey (Eds.), *The handbook of social psychology* (3–40). McGraw-Hill.

Gaumer Erickson, A. S., Noonan, P. M., Monroe, K., & McCall, Z. (2016). Assertiveness Formative Questionnaire. In P. M. Noonan & A. S. Gaumer Erickson (2017), *The skills that matter: Teaching interpersonal and intrapersonal competencies in any classroom* (pp. 181–182). Corwin.

Hall, J. A., & Gunnery, S. D. (2013). Gender differences in nonverbal communication. In J. A. Hall & M. L. Knapp (Eds.), *Nonverbal communication* (639–669). De Gruyter Mouton. https://doi.org/10.1515/9783110238150.639

Holmes, J. G., & Murray, S. L. (1996). Conflict in close relationships. In E. T. Higgins & A. W. Kruglanski (Eds.), *Social psychology: Handbook of basic principles* (622–654). Guilford Press.

Levenson, R. W., & Gottman, J. M. (1983). Marital interaction: Physiological linkage and affective exchange. *Journal of Personality and Social Psychology, 45*(3), 587–597. https://doi.org/10.1037/0022-3514.45.3.587

Overall, N. C., & McNulty, J. K. (2017). What type of communication during conflict is beneficial for intimate relationships? *Current Opinion in Psychology, 13*, 1–5. https://doi.org/10.1016/j.copsyc.2016.03.002

Rusbult, C. E., Martz, J. M., & Agnew, C. R. (1998). The Investment Model Scale: Measuring commitment level, satisfaction level, quality of alternatives, and investment size. *Personal Relationships, 5*(4), 357–391. https://doi.org/10.1111/j.1475-6811.1998.tb00177.x

Russell, D. W. (1996). UCLA Loneliness Scale (Version 3): Reliability, validity, and factor structure. *Journal of Personality Assessment, 66*(1), 20–40. https://doi.org/10.1207/s15327752jpa6601_2

Russell, D., Peplau, L. A., & Cutrona, C. E. (1980). The revised UCLA Loneliness Scale: Concurrent and discriminant validity evidence. *Journal of Personality and Social Psychology, 39*(3), 472–480. https://doi.org/10.1037/0022-3514.39.3.472

CHAPTER 5

Learn Your Way

Author's Introduction

"No matter what your current ability is, effort is what ignites that ability and turns it into accomplishment."

—Carol Dweck

CHAPTER OUTLINE	LEARNING OBJECTIVES
Envision, Pursue, and Persist: Amy Cuddy	
Module 5.1 Understanding Learning Models of Learning *Make It Personal: Setting Goals* Learning Styles *Test Yourself: What's Your Learning Style?* Using Learning Styles to Maximize Success *Think Deeper: Preparing for Exams*	**LO 5.1** To understand how learning styles influence academic success
Module 5.2 Defining Multiple Intelligences Types of Intelligence *Test Yourself: What Are Your Intelligence Strengths?* *Think Deeper: Understanding Your Strengths* Evaluating Multiple Intelligences	**LO 5.2** To define different types of intelligence
Module 5.3 Understanding Mindset Types of Mindsets *Test Yourself: What's Your Mindset?* Mindset Matters Changing Your Mindset *Make It Personal: Shift Your Fixed Mindset* *Think Deeper: Responding to New Challenges*	**LO 5.3** To examine the role of mindset in learning
Think Ahead: Career and Lifelong Applications	
Take Some Action: Here and Now	
Chapter Summary Key Terms Resources References	

Envision, Pursue, and Persist | Amy Cuddy

ZUMA Press, Inc./Alamy Stock Photo

In 1992, Amy Cuddy was a sophomore in college studying theater and history when she was in a car accident that changed the course of her life. Late one night, she was asleep in the backseat of a friend's car when the driver nodded off. The car ran off the road and rolled over three times. Amy was thrown out of the window. When she awoke in the hospital, she learned that she had experienced a traumatic brain injury and that her IQ had dropped thirty points. The doctors warned her that it was unlikely that she would be able to finish college. Amy did return to college, but she struggled to read and retain information. "It was very hard for me to sit in a lecture," she says. "I would take copious notes and still couldn't make sense of what I was hearing." She dropped out several times, but after six years she finally received her degree.

Amy's experience with recovering from her injury led to an interest in how the brain works. After graduation, she worked as a research assistant with a psychology professor. She then decided to pursue graduate work in psychology. She received her PhD from Princeton University and today teaches leadership at Harvard University. Her research examines how people have the power to influence their own thoughts, feelings, and performance. Amy has received numerous awards for her research and was named one of the BBC 100 Women of 2017. Amy's self-help book *Presence: Bringing Your Boldest Self to Your Biggest Challenges* appeared on the *New York Times* Best Seller list.

This chapter examines factors that influence how people learn, which is an essential component of college success. First, you'll read about how different people learn most effectively in different ways and how to figure out your own best learning style. This knowledge will help you master and retain information. Next, you'll learn intelligence is not just one dimension. Instead, all people have different types of strengths, or intelligences, in different areas. The final section of this chapter will describe how the mindset you adopt when facing both academic and personal challenges has a substantial impact on your success. You'll also learn specific strategies you can use to adopt a more positive approach to learning.

Module 5.1 Understanding Learning

LO 5.1.1 To understand different models of learning

LO 5.1.2 To examine different learning styles

LO 5.1.3 To review how learning styles can maximize success

When you are trying to learn new information, what approach do you generally try? Do you read material quietly to yourself? Discuss material with classmates? Create diagrams or pictures of the material? These different approaches to mastering information are called **learning styles**, meaning our individual preferences about acquiring, organizing, and retaining information.

Models of Learning

VIDEO CONTENT

We all learn things every single day. We meet a new person and remember their name. We hear a new song and remember the lyrics. We watch a new television show and remember the plot. All of these examples illustrate types of **learning**, meaning acquiring new, or modifying existing, knowledge, skills, values, or behavior. Learning is particularly important because it enables us to adapt to new situations. For example, you may have learned that you tend to do better in small classes in which you can actively participate. Or you may have learned that you study most effectively in quiet rooms with few distractions. These are both examples of how learning helps us adapt to and succeed in our environment. This section will focus on the three most commonly used models to explain how learning occurs: classical conditioning, operant conditioning, and observational learning.

Classical Conditioning

Classical conditioning is a type of learning that occurs when a previously neutral stimulus over time starts to elicit a response. Although this definition can be confusing, here's a simple example. Can you imagine the sound of a drill at the dentist's office? For many people, just imagining that sound can lead to negative emotions and unpleasant arousal. This response occurs because you've learned to associate the sound of the drill with experiencing pain.

This process of classical conditioning was initially discovered entirely by accident by Ivan Pavlov, a Russian scientist. He was conducting a study to examine how dogs automatically start to produce saliva when they see or smell food. But he found that sometimes dogs produced saliva even before he presented the food. Instead, they would start to produce saliva when they saw him arrive in the lab or when they heard his footsteps. In this case, the previously neutral stimulus—seeing or hearing a person—starts to elicit a response—salivation—because the dogs have learned to associate the person with receiving the food.

How does classical conditioning relate to learning in college? Just as dogs can form an association between footsteps and food, and therefore start to produce saliva at the sound or sight of a person approaching, students also can learn associations that help or hurt academic performance. If you received a bad grade on one of the first quizzes in a class, you may develop anxiety about taking future quizzes. This anxiety can then interfere with your ability to do well. Developing strategies to form new associations is therefore important. For example, you could work to develop new associations by giving yourself practice quizzes and pairing taking those quizzes with relaxation or positive thinking.

Operant Conditioning

Have you ever received a trophy for most improved player, a reward for returning a lost wallet, or positive comments from a teacher on your paper? If so, you've already experienced the benefits of operant conditioning.

Operant conditioning theory states that behavior can be more or less likely to occur depending on the presence of reinforcements. When people receive positive reinforcements, or rewards, for behaving in a certain way, they are more likely to continue that behavior. If you used a particular study technique and then received an A on an exam, you will probably use that same technique in the future. Rewards therefore strengthen the behavior.

Operant conditioning can also lead to decreases in behavior. Imagine you are speeding on your way to class one day and a police officer pulls you over and gives you a ticket. Your behavior—driving too fast—resulted in a negative outcome. This should reduce that behavior in the future.

You can use operant conditioning to improve your own academic performance by creating reinforcements, or rewards, for engaging in particular types of behavior. For example, you could reward yourself with something desirable—having a snack, checking your social media, playing video games—after you finish reading a chapter, completing a homework assignment, or making an outline for your paper. The essential part of operant conditioning is that you receive these rewards only *after* you've finished the behavior you've set out to do.

Operant conditioning can help you improve any type of behavior, from improving your study habits to cleaning your room to exercising regularly. Write down a few goals you have. Then write down some type of reward you could give yourself for accomplishing each goal.

Make It Personal | Setting Goals

DOWNLOAD DOCUMENTS & TEMPLATES

Goals	Reward
1.	
2.	
3.	
4.	

Observational Learning The theory of **observational learning** states that people learn by observing and imitating, or modeling, other people's behavior. We are especially likely to watch those who are older than us or who have more experience in an environment. You might remember times when you observed an older sibling's attitudes or behaviors to learn how to feel or act. Or, if you are the firstborn, you might remember your younger siblings modeling your behavior.

We also observe the consequences—positive or negative—that people experience from engaging in particular behaviors. For example, a college student who sees an instructor criticizing another student for coming late to class, or using a phone during class, will likely remember that interaction. It will also motivate them to avoid engaging in those behaviors, at least during that instructor's class.

Observational learning can lead to positive academic outcomes. If you have a close friend or roommate who studies regularly, turns in assignments on time, and seeks help from the instructor when it's needed, you may model this same type of strong work ethic. This choice will almost certainly lead you to experience better success in all of your classes.

Unfortunately, observational learning can also lead to negative academic outcomes. If many of your peers only start studying the night before a test, spend large amounts of time playing video games or checking the internet, and refuse to reach out for help when they are struggling, you may start to model those behaviors. It's therefore really important to make sure to spend time with people who share your desire for academic success so that you can model positive behaviors instead of negative ones.

Learning Styles

VIDEO CONTENT

There are many different models that categorize people's learning styles in different ways. But all of these models are based on the same underlying theory: each person has a specific learning style, and we learn best when we use our own style to learn. Perhaps you learn more from talking about material in a class with other students, but your roommate learns better by reading the textbook on their own. The assumption is that students need to figure out their preferred style so that they can learn in the most effective way.

Common Learning Styles Models One of the most popular learning styles models is the *VARK model*, which stands for visual, auditory, reading, and kinesthetic (see **Figure 5.1**). This model was developed by Neil Fleming, a teacher in New Zealand. According to the VARK model, there are four different types of learning styles:

1. Visual—when information is presented in a diagram or picture
2. Auditory—when information is described aloud
3. Reading—when information is given in a written form
4. Kinesthetic (Doing)—when students can actively try something out in a demonstration

The VARK model emphasizes that students who adapt their study style to their preferred method of learning will find it easier to learn and retain information. For example, a student who is a reading learner, would prefer to read the textbook and lecture notes when preparing for an exam. A student who is a visual learner, on the other hand, would learn best by creating pictures, charts, or graphs of course material.

Another popular learning styles model was developed by psychologist David Kolb. According to his Learning Style Inventory (LSI), people vary based on two dimensions. One of these dimensions is active versus reflective. This means how much someone likes to actively practice what they are learning versus thinking about it on their own. The other dimension is abstract versus concrete. This means how much

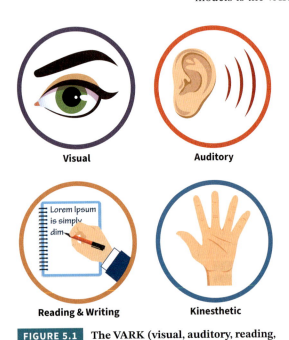

FIGURE 5.1 The VARK (visual, auditory, reading, kinesthetic) model.

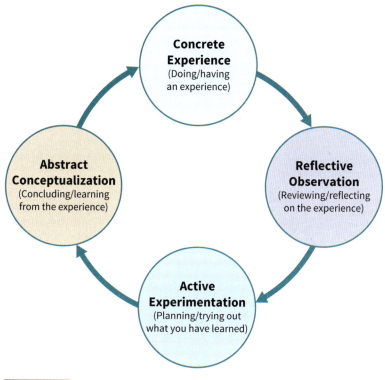

FIGURE 5.2 Kolb's Learning Styles Inventory (LSI) model.

someone prefers learning by thinking about abstract concepts versus things that have personal meaning. These two dimensions create four distinct types of abilities, as shown in **Figure 5.2**: concrete experience, reflective observation, abstract conceptualization, active experimentation.

This approach focuses on helping people develop skills in all of these areas. This makes sense because different types of courses in college require each of these abilities. Courses in the sciences, for example, often require skills in active experimentation. On the other hand, courses in the humanities and social sciences may emphasize reflective observation. Kolb's inventory of learning styles emphasizes the need for people to understand their strengths. It also proposes that people should gain skills in areas in which they are less strong so they can be successful in all courses.

A different type of learning styles model, the Myers-Briggs Type Indicator, was initially developed to test personality traits. In fact, it is probably the best known and most widely used model of personality. According to the Myers-Briggs test, people can be grouped into sixteen different personality types, assessing four distinct dimensions: extraversion (E) versus introversion (I); sensing (S) versus intuition (N); thinking (T) versus feeling (F); and judging (J) versus perceiving. These dimensions are combined into types as shown in **Figure 5.3**.

The Minnesota Multiphasic Personality Inventory (MMPI) is another model for testing personality traits. Although it isn't focused on learning styles, it is still used in that area, because people with different personality types are thought to learn best in different ways. Specifically, these personality styles may influence how people take in information and form conclusions. Many businesses give the MMPI test to employees to help them understand how they perceive the world, get along with people, and make decisions.

Although different models vary in their specific dimensions, they all share the same fundamental assumptions. First, they describe how people differ on various dimensions, such as learning preferences and/or personality traits. Second, they emphasize that understanding your own distinct learning orientation can help you master and retain information more effectively.

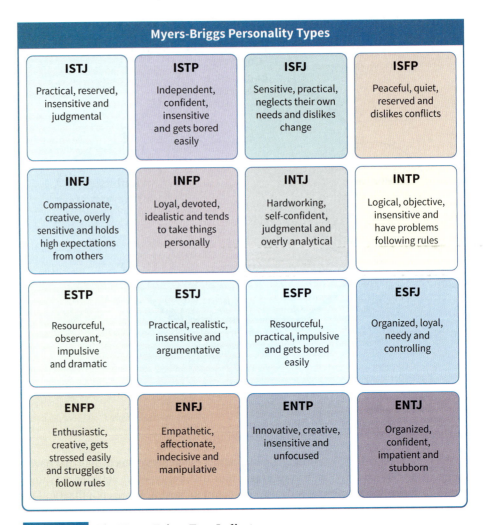

FIGURE 5.3 The Myers-Briggs Type Indicator.

Evaluating Common Learning Styles Models
Learning styles models are very appealing to people for many different reasons. We are often interested in trying to understand ourselves—and other people—better. Models that let us rate ourselves and provide quick solutions telling us "how to learn better" are therefore seen as extremely helpful. This is one reason why online quizzes are so popular! These models also acknowledge that people differ from one another and have unique strengths and preferences in terms of how they learn. Perhaps most important, these models all provide hope: they suggest that we all have the ability to learn and master information but may do so most effectively in a particular way.

But the most important question, of course, is whether they work. In other words, does your learning style predict how you will best master material and how well you will perform in a particular class or job? Unfortunately, there is not much evidence that most learning styles models actually predict performance.

In 2009, cognitive psychologists reviewed all of the research on learning styles. The goal of this project was to evaluate whether scientific evidence supports using learning styles to improve learning. Their findings provided no evidence that people with different learning styles learn better when they are taught—or study on their own—in ways that match their learning style. People do have definite preferences for how they learn new information. But people who are taught according to these preferences do not actually experience better educational outcomes.

Similarly, although the Myers-Briggs test is commonly used by many companies, there is no evidence from scientific research showing that these sixteen different personality types actually exist. Even more important, there is no evidence that scores on this test can predict people's success in a given job or career.

Index of Learning Styles	
Active	**Reflective**
Doing something active with it. Discussing, applying, or explaining it to others.	Thinking about it quietly first.
Sensing	**Intuitive**
Learning facts.	Discovering possibilities and relationships.
Visual	**Verbal**
See—pictures, diagrams, flow charts, time lines, films, and demonstrations.	Words—written and spoken explanations.
Sequential	**Global**
Gain understanding in linear steps.	Learn in large jumps, suddenly "getting it."

FIGURE 5.4 The Index of Learning Styles (ILS) model.

INTERACTIVE FIGURES, CHARTS, & TABLES

Can learning styles ever be useful in categorizing people and improving academic outcomes? Yes. The Index of Learning Styles (ILS) model, developed by Richard Felder (an engineering professor) and Barbara Silverman (an educational psychologist), is supported by scientific research. As shown in **Figure 5.4**, this model divides people based on four different ways in which they process and organize information: active-reflective, sensing-intuitive, verbal-visual, and sequential-global.

Let's examine each of these dimensions.

1. **Active versus reflective**—Active learners learn best by doing something active with information, such as discussing it, applying it, or explaining it. Not surprisingly, they like and learn well from group work. Reflective learners prefer to think quietly and on their own about information and tend to do better when working alone.

2. **Sensing versus intuitive**—Sensing learners like learning facts, memorizing information, and using well-established methods to solve problems. Intuitive learners like discovering new possibilities and trying innovative and novel approaches; they are comfortable with abstract thinking.

3. **Visual versus verbal**—Visual learners remember best when they can see information presented, such as in pictures, diagrams, flowcharts, time lines, films, and demonstrations. Verbal learners remember best when they can read or hear explanations.

4. **Sequential versus global**—Sequential learners prefer gaining knowledge in a linear fashion, with each step following logically from the prior one. Global learners tend to gain knowledge in large jumps, by absorbing different pieces of material and then all of sudden seeing how this material all fits together.

Are you interested in assessing your own learning style? Complete the *Test Yourself* that follows to learn how you score on each of these dimensions.

Knowing your preferred learning style can help you master course material more effectively. For example, visual learners might find that creating diagrams or charts is a helpful way for them to remember course material. Verbal learners, on the other hand, often find that reading material, either silently or aloud, is the most effective way to retain information.

Test Yourself | What's Your Learning Style?

Each of the following statements has two possible endings. Select the option that best describes you.

1. I understand something better after I **a.** try it out or **b.** think it through.
2. I would rather be considered **a.** realistic or **b.** innovative.
3. When I think about what I did yesterday, I am most likely to get **a.** a picture or **b.** words.
4. I tend to **a.** understand details of a subject but may be fuzzy about its overall structure or **b.** understand the overall structure but may be fuzzy about details.
5. When I am learning something new, it helps me to **a.** talk about it or **b.** think about it.
6. If I were a teacher, I would rather teach a course **a.** that deals with facts and real-life situations or **b.** that deals with ideas and theories.
7. I prefer to get new information in **a.** pictures, diagrams, graphs, or maps or **b.** written directions or verbal information.
8. Once I understand **a.** all the parts, I understand the whole thing or **b.** the whole thing, I see how the parts fit.
9. In a study group working on difficult material, I am more likely to **a.** jump in and contribute ideas or **b.** sit back and listen.
10. I find it easier **a.** to learn facts or **b.** to learn concepts.
11. In a book with lots of pictures and charts, I am likely to **a.** look over the pictures and charts carefully or **b.** focus on the written text.
12. When I solve math problems, I **a.** usually work my way to the solutions one step at a time or **b.** often just see the solutions but then have to struggle to figure out the steps to get to them.
13. In classes I have taken, I **a.** have usually gotten to know many of the students or **b.** have rarely gotten to know many of the students).
14. In reading nonfiction, I prefer **a.** something that teaches me new facts or tells me how to do something or **b.** something that gives me new ideas to think about.
15. I like teachers who **a.** put a lot of diagrams on the board or **b.** spend a lot of time explaining.
16. When I'm analyzing a story or a novel, I **a.** think of the incidents and try to put them together to figure out the themes or **b.** just know what the themes are when I finish reading and then I have to go back and find the incidents that demonstrate them.
17. When I start a homework problem, I am more likely to **a.** start working on the solution immediately or **b.** try to fully understand the problem first.
18. I prefer the idea of **a.** certainty or **b.** theory.
19. I remember best **a.** what I see or **b.** what I hear.
20. It is more important to me that an instructor **a.** lay out the material in clear sequential steps or **b.** give me an overall picture and relate the material to other subjects.
21. I prefer to study **a.** in a study group or **b.** alone.
22. I am more likely to be considered **a.** careful about the details of my work or **b.** creative about how to do my work.
23. When I get directions to a new place, I prefer **a.** a map or **b.** written instructions.
24. I learn **a.** at a fairly regular pace. If I study hard, I'll "get it." or **b.** in fits and starts. I'll be totally confused and then suddenly it all "clicks".
25. I would rather first **a.** try things out or **b.** think about how I'm going to do it.
26. When I am reading for enjoyment, I like writers to **a.** clearly say what they mean or **b.** say things in creative, interesting ways.
27. When I see a diagram or sketch in class, I am most likely to remember **a.** the picture or **b.** what the instructor said about it.
28. When considering a body of information, I am more likely to **a.** focus on details and miss the big picture or **b.** try to understand the big picture before getting into the details.
29. I more easily remember **a.** something I have done or **b.** something I have thought a lot about.
30. When I have to perform a task, I prefer to **a.** master one way of doing it or **b.** come up with new ways of doing it.

31. When someone is showing me data, I prefer **a.** charts or graphs or **b.** text summarizing the results.
32. When writing a paper, I am more likely to **a.** work on [think about or write] the beginning of the paper and progress forward or **b.** work on [think about or write] different parts of the paper and then order them.
33. When I have to work on a group project, I first want to **a.** have group brainstorming where everyone contributes ideas or **b.** brainstorm individually and then come together as a group to compare ideas.
34. I consider it higher praise to call someone **a.** sensible or **b.** imaginative.
35. When I meet people at a party, I am more likely to remember **a.** what they looked like or **b.** what they said about themselves.
36. When I am learning a new subject, I prefer to **a.** stay focused on that subject, learning as much about it as I can or **b.** try to make connections between that subject and related subjects.
37. I am more likely to be considered **a.** outgoing or **b.** reserved.
38. I prefer courses that emphasize **a.** concrete material [facts, data] or **b.** abstract material [concepts, theories].
39. For entertainment, I would rather **a.** watch television or **b.** read a book.
40. Some teachers start their lectures with an outline of what they will cover. Such outlines are **a.** somewhat helpful to me **b.** very helpful to me.
41. The idea of doing homework in groups, with one grade for the entire group **a.** appeals to me **b.** does not appeal to me.
42. When I am doing long calculations, I **a.** tend to repeat all my steps and check my work carefully or **b.** find checking my work tiresome and have to force myself to do it.
43. I tend to picture places I have been **a.** easily and fairly accurately or **b.** with difficulty and without much detail.
44. When solving problems in a group, I would be more likely to think of **a.** the steps in the solution process or **b.** possible consequences or applications of the solution in a wide range of areas.

After completing these items, add up how many a. and b. answers you chose on each of the four subscales using the following items:

Sensing-intuitive: 2, 6, 10, 14, 18, 22, 26, 30, 34, 38, 42 (more **a** answers indicates sensing; more **b** answers indicates intuitive)

Visual-verbal: 3, 7, 11, 15, 19, 23, 27, 31, 35, 39, 43 (more **a** answers indicates visual; more **b** answers indicates verbal)

Sequential-global: 4, 8, 12, 16, 20, 24, 28, 32, 36, 40, 44 (more **a** answers indicates more sequential; more **b** answers indicates global)

Active-reflective: 1, 5, 9, 13, 17, 21, 25, 29, 33, 37, 41 (more **a** answers indicates active; more **b** answers indicates reflective)

Which is your highest scale(s)? That scale (or combination of scales) indicates your preferred learning style.

Felder, F.M., & Soloman, B.A. (1991). Index of Learning Styles. North Carolina State University.

Using your preferred learning style can also help you stay interested and engaged in studying. Students who find ways to study material that matches their preferred learning style may study for longer periods of time and in more focused ways. Not surprisingly, more and better studying can really pay off.

Using Learning Styles to Maximize Success

While most popular learning style models are not supported by scientific evidence, the Index of Learning Styles model is, and understanding learning style models *can* help you master information. Here is some general guidance that you can use to enhance your learning, regardless of your preferred style:

- **Think visually**—People who see information presented in a diagram or flowchart are better able to retain that information. Visual models provide an overall picture of how concepts and information fit together. This helps promote

longer retention of information. It also makes it easier to access, or retrieve, that information when you need it.

- **Match learning style to material**—Material in different courses needs to be approached in different ways. If you are taking an English class, using a verbal learning style may best help you read novels and poems. If you are learning a foreign language, you probably need to use an active learning style to practice speaking that language. Think about the right way to approach the material in each class so that you can best learn and retain information.
- **Use different learnings styles**—People retain information best when they use different types of learning styles; doing so activates different parts of the brain. This makes it easier to retain information over time. In your science class, you might start by reading a chapter describing a new concept and then create a visual diagram of what you've learned. Later on, you might use active learning to carry out a test of that concept in an experiment. Try to use multiple learning styles to really solidify the material in your mind, which will help you retain it over time.

Think Deeper | Preparing for Exams

Think about your last exam and the study strategies you used to prepare. Then consider the following questions:

1. What strategies did you use to study information?
2. Which approaches did you find most effective?
3. How could you use a different approach, or multiple approaches, in the future to experience greater success?

Reflecting on the types of learning styles you used—and could use in the future—can help you better plan for future academic work in ways that will help you succeed.

Review, Discuss, and Apply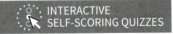

Discussion Questions

1. What types of reinforcements or rewards have you received for learning? How have these rewards influenced your motivation to learn?
2. Why are many models of learning styles so appealing, even when the evidence doesn't support their use?
3. People differ on the four dimensions of the Index of Learning Styles model. What factors contribute to these differences?

Module 5.2 | Defining Multiple Intelligences

LO 5.2.1 To describe different types of intelligence

LO 5.2.2 To examine evidence for multiple intelligences

What do you think of when you hear the word *intelligent*? Most people think about a person who performs well on traditional measures, such as getting As on tests. This type of intelligence, or intellectual potential, is often seen as something that a person is born with. It can also be measured by standardized tests or IQ tests.

But research in psychology now tells us that intelligence is not just one thing. In fact, all of us are intelligent in some ways—and not so intelligent in others. In this section, you'll learn about the theory of **multiple intelligences**. According to this theory, developed by psychologist Howard Gardner, all people have different kinds of "intelligence" or strengths in different areas. You'll also learn about how understanding your own types of intelligence can help you in college and your career.

Types of Intelligence

Think about your overall strengths, including academic subjects that tend to come easily to you or abilities outside the classroom. Are you good at singing? Playing basketball? Remembering people's names? Now think about your weaknesses, or things that you may struggle to accomplish. According to the theory of multiple intelligences, all people show different kinds of strengths or abilities (see **Figure 5.5**).

Types of intelligence include the following:

- **Visual-spatial intelligence**—People who are strong in visual-spatial intelligence are good at visualizing things; they are often good at interpreting graphs and charts, putting together puzzles, drawing, and painting.
- **Linguistic-verbal intelligence**—People who are strong in linguistic-verbal intelligence are able to use words well; they are often good at writing, reading, and debating or giving speeches.
- **Logical-mathematical intelligence**—People who are strong in logical-mathematical intelligence are good at reasoning and analyzing problems; they are often good at solving problems, conducting scientific experiments, and thinking about abstract ideas.
- **Bodily-kinesthetic intelligence**—People who are strong in bodily-kinesthetic intelligence are good at body movement and physical coordination; they are often good at dancing, playing sports, and creating things with their hands.
- **Musical intelligence**—People who are strong in musical intelligence are good at thinking in patterns, rhythms, and sounds; they are often good at singing, playing musical instruments, and remembering songs and melodies.

Visual-spatial

Linguistic-verbal

Interpersonal

Intrapersonal

Logical-mathematical

Musical

Bodily-kinesthetic

Naturalistic

FIGURE 5.5 Different types of intelligence.

- **Interpersonal intelligence**—People are who are strong in interpersonal intelligence are good at understanding and interacting with other people; they are often good at communicating verbally, resolving conflicts in groups, and creating positive relationships.
- **Intrapersonal intelligence**—People who are strong in intrapersonal intelligence are good at self-reflection and being aware of their own emotions and motivations; they are often good at analyzing theories and ideas, understanding their own strengths and weaknesses, and interpreting their own motivations and feelings.
- **Naturalistic intelligence**—People who are strong in naturalistic intelligence are good at categorizing information and exploring the outdoors; they are often good at gardening, learning about other species, hiking, and camping.

According to this theory, we all might be particularly strong in one area. But we also might have strengths in several types of intelligence. So, you might be particularly strong in linguistic-verbal intelligence but also show relative strengths in interpersonal intelligence, musical intelligence, and naturalistic intelligence. You can test your own intelligence strengths using the following *Test Yourself*.

Test Yourself | What Are Your Intelligence Strengths?

 INTERACTIVE SELF-ASSESSMENTS

Are you interested in figuring out your intelligence strengths? Read each of the following statements below and rate yourself using a 1–5 scale, as follows:

No, the statement is not at all like me. 1	The statement is a little like me. 2	The statement is somewhat like me. 3	The statement is a lot like me. 4	Yes, the statement is definitely me. 5

Verbal/Linguistic
- I can use lots of different words to express myself.
- I feel comfortable working with language and words.
- I enjoy crosswords and other word games like Scrabble.
- I tend to remember things exactly as they are said to me.
- I enjoy participating in debates and/or discussions.
- I find it easy to explain things to others.
- I enjoy keeping a written journal and/or writing stories and articles.
- I like to read a lot.

Logical/Mathematical
- I work best in an organized work area.
- I enjoy math and using numbers.
- I keep a "things to do" list.
- I enjoy playing brainteasers and logic puzzles.
- I like to ask "Why?" questions.
- I work best when I have a day planner or timetable.
- I quickly grasp cause-and-effect relationships.
- I always do things one step at a time.

Visual/Spatial
- I understand color combinations and what colors work well together.
- I enjoy solving jigsaw, maze, and/or other visual puzzles.
- I read charts and maps easily.
- I have a good sense of direction.
- I like to watch the scenes and activities in movies.
- I am observant. I often see things that others miss.
- I can anticipate the moves and consequences in a game plan (i.e., hockey sense, chess sense).
- I can picture scenes in my head when I remember things.

No, the statement is not at all like me. 1	The statement is a little like me. 2	The statement is somewhat like me. 3	The statement is a lot like me. 4	Yes, the statement is definitely me. 5

Interpersonal
- I can sense the moods and feelings of others.
- I work best when interacting with people.
- I enjoy team sports rather than individual sports.
- I can sort out arguments between friends.
- I prefer group activities rather than ones I do alone.
- I enjoy learning about different cultures.
- I enjoy social events like parties.
- I enjoy sharing my ideas and feelings with others.

Musical
- I often play music in my mind.
- My mood changes when I listen to music.
- It is easy for me to follow the beat of music.
- I can pick out different instruments when I listen to a piece of music.
- I keep time when music is playing.
- I can hear an off-key note.
- I find it easy to engage in musical activities.
- I can remember pieces of music easily.

Naturalistic
- Pollution makes me angry.
- I notice similarities and differences in trees, flowers, and other things in nature.
- I feel very strongly about protecting the environment.
- I enjoy watching nature programs on television.
- I engage in "clean-up days."
- I like planting and caring for a garden.
- I enjoy fishing, hiking, and bird-watching.
- When I leave school, I hope to work with plants and animals.

Body/Kinesthetic
- I like to move, tap, or fidget when sitting.
- I enjoy participating in active sports.
- I am curious as to how things feel, and I tend to touch objects and examine their texture.
- I am well coordinated.
- I like working with my hands.
- I prefer to be physically involved rather than sitting and watching.
- I understand best by doing (i.e., touching, moving, and interacting).
- I like to think through problems while I walk or run.

Intrapersonal
- I know myself well.
- I have a few close friends.
- I have strong opinions about controversial issues.
- I work best when the activity is self-paced.
- I am not easily influenced by other people.
- I have a good understanding of my feelings and how I will react to situations.
- I often raise questions concerning values and beliefs.
- I enjoy working on my own.

What do your scores illustrate about your own intelligence strengths? In what area(s) are you particularly strong?

Gardner, H. (2006). *Multiple intelligences: New horizons in theory and practice*. Basic Books.

Evaluating Multiple Intelligences

The theory of multiple intelligences has made a major contribution to how we think about intelligence. This theory pushes us to think more broadly about our abilities and talents. It can help us figure out the classes and majors where we will experience the most success. It can also provide insight into careers that best fit our natural interests.

The theory of multiple intelligences has also received some criticism. Some people believe that these different dimensions aren't really types of intelligence. Perhaps instead they should be seen as types of talents, abilities, or personality traits. There also is not a lot of scientific evidence supporting this theory.

Overall, many educators and college students find this theory very useful. Instructors, advisers, and career counselors often encourage students to think about their own distinct types of intelligence. Students often recognize their own strengths—and weaknesses—in these different types. It is also clear that reflecting on the types of material that you find most interesting can help you experience more success in your college classes. Use the following *Think Deeper* to help you better understand how learning about strengths can help you succeed in college.

> ### Think Deeper | Understanding Your Strengths
>
> Think about the different academic classes you took in high school. Then consider the following questions:
>
> 1. Which classes and subjects did you particularly enjoy? What were the common features of those classes?
> 2. Now, think about the classes and subjects with which you struggled. What types of material did those classes cover?
> 3. What does this reflection tell you about the types of classes you should take in college in order to experience success?
>
> Reflecting on the types of academic experiences you've had in the past—both positive and negative—can help you develop a plan for making the most of your college experience.

Review, Discuss, and Apply

Discussion Questions

1. Think of people in your own life, such as parents or guardians, siblings, and friends. What types of multiple intelligences do you recognize in each of them?
2. What do you think leads to people's strengths in different types of intelligences? Are these differences due to nature (our genes) or nurture (our environment)?

Module 5.3 | Understanding Mindset

LO 5.3.1 To review different types of mindsets

LO 5.3.2 To describe how mindset matters

LO 5.3.3 To examine strategies for changing mindset

Another factor that influences learning is the **mindset**, or mental frame, we adopt about ourselves and the world. Our mindsets—which include thoughts, beliefs, and expectations—determine how we perceive and respond to events in our lives. In this first section, you'll learn about different types of mindsets people hold about themselves and the world and the benefits of adopting particular types of mindsets. Next, you'll learn about the role mindset plays in the goals you set and how these goals influence academic and professional success. In the final section, you'll learn some specific strategies for adopting a more positive mindset, no matter what your natural tendency is.

Types of Mindsets

We all hold distinct views about ourselves and the world that influence virtually all aspects of our lives. These mindsets include how we explain our successes and failures. They also include expectations we hold about our abilities, traits, and characteristics. Are we optimistic or pessimistic? Good at math or terrible with numbers? A people person or a shy introvert? These beliefs we hold about ourselves have a major influence on how we learn and retain information. They also influence how we respond to setbacks and disappointments.

Carol Dweck, a psychology professor at Stanford University, has conducted extensive research on the different types of mindsets that people hold. This work has shown that people generally hold one of two sets of beliefs about their basic abilities (see **Figure 5.6**).

- People with a **fixed mindset** believe that their basic qualities, like their intelligence or talent, are stable over time. They tend to agree with statements like "You have a certain amount of intelligence, and you can't really do much to change it" and "You can do things differently, but the important parts of who you are can't really be changed."
- People with a **growth mindset** believe that their basic qualities can change over time through effort and hard work. They tend to agree with statements like "No matter who you are, you can significantly change your intelligence level" and "No matter what kind of person you are, you can always change substantially."

The type of mindset you adopt influences how you approach new situations, how you react to mistakes and failures, and how you respond to challenges.

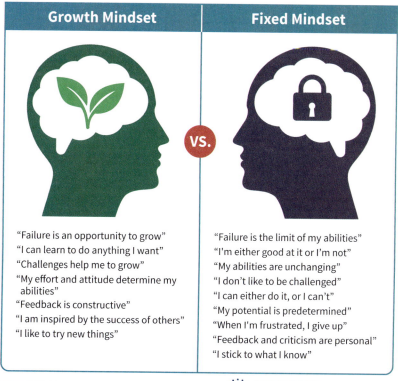

FIGURE 5.6 Growth versus fixed minset.

People who adopt a fixed mindset are very worried about failing, since they believe a single bad outcome predicts their entire future. After all, if you see ability in math as fixed and you do poorly on one test, then this news may be devastating. A fixed mindset leads people to avoid difficult challenges. Unfortunately, this means you don't have the opportunity to learn and grow. As Robert Sternberg, former dean of the School of Arts and Sciences at Tufts University, notes, "If you're afraid of making mistakes, you'll never learn on the job, and your whole approach becomes defensive: 'I have to make sure I don't screw up.'"

On the other hand, people who adopt a growth mindset see mistakes as opportunities to learn and grow. This belief leads them to pursue challenging tasks in order to develop new strengths. They are willing to risk failure and disappointment because they understand that these experiences are an essential part of mastering new tasks and skills.

Are you interested in assessing your own mindset? Use the following *Test Yourself* to see what mindset you tend to adopt.

Test Yourself | What's Your Mindset?

 INTERACTIVE SELF-ASSESSMENTS

To figure out your mindset, answer these questions using a 1–6 scale, where 1 = strongly disagree and 6 = strongly agree.

1. The kind of person someone is is something very basic about them and it can't be changed very much.
2. People can do things differently, but the important parts of who they are can't really be changed.
3. Everyone, no matter who they are, can significantly change their basic characteristics.
4. As much as I hate to admit it, you can't teach an old dog new tricks. People can't really change their deepest attributes.
5. People can always substantially change the kind of person they are.
6. Everyone is a certain kind of person, and there is not much that can be done to really change that.
7. No matter what kind of person someone is, they can always change very much.
8. All people can change even their most basic qualities.

First, add up your scores on questions 1, 2, 4, and 6. This total is your fixed mindset score. Next, add up your score on questions 3, 5, 7, and 8. This total is your growth mindset score. Which score is higher? That will tell you what mindset you tend to adopt.

Dweck, C. (2006). *Mindset: The new psychology of success.* Random House.

Mindset Matters

 VIDEO CONTENT

Adopting a growth mindset can lead to substantial benefits, not only in your academic life but in other areas of your life as well. Here are some of the advantages of adopting a growth mindset.

- Students who adopt a growth mindset show increases in grades during the first two years of middle school—when schoolwork becomes more challenging and grading standards become more rigorous. Students without such beliefs show no such improvements.
- Athletes who adopt a growth mindset understand that talent alone is insufficient, and that serious effort and rigorous training are the keys to success, achieve at higher levels.

- Giving teenagers (who were all already experiencing mental health problems) a thirty-minute lesson about growth mindset, and our ability to change and improve over time, led to lower levels of anxiety and depression as long as nine months later.
- Teaching high school students to adopt a growth mindset about intelligence and personality leads to lower levels of stress and physical illness.

In sum, adopting a mindset focused on the power and potential for change results in substantial benefits, for your academic performance as well as your psychological and physical well-being.

Mindset and Goals

The mindset you adopt has a major influence on how you approach learning. People with different types of mindsets focus on different goals when trying to master new material. These goals, in turn, influence how well you can learn new information and skills.

One way in which mindsets influence how you approach learning is through the types of goals you set. These goals can focus on either the outcome of learning or the process of learning. Let's examine these differences.

- **Performance goals** are about appearing good to others. People with these goals are focused on showing other people—and themselves—that they are smart and capable. They are concerned with looking dumb or incompetent, so they tend to play it safe.
- **Learning goals** are about increasing your competence. People with these goals are focused on learning new skills, mastering new tasks, and understanding new things. They understand that this process often involves confusion and failure and therefore aren't worried about how they appear to others.

Think about the types of goals people with different mindsets about learning tend to set when they approach a new task, whether it's speaking a new language or trying to master juggling.

People with a fixed mindset believe that their abilities don't really change. They tend to set performance goals, since they don't really believe people can develop new skills. They also worry that if they try something and fail, then that will prove they can't do something. This fear leads them to avoid attempting new things. Instead, they choose easy or familiar tasks that they know will bring them success. People with this mindset basically take a play-it-safe approach.

People with a growth mindset understand that their abilities can change with effort. They tend to set learning goals because they believe that trying new things can pay off over time. They aren't worried about how they appear to others because they understand that everyone initially struggles with learning new things.

Goals Influence Learning

As you can probably predict, the type of goal you set when approaching new material or needing to master new skills really matters.

People who adopt performance goals worry about appearing dumb or incompetent to others. They therefore tend to select easy tasks in which they are already pretty sure they can succeed. For example, they might take a college class that mostly reviews material they already know from high school. But this choice means they aren't learning new things. Instead, they are just continuing to work on areas in which they are already very strong.

People who adopt learning goals are focused on improving their understanding, competence, and skills. They therefore tend to select challenging tasks in which they can push themselves to master new things. For example, they might push themselves to take a college course about something they don't know much about. This choice naturally leads to periods of confusion and mistakes. But this process over time also leads people to develop new abilities.

Perhaps most important, the types of goals people set have a strong influence on how they respond to failure. People who set performance goals are highly concerned about doing poorly. When they initially experience difficulty when trying something new, they tend to give up and withdraw effort. They might drop a class or quit the new sport they are trying. This choice allows them to blame future mistakes on a lack of effort.

People who set learning goals respond to setbacks in a dramatically different way. They continue to stay focused on the task and try new strategies to see if a different approach can

lead to better outcomes. If they are struggling with a homework assignment, they might meet with the professor for advice on how to better prepare. If they are having trouble getting a campus job, they might ask an older student for advice on where to look. This greater persistence helps them maintain effort and develop new skills.

Changing Your Mindset

If you already hold a growth mindset, congratulations! You understand the importance of hard work and effort and how they lead to success. This view will help you overcome challenges you face and help you persist even when things are hard.

But for those who don't already hold a growth mindset, here's the good news: there are absolutely steps you can take to shift your mindset and experience greater success. Here's what you can do:

- **Recognize—and stop—fixed mindset thoughts**—Pay attention to thoughts you might have when you approach a difficult task, like "I've never been good at writing" or "Math is just not my thing." As soon as you find yourself thinking these types of negative thoughts, which reflect a fixed mindset, stop yourself. If this is your natural tendency, the first step is learning to identify these negative thoughts, and then immediately stop them.
- **Change your thought patterns**—Replace maladaptive fixed mindset thoughts with more positive growth mindset ones. Remind yourself that learning new things and developing new skills takes time for everyone. Remember that with time and effort, you can master difficult material. College work is an adjustment for all students. Adopt a growth-focused mantra that works for you, such as "I can do this" or "Learning takes time."
- **Focus on the good**—Some people tend to focus on what's going poorly in their lives—their problems, disappointments, and rejections. They repeatedly think about a fight they had with a friend or a C grade they received on a test. Not surprisingly, this approach doesn't help them feel better. If you have this tendency, a good strategy is to start by focusing on what's going well in your life and reminding yourself that there's a lot of good in your life.
- **Accept that change takes time**—When things don't go your way, accept that achieving success almost always takes considerable time and effort. If you are trying to master college-level math or become a stronger writer, it won't happen overnight. Recognize that setbacks are a normal and natural part of life and that change takes time.

- **Focus on learning goals, not performance goals**—Emphasize the process of learning new things, such as how to write more effectively, share your thoughts in class, or comprehend a foreign language. Acknowledge the steps you've made in getting better at these tasks, instead of focusing only on the grade you will receive on your latest assignment.
- **Seek feedback from others**—If you find yourself getting stuck in a cycle of negative thoughts, talk to people you trust, such as instructors, career counselors, or academic advisers. These people can help you understand that learning is a process for almost everyone, and that they too may well have experienced struggles and setbacks to get where they are today.

How well can you shift your mindset? Take each of the fixed mindset statements that follow and shift them to form a growth mindset.

Fixed-Mindset Statements	Growth Mindset
I've never been good at science.	
If I try and fail, I'll be a failure.	
If I don't try, I won't embarrass myself when I fail.	
People with talent find this really easy.	

DOWNLOAD DOCUMENTS & TEMPLATES

Think Deeper | Responding to New Challenges

Think about the last time you struggled with completing an academic task, such as writing a paper or studying for a test. Then consider the following questions:

1. What mindset did you use when approaching this task?
2. How did using this mindset help you or hurt you in working on the task?
3. If this mindset hurt you, how could adopting a growth mindset help you experience greater success in the future?

Reflecting on the type of mindset you most commonly use when you succeed at a difficult academic challenge can help you understand why that approach was the right one. It can also help you understand why adopting a better approach on future tasks may be a good idea.

Review, Discuss, and Apply

INTERACTIVE SELF-SCORING QUIZZES

Discussion Questions

1. Thinking about yourself as a high school student, did you adopt more of a fixed mindset or a growth mindset about your academic work? Where do you think this type of mindset came from?
2. What factors might lead people to adopt learning goals versus performance goals?
3. Which of the strategies for shifting your mindset do you see as most helpful? Which will you try?

Think Ahead | Career and Lifelong Applications

People's mindset influences virtually all aspects of their personal and professional lives. People who adopt a growth mindset tend to achieve more in their careers. They also experience closer relationships, less stress, and better health. What explains these benefits? Here are some of the advantages:

Goal Setting—People with a growth mindset set more challenging goals. They set more ambitious goals in their careers, which often leads them to achieve at a higher level. They also set ambitious goals in their personal lives, such as exercise regimens, saving money, or pursuing hobbies.

Seventyfour/Adobe Stock

Enjoyment—People with a growth mindset enjoy learning new things. This leads them to take on more responsibility in their careers and to develop new skills in their personal lives.

Persistence—People with a growth mindset believe that effort pays off. This belief leads them to persist over time, even when things don't initially go well.

Response to failure—People with a growth mindset understand that setbacks are simply a part of life. This belief leads them to persist even when they face challenges and disappointments.

As you can see, adopting a growth mindset helps people succeed in many different types of environments. People with a growth mindset set more ambitious goals, in part because they enjoy learning new things. They also persist with these goals, even when things aren't going well. This mindset helps them achieve more success in their careers. It also helps them achieve goals in their personal lives, such as learning a new language, training to run a marathon, or saving money to buy a house.

What Would You Do?

In this chapter, Aiden and Julia need your advice.

VIDEO CONTENT

AIDEN

Aiden just had some of his ideas for the hardware store shot down by his uncle and his mother. How should he respond?

Watch Aiden's video: **Push Forward or Retreat?**

JULIA

Julia picked up an accordion at a second-hand store on a whim and started learning how to play it. She has learned a little bit but is thinking about giving up on it.

Watch Julia's video: **Always Learning**

What would you tell Aiden? What would you tell Julia?

Take Some Action | Here and Now

DOWNLOAD DOCUMENTS & TEMPLATES

We all have strengths and weaknesses when it comes to knowing how we learn best and developing the right mindset. Being aware of those strengths and weaknesses is key to success in college, in the workplace, and in life.

Review your outcomes on the *Test Yourself* assessments throughout this chapter and your responses to the *Think Deeper* questions. Reflect on your results and responses, and then answer these questions:

1. What are your strengths with respect to being in touch with your best learning styles? How will you put those strengths to work for you toward succeeding in college? How will sharpening those strengths in college help you be successful in the workplace?

2. How do you want to improve your strengths when it comes to mindset?

3. Review the suggested action steps in that area and choose two or three of those to commit to here and now, and for each, say how taking that action step will help you succeed in college and beyond.

Share and discuss your responses to these questions with a friend, classmate, or family member.

Chapter Summary

INTERACTIVE SELF-SCORING QUIZZES
Chapter 5 Practice Quiz

Module 5.1 Understanding Learning

- Several different models explain how learning occurs: classical conditioning, operant conditioning, and observational learning. Classical conditioning is a type of learning that occurs when a previously neutral stimulus over time starts to elicit a response. This type of learning occurs when people associate—connect—different things, such as taking a quiz and feeling anxious. Operant conditioning theory states that behavior can be more or less likely to occur depending on the presence of reinforcements. When people receive positive reinforcements, or rewards, for behaving in a certain way, they are more likely to continue that behavior. When people receive a punishment for a behavior, they are less likely to continue that behavior. The theory of observational learning states that people learn by observing and imitating, or modeling, other people's behavior. We also observe the consequences—positive or negative—that people experience from engaging in a particular behavior.

- There are many different models that categorize people's learning styles in different ways. One of the most popular models of learning styles is the VARK model, which stands for visual, auditory, reading, and kinesthetic. Another popular model of learning styles is Kolb's Learning Style Inventory (LSI), which states that people vary based on two dimensions: active versus reflective and abstract versus concrete. According to the Myers-Briggs Type Indicator, people can be grouped into sixteen different personality types, assessing four distinct dimensions: valuing, visioning, relating, and directing.

- Although models of learning styles are very appealing to people for many different reasons, there is not much evidence that most such models actually predict performance. However, there is empirical support for the Index of Learning Styles (ILS) model, which divides people based on four different ways of processing and organizing information: active-reflective, sensing-intuitive, verbal-visual, and sequential-global. The following strategies can help enhance your learning, regardless of your preferred style: think visually, match learning style to the material, and use different learning styles.

Module 5.2 Defining Multiple Intelligences

- According to the theory of multiple intelligences, all people have different kinds of intelligence or strengths in different areas. These different types of intelligence include visual-spatial, linguistic-verbal, logical-mathematical, bodily-kinesthetic, musical, interpersonal, intrapersonal, and naturalistic. People may show a particular strength in one area, or relative strengths in several areas.

- The theory of multiple intelligences pushes people to think more broadly about their abilities and talents. Many people find it useful. However, some people have raised concerns about whether these different dimensions are actually types of intelligence and whether this theory is supported by scientific research.

Module 5.3 Understanding Mindset

- Another factor that influences learning is the mindset, or mental frame, we adopt about ourselves and the world. People with a fixed mindset believe that their basic qualities, like their intelligence or talent, are stable over time. People with a growth mindset believe that their basic qualities can change over time through effort and hard work. The type of mindset you adopt influences how you approach new situations, how you react to mistakes and failures, and how you respond to challenges.

- Adopting a growth mindset can lead to substantial benefits. People with a growth mindset have better grades, achieve better athletic performance, have better psychological well-being, and have lower rates of stress and illness. Mindsets influence the types of goals people set. People with a fixed mindset tend to set performance goals, which focus on appearing good to others. People with a growth mindset tend to set learning goals, which focus on increasing their competence. Mindsets also influence how people approach learning new material, mastering new skills, and responding to setbacks.

- You can take steps to change your mindset and experience greater success. Strategies you can use include recognizing (and stopping) fixed mindset thoughts, changing your thought patterns, focusing on the good, accepting that change takes time, focusing on learning (not performance) goals, and seeking feedback from others.

Key Terms

Classical conditioning A type of learning that occurs when a previously neutral stimulus over time starts to elicit a response

Fixed mindset A belief that a person's basic qualities are stable over time

Growth mindset A belief that a person's basic qualities can change over time through effort and hard work

Learning Acquiring new, or modifying existing, knowledge, skills, values, or behavior

Learning goals Goals focused on increasing your own competence

Learning styles A person's preferences about acquiring, organizing, and retaining information

Mindset A mental frame, or thought pattern, people hold about themselves and the world

Multiple intelligences A theory that all people have different kinds of intelligence or strengths in different areas

Observational learning A type of learning that occurs when people observe and imitate, or model, other people's behavior

Operant conditioning A type of learning that occurs when people receive rewards or punishments for engaging in a behavior

Performance goals Goals focused on appearing good to others

Resources

Cherry, K. (2022, November 18). What is the MMPI test? What to know about the Minnesota Multiphasic Personality Inventory. *Verywell Mind.* Retrieved from https://www.verywellmind.com/what-is-the-minnesota-multiphasic-personality-inventory-2795582

Cherry, K. (2023, March 11). Gardner's theory of multiple intelligences. *Verywell Mind.* Retrieved from https://www.verywellmind.com/gardners-theory-of-multiple-intelligences-2795161

Dweck, C. (2016, January 13). What having a 'growth mindset' actually means. *Harvard Business Review.* Retrieved from https://hbr.org/2016/01/what-having-a-growth-mindset-actually-means

Dweck, C. S. S. (2007). *Mindset: The new psychology of success.* Ballantine Books.

Gardner, H. (1983). *Frames of mind: The theory of multiple intelligences.* Basic Books.

Willingham, D. T. (2018, October 4). Are you a visual or an auditory learner? It doesn't matter. *The New York Times.* Retrieved from https://www.nytimes.com/2018/10/04/opinion/sunday/visual-learner-auditory-school-education.html

References

Dweck, C. (2006). *Mindset: The new psychology of success.* Random House.

Dweck, C. S., & Leggett, E. L. (1988). A social-cognitive approach to motivation and personality. *Psychological Review, 95*(2), 256–273. https://doi.org/10.1037/0033-295X.95.2.256

Felder, F. M., & Soloman, B. A. (1991). Index of Learning Styles. North Carolina State University.

Felder, R. M., & Silverman, L. K. (1988). Learning and teaching styles in engineering education. *Engineering Education, 78,* 674–681.

Gardner, H. E. (2006). *Multiple intelligences: New horizons in theory and practice.* Basic Books.

Husmann, P. R., & O'Loughlin, V. D. (2019). Another nail in the coffin for learning styles? Disparities among undergraduate anatomy students' study strategies, class performance, and reported VARK learning styles. *Anatomical Sciences Education, 12*(1), 6–19. https://doi.org/10.1002/ase.1777

Nancekivell, S. E., Shah, P., & Gelman, S. A. (2020). Maybe they're born with it, or maybe it's experience: Toward a deeper understanding of the learning style myth. *Journal of Educational Psychology, 112*(2), 221–235. https://doi.org/10.1037/edu0000366

Pashler, H., McDaniel, M., Rohrer, D., & Bjork, R. (2008). Learning styles: Concepts and evidence. *Psychological Science in the Public Interest, 9*(3), 105–119.

Pittenger, D. J. (1993). The utility of the Myers-Briggs Type Indicator. *Review of Educational Research, 63*(4), 467–488. https://doi.org/10.2307/1170497

Schleider, J. L., & Weisz, J. R. (2016). Reducing risk for anxiety and depression in adolescents: Effects of a single-session intervention teaching that personality can change. *Behaviour Research and Therapy, 87,* 170–181. https://doi.org/10.1016/j.brat.2016.09.011

Yeager, D. S., Johnson, R., Spitzer, B. J., Trzesniewski, K. H., Powers, J., & Dweck, C. S. (2014). The far-reaching effects of believing people can change: Implicit theories of personality shape stress, health, and achievement during adolescence. *Journal of Personality and Social Psychology, 106*(6), 867–884. https://doi.org/10.1037/a0036335

CHAPTER 6

The Power of Emotional Intelligence

VIDEO CONTENT
Author's Introduction

"Do not judge me by my success, judge me by how many times I fell down and got back up again."
—Nelson Mandela, former president of South Africa

CHAPTER OUTLINE	LEARNING OBJECTIVES
Envision, Pursue, and Persist: Oprah Winfrey	
Module 6.1 **Understanding Emotional Intelligence**	**LO 6.1** To understand the influence of emotional intelligence
Components of Emotional Intelligence	
Test Yourself: What's Your Emotional Intelligence?	
The Role of Empathy	
Test Yourself: How Empathetic Are You?	
Strategies for Increasing Emotional Intelligence	
Think Deeper: Motivation Matters	
Module 6.2 **Understanding Grit**	**LO 6.2** To examine the power of grit
Components of Grit	
Make It Personal: Showing Perseverance	
How Grit Predicts Success	
Test Yourself: How Gritty Are You?	
Strategies for Increasing Grit	
Think Deeper: Achieve Your Goals	
Module 6.3 **Understanding Resilience**	**LO 6.3** To develop strategies for building resilience
The Value of Resilience	
Test Yourself: How Resilient Are You?	
The Upside of Adversity	
Think Deeper: Responding to Difficult Life Events	
Strategies for Building Resilience	
Make It Personal: Reframing Challenges	
Make It Personal: Goal Planning	
Test Yourself: Do You Practice Self-Compassion?	

Think Ahead: Career and Lifelong Applications
Take Some Action: Here and Now

Chapter Summary
Key Terms
Resources
References

Envision, Pursue, and Persist | Oprah Winfrey

Featureflash Photo Agency/Shutterstock.com

Oprah Winfrey was born in 1954 to a teenage mother living in a rural town in Mississippi. Throughout her childhood, she experienced numerous hardships. These included living in poverty, suffering sexual abuse, and becoming pregnant at age fourteen.

Despite these very difficult life circumstances, Oprah persisted. She moved to Tennessee to live with her father and focused intently on her schoolwork. She worked part-time at a local radio station to help pay for college.

As a student at Tennessee State University, Oprah majored in communications. She was hired by a television station in Nashville after graduation. This eventually led to a job in Baltimore with ABC. Only a few years after graduating from college, Oprah became the prime-time news coanchor. But this exciting career opportunity didn't last: the show had poor ratings and was cancelled (with Oprah receiving much of the blame).

How did she respond to this major career disappointment? Oprah thought about what she liked—and didn't like—about journalism. She realized that she loved working in television, but she wasn't interested in the so-called "hard news." Instead, she preferred focusing on human-interest stories.

Oprah's self-awareness about her strengths and interests led to yet another career move: co-hosting a low-rated morning talk show called *AM Chicago*. Within a few months, this show became the highest-rated talk show in Chicago. Oprah had found her calling.

She was then recruited to start her own show, which began broadcasting on September 8, 1986. Within a few years, this show, *The Oprah Winfrey Show*, became the top-rated daytime talk show in America. What made this show so successful? Oprah's empathy for her guests and openness with her own personal challenges—such as her struggle to lose weight—clearly played a role.

Oprah's story clearly demonstrates that success often doesn't come quickly or easily. Instead, success involves learning from failure, understanding your strengths, and persevering even when things are hard. This chapter will examine all of these topics, including how you can develop these abilities and thereby experience better success in college. As Oprah herself notes, "Turn your wounds into wisdom. You will be wounded many times in your life. You'll make mistakes. Some people will call them failures, but I have learned that failure is really God's way of saying, 'Excuse me, you're moving in the wrong direction.' It's just an experience, just an experience."

Module 6.1 | Understanding Emotional Intelligence

LO 6.1.1 To describe the distinct components of emotional intelligence

LO 6.1.2 To understand the value of empathy

LO 6.1.3 To review strategies for increasing emotional intelligence

---

Do you know people who always seem positive, calm, and in control of their emotions even in stressful situations? Do you know people who sense that you are feeling down, even before you say anything to them? People with these types of characteristics have high **emotional intelligence** (or EI). People who have high EI tend to be more successful in school, work, and interpersonal relationships. They also experience greater mental and emotional health. Therefore, developing skills in EI can help people succeed in all aspects of life. In this section, you'll learn about the components of emotional intelligence and the benefits of emotional intelligence for your personal and professional lives.

Components of Emotional Intelligence

Emotional intelligence refers to the ability to identify and manage emotions, not only your own emotions but also those of other people around you. People who are emotionally intelligent are aware of their emotions and are able to regulate or manage the emotions they feel. They are able to help other people with regulating their own emotions.

Why is understanding and regulating emotions so important? One reason is that it helps people avoid conflicts and misunderstandings. Let's say you are feeling frustrated that one of your good friends never seems to make time for you. Someone who is low in emotional intelligence might respond to this situation in ways that hurt the friendship. For example, they might become angry and rude to their friend. Or they might just pull away from the friendship completely.

In contrast, someone who is high in emotional intelligence will likely share their feelings honestly and openly with their friend. This approach lets the friend know how they feel, but it doesn't create conflict or hurt feelings. They would also have empathy for what their friend might be going through. Perhaps their friend is struggling with a personal issue that is taking up a lot of their time. A person who is high in emotional intelligence might also suggest solutions that would help maintain the friendship over time.

People who are high in emotional intelligence understand their own emotional states, which helps them manage their feelings. Have you ever lashed out at a friend, sibling, or dating partner because you were feeling really tired or hungry? That's an example of how our emotional states can influence our relationships. People who are high in emotional intelligence are better at understanding whether they are really feeling angry, or instead are just feeling exhausted. As you can probably imagine, having this type of awareness of what you are feeling helps in all types of relationships.

People who have high EI also show other distinct strengths and abilities, including the following (**Figure 6.1**):

- **Self-awareness**—People with high EI understand what they are feeling and how their emotions influence themselves and people around them. They have a good sense of their own strengths and weaknesses.
- **Self-regulation**—People with high EI are good at managing their emotions, even when in stressful situations. They can control their feelings and think before acting.
- **Internal motivation**—Recall from Chapter 1 that motivation may be intrinsic (based on internal rewards) or extrinsic (based on external rewards). People with high EI are internally motivated to pursue their goals, which leads to better results.
- **Social skills**—People with high EI are able to understand and influence the emotions of people around them. This ability helps them work well with other people, build and maintain relationships, and resolve conflicts in constructive ways.
- **Empathy**—People with high EI have high levels of social awareness and empathy, meaning they can easily put themselves in someone else's shoes. They understand how other people are feeling and therefore are really good at supporting their friends when they are in need.

INTERACTIVE FIGURES, CHARTS, & TABLES

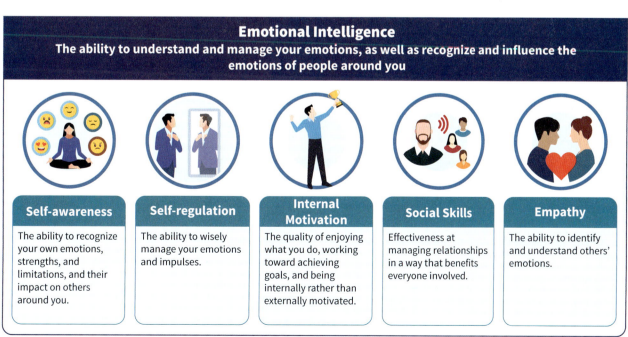

FIGURE 6.1 The five distinct components of emotional intelligence.
Source: Adapted from: https://venngage.com/templates/mind-maps/dark-emotional-intelligence-mind-map-62a9563e-6b9b-4c5c-9ff3-eac57073c288

Are you interested in learning about your own emotional intelligence? Use the following *Test Yourself* to rate yourself on the various competencies of emotional intelligence.

> **Test Yourself | What's Your Emotional Intelligence?** 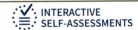 INTERACTIVE SELF-ASSESSMENTS
>
> Read each of the following statements and rate how much it applies to you on a scale of 1 to 5. Give yourself a 1 if you disagree strongly and a 5 if you agree strongly.
>
> 1. I know why my emotions change.
> 2. I easily recognize my emotions as I experience them.
> 3. I can tell how people are feeling by listening to the tone of their voice.
> 4. By looking at their facial expressions, I recognize the emotions people are experiencing.
> 5. I seek out activities that make me happy.
> 6. I have control over my emotions.
> 7. I arrange events others enjoy.
> 8. I help other people feel better when they are down.
> 9. When I am in a positive mood, I am able to come up with new ideas.
> 10. I use good moods to help myself keep trying in the face of obstacles.
>
> This scale assesses five different components of emotional intelligence: understanding one's own emotions, understanding other people's emotions, regulating one's own emotions, regulating other people's emotions, and using positive emotions in a good way. Higher scores on this scale indicate higher overall emotional intelligence. But don't worry about your score: later in this chapter, you'll learn how to increase emotional intelligence.
>
> Schutte, N. S., Malouff, J. M., Hall, L. E., Haggerty, D. J., Cooper, J. T., Golden, C. J., & Dornheim, L. (1998). Development and validation of a measure of emotional intelligence. *Personality and Individual Differences, 25*(2), 167–177. https://doi.org/10.1016/S0191-8869(98)00001-4

Guillermo Spelucin/Adobe Stock

The Role of Empathy

 VIDEO CONTENT

The term *empathy* describes the ability to understand and share the feelings of another person. People who have an abundance of empathy can easily imagine the world from another person's point of view. They can even experience the same emotions a person is feeling. This explains why people who have a great deal of empathy may cry watching a fictional character in a movie or television show. They can clearly imagine being in that person's situation.

How able are you to do this type of perspective-taking? Rate yourself using the following *Test Yourself*.

People who have a lot of empathy often build very close relationships because they take the time to understand how other people are thinking and feeling. This ability helps them get along with people from different backgrounds. Empathy helps people form better relationships in ways that include the following:

- An ability to make other people trust them and feel comfortable confiding in them.
- A focus on what they share with other people, rather than what differences they may have.

- A better ability to work through conflict in relationships. This is because they can imagine the conflict from the other person's perspective.
- A sincere interest in understanding other people's experiences and perspectives. They recognize that people from different backgrounds have different views of the world. They also enjoy learning about these different perspectives.
- A willingness to get to know people as individuals and accept them for who they are. They avoid making assumptions about people or relying on stereotypes based on race, nationality, sex, gender identity, sexual orientation, or other characteristics.

Test Yourself | How Empathetic Are You?

Read each of the following statements and rate how frequently you feel or act in the manner described. Use the following scale to rate your answers:

Never	Rarely	Sometimes	Often	Always
0	1	2	3	4

1. When someone else is feeling excited, I tend to get excited, too.
2. Other people's misfortunes do not disturb me a great deal.
3. It upsets me to see someone being treated disrespectfully.
4. I remain unaffected when someone close to me is happy.
5. I enjoy making other people feel better.
6. I have tender, concerned feelings for people less fortunate than I.
7. When a friend starts to talk about their problems, I try to steer the conversation toward something else.
8. I can tell when others are sad even when they do not say anything.
9. I find that I am "in tune" with other people's moods.
10. I do not feel sympathy for people who cause their own serious illnesses.
11. I become irritated when someone cries.
12. I am not really interested in how other people feel.
13. I get a strong urge to help when I see someone who is upset.
14. When I see someone being treated unfairly, I do not feel very much pity for them.
15. I find it silly for people to cry out of happiness.
16. When I see someone being taken advantage of, I feel kind of protective toward them.

First, add up your total scores on items: 1, 3, 5, 6, 8, 9, 13, and 16. Next, add up your scores on the following items: 2, 4, 7, 10, 11, 12, 14, and 15. Then subtract your total sum on the second set of items from your total sum on the first set of items. This will give you a total score on empathy, with higher scores indicating a greater tendency to feel empathy for others.

Davis, M. H. (1983). Measuring individual differences in empathy: Evidence for a multidimensional approach. *Journal of Personality and Social Psychology, 44*(1), 113–126. https://doi.org/10.1037/0022-3514.44.1.113

Strategies for Increasing Emotional Intelligence

No matter our natural tendency, we can all take steps to increase our own emotional intelligence. Developing these skills can help you be a better friend, parent, leader, and romantic partner. Simply understanding the importance of these skills is an important first step.

Here are some other strategies you can use:

- **Become more self-aware**—Pay attention to your feelings and what may be causing them. Being mindful of your own emotions will help you identify how you feel and how you respond to other people. It will also help you be more aware of other people's emotions.
- **Discover your passions**—Think about what makes you feel excited, including in your classes, job, volunteer work, and hobbies. Most people have a passion for some type of activity, work, or hobby. This passion helps them to maintain interest and focus over time. Spend some time thinking about where your passion lies, and then try to find ways to pursue it.
- **Focus on internal motivation**—People who are high in emotional intelligence work on things they find internally motivating, meaning enjoyable, interesting, and challenging. As we noted earlier, internal motivation tends to lead to better outcomes. People who pursue things based on external motivation, meaning a desire for external rewards or out of obligation or pressure, have less fun and tend to do less well.
- **Understand your strengths and weaknesses**—Think about where your strengths lie, and try to find opportunities to use those strengths in your daily life. People who figure out their strengths can make better choices about what they pursue, and they tend to experience more success.
- **Develop empathy**—People who are able to see the world from another person's perspective can build closer personal relationships, including with family members, friends, and romantic partners. They also tend to be more effective in their work relationships. You can increase your own level of empathy by paying attention to other people, including what they say verbally as well as their nonverbal messages.
- **Manage your emotions**—Learn to control your emotions, instead of letting them control you. This type of self-regulation can help you cope better, even in stressful situations. If you are feeling angry or sad, recognize what you are feeling and then think about what is causing that emotion. Next, remind yourself that you can control your feelings and take steps to shift that emotion if you'd like to do so. For example, if you recognize that you feel lonely, you could make a plan with a friend to do something.
- **Practice social responsibility**—People who are high in emotional intelligence care about other people. They therefore take steps to help other people in various ways. This could include donating money to a charitable cause, volunteering, or helping out a friend or family member. Think about a cause that is personally meaningful to you, such as homelessness, climate change, child abuse, or a specific disease. Then, find ways to contribute to that cause, such as by giving money, volunteering time, or increasing awareness of the issue.
- **Pursue happiness**—People who are high in emotional intelligence search out things that make them happy. Their general tendency to feel happy makes them more pleasant for other people to be around. It also allows them to manage stressors and challenges when they do occur. A great way to increase your own emotional intelligence is therefore to find ways to pursue happiness in your own life. (You'll learn more about this important topic in **Chapter 10: Find Your Happiness**.)

> **Think Deeper** | Motivation Matters
>
> Think about different types of activities in which you participated during high school, including your academic classes and extracurricular activities. Then consider the following questions:
>
> 1. What things did you find enjoyable, fun, and challenging to pursue?
> 2. What things did you do out of a feeling of pressure or hope for external rewards?
> 3. How can you focus more in college on the activities and interests that you found internally motivating?
>
> Reflecting on the types of experiences you had during high school can help you find classes and activities that you find personally interesting and enjoyable. You'll probably also experience more success.

Review, Discuss, and Apply

Discussion Questions

1. Why are people with high EI more successful in their personal and professional relationships?
2. Which of the components of emotional intelligence do you find most important, and why?
3. Why do people vary in their level of empathy? What explains such differences?
4. Which strategy for increasing your emotional intelligence are you most likely to try?

Module 6.2 Understanding Grit

LO 6.2.1 To define the different components of grit
LO 6.2.2 To examine the link between grit and success
LO 6.2.3 To understand strategies for increasing grit

We often believe that people who accomplish great things must be very smart or naturally talented. But what research shows again and again is that other factors can play a substantial role in whether we succeed. Research by Angela Duckworth, a psychology professor at the University of Pennsylvania, has shown that people who achieve great things are typically high in **grit**—meaning that they tend to work diligently on something they feel passionately about and to stick with it, even when facing difficulty or failure.

Think about Oprah's persistence over time: her first television show failed, but instead of giving up, she shifted her focus from hard news to human interest. And that shift clearly paid off. Other people who have achieved great success in their careers often had similar types of setbacks (see **Figure 6.2**). In this section, you'll learn about the components of grit, how grit predicts success, and strategies you can use to develop grit.

 **Steven Spielberg**—This Oscar-award-winning film director was rejected three times from the University of Southern California School of Theater, Film, and Television (now the School of Cinematic Arts).

 **Diana Nyad**—At age 64, this woman became the first person to swim from Cuba to Florida, spending over 50 hours swimming 110 miles in waters full of sharks and jellyfish. She had failed to complete the swim on her four previous attempts.

 **Amelia Earhart**—The first woman to fly across the Atlantic Ocean worked multiple jobs to pay for flight school, was told to stop doing "boy things" when she said she wanted to be a pilot, and was told that she would never be able to successfully fly across the Atlantic.

 **Jim Carrey**—This award-winning comedic actor dropped out of high school at age fifteen to work as a janitor to help support his low-income family, was booed off stage during his first comic stand-up at a club, and was rejected following his audition for *Saturday Night Live*.

 **Steph Curry**—This National Basketball Association Most Valuable Player played junior varsity during his freshman year of high school and attended a Division III college (after not being recruited by any Division I programs).

 **Sonia Sotomayor**—This Supreme Court Justice grew up in poverty and struggled to manage her juvenile diabetes before graduating from Princeton University and Yale Law School.

FIGURE 6.2 Real world examples of showing grit when facing setbacks.

Components of Grit

Psychologists describe grit as passion and perseverance for long-term and meaningful goals (see **Figure 6.3**). As you can tell from this definition, grit has two distinct components:

1. **Passion**—People who are high in grit focus on their passion for achieving a particular long-term goal. They are deeply committed to pursuing this goal. They are willing to give up other things in order to devote time and energy to it. They also stay focused on what they want to achieve even when they feel bored, tired, or overwhelmed.

2. **Perseverance**—People who are high in grit show resilience even in the face of failure or adversity. They continue to work toward their goals, no matter what. If necessary, they find new ways to work toward achieving them instead of simply giving up.

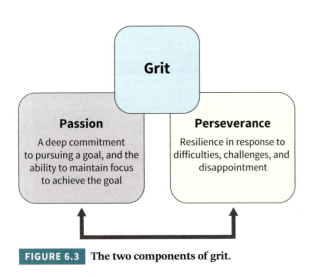

FIGURE 6.3 The two components of grit.

These two components help people with grit stick with their goals, even when things don't initially go their way. Let's say a first-year college student gets a failing grade on their first exam. How do they respond? Someone who is low in grit might decide to just give up and drop that class. They might even decide they aren't cut out for college. Someone who is high in grit would take a very different approach. They might meet with the professor to learn how to prepare better for the next exam. They might change their study habits to better master the material. These choices would probably lead to a better outcome on the next exam.

How do you respond when things don't initially go your way?

Make It Personal | Showing Perseverance

For each of these challenging situations you might face in college, write down how you could respond in a positive way, showing perseverance. Think of challenging situations that might apply more personally to you and write down your strategies for those as well.

Challenging Situation	Strategy
You audition for a play and don't get the part.	
You get a C on a paper.	
You are cut from the basketball team.	
You apply for a part-time job and don't get it.	

How Grit Predicts Success

One of the first studies to demonstrate the power of grit examined data collected from students at West Point Military Academy. Admission to West Point is very competitive: applicants submit not only SAT scores and grades but also measures of physical fitness and leadership ability. All students also undergo an extensive summer of training right before they start their first year.

At the start of the summer, researchers in this study gave all students a short assessment measuring their level of grit. Then they examined whether scores on this assessment would predict which students dropped out of the program, even before starting college. Given what you've just learned about grit, can you predict their findings?

Grit was a stronger predictor of whether students stayed with the program than any other measure. This included measures of physical fitness, IQ, or conscientiousness. This doesn't mean that those factors aren't important, but it does show that grit is also an important factor in predicting success. In other words, grit matters.

Grit also predicts success in other types of situations. Students who are high in grit are more likely to graduate from college. First-year teachers who are high in grit are more likely to stick with their job, even if they are working in tough schools.

What's the key finding of all this research? We often assume that people who succeed must be very smart, or very talented, or very lucky. But personal factors, including hope, optimism, and self-confidence, also have a strong influence on how we perform.

If you are interested in seeing how you score on grit, take the following *Test Yourself*.

Test Yourself | How Gritty Are You?

Read each of the following items, and rate how much it applies to you on a scale of 1 to 5. Give yourself a 1 if it is not like you at all and a 5 if it is very much like you.

1.	New ideas and projects sometimes distract me from previous ones.
2.	Setbacks don't discourage me.
3.	I have been obsessed with a certain idea or project for a short time but later lost interest.
4.	I am a hard worker.
5.	I often set a goal but later choose to pursue a different one.
6.	I have difficulty maintaining my focus on projects that take more than a few months to complete.
7.	I finish whatever I begin.
8.	I am diligent.

Add up your scores on items 2, 4, 7, and 8. Then add up your scores on items 1, 3, 5, and 6. Subtract your total on the second set of items from your total on the first set of items to get your total grit score. Higher numbers indicate more grittiness.

Duckworth, A. L., & Quinn, P. D. (2009). Development and validation of the Short Grit Scale (GRIT–S). *Journal of Personality Assessment, 91*(2), 166–174. https://doi.org/10.1080/00223890802634290

There clearly isn't only one variable that predicts success. It probably does help to be smart and talented. But even people who have these natural advantages may not succeed if they don't keep trying when things don't go well. And even people without these advantages may achieve great things.

Think Deeper | Achieve Your Goals

Think about a time you've set and then worked through a personal goal. It could be learning to play the guitar, saving money to buy a car, or getting into college. Then consider the following questions:

1. How did you choose your goal? What motivated this decision?
2. What challenges or obstacles did you experience along the way?
3. How did you overcome these roadblocks and stay focused on what you wanted to achieve?

Reflecting on the types of goals you've successfully worked toward in the past can help you figure out good strategies for the future. This self-knowledge can then help you achieve other goals during college and beyond.

Strategies for Increasing Grit

Some people—like Oprah—seem to be naturally high in grit. But no matter your tendency, you can take steps to increase your grit. Here are some strategies you can use.

- **Find a purpose**—It's much easier to keep working on something that you really care about. In all classes, you may find some material that is less interesting. Similarly, all jobs have some parts that may feel boring. But if you see what you are working on as having meaning, you will find it much easier to keep going. Think about the class you are taking as building up to your very meaningful college degree. Think about the job you are doing as an important stepping stone toward your dream career.

- **Develop your talent**—We often assume that some people are just talented in a given area, and others aren't. But the reality is that all of us can develop skills in any area, as long as we practice. Find something that you want to pursue, and work on developing your own skills in that area.
- **Have a growth mindset**—As you learned in Chapter 5, people with a growth mindset understand that effort and hard work matter. They stay focused on their goals, even when they experience setbacks and obstacles. In fact, they recognize that failures are just a natural part of mastering new skills. This mindset helps them persevere, no matter what.
- **Learn from others**—Recognize that feedback from other people can help you develop new skills. Be receptive to advice from people around you. They may have suggestions that can help you achieve your goals.
- **Work on your weaknesses**—It often feels good to spend time doing what comes easiest to you. But an important part of developing grit is also focusing on your weaknesses. Figure out what things are hard for you and spend some time trying to strengthen these areas. Do you hate writing, so you avoid classes that require papers? This isn't a good strategy for improving your writing! Instead, try things that challenge you and help you develop new skills. This approach can really pay off over time.

Which strategy is being used in each of the following situations?

Marisol realizes that writing term papers makes her anxious. She therefore makes an appointment with her school's writing center whenever an instructor assigns a paper.

INTERACTIVE FIGURES, CHARTS, & TABLES

Jayden isn't really enjoying his science class. He reminds himself regularly that this class is a required course for his degree in physical therapy.

Brooklyn struggled with managing their time well during the first few weeks of college. Then they reached out to other students in their major for some advice, which was really helpful.

In the first few weeks of college, Akito struggled a lot with her accounting class. Then she started coming regularly to office hours and spending more time reviewing her notes. Akito is now doing very well in this class.

Noah joined his friend's basketball team as a way of meeting people and getting some exercise. After seeing that most of the other players were much better than he was, Noah spent more time practicing on his own. He now feels much more confident about his basketball skills.

Review, Discuss, and Apply

Discussion Questions

1. Think about your own life. What are the areas where you demonstrate the greatest amount of grit (e.g., competitive sports, academic achievement, playing a musical instrument)? Conversely, what are some places where you may tend to give up without much effort or thought?
2. Who are the people in your life who encourage you to keep going when things get tough?

Module 6.3 Understanding Resilience

LO 6.3.1 To understand the value of resilience

LO 6.3.2 To examine the role of adversity in creating resilience

LO 6.3.3 To review strategies for building resilience

No one wants to experience negative life events, such as a serious injury or illness, violent crime, or the death of a family member. But unfortunately, we all will at times experience extremely difficult events. And as you'll learn in this section, difficult life events can help us learn to develop important coping skills. In fact, people who have experienced more difficult events often show higher levels of **resilience**, meaning an ability to recover from traumatic and stressful events.

The Value of Resilience

People with resilience show a remarkable ability to bounce back from major life stressors, including serious health problems, financial stress, physical trauma, and relationship problems.

People who have a lot of resilience show particular characteristics, which include the following:

- An ability to make plans and successfully carry them out
- Positive views of themselves and self-confidence in their strengths and abilities
- Skills in communicating with others and solving problems
- The ability to manage strong feelings and impulses

The characteristics of resilience can all be developed with practice. In fact, experiencing some adversity gives people an opportunity to develop important skills for coping when future challenges arise. This means they are better able to recover from future difficult events.

Dizain/Adobe Stock

Do you want to assess your own level of resilience? Use the following *Test Yourself* to measure your resilience.

> **Test Yourself | How Resilient Are You?**
>
> Respond to these six items using a scale of 1 to 5, with 1 meaning strongly disagree and 5 meaning strongly agree.
>
> 1. I tend to bounce back quickly after hard times.
> 2. I have a hard time making it through stressful events.
> 3. It does not take me long to recover from a stressful event.
> 4. It is hard for me to snap back when something bad happens.
> 5. I usually come through difficult times with little trouble.
> 6. I tend to take a long time to get over setbacks in my life.
>
> Now, add up your scores on all the odd-numbered items. Then, reverse-score all your answers on the even-numbered items, meaning give yourself the opposite, or reverse, number of your answer (meaning a 5 becomes a 1, a 4 becomes a 2, a 3 stays a 3, a 2 becomes a 4, and a 1 becomes a 5). Then add up all these numbers, and add them to the total score of your odd-numbered items. Higher numbers on this combined scale indicate higher levels of resilience. Where do you stand?
>
> Smith, B. W., Dalen, J., Wiggins, K., Tooley, E., Christopher, P., & Bernard, J. (2008). The brief resilience scale: Assessing the ability to bounce back. *International Journal of Behavioral Medicine, 15*(3), 194–200. https://doi.org/10.1080/10705500802222972

The Upside of Adversity

As we already mentioned, no one wants bad things to happen to them or to people they care about. But experiencing some difficult life events can actually have important benefits (see **Figure 6.4**). People who undergo some adversity—such as coping with a serious injury or illness, struggling with financial pressure, or experiencing the death of a loved one—are better able to cope with future difficult events. Adverse events provide people with opportunities to practice coping with trauma. This helps them develop strategies for managing later problems they experience.

Researchers in one study surveyed nearly 2,000 adults to assess how their well-being changed over time. They were asked about any difficult life events they had experienced. These events included divorce, deaths of loved ones, serious illnesses, and natural disasters. They then examined these people's overall psychological well-being.

You might expect that people who had avoided major stresses would have greater life satisfaction. However, those who had experienced only one—or no—difficult experiences were no happier than those who had experienced many difficult life events.

Who was the happiest? Those who had experienced some, but not too many, stressful events (two to six) were the happiest. Researchers believe that people who experience some negative events develop skills and strategies for coping. They are therefore better able to cope when they experience other negative events.

Resilience doesn't happen—at least for most of us—by accident. Instead, we get better at recovering from difficult events with practice. Experiencing some challenges gives us a chance to develop skills for coping with other events later on. This means we can recover better from future difficult events. People who've managed to avoid major stressors haven't had a chance to develop these skills. So, when difficult things do happen, they have trouble coping.

As Roxanne Cohen Silver, a psychologist at the University of California, Irvine, notes, "Each negative event a person faces leads to an attempt to cope, which forces people to learn about their own capabilities, about their support networks—to learn who their real friends are. That kind of learning, we think, is extremely valuable for subsequent coping."

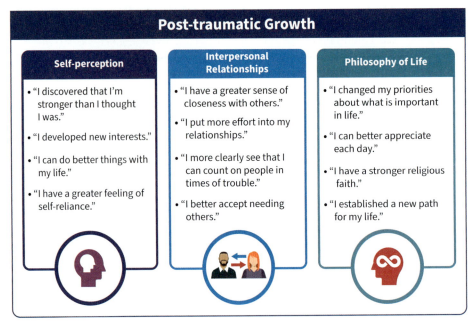

FIGURE 6.4 The benefits of post-traumatic growth.
Source: Adapted from: https://www.sketchbubble.com/en/presentation-posttraumatic-growth.html

DOWNLOAD DOCUMENTS & TEMPLATES

> **Think Deeper** | Responding to Difficult Life Events
>
> Think about a difficult life event that you experienced, such as the death of a loved one, a serious academic or professional disappointment, or a major injury, illness, or assault. Then consider the following questions:
>
> 1. What did you learn or gain from this event?
> 2. Can you find any positive outcomes that resulted from the event, such as a closer relationship with a friend, stronger spiritual beliefs, or a shift in life priorities and goals?
> 3. What did this experience teach you about yourself that could help you cope more effectively with other life challenges?
>
> Reflecting on the benefits of difficult life experiences can help you cope more effectively with these challenges and lead to benefits in psychological and even physical well-being.

Strategies for Building Resilience

VIDEO CONTENT

Everyone at some point goes through difficult experiences, including academic disappointments, family problems, or health concerns. It's therefore important to build resilience so that you can manage such experiences when they do arrive. People can develop the characteristics of resilience with practice. Here are some strategies developed by the American Psychological Association for building your resilience.

Make Connections One of the best strategies for building resilience is to develop and maintain strong relationships. People who have a strong support network can manage difficult experiences because they know they can rely on other people for help. For example, if your car breaks down and you can't get to your job, a close friend or dating partner might be able to give you a ride. This type of support makes difficult situations feel much less stressful.

Social support also helps people cope with very serious events, such as natural disasters, injury or illness, or the death of a loved one. Simply having people to talk to about difficult experiences can reduce stress.

Making connections beyond your immediate circle of close friends and family members can also help increase your resilience. People who join groups, such as clubs, religious organizations, or volunteer communities, can find that this type of belonging helps them cope when times are tough. Helping other people can also make us feel better about ourselves, which in turn increases resilience.

Reframe Crises   You can't go through life avoiding all stress and adversity. But you can shift how you think about and interpret negative events. People who are resilient can find positive ways to think about difficult experiences. They see problems as opportunities and feel optimistic that, over time, they will adapt to these changes. The following *Make It Personal* gives some examples of situations in which you can shift your mindset.

Make It Personal | **Reframing Challenges**   ⬇ DOWNLOAD DOCUMENTS & TEMPLATES

For each of these challenging situations, write some type of positive statement to reframe the challenge.

Challenging Situations	Positive Reframe
Your dating relationship ends.	
You receive a poor grade on a test.	
You don't get the summer internship you wanted.	
You had a fight with a friend.	
You have to give a presentation in class next week.	

Embrace—or at Least Accept—Change   For most people, change is really hard. Many college students experience at least some major life changes, such as the divorce of their parents, a serious illness or injury, or even the death of a loved one. Keep in mind that change is hard for everyone initially, but over time, you can adjust and feel better.

When changes happen, try to distinguish between things you can't do anything to change and things over which you have some control. For things that are within your control, take active steps to help these events go better in the future. If your past romantic relationship didn't go well and has ended as a result of constant conflict, think about ways you could develop skills to handle conflict more effectively so that a future relationship may last. On the other hand, work on accepting and coping with the events that are beyond your control. How? You'll learn some strategies in **Chapter 10: Find Your Happiness**.

Pursue Goals   Working toward goals feels good and keeps you focused on moving forward in some way. Think about goals you would like to accomplish in your academic, personal, and/or professional life. These can be personal goals, such as running a 5K race, buying a car, or learning to play the guitar. They can also be academic or professional goals, such as graduating from college, earning a scholarship, or getting a new job.

Next, develop a plan for working toward these goals. Write down a few realistic goals you'd like to work toward. Post these in a place where you see them regularly—in your bathroom, on your phone, or on your refrigerator. Working toward goals, and making even small amounts of progress, can increase your self-confidence. Remember that each step you take to complete a goal is a positive step, even if it takes time to fully achieve your goal. If you miss a goal, reevaluate your progress and adjust your goals as needed.

Working toward goals involves making a plan and getting started. Even taking a small step moves you in the right direction. Use the following *Make It Personal* to write down a few goals you have—in your personal or professional life. Then write down the first two steps you should take to achieve them.

Make It Personal | **Goal Planning** ⬇ DOWNLOAD DOCUMENTS & TEMPLATES

List a Goal	First Step	Second Step
1.		
2.		
3.		
4.		

Take Decisive Actions When you experience a setback, it's often tempting to just give up or wish the problem would go away. But this stick-your-head-in-the-sand approach doesn't let you learn and grow from this experience. Instead, make a plan to work toward a different outcome in the future. For example, if you are disappointed with the amount of playing time your coach gives you or wish you'd received a better grade on your last paper, think about what you can do differently next time. Talk to your academic advisor, professor, or older students about strategies you could use in the future that might help the outcome go better the next time.

Focus on Self-Discovery None of us wants bad things to happen. But the reality is that we often learn something about ourselves when we experience difficult circumstances. Many people who have experienced hardship and even tragedy report some positive outcomes. This could include developing stronger relationships, feeling a greater sense of strength, or having a greater appreciation for the small joys of life. When you experience a bad outcome, try making a list of any positive effects that may emerge, even if they are very small. For example, you might feel upset after a fight with a friend, but you also recognize that you now have a better understanding of their perspective on the issue, which could help you become closer in the future. This ability to find some good, no matter the situation, can help you take negative events in stride.

Nurture Self-Compassion When things work out well, it's easy to celebrate. But how do you respond when things don't go your way? People differ a lot in how they think about the causes of disappointments and failures in their own life.

- Some people blame negative events on themselves and on their flaws and inadequacies. They think long and hard about these bad outcomes and beat themselves up when things don't go their way. Not surprisingly, this type of self-criticism makes it really hard to feel better.
- Other people adopt a much more positive approach in responding to failures and disappointments. They recognize that difficulties happen to everyone and see disappointments as opportunities to learn and grow.

As you can probably imagine, people who show **self-compassion**, meaning treating themselves with kindness and understanding, in the face of negative events feel better. People who practice self-compassion forgive themselves when things don't go well. They focus on what they've learned from the experience and how they could do things differently the next time. They have lower levels of anxiety and depression and overall feel happier and more optimistic about the future. For example, first-year college students who are higher in self-compassion show greater engagement and motivation with college life. People who cut themselves some slack when disappointments happen also experience better physical health.

> **Test Yourself** | **Do You Practice Self-Compassion?**  INTERACTIVE SELF-ASSESSMENTS
>
> Answer each of these ten questions using a scale of 1 to 5, with 1 meaning less likely to feel that way and 5 meaning very likely to feel that way.
>
> 1. I'm disapproving and judgmental about my own flaws and inadequacies.
> 2. When I'm feeling down, I tend to obsess and fixate on everything that's wrong.
> 3. When I fail at something important to me, I become consumed by feelings of inadequacy.
> 4. When times are really difficult, I tend to be tough on myself.
> 5. When I see aspects of myself that I don't like, I get down on myself.
> 6. When things are going badly for me, I see the difficulties as part of life that everyone goes through.
> 7. When something upsets me, I try to keep my emotions in balance.
> 8. When something painful happens, I try to keep a balanced view of the situation.
> 9. When I fail at something important to me, I try to keep things in perspective.
> 10. I'm tolerant of my own flaws and inadequacies.
>
> The first five items measure whether you are pretty hard on yourself; the next five measure whether you practice self-compassion. For those with relatively low scores on the first items and high scores on the second set of items, congratulations! People with this score pattern are doing a good job of adopting a positive mindset in the face of disappointment. But if you have high scores on the first five items, coupled with low scores on the next set of items, you need to develop skills and strategies for treating yourself better. Don't worry—you'll learn about such approaches in the next section.
>
> Neff, K. D. (2003). The development and validation of a scale to measure self-compassion. *Self and Identity, 2*(3), 223–250. https://doi.org/10.1080/15298860309027

An easy way to feel happier and be healthier is to forgive yourself, be kind to yourself, and treat yourself with care and compassion. See the *Test Yourself* above for a simple test you can take to figure out how you think about yourself—whether you beat yourself up when things don't go well or give yourself a break.

Keep Things in Perspective

Even when facing disappointments and setbacks, try to avoid blowing the event out of proportion. A single bad grade on an exam, or even in a class, doesn't mean that you can't be a successful college student. Experiencing the breakup of a romantic relationship doesn't mean that you will spend your life alone. Remember that setbacks are temporary and that you can move past them.

Maintain a Hopeful Outlook

People who are resilient approach daily life with an optimistic outlook. They stay positive, even when difficult things happen. They expect that, over time, things will get better. For example, a college student who gets a C grade on their first paper can feel disappointed but also feel hopeful. The student can be confident that, with more effort, a better grade on the next paper is possible.

Take Care of Yourself

It's hard to practice resilience when you feel exhausted, run-down, and sick. Make sure to take care of yourself so that you have the physical and psychological strength to cope when things don't go your way. This includes getting enough sleep, eating healthy foods, exercising regularly, and avoiding substance use and abuse. Other strategies for taking care of yourself could include writing in a journal, meditating, or talking with friends.

Ivan/Adobe Stock

Figure 6.5 summarizes the ten strategies for building resilience that we have just examined.

1	**Make Connections** — Social support helps people cope with serious events. Simply having people to talk to about difficult experiences or rely on for help can reduce stress.	**6**	**Focus on Self-Discovery** — When you experience a bad outcome, think about any positive effects, even small ones, that may emerge. This can help you take negative events in stride.
2	**Reframe Crises** — People who are resilient can see problems as opportunities and feel optimistic that, over time, they will adapt to changes.	**7**	**Nurture Self-Compassion** — People who treat themselves with kindness and understanding feel better when they experience failures and disappointments.
3	**Embrace Change** — Keep in mind that change is hard for everyone initially, but over time, you can adjust and feel better.	**8**	**Keep Things in Perspective** — Even when facing disappointments and setbacks, try to avoid blowing the event out of proportion. Setbacks are temporary and you can move past them.
4	**Pursue Goals** — Working toward goals feels good and keeps you focused on moving forward in some way. Even taking a small step moves you in the right direction.	**9**	**Maintain a Hopeful Outlook** — Resilient people have an optimistic outlook, staying positive even when difficult things happen and expecting that, over time, things will get better.
5	**Take Decisive Actions** — When you experience a setback, think about what you can do differently next time. Make a plan to work toward a different outcome in the future.	**10**	**Take Care of Yourself** — It is hard to be resilient when you feel exhausted, run-down, and sick. Take care of yourself so that you have the strength to cope when things don't go your way.

FIGURE 6.5 Strategies for building resilience.

Review, Discuss, and Apply

Discussion Questions

1. Are some types of difficult events more likely to foster resilience than others? Are some less likely to foster resilience?
2. Why do people vary in their tendency to show self-compassion? What explains such differences?
3. Which strategy for increasing resilience do you find most helpful, and why?

Think Ahead | Career and Lifelong Applications

People who are high in EI experience many benefits in their careers, regardless of the area in which they work. They have greater job satisfaction and tend to advance higher in their careers and earn higher salaries. People who are high in EI also experience benefits in their personal lives. Why? The ability to understand and manage emotions helps people build good relationships with friends and family members as well as colleagues. How does EI pay off? Here are some of the advantages:

Strong social skills—We all interact with other people all the time. This can include coworkers, bosses or supervisors, neighbors, and friends. People who are high in EI are more successful working with people because they have good social skills. They respect different points of view and make sure everyone feels heard and understood.

Ability to manage stress—People who are high in EI can focus on the task at hand, even when facing pressure, deadlines, and problems. This helps them stay calm and make clear and careful decisions instead of acting impulsively or feeling overwhelmed.

Empathize with others—Most people regularly interact with people from different backgrounds and experiences. People who are high in EI take time to get to know people around them. They are also better able to see other people's perspectives and feel empathy. This lets them get along with other people in different settings.

Communicate effectively—People who are high in EI are able to understand and influence other people's emotions. This ability helps them share disappointing news in a more sensitive manner. They can also understand and manage their own emotions, which helps them respond effectively, even when others show anger and frustration.

As you can probably imagine, these skills help people succeed in all different types of environments. People who are high in EI are better at working with people—and getting other people to want to work with them—and therefore tend to get more done. This helps explain why people who are high in EI also tend to have higher salaries. This also helps explain why people high in EI have better relationships with friends, family members, and romantic partners.

144 CHAPTER 6 The Power of Emotional Intelligence

What Would You Do?

In this chapter, Olivia and William need your advice.

OLIVIA
Olivia is planning to attend the funeral for a friend's father and isn't sure what to say to her friend and his family when she gets to the funeral home.

Watch Olivia's video: **"Sorry for Your Loss"**

WILLIAM
William is working a temp job to make some money for his backpacking trip, and it's making him realize he wants to brush up on his people skills.

Watch William's video: **People Conscious**

What would you tell Olivia? What would you tell William?

Take Some Action | Here and Now

We all have strengths and weaknesses when it comes to emotional intelligence. Being aware of those strengths and weaknesses is key to success in college, in the workplace, and in life.

Review your outcomes on the *Test Yourself* assessments throughout this chapter and your responses to the Think Deeper questions. Reflect on your results and responses, and then answer these questions:

1. What are your strengths with respect to emotional intelligence, grit, and resilience? How will you put those strengths to work for you toward succeeding in college? How will sharpening those strengths in college help you be successful in the workplace?

2. How do you want to improve your strengths when it comes to emotional intelligence? How do you want to improve your strengths when it comes to demonstrating grit and resilience?

3. Review the suggested action steps in that area and choose two or three of those to commit to here and now, and for each, say how taking that action step will help you succeed in college and beyond. Share and discuss your responses to these questions with a friend, classmate, or family member.

Chapter Summary

INTERACTIVE SELF-SCORING QUIZZES
Chapter 6 Practice Quiz

Module 6.1 Understanding Emotional Intelligence
- Emotional intelligence refers to the ability to identify and manage emotions. People who are emotionally intelligent are aware of their emotions, are able to regulate or manage the emotions they feel, and can help other people with regulating their own emotions. They also have other distinct strengths and abilities, including greater self-awareness, the ability to self-regulate, high internal motivation, strong social skills, and empathy.
- People who have high EI tend to be more successful in school, work, and interpersonal relationships. They also experience greater mental and emotional health. Developing skills in EI can therefore help people succeed in all aspects of life.
- No matter our natural tendency, we can all take steps to increase our own emotional intelligence. Strategies for increasing emotional intelligence include becoming more self-aware, discovering your passions, focusing on internal motivation, understanding your strengths and weaknesses, developing greater empathy, learning to manage your emotions, practicing social responsibility, and pursuing happiness.

Module 6.2 Understanding Grit
- Grit refers to a tendency to work diligently on something you feel passionately about and to stick with it, even when facing difficulty or failure. Grit has two distinct components. People high in grit feel passion, meaning a focus on and commitment to pursuing a goal. They also show perseverance, meaning an ability to continue working toward their goals even in the face of failure or adversity.
- Grit predicts success in a variety of different life domains. Students who are high in grit are more likely to graduate from college. People who are high in grit are more likely to stick with their jobs, even when they face challenges at work.
- We can all take steps to increase grit. Strategies for increasing grit include finding purpose in our lives, developing our particular talents, adopting a growth mindset, learning from those around us, and working on our weaknesses.

Module 6.3 Understanding Resilience
- People who are high in resilience can bounce back from significant life stressors, including serious health problems, financial

- stress, physical trauma, and relationship problems. They also have particular characteristics, such as an ability to make and carry out plans. They feel confident in themselves and their strengths and abilities to communicate with others and solve problems and manage strong feelings and impulses.
- Experiencing adverse events can provide people with opportunities to develop strategies for managing problems. This helps people learn and practice skills in resilience. They are then better able to manage other adverse events they face in the future.
- People can develop the characteristics of resilience with practice. Strategies for building your resilience include making connections, reframing crises as opportunities, embracing—or at least accepting—change, setting and working toward valued goals, taking some action when experiencing a setback, focusing on learning more about yourself, nurturing self-compassion when things don't go your way, keeping things in perspective when facing disappointments and setbacks, maintaining a hopeful and positive outlook, and taking care of yourself to maintain physical and psychological strength.

Key Terms

Emotional intelligence The ability to identify and manage emotions, not only your own emotions but also those of other people around you.

Empathy The ability to understand and share the feelings of another person.

Grit A tendency to work diligently on something you feel passionately about, and to stick with it, even when facing difficulty or failure.

Resilience An ability to recover from traumatic and stressful events.

Self-awareness An ability to understand your feelings and your own strengths and weaknesses.

Self-compassion An ability to treat yourself with kindness and understanding.

Self-regulation An ability to manage emotions, even when in stressful situations.

Social skills The skills that people use to interact and communicate effectively with others.

Resources

Abramson, A. (2021). Cultivating empathy. *Monitor on Psychology, 52*(8), 44–52. https://www.apa.org/monitor/2021/11/feature-cultivating-empathy

American Psychological Association. (2020, February 1). Building your resilience. https://www.apa.org/topics/resilience/building-your-resilience

Bariso, J. (2020, November 29). *Should I abbreviate emotional intelligence as EI or Eq? there's only 1 right answer.* Inc.com. Retrieved November 2, 2021, from https://www.inc.com/justin-bariso/should-i-abbreviate-emotional-intelligence-as-ei-or-eq-theres-only-1-right-answer.html

Carey, B. (2011, January 3). On-road to recovery, past adversity provides a map. *The New York Times.* Retrieved October 24, 2021 from https://www.nytimes.com/2011/01/04/health/04mind.html

Duckworth, A. (2016). *Grit: The power of passion and perseverance.* Scribner/Simon & Schuster.

Goleman, D. (2007). *Emotional intelligence* (10th ed.). Bantam Books.

Neff, K. (2011). *Self-compassion: Stop beating yourself up and leave insecurity behind.* William Morrow.

Sanderson, C. A. (2019). *The positive shift: Mastering mindset to improve happiness, health, and longevity.* BenBella Books.

References

Brackett, M. A., Rivers, S. E., & Salovey, P. (2011). Emotional intelligence: Implications for personal, social, academic, and workplace success. *Social and Personality Psychology Compass, 5*(1), 88–103. https://doi.org/10.1111/j.1751-9004.2010.00334.x

Davis, M. H. (1983). Measuring individual differences in empathy: Evidence for a multidimensional approach. *Journal of Personality and Social Psychology, 44*(1), 113–126. https://doi.org/10.1037/0022-3514.44.1.113

Duckworth, A. L., Peterson, C., Matthews, M. D., & Kelly, D. R. (2007). Grit: Perseverance and passion for long-term goals. *Journal of Personality and Social Psychology, 92*(6), 1087–1101. https://doi.org/10.1037/0022-3514.92.6.1087

Duckworth, A. L., & Quinn, P. D. (2009). Development and validation of the Short Grit Scale (GRIT–S). *Journal of Personality Assessment, 91*(2), 166–174. https://doi.org/10.1080/00223890802634290

Duckworth, A. L., Quirk, A., Gallop, R., Hoyle, R. H., Kelly, D. R., & Matthews, M. D. (2019). Cognitive and noncognitive predictors of success. *Proceedings of the National Academy of Sciences of the United States of America, 116*(47), 23499–23504. https://doi.org/10.1073/pnas.1910510116

Gunnell, K. E., Mosewich, A. D., McEwen, C. E., Eklund, R. C., & Crocker, P. R. E. (2017). Don't be so hard on yourself! Changes in self-compassion during the first year of university are associated with changes in well-being. *Personality and*

Individual Differences, *107*, 43–48. https://doi.org/10.1016/j.paid.2016.11.032

MacCann, C., Jiang, Y., Brown, L. E. R., Double, K. S., Bucich, M., & Minbashian, A. (2020). Emotional intelligence predicts academic performance: A meta-analysis. *Psychological Bulletin*, *146*(2), 150–186. https://doi.org/10.1037/bul0000219

Neff, K. D. (2003). The development and validation of a scale to measure self-compassion. *Self and Identity*, *2*(3), 223–250. https://doi.org/10.1080/15298860309027

Neff, K. D., Hsieh, Y.-P., & Dejitterat, K. (2005). Self-compassion, achievement goals, and coping with academic failure. *Self and Identity*, *4*(3), 263–287. https://doi.org/10.1080/13576500444000317

Schutte, N. S., Malouff, J. M., Hall, L. E., Haggerty, D. J., Cooper, J. T., Golden, C. J., & Dornheim, L. (1998). Development and validation of a measure of emotional intelligence. *Personality and Individual Differences*, *25*(2), 167–177. https://doi.org/10.1016/S0191-8869(98)00001-4

Seery, M. D., Holman, E. A., & Silver, R. C. (2010). Whatever does not kill us: Cumulative lifetime adversity, vulnerability, and resilience. *Journal of Personality and Social Psychology*, *99*(6), 1025–1041. https://doi.org/10.1037/a0021344

Smith, B. W., Dalen, J., Wiggins, K., Tooley, E., Christopher, P., & Bernard, J. (2008). The brief resilience scale: Assessing the ability to bounce back. *International Journal of Behavioral Medicine*, *15*(3), 194–200. https://doi.org/10.1080/10705500802222972

Tugade, M. M., & Fredrickson, B. L. (2004). Resilient individuals use positive emotions to bounce back from negative emotional experiences. *Journal of Personality and Social Psychology*, *86*(2), 320–333. https://doi.org/10.1037/0022-3514.86.2.320

CHAPTER 7

Engage with Digital Technology

Author's Introduction

"Before you become too entranced with gorgeous gadgets and mesmerizing video displays, let me remind you that information is not knowledge, knowledge is not wisdom, and wisdom is not foresight. Each grows out of the other, and we need them all."

—Arthur C. Clarke, British science fiction writer (1917–2008)

CHAPTER OUTLINE	LEARNING OBJECTIVES
Envision, Pursue, and Persist: Paul Otlet	
Module 7.1 Living in a Digital World Technology: Love It or Leave It? *Test Yourself: Are You a Technophobe?* *Test Yourself: Are You a Technophile?* Bridging the Digital Divide *Think Deeper: Engaging with Technology*	**LO 7.1** To examine the role of digital technology in our daily lives
Module 7.2 Technology in Higher Education Campus- and Course-Based Resources *Make It Personal: Taking Full Advantage* *Test Yourself: Do You Have the Best Tools for the Job?* Evaluating Digital Content in an Information-Rich Environment *Test Yourself: Are You a Content Curation Guru?* *Make It Personal: A Plan of Attack*	**LO 7.2** To identify the variety of digital resources available to students on your campus and understand how to evaluate and use digital content
Module 7.3 Leaving a Credible Digital Footprint Long-Term Impact Safety and Security Your Image on Social Media *Test Yourself: What About Your Digital Footprint?* *Think Deeper: Social Media Audit*	**LO 7.3** To develop an awareness of the importance of a credible digital footprint
Think Ahead: Career and Lifelong Applications Take Some Action: Here and Now	
Chapter Summary Key Terms Resources References	

Envision, Pursue, and Persist | Paul Otlet

Mundaneum/Wikimedia Commons

Paul Otlet, born in 1868, was a librarian in Brussels, Belgium. He had a big dream. In 1898, he announced the idea of bringing together all the information in the world in every language. Here is how he described his dream:

Everything in the universe, and everything of man, would be registered at a distance as it was produced. In this way, a moving image of the world would be established, a true mirror of his memory. From a distance, everyone will be able to read text, enlarged and limited to a desired subject, projected on an individual screen. In this way, everyone from his armchair will be able to contemplate creation, in whole or in certain parts (https://www.brainpickings.org/2014/06/09/paul-otlet-alex-wright/).

In the book *Cataloguing the World: Paul Otlet and the Birth of the Information Age,* Alex Wright reported that Otlet's dream went even further to envisioning the ability to upload files to central servers and communicate through wireless networks. This pronouncement was made more than fifty years before the internet's creation.

Otlet and a colleague formed the Institut International de Bibliographie. Along with their staff, they began to collect information on every conceivable topic and to record that data on small index cards. These cards were then stored in file cabinets according to subject areas. At its peak, this collection included over fifteen million individual index cards. Individuals worldwide would write letters to Otlet requesting information on a specific topic. The library staff would research the answer by sifting through their collection of subject matter cards, copying that information, and returning it by mail to the person asking the question. It is reported that by 1912, the library responded to more than 1,500 information requests per year.

Fast-forward to the twenty-first century, where we have more information available to us than at any time in the history of the world:

- Over 1.88 billion websites housing more than 130 trillion web pages are available.
- An estimated 129 million different books have been published in the world.
- Each year, at least 1.7 million books are self-published.
- There are over 2.9 billion monthly active Facebook users.
- The percentage of Facebook users who access the app on both phones and computers is 16.7.
- On average, X users send about 6,000 x's every second, or about 500 million x's per day.
- Over 2 billion people use YouTube, with over 30 million visitors every day.
- Currently, over 300 hours of video are uploaded to YouTube every minute.
- Every day, 4.4 million blog posts are written.
- An estimated 333.2 billion emails are sent every day (i.e., 3.5 million emails per second).
- Instagram is the seventh most visited website on the internet and the ninth most Google-searched term.
- TikTok has over 500 million monthly active users and is available in over 200 countries.
- LinkedIn has over 850 million users.

This trend will only continue to grow at exponential rates. In your personal life, your college career, and current or future employment, it will be critical that you develop a variety of digital skills.

Module 7.1 | Living in a Digital World

LO 7.1.1 To reflect on the level at which digital technology impacts our daily lives
LO 7.1.2 To examine personal biases and habits related to the use of technology

You undoubtedly use digital technology in various ways in your everyday life. They may include the following:

- Communicating with friends and family through email, texts, Facebook, and Instagram
- Creating documents
- Streaming video content on YouTube, Netflix, or Hulu
- Listening to music on iTunes or Spotify
- Tracking your appointments on a digital calendar
- Googling for answers to questions and needed information
- Finding your way to desired locations using a GPS app on a phone
- Buying needed products on Amazon or similar digital marketplaces

These common practices have become second nature, and it is sometimes difficult to think about how we would survive without them. We become keenly aware of this reality when the electricity goes off in our homes for a brief time, or our internet service has a period of interruption. Time stands still as we lose access to these vital tools and pastimes.

As a college student as you complete assigned tasks in your courses (and in life in your chosen career), you will make constant use of several digital tools and resources:

- Using an e-textbook
- Using online databases and other resources provided through your campus library
- Writing a paper and making corrections using writing tools like Grammarly
- Keeping your résumé up to date on LinkedIn
- Creating PowerPoint presentations
- Participating in courses that include an online component
- Keeping up to date with scheduled class due dates
- Remaining aware of campus activities
- Making digital appointments to meet with classmates on group projects
- Texting and emailing with classmates (e.g., "Hey, when is that paper due?")

This is an excellent time to begin thinking about what you know about technology and what you need to learn.

It is relevant to note how employers identify digital skills as the most important in hiring decisions. A recent survey by LinkedIn identified several vital skills that fall into this category, including cloud computing, artificial intelligence, analytical reasoning, user experience design, and mobile application development. These skill sets may not align with your chosen academic and career path. Still, it is safe to say that digital technology is here to stay and will become increasingly important across virtually every job classification.

Technology: Love It or Leave It?

VIDEO CONTENT

As you read about the role of technology in our culture, you might greet that information with either a big thumbs-up, a shrug, or a thumbs-down. Some people love technology dearly, while others see it as a total pain and wish to ignore or avoid it. Still others view it as a necessary evil and simply shrug their shoulders and tolerate it. This reality has prompted researchers to develop various classifications that define groups of people and their attitudes toward technology. Marc

Prensky developed one of the first classification systems in 2001 when he proposed that every citizen could be labeled a **digital native** or a **digital immigrant**. Digital natives are generally described as people who were born after 1982 and who have lived their entire lives in a digital world. They have never known a world without the internet and a collection of digital devices. This reality is most easily observed watching a two-year-old child while they play with their parent's tablet. They swipe their fingers across the screen just like they have seen their parents do on numerous occasions. They give a distinct impression that they might be searching for a specific item like a picture or video (which could be the case).

The second grouping proposed by Prensky is the digital immigrant. He suggested that this group, presumably born before 1982, has an ongoing learning curve to acquire technology skills. There is also a hint that members of this group may not be entirely as digitally competent as their digital native counterparts. Maybe, maybe not. It is, however, possible that the divide between those who like technology and those who do not has more digital immigrants on the "do not" side of the divide.

As you read these descriptions and place yourself into one of these two groups, consider the level at which these generalizations about natives or immigrants are accurate to your preferences and digital skills. You could, for example, be a digital immigrant and love technology. At the same time, you could be a digital native with no interest in using technology regularly. In some ways, this classification system has outlived its usefulness as technology has become more of a necessity than an optional experience.

Perhaps a more personal way of thinking about your feelings about using technology is the technophobe/technophile continuum. A **technophobe** is a person who fears, dislikes, or avoids using technology. A **technophile**, however, is at the other end of the continuum and loves technology and cannot get enough of it. Let's consider some of the typical characteristics of individuals at either end of this continuum.

The following *Test Yourself* activities are intended to give you a sense of your approach to engaging with technology. Take a minute to complete these surveys and determine your tendencies to be a technophobe or technophile. For example, if you recorded "yes" in response to the statement "At the end of the day, you are comfortable in a life without the interference

Test Yourself | Are You a Technophobe?

INTERACTIVE SELF-ASSESSMENTS

Consider the following descriptors of people who might be classified as technophobes. How many of these sound like you and your approach to technology? For each statement that follows, respond yes if the information is true for you and no if the statement is not true for you.

	Texting is a big challenge.
	You have not bought anything online in a long time.
	You are reluctant to update the software on your computer, tablet, or smartphone. Perhaps a related sign is the fact that you do not have or need to have multiple devices.
	You have trouble reprogramming your microwave and digital clocks when there is a time change.
	You are reluctant to buy an e-book because you like to turn pages.
	When people use digital terms like RAM, gigabyte, and WAN, you think to yourself "WTF!" (i.e., wanting technology finished!).
	Part of you envies others who can use technology for a variety of purposes.
	You are reluctant to get a subscription to Netflix, Hulu, or Amazon Prime.
	At the end of the day, you are comfortable in a life without the interference of technology.

The higher number of "yes" responses you gave, the more likely it is that you are a technophobe.
If "no" was your most frequent response, you are not a technophobe!

Module 7.1 Living in a Digital World 151

> **Test Yourself** | Are You a Technophile?
>
> You may consider yourself to be a technophile. For each statement that follows, respond yes if the information is true for you and no if the statement is not true for you.
>
> | | |
> |---|---|
> | | You find yourself experiencing Gear Acquisition Syndrome (GAS: This is a nagging feeling that you absolutely must have the latest and greatest technology). |
> | | If a friend or family member needs help with technology, you are the go-to person. At the same time, you become upset when they can't learn a new skill as quickly as you do. |
> | | You are an avid user of social media. Most of your connections with friends and family are done on Facebook, Instagram, and TikTok. |
> | | You frequently hear people asking, "Is that the latest version of _____?" when you are engaged with technology daily. This makes you happy because it is, in fact, the latest version. You downloaded it on the day it became available. |
> | | You've lost track of how many online accounts you have and cannot remember all your usernames and passwords. |
> | | You are upset when someone has a newer version of a device or software. |
> | | You experience anxiety over the fear of missing out. |
> | | At the end of the day, you can't imagine a day without technology. |
>
> The higher your positive score, the more likely it is that you are a technophile.
> If your score is negative, you are not a technophile!
> **Source:** Adapted from "8 Signs You're a Technophile" https://www.movaglobes.com/blog/8-signs-youre-a-technophile/.

of technology," ask yourself how that might impact your life moving forward. You may be comfortable not using technology, but at what point in your life and career might that mindset hold you back from more efficiency in your personal life and advancement in your career? Consider each of the statements where you recorded a "yes" in *Test Yourself: Are You a Technophobe* and begin to make plans to learn the skills associated with that statement.

So, what do you think? Are you somewhat reluctant to engage with technology? Although it is wise to maintain a balanced approach to the use of technology, skills in this area will likely continue to be increasingly important well into the future. You may decide that technology will not be part of your daily activities. That is your prerogative. At the same time, it is a virtual certainty that technology will be an essential part of your chosen career. In any case, you must remain aware of your chosen career field's technological demands and expectations.

Considering these statements, how much influence does technology have in your life?

Is it possible to get too much of a good thing like technology? Probably, yes! The use of technology can sometimes creep up and overwhelm us. Look around you and observe people constantly staring at their phones to stay in touch with all that is happening in the world. Keeping up to date is good, but not to the detriment of living and being present in the real world. Balance is the key.

Do you see yourself in either of these categories? This conversation about technophobes and technophiles should be viewed as the extreme ends of the continuum of technology use. Most of us fall somewhere between these two extremes. For all of us, however, it is critically important to learn the skills necessary to curate effectively and examine all the information that comes our way through digital channels.

There is often a tendency to devalue and criticize technophobes while celebrating the digital prowess of technophiles. It may be reasonable to argue that these two diverse groups could learn something from one another. Technophobes could, perhaps, consider how expanded use of the technology might benefit them. They might gradually become involved, deciding to include the internet for specific tasks (e.g., making airline reservations, finding the schedules for their favorite athletic teams, and looking up definitions or weather forecasts). Technophiles, on the other hand, may want to embrace some of the hesitancies that technophiles have about using technology, such as using more caution in searching and not accepting everything posted on the internet as accurate.

XaMaps/Adobe Stock

> **Think Deeper | Engaging with Technology**  DOWNLOAD DOCUMENTS & TEMPLATES
>
> As you think about your feelings about technology, and your skills in using those tools, consider these four questions:
>
> 1. How do you feel about your current skill level in using digital technology that might be relevant to the current demands of your life?
> 2. Are there specific digital tools or skills that you would like to acquire?
> 3. What are the resources available to you as a way of acquiring new digital skills?
> 4. What strategies could you put in place to maintain balance in your use of digital technology?

Bridging the Digital Divide

 VIDEO CONTENT

It is also worth noting that some individuals do not have total control over the level at which they can engage with digital technology. The term **digital divide** describes the level at which certain groups of individuals, along socioeconomic, geographic, educational, racial, and gender lines, are denied access or limited in their abilities to engage with digital technology. Recent data indicate that roughly 58.4 percent of the world's population has access to the internet, including the regions shown in **Table 7.1**. These statistics, although perhaps somewhat surprising, reflect a dramatic period of growth between the years 2000–2019.

TABLE 7.1. Internet Access Around the World

Region	Internet Access	20-Year Growth
Africa	39.5%	11,454%
Asia	53.6%	1,891%
Europe	87.7%	592%
Latin America/Caribbean	68.9%	2,411%
Middle East	67.9%	5,243%
North America	89.4%	203%
Oceania/Australia	68.4%	276%

The internet can provide a means to facilitate communication and the sharing of ideas among all global citizens. Currently, initiatives are under way to classify internet access as a fundamental human right connected with the freedoms of speech, economic development, and assembly. These initiatives, however, will be impacted by political and socioeconomic realities in individual countries and regions around the world.

One exciting example is the website Alison.com. Founded in 2007, this website was created to offer large volumes of information on various vital topics for free to the world at large. This site boasts 30 million learners, over 6 million graduates, over 4,000 courses, and participants from 195 countries. Topics include the following:

- Diplomas in public relations, health studies, and information technology management, and Amazon Web Services
- Transformational leadership
- Foods and beverages, arts and crafts, and skilled trades
- Language courses in English, Spanish, German, Irish, French, Chinese, Arabic, Swedish, and Japanese
- Supply chain, risk management, and quality control

It has been noted that Alison courses have become generally recognized by many employers, particularly in occupations and disciplines where no external postgraduate certification by professional bodies is available. Since its founding, nearly half of the participants in Alison courses have come from developing countries. Moving forward, digital technology may offer a pathway to learning for individuals who cannot afford to attend a more formalized college or university training program.

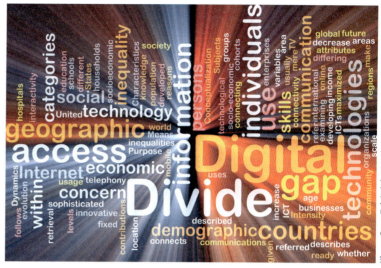

Another related example, reported by Sugata Mitra, is seen in India, where *Hole in the Wall* kiosks provide opportunities for impoverished children to play with computers. Here is Mitra's 2012 account of this remarkable experience:

> What happened next astonished us. Children came running out of the nearest slum and glued themselves to the computer. They couldn't get enough. They began to click and explore. They began to learn how to use this strange thing. A few hours later...the children were actually surfing the Web.
>
> We left the PC where it was, available to everyone on the street, and within six months the children of the neighborhood had learned all the mouse operations, could open and close programs, and were going online to download games, music, and videos. We asked them how they had learned all of these sophisticated maneuvers, and each time they told us they had taught themselves.

The designers of the initiative have heralded the *Hole in the Wall* project as a dramatic breakthrough demonstrating how children can teach themselves basic computer skills and then take that a step further by teaching one another.

Related to access to digital technology is the level at which individuals have the skills necessary to engage with technology. Researcher Eszter Hargittai has identified this gap as a **second-level digital divide**. So, even though individuals may have access to digital technology, they do not have the skills needed to take advantage of that opportunity. This reality is also commonly driven by socioeconomic status, geography, educational opportunities, race, and gender. So, for example, it might be present in cultures where women or members of certain political or religious groups have fewer privileges and opportunities.

Review, Discuss, and Apply

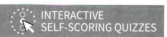

Discussion Questions

1. How would you describe your relationship with technology?
2. What are your preferred activities using digital technology?
3. What are your greatest challenges in using technology?

Module 7.2 | Technology in Higher Education

LO 7.2.1 To identify the variety of digital resources available to students on your campus

LO 7.2.2 To articulate plans for continued growth using digital tools

Technology is playing an increasingly important role in higher education. As a student, knowing what technology is available to you and how to access and use these resources can contribute significantly to your opportunities for success. Preparing for this reality requires that you take stock of your digital tools and skills while also becoming fully aware of the digital opportunities your school provides to help you learn and succeed. Let's begin this conversation by examining the digital resources that will be part of your college experience and then discuss how you might take full advantage of these learning tools.

Campus-and Course-Based Resources

Colleges and universities have realized the power of digital resources to help students learn more effectively inside and outside the classroom. As a student, it is in your best interests to take full advantage of these resources. Knowing how and where to find information and how to use it effectively will help you as a student and in your career.

Password-Protected Web Portals All colleges and universities have password-protected portals designed to provide 24/7 as-needed information to their students. After logging in with your username and password, you are given access to a variety of resources, including the following:

- Course offerings and schedules
- University departments and policies (e.g., financial aid)
- Student handbook containing institutional policies
- Online registration tools
- Financial aid information
- Application for graduation
- Campus employment opportunities
- Grade reports

Make It Personal | Taking Full Advantage — DOWNLOAD DOCUMENTS & TEMPLATES

Take a few minutes to find these resources on your campus website:

Campus Internet Resources	Found It!
The beginning and end dates of the current semester	☐
Campus holidays during the current semester	☐
Syllabi for all your current courses	☐
A journal article on a topic of interest using your library databases	☐
The operating hours of your campus dining facilities	☐
The listing of courses that are required for a degree in your area of study	☐
The web page of your favorite professor	☐
Where to get help on LMS activities that seem challenging	☐
Any software tools that may be available to students for a free download	☐
Upcoming dates for registering for the next semester	☐

These and other questions can often be answered quickly and efficiently by using the digital resources offered on your campus. Stay aware and take full advantage of these resources. For questions to which you were unable to respond "Found It!", seek out people who can help you move forward.

- Campus calendars, activities, and deadlines
- Parking, food service, health services, and recreational opportunities
- Academic advising

As a student, it will benefit you to become thoroughly acquainted with the tools and resources on your school's web portal. Being able to navigate this portal will save you time and prevent unneeded worries.

Learning Management System Virtually every college or university uses a **learning management system (LMS)** as a resource for students and faculty. Popular LMSs include Blackboard, Canvas, Edmodo, Moodle, and Schoology. This software is often password protected and can be a vital tool for learning in your courses. Once inside, you will have access to various resources using your assigned username and password. For example, in the courses that you are taking, a variety of resources and activities may be posted to enhance your learning, including the following:

- Course syllabus
- College/university policies
- Course policies on attendance and late assignments
- Gradebook
- Announcements
- Links to videos, journal articles, and other web-based resources
- Supplementary materials to support your learning
- Links to tutorial resources
- Discussion forums where you interact with classmates around course content and build relationships
- Online quizzes
- A place to submit written assignments

Generally, faculty are free to choose the level at which they take advantage of the tools and resources in your school's LMS. As you begin every course, checking out the LMS to see what course-related resources are available (or required) for your use is critically important.

Campus Library Historically, college libraries were locations students had to physically visit to take advantage of books, journals, videos, and other learning resources. Those times have changed. Although campus libraries still maintain a variety of hard-copy resources that will aid your learning (e.g., books, professional journals, videos), they have also moved into the digital age by providing a wealth of digital resources that can be accessed remotely. These resources, often accessed using your username and password, may include the following:

- E-books
- **Academic databases** that connect with hundreds of electronic journals across a variety of academic disciplines
- The ability to request copies of journal articles, books, and other resources that may not be held at your campus library
- Chat tools that provide students with the opportunity to engage remotely with librarians in real time
- Subscription services that provide students with access to video- and audio-based learning tools

It is strongly suggested that you begin your college career by acquainting yourself with what your library offers on the courses you will be taking. This can be accomplished very easily by visiting the library website. If you have questions, librarians are often available in person and online to assist you.

Test Yourself | Do You Have the Best Tools for the Job?

INTERACTIVE SELF-ASSESSMENTS

Developing your digital skills is a valuable pursuit for both your college success and your transition to employment. Consider these questions as a starting point for assessing the skills you have and those you need to develop:

Technical Skills	Of Course, I Can!	Not Yet
1. Can you start and quit a program stored on the drive?	☐	☐
2. Can you save and retrieve files to and from a flash drive or hard drive?	☐	☐
3. Can you cut/copy text from one source and paste it to another?	☐	☐
4. Can you open, close, and minimize menus and windows?	☐	☐
5. Can you move windows around on your desktop?	☐	☐
6. Can you resize windows on your desktop?	☐	☐
7. Can you create folders?	☐	☐
8. Can you navigate a directory structure to find files?	☐	☐
9. Can you rename files?	☐	☐
10. Can you delete files?	☐	☐
11. Do you have keyboard skills to produce at least 30–40 words per minute?	☐	☐
12. Can you create a Word document using the various editing and formatting features?	☐	☐
13. Can you print a word-processing document?	☐	☐
14. Can you convert a Word document to a pdf?	☐	☐
15. Can you use spell and grammar checking to revise your work?	☐	☐
16. Do you know how to retrieve and delete email messages?	☐	☐
17. Can you cut, paste, insert, and resize images inside a Word document?	☐	☐
18. Can you create and format a spreadsheet?	☐	☐
19. Can you create a table and paste it into a Word document?	☐	☐
20. Can you create and format a PowerPoint presentation?	☐	☐
21. Can you insert audio and video components into a PowerPoint presentation?	☐	☐
22. Can you create, send, forward, reply to, and save email messages?	☐	☐
23. Can you distinguish between an email address and a web address?	☐	☐
24. Can you send group emails?	☐	☐
25. Do you know how to post messages to discussion lists?	☐	☐
26. Can you locate and access needed information using a search engine?	☐	☐
27. Do you know how to check the credibility of internet sources?	☐	☐
28. Can you "talk" or "chat" for real-time communication?	☐	☐
29. Are you familiar with and do you abide by standard acceptable etiquette on the internet?	☐	☐
30. Can you create internet bookmarks?	☐	☐
31. Can you create accounts on social media platforms?	☐	☐
32. Can you locate and use appropriate computer resources and technologies (e.g., online databases, periodical indexes, full-text resources, multimedia resources) available at your campus library?	☐	☐

Remember, these are the basics. It is important to assume a mindset that says, "I will be a lifelong digital learner".

After answering the questions about your digital skills in the preceding *Test Yourself*, you can use the following guide to evaluate your results:

28–22: Excellent—More than likely, you have the necessary digital skills.

21–17: Fair—Your digital skills may be marginal, and your lack of skill in technical areas of using a computer to communicate and navigate the internet may jeopardize your ability to be successful as a learner.

16 or less: Needs improvement—It is recommended that you access coursework, workshops, or tutorials that will help you improve your basic computer and internet skills.

Add a point for every time you answer "Of course, I can!" "Not yet" answers do not receive points.

Course-Based Resources In addition to attending classes and reading your textbook, you may need to consult other resources as part of your course assignments. It is becoming increasingly common for faculty to move beyond the basics of lectures and textbooks and include website resources, videos, and other online learning tools to enhance opportunities for your success. You will be able to identify these resources by consulting your course syllabus. It is important to remember that as a student, you will be held responsible for anything your instructor includes in the course syllabus.

Evaluating Digital Content in an Information-Rich Environment

There is a vast and ever-growing volume of information available on the internet. When we search on the internet, for example, we are greeted with millions of possible responses to our query in less than a second. The challenge becomes sorting through that content to determine what is truthful, accurate, and valuable. As a college student and throughout your life as an internet user and information consumer, developing skills related to **digital content curation** *is essential*. Your author, Brad Garner (2019) defined the elements of digital content curation to include the following components:

- **Specify**—To articulate what is to be accomplished by searching, examining, and using internet content
- **Survey**—To choose the tools to accomplish the identified outcomes
- **Search**—To query the internet, using chosen search tools, to gather information related to research questions and hypotheses
- **Select**—To choose the most relevant and most accurate content derived from the search process
- **Synthesize**—To precisely consider how all pieces fit together to communicate a logical, coherent, and accurate result
- **Share**—To determine the most effective and appropriate format for distribution to external audiences and create a final product in that venue
- **Steward**—To make consistent decisions about how and where to store digital resources

For example, imagine that your course title is "A Survey of American History: 1865–1965." Your instructor has assigned you the task of creating a twenty-page research paper. Your chosen topic is "A History of Civil Rights: 1865–1965." Let's walk through each element of the digital content curation model and see how each applies to this assignment and how you might complete it efficiently, effectively, and on time.

Specify Given this assignment, it will first be essential to identify your paper's topics and generate specific research questions and hypotheses that you will work to answer. This crucial first step will focus on completing your assigned research paper. At the **specify** level, the goal is for users to specify what they hope to accomplish by searching, examining, and using internet content. Taking time to engage in this process will sharpen and focus all that follows when curating digital content.

As you engage with higher education, you will find that faculty have high expectations for scholarly products like research papers and essays on topics related

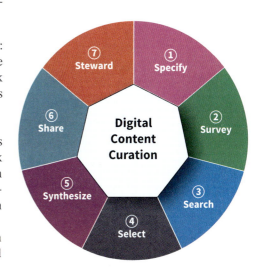

to your academic discipline. The other thing to note is that faculty habitually keep up with the latest research in the field. Additionally, faculty will not be satisfied with Google searches that turn up web pages as your sources for the papers that you write. They will want you to dig deeper into actual research and scholarly writings. For this reason, it is essential for you to have a clear sense of what you hope to accomplish before launching into searches of the internet and academic databases.

Consider these tips:

- Begin with the end in mind. Ask yourself, "What do I intend to communicate?"
- Develop a hypothesis for research-based assignments.
- Create research questions that will aid in the process of seeking internet-based information.
- These questions serve as a guide for all the activities that follow.
- At the end of this process, you should be able to confidently answer these questions.

Survey   Now that you have created research questions to guide and focus your activities, it's time to **survey**, or think about identifying the search tools that will best contribute to gathering information. For most of us, the go-to tools might be Google, Google Scholar, or Wikipedia. These are excellent resources as you begin the search for relevant resources. However, you will also want to use other, more specialized search tools to dig deeper. Your school's library likely has subscriptions to various academic databases like EBSCOhost, PsycInfo, and PubMed/MEDLINE that are free to use and will connect you with discipline-specific journals and other resources. These tools are available online and often allow you to download chosen journal articles to your computer. This resource makes it much easier to conduct necessary research from any location.

Consider your most common practices for surveying available information on a research topic. Do you rely on your internet browser to do the work and limit yourself to the first page of search results? That may be an excellent way to acquaint yourself, in general terms, with the topic you are exploring. Or you may even check out a relevant *Wikipedia* page to get the names of key people and events related to your topic. Those activities, however, are only a starting point. You must rely on various search tools to create a serious and credible product. Consider these tips:

- First, ask yourself what types of information are being sought (e.g., general information queries, academic journals, books, conference presentations, video/audio).
- Check out your campus library website to determine if any academic databases are related to the search topic or question. A specific database related to your topic or academic discipline will help you dig deeper more efficiently.

Search   Sometimes we just want to know trivia like "Who is the front man for the band Imagine Dragons?" Those searches are relatively straightforward and have a direct answer. For much of the class-related work you will be doing, however, the information you are seeking is often more theoretical and clouded by various perspectives on the "right" answer or approach to your topic. After surveying the available search tools, you can explore the internet to find those resources that will help you create your research paper. Queries or search terms guide the search process. Guinee, Eagleton, and Hall (2003) described the most common strategies for finding information on the internet:

- **Dot-com formula**—Searching by stating the search term in a dot-com format (e.g., www.astronomy.com, www.impeachment.com)
- **Shopping mall approach**—Searching by entering informational categories related to the topic of interest (e.g., "planets" to find their relative sizes, "presidents" to see the names of those who have been impeached)
- **Typical strategies**—Using an internet-based search engine using a search term. (These authors also described how search strings are often constructed.)

- **Term**—A search that relies on using a broad research topic (e.g., presidents, climate change, astronomy)
- **Topic and focus**—Using the combination of a subject (e.g., presidents) and a focus (e.g., James Garfield) to search the internet
- **Multiple terms**—Using more than one discrete term to search for content (e.g., Batman + actors + roles)
- **Phrase**—Searches that employ a phrase (e.g., arguments for climate change) to seek information
- **Question**—Formatting the search as a question (e.g., What grounds for impeaching a president of the United States?)
- **Combination**—Using, for example, a phrase and a question to search for content
- **Repeated concept**—Repeating, in different forms, varying parts of a search query (e.g., Clinton + Nixon + grounds for impeachment)

We all have developed certain search habits we routinely rely on to get us what we need. Again, for most purposes, those techniques work beautifully and efficiently. To add more depth to your search process, however, consider these tips:

- Try using several different search queries described above to see if you get different or additional results.
- If you are using an academic database, you can often narrow your results by setting conditions, including:
  — Scholarly articles, books, and e-books; e-books only; print books only; pdf only
  — Only refereed journal articles (i.e., blind-reviewed before publication)
  — By date (e.g., 2010–2022)
  — Only articles that can be downloaded as pdf

These delimiters will impact the number of sources that appear in your search results.

Select Now that you have gathered information using digital resources, the challenge becomes selecting the most relevant and accurate content. To **select** is a critical-thinking task. You must thoughtfully assess the information you are reviewing by evaluating the validity of the content, make connections or discover disconnections among the works of various researchers and theorists, and choose resources for your research project.

Not all the information on the internet is valid, reliable, and worthwhile. Two significant categories of information fall into the category of being inaccurate, false, and misleading: **misinformation** and **disinformation**. Misinformation is wrong information that is unintentionally reported in a variety of ways. It includes "incomplete information, pranks, contradictions, out-of-date information, improperly translated data, software incompatibilities, unauthorized revisions, factual errors, biased information, and scholarly misconduct." Research by Stephan Lewandowsky and his colleagues (2012) identified four primary sources of misinformation:

- **Rumors and fiction**—Individuals and organizations are inclined to share information even at the risk of sharing something inaccurate or incomplete.
- **Governments and politicians**—Both can be sources or targets of misinformation and may have motivations related to policies and decisions.
- **Vested interest groups and nongovernmental organizations**—These organizations may spread misinformation as a strategy or tool to create interest and affect thoughts or feelings about issues.
- **The media**—Media representatives are always interested in creating additional viewership and may spread misinformation in haste without considering all the details.

Remember that when these sources spread misinformation, they do not intend to deceive the audience.

Unlike the posting of misinformation, the posting of disinformation is an intentional act to deceive and mislead readers. The intentionality of disinformation creates the most significant concern when an individual or a group purposely plans to provide internet searchers with faulty information that will be consumed and believed. This process may seem relatively straightforward. However, the path to creating effective disinformation can be deceptive and hard to trace. James Fetzer (2012) identified five types of disinformation:

- Purposeful selection and reporting of information to mislead the reader
- A highly biased perspective that ignores essential and relevant aspects of the available information
- Attacks on the author of previously published materials as a way of discrediting that author's work
- Dismissal of pertinent information that could contribute to a discussion
- Assertions made by incompetent individuals or those who lack the qualifications to offer valid opinions

As a student and throughout your life, it will be important to develop your skills in assessing the reliability of information found on the internet.

Wathen and Burkell (2002) argued that credibility is equivalent to believability. The credibility of internet content can be affected by a variety of factors, including the following:

- **Source** (e.g., expertise/knowledge, trustworthiness, credentials, attractiveness)
- **Receiver** (e.g., issue relevance, prior knowledge of the issue, values/belief/situation, stereotypes about source or topic)
- **Message** (e.g., topic/content, plausibility of arguments, repetition/familiarity, ordering)
- **Medium** (e.g., organization, usability, presentation, vividness)
- **Context** (e.g., distraction/noise, time since message encountered)

Several internet resources provide practical strategies for the assessment of web-based content, including the following:

- **The Baloney Detection Kit** (available at https://www.themarginalian.org/2014/01/03/baloney-detection-kit-carl-sagan/)
- **Crap Detection and Other Essential Network Skills** (available at https://socialreporter.com/2012/03/06/crap-detection-and-other-essential-network-skills/)
- **Crap-Detection Mini-Course** (check out the Crap Detection Resources tab), available at https://rheingold.com/2013/crap-detection-mini-course/)

Be aware of these traps as you engage in research and the creation of written products or presentations. Consider these tips:

- Try using several different search queries described above to see if you get different or additional results.
- If you are using an academic database, you can often narrow your results by setting conditions, including the following:
  — Scholarly articles, books, and e-books; e-books only; print books only; pdf only
  — Only refereed journal articles (i.e., blind-reviewed before publication)

Synthesize   As you progress toward writing your research paper, you will have gathered a sizable collection of resources, including journal articles, videos, website resources, and excerpts of books on the topic. Now the task becomes one to **synthesize**, or combine the pieces in a way that tells a story concerning the research questions.

One tool that you may want to consider using in the synthesis process is a **mind map**, which organizes words, thoughts, ideas, tasks, activities, and more in the form of a diagram. ...start with a key or main idea in the center with subtopics [arranged] radially around the main idea. The subtopics group and cluster similar ideas, and they branch out to lower-level topics, guiding you to wherever your thought processes lead you (Arthur, 2012, p. 9).

The mind map provides a visual picture of how the pieces of your writing project fit together and will help to organize your writing. A variety of digital tools are available on the internet that provide a format for creating a mind map. Educational consultant Tony Buzan compared the mind map with the map of a city:

FIGURE 7.1   Using a mind map to organize thinking and content.

> The centre of your Mind Map is like the centre of the city. It represents your most important idea. The main roads leading from the centre represent the main thoughts in your thinking process; the secondary roads represent your secondary thoughts, and so on. Special images or shapes can represent sites of interest or exciting ideas (Buzan, 1974, p. 6).

Tsinakos and Balafoutis (2009), summarizing current research on mind maps, suggested the following process for creating a mind map:

- Begin with a blank (preferably large) sheet of paper.
- Place the main topic of the map in the center of the page. The topic should be depicted in a large, colorful manner and accompanied by a graphic design or picture.
- Draw radiating, curved lines (called branches) from the main topic to represent key ideas. Branches should be drawn in bright colors; identified with one-word labels; and, if the content is sequential in some way, numbered in a clockwise manner.
- Add subbranches, as necessary, to clarify and define the topic.
- Use arrows, geometric figures, punctuation marks, symbols, and pictures to prioritize the importance of the content.

Investing time using a mind map or an outline will pay great benefits when you move on to writing your research paper (see **Figure 7.1**).

One important thing to consider, particularly when using a variety of digital resources, is the possibility of **plagiarism**. Plagiarism is drawing any idea or any language from someone else without adequately crediting that source in your work. There is research to indicate that college students often engage in plagiarism. Although it can be done intentionally, it also occurs incidentally as part of our copy-and-paste culture. It is customary to copy information from a journal article or website into a research paper and then fail to provide a reference citation. With increasing frequency, there are electronic tools that can assist you in detecting inappropriate source citations and plagiarism. These programs scan the internet for phrases, sentences, and content that match your written work. Although imperfect, these tools can significantly enhance the efficiency of identifying suspicious content and help you avoid plagiarism. Examples of free or low-cost programs include the following:

- **Dupli Checker** (http://www.duplichecker.com/)
- **Plagiarisma** (http://plagiarisma.net/)
- **Viper** (https://www.scanmyessay.com/)

As a student, it will be very important for you to carefully document all the resources and content that you include in your written assignments.

It is very unlikely that once you leave college, you will ever again need to write a research paper formatted in the way that you complete current assignments. At the same time, you may be asked to compile a project plan or executive summary on a topic of interest to your employer. Being able to synthesize content in a readable and comprehensive manner quickly is a skill that will serve you well throughout your career.

Consider these tips:

- Reflect on your most recent writing assignment. What parts of that process were the easiest and the most difficult?
- Are you taking full advantage of writing tools (e.g., Grammarly, ProWritingAid, and Linguix) to correct grammar, formatting, spelling, and punctuation? Even the most seasoned writers are taking advantage of these tools.
- First, check whether your school provides a free grammar-checking tool. If not, it is a wise investment to improve your writing dramatically.

Share Now, with your preparatory work, you will begin constructing your assigned research paper in order to **share** your findings. Quite often, this is the most challenging part of the process. However, planning well and doing the necessary research before this stage will make this much more manageable. As you proceed through your academic program, you will undoubtedly be assigned to complete several writing assignments. These experiences will help you to develop skills in gathering and evaluating research as you create authentic products. In the digital age in which we live, building your skills in creating other products like presentations, websites, blogs, wikis, podcasts, audio, and video products is essential. Moving beyond written research papers into digital venues will require the development of new skill sets and a sense of judgment over how, when, and where to share results and conclusions.

Consider these tips:

- Getting caught up in the details of preparing a written product is easy. However, those details (e.g., reference format, page length, title page requirements) can impact your grade on the final product.
- Schools, programs, and disciplines generally adopt a specific format for written assignments (e.g., American Psychological Association, *Chicago Manual of Style*, Turabian). Make yourself familiar with the chosen style guide and available resources.
- The Purdue University Writing Lab offers a free online resource that covers all the basics of the writing style formats (https://owl.purdue.edu/).
- Examine the final product to make sure that it meets the criteria established by your instructor (e.g., length, number of sources, and formatting).
- Think about the types of additional skills that may be needed for success on projects and assignments.
- Also, consider that in the digital age, it is common to share developed content on various venues (e.g., websites, videos, podcasts, and conference presentations). When possible, explore how you might take advantage of these opportunities.

Steward To **steward** something means to look after and take care of it. As digital creators and consumers, we struggle to manage the digital information available and determine which content we should save (i.e., short-term and long-term) or which can be discarded immediately after use. These decisions are subject to considerations about access to storage devices, capacity, cost, and whether saved content is secure from unauthorized access.

Over the past several years, there have been dramatic shifts in the availability of storage devices for digital content (i.e., 8-inch floppy disks, 5¼-inch floppy disks, 3½-inch disks, USB flash drives, external hard drives, the cloud). Where we used to talk about digital storage in terms of megabytes, we now casually compare storage capabilities in gigabytes, terabytes, petabytes, and exabytes. Stay tuned, as additional levels of storage capability will undoubtedly be added to this list soon. Consumers found greater freedom to store ever-increasing content as each change was made. Many of our students, who did not live through these transitions, have seldom found it necessary to decide what to save and delete. In the latest rendition of digital storage, cloud-based venues, consumers can purchase vast amounts of storage space, making it incredibly easy to maintain digital possession of virtually anything and everything

Consider these tips for systematically storing and labeling your information:

- Systematically create desktop folders to keep digital content.
- Name files that are on your computer in a manner such that you can easily retrieve them.
- Create designated names for versions of the documents you prepare by version sequence (e.g., V1, V2) or date (e.g., 9.2.25).
- Create a strategy for storing links to web-based resources.
- Choose a storage strategy like an external hard drive or cloud-based service for items that you wish to save on a long-term basis.
- Use portable flash drives to store items that will be useful only on a short-term basis.

Test Yourself | Are You a Content Curation Guru?

 INTERACTIVE SELF-ASSESSMENTS

Things That Effective Content Curators Do	Always	Sometimes	Never
1. I create research questions that will aid in seeking internet-based information.	☐	☐	☐
2. I ask myself what types of information are being sought.	☐	☐	☐
3. I consult with reference librarians to gain ideas and insights on available resources.	☐	☐	☐
4. I use a variety of search queries.	☐	☐	☐
5. I search on multiple databases for information related to my topic.	☐	☐	☐
6. I use a variety of resources, including journal articles, books, websites, and e-books.	☐	☐	☐
7. I thoroughly examine the credibility of potential sources and references.	☐	☐	☐
8. I am always on my guard against misinformation and disinformation.	☐	☐	☐
9. I develop an outline or mind map to guide my writing.	☐	☐	☐
10. I have a system for collecting and storing my reference materials.	☐	☐	☐
11. I check and double-check my written products for accuracy.	☐	☐	☐
12. I use grammar-checking tools	☐	☐	☐
13. I systematically label my files for storage and retrieval.	☐	☐	☐
14. I plan for ways to back up my work to flash drives or cloud-based storage sites.	☐	☐	☐

Ideally, you were able to report that you Always engage in each of these activities related to these best practices of digital content curation. If you recorded Sometimes or Never, it is recommended that you reconsider how you might include these activities in writing your next research paper.

Make It Personal | A Plan of Attack

 DOWNLOAD DOCUMENTS & TEMPLATES

You will soon be, or have already been, assigned the task of writing a research paper. This will be the first of many such assignments over the span of your college career. It is always wise to make a plan for attacking a major assignment like a research paper. Given that, identify the first steps that you will take and the resources that might help you along:

Steps That I Will Take:	Resources That Might Help Me:
1.	1.
2.	2.
3.	3.
4.	4.
5.	5.

Review, Discuss, and Apply

 INTERACTIVE SELF-SCORING QUIZZES

Discussion Questions

1. Think about the assignments that you must complete before the end of the semester. What are some ways that a campus librarian might be of assistance to you?
2. How often are you checking into your LMS to stay on top of assignments and feedback from your instructors?
3. When faced with the challenge of writing a research paper on a new and unfamiliar topic, what are your first steps?
4. When you have a question that is begging for an answer, where do you go? If that location is an internet browser, how often do you look beyond the first page of search results?

Module 7.3 Leaving a Credible Digital Footprint

LO 7.3.1 To understand the long-term impact of a digital footprint on our identity

LO 7.3.2 To examine measures that can be taken to improve safety and security when using digital devices

LO 7.3.3 To examine personal practices that may influence your digital footprint

---

Imagine sitting at home searching on Amazon.com for a new pair of shoes. You only look casually and do not find the exact pair of shoes you want. Moments later, as you check out what is happening on Facebook, you somehow see an advertisement for several of the shoes you were just considering for purchase. This shared experience is an example of your **digital footprint**, defined as the information you leave behind as a trail of your activity on the internet, including social media, websites visited, online shopping, and emails. Our internet service provider could track or record many of these activities in a database. Unfortunately, many of us engage casually with the internet as if we were invisible and with little regard for the nature of our digital footprint.

Long-Term Impact

 VIDEO CONTENT

Our culture has made digital interactions a centerpiece of our daily activities. For example, estimate how many hours a day you engage with a digital screen, including your phone, tablet, or laptop. There are estimates that, on average, students spend roughly ten hours per day engaging with these various devices. Your initial reaction may be "Whoa, that's not me!" and perhaps you are correct. At the same time, however, we could all probably acknowledge that we often pick up and use these devices for various purposes every day without thinking much about it.

The first long-term impact of our engagement with digital technology is related to creating a sense of balance. Acknowledging the role of digital technology can promote efficiency and productivity. Technology can also become a preoccupation and a hindrance to face-to-face interactions with classmates, friends, and family. Google has referred to this balance as "digital well-being," which they describe in the following :

> As technology becomes more and more integral to everything we do, it can sometimes distract us from the things that matter most to us. We believe technology should improve life, not distract from it. We're committed to giving everyone the tools they need to develop their sense of digital well-being. So that life, not the technology in it, stays front and center.

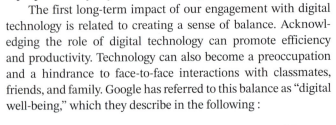
aleutie/Adobe Stock

In line with this thinking, some digital providers have started sending out weekly notices to remind users of their weekly use of technology.

Safety and Security

We have all heard of, and maybe you have experienced, a breach of security where someone or some group gains access to passwords and other measures designed to protect our digital security. The website *Mental Floss* recommended some basic things that all of us can do to maintain the safety of our digital devices:

- Always keep track of your digital devices
- Use available apps on your mobile devices like phones and tablets to maintain an awareness of where all your devices are located
- When you leave your devices, make sure they are in a secure locked location

The publication *Forbes* suggested some additional measures that all of us can consider:

- Adopt a "pass phrase" (e.g., four or more randomly chosen words) rather than a password
- Keep your software current by downloading every update
- Be selective about what you download and the source of that content
- Back up your data regularly to a secure location

Best advice: Do not be lulled into thinking, "That could never happen to me!" Everyone who has had their digital security breached has undoubtedly believed the same. Be proactive in protecting yourself and your data.

Your Image on Social Media

Social media has become a meaningful way to connect with family, friends, and classmates and communicate the events of our lives. Apps like Facebook, Snapchat, Instagram, X, and WhatsApp help provide a means for communicating in real time. At the same time, however, social media sites have become a breeding ground for negativity, misinformation, and ugly dialogues.

There are several things that you can do to protect your identity on social media and put forward a brand that represents who you are:

- **Choose a "voice" that represents you**—Ask yourself, "How do you wish to be represented?" For example, do you wish to be considered serious, informative, thoughtful, or encouraging? Choose one that is consistent with who you are. Make your social media entries consistently represent that voice.
- **Be selective about the information that you share**—Although we tend to believe that our posts are restricted to friends and family, nothing could be further from the truth. It is common for people who may not know you to look at your profile and what you post.
- **Make sure that the pictures posted are those you would not mind having on the front page of your local newspaper**—This is a good rule of thumb for all the posts that you make on social media.
- **Refrain from endless arguments over personal beliefs, religion, and politics**—You might find yourself baited into these conversations. Resist the temptation.

A Bottom Line to Consider Your choices about engaging with the internet and social media are more than a personal preference. A 2018 survey by the Harris Poll on behalf of CareerBuilder indicated that 70 percent of employers who responded were checking the social media profiles of potential employees. This phenomenon also applies to current employees and their interaction with social media. Consider these examples from the *American Business Law Journal*:

> Accounts of employees discrediting themselves and their employers via postings on social networking and media sites have become ubiquitous. A high school teacher was dismissed after posting on her Facebook page that she thought residents of the school district were "arrogant and snobby" and that she was "so not looking forward to another year [at the school]." A flight attendant was fired for posting suggestive pictures of herself in her company uniform. A study reported medical students engaged in unprofessional banter and disclosure about patients on their social networking profiles. Two pizza chain employees were fired after posting a "prank" video on YouTube that showed them preparing sandwiches at work while one put cheese up his nose and mucus on the food. Whether these well-documented anecdotes reflect ill-advised judgment of employees or overly aggressive responses by employers, they exemplify the tension between employer interests and employee privacy and speech rights (Abril et al., 2012).

What we do on social media is easily found, read, and observed by virtually anyone, anywhere, at any time. Keep that in mind the next time you are tempted to post a picture of yourself and your friends at a party. A corollary piece of advice is to show the same level of respect for your friend in terms of what you say or offer their behaviors and choices.

Test Yourself | What About Your Digital Footprint?

INTERACTIVE SELF-ASSESSMENTS

Given our voracious digital content consumption, we all have a digital footprint. Sadly, there is also a tendency to believe that we are invisible as we search and browse the internet. There are some things we can easily do to protect and enhance our digital footprints. How well are you doing?

Digital Footprint Protection Strategy	Yes	No
I create strong passwords that are difficult to predict.	☐	☐
I routinely change my passwords and check internet browser security settings.	☐	☐
I routinely check the level at which I use applications on my computer and delete those that I seldom use.	☐	☐
I routinely unsubscribe from unwanted mailing lists that routinely send me emails.	☐	☐
I think twice before posting a picture or message on my social media sites, asking myself, "Does this portray an image that best represents who I am?"	☐	☐
I routinely do an online search of my name to see what types of information are being distributed.	☐	☐
I limit the number of online accounts that I use (e.g., limiting the number of email accounts).	☐	☐
If a website URL begins with HTTP instead of HTTPS, I reconsider entering any personal information there. The *S* in the URL stands for *secure*.	☐	☐
I am careful where I click and do not download anything when I am unsure of the sender.	☐	☐
I do not open emails or attachments when I am unsure of the sender.	☐	☐

The best-case scenario is that you answered Yes to all these best practices in protecting your digital footprint. For those where you answered No, consider changing your current practices.

Module 7.3 Leaving a Credible Digital Footprint

Think Deeper | Social Media Audit

Having an opinion about our social media presence and how well it represents who we are is one thing. Reality, however, may be a different story. As we have discussed, it is becoming a more common practice for employers to check out the social media presence of job applicants. Why not get a head start on this by doing a social media audit? To accomplish this task, ask a friend or classmate to examine your postings on Facebook, X, or Instagram. After they have reviewed your postings, discuss the following topics:

- What is the one word that you would use to describe the postings?
- If I had written the postings and you were considering me for a job, would any of the postings be of concern?
- Do you have any suggestions on ways to create a better image for myself on social media?

Review, Discuss, and Apply

Discussion Questions

1. If we have never met and I decided to check you out on social media, what types of conclusions could I draw about the kind of person you are?
2. What guides your decision making about what to post on social media?
3. Is your social media profile more a reflection of who you really are or an image that you would like to portray to others?

Think Ahead | Career and Lifelong Applications

Technology will play a key role in your future, both during college and in the workplace. That reality will continue to be more important as digital tools and resources continue to grow, develop, and become more influential in every aspect of our lives. Now is the time to begin thinking about how you might stay current in the use of technology. Consider the following as you plan for your digital future:

It is very likely that you have been exposed to technology for a major portion of your life. Having grown up with technology, you know how to use a variety of tools and apps. Have you ever stopped to think about how you feel about technology and the influence it has in your life? That is an important thing to consider moving forward. Is technology a tool that you use to accomplish needed tasks or is it more of an obsession? Are you constantly looking at your phone, always checking for the latest updates on social media? Begin now to work on maintaining a balanced view of technology. It is a valuable tool, but don't let it rule your life.

artpaper/Adobe Stock

So, where to begin? You know the value of keeping up with the latest digital tools. But how to keep up with the latest and greatest apps is always a challenge. Here is a possible plan to consider:

- Identify the types of technology that are required in your chosen field of study.
- Make it a regular routine to review new tools that might enhance your performance.
- Check out the many online resources available to teach you new skills and increase your efficiency in using your current tools.

In our digital world, this should be a constant process, during college and in your work life.

When is the last time you visited an actual physical library? We often think of a library as a building that stores a vast collection of books. That is partially true. There are rows and rows of books in your library. At the same time, however, librarians have been smart enough to keep pace with digital technology. Your college or university has subscriptions to digital databases, and librarians are available (in person and online) to help you research topics of interest. Take advantage of that resource during your time in college. Also, however, watch and learn as they show you how to find accurate, up-to-date information on the topics you are researching. Learning those skills can be of great help moving forward as you will always need the latest information during your work career.

We often think of social media as an enjoyable way of sharing the highlights of our lives, while also keeping up and connecting with friends and family. There is always, however, the temptation to post something amusing or a picture of yourself doing something that may be a little edgy or provocative. Those decisions, made in a second, could have long-term impact. Many companies are now employing individuals who search out the social media profiles of prospective employees. What would your social media profile say about the person you are? Is that profile an accurate depiction of your character?

What Would You Do?

In this chapter, Aiden and Imani need your advice.

AIDEN

Aiden was excited about a job interview he had, but then he got some troubling news from the human resources team at the company.

Watch Aiden's video: **Social Media Challenge**

IMANI

Imani feels like she needs to improve her skills with using new technology so that she can be more productive.

Watch Imani's video: **Tech Skills**

What would you tell Aiden? What would you tell Imani?

Take Some Action | Here and Now

We all have strengths and weaknesses when it comes to using technology. Awareness of those strengths and weaknesses is critical to success in college, the workplace, and life.

Review your outcomes on the *Test Yourself* assessments throughout this chapter and your responses to the *Think Deeper* questions. Reflect on your results and reactions, and then answer these questions:

1. What are your strengths in using technology?
2. How will you put those strengths to work for you toward succeeding in college?
3. How will sharpening those strengths in college help you be successful in the workplace?
4. In what aspects of technology use do you want to improve your strengths?
5. Review the suggested action steps in that area and choose two or three of those to commit to here and now, and for each, say how taking that step will help you succeed in college and beyond.

Share your responses to these questions with a friend, classmate, or family member.

Chapter Summary

Module 7.1 Living in a Digital World

- Technology is everywhere and an ever-present element of our lives.
- There are a variety of perspectives on the level at which technology is helpful and valuable. Some people avoid technology at any cost; we call them technophobes. At the other end of the continuum are people who simply cannot get enough of technology and spend their days interacting with digital devices and various digital tools. We refer to these individuals as technophiles. Most of us are probably somewhere between these two ends of the digital use continuum.
- At any rate, each of us needs to make serious decisions about the level at which we will learn to take advantage of technology as part of our personal and professional lives.

Module 7.2 Technology in Higher Education

- Technology has also become a more critical part of the higher education culture. This was especially true during the pandemic when colleges and universities were forced to move to emergency remote teaching.
- One of the primary platforms that colleges and universities use to offer course-related materials and assessments is a learning management system (LMS). Knowing how to capitalize on the tools and resources provided by your campus LMS will significantly enhance your opportunities for success.
- Colleges and universities store vast amounts of information on their websites and password-protected web pages. This includes information related to degree requirements, academic

- calendars, advising tools, grades, and information regarding campus activities, to name a few.
- The library on your campus (and the related web-based resources) can significantly help you gather information for assigned tasks.
- The volume of information available on the internet is overwhelming and continuously growing.
- A wise digital content consumer needs to remain vigilant and aware of misinformation and disinformation that appears in response to internet searches.
- Having well-developed skills in curating digital content from the internet is crucial in college and beyond.
- There is a logical and sequential strategy for curating digital content: specify, survey, search, select, synthesize, share, and steward.

Module 7.3 Leaving a Credible Digital Footprint
- Your digital footprint is a commodity that you will want to protect and nurture. At an increasing rate, employers are evaluating the digital footprint of prospective employees.
- Protecting passwords and keeping track of your digital devices is critical to internet safety.
- As a wise internet and social media user, it is essential to be careful about the level at which posted pictures and messages are compatible with the image you wish to portray.

Key Terms

Academic databases Electronic collections, often subscription-based, of journal articles, books, videos, and other content

Digital content curation The process of systematically searching for, selecting, using, sharing, and storing digital information

Digital divide The gulf between people with ready access to computers and the internet and those without access

Digital footprint Information about an individual that exists on the internet as a result of their online activity

Digital immigrant A person born and brought up before the widespread use of digital technology

Digital native A person born and brought up during the age of digital technology who is familiar with the use of computers and the internet

Disinformation Incorrect or inaccurate information that is shared intentionally

Learning management system (LMS) A software application or web-based technology used to deliver course-based resources, content, and assessments

Mind map A type of diagram that visually organizes and presents a body of information

Misinformation Incorrect or inaccurate information that is shared inadvertently

Plagiarism Using someone else's work or ideas and claiming them as one's own

Second-level digital divide The gulf that exists between people who have access to computers and the internet but do not have the skills or training to access those tools

Select To choose the most relevant and most accurate content derived from the search process

Share To determine the most effective and appropriate format for distribution to external audiences and create a final product in that venue

Social media A collection of interactive websites that provide opportunities for participants to network, make connections, and share life events in the form of posts and responses.

Specify To articulate what is to be accomplished by searching, examining, and using internet content

Steward To make decisions regarding which digital content will be discarded and which will be retained, and in what format

Survey To choose the tools to accomplish the identified outcomes

Synthesize To precisely consider how all pieces fit together to communicate a logical, coherent, and accurate result

Technophile A person who loves, loves, loves technology and cannot get enough of it

Technophobe A person who fears, dislikes, or avoids using technology

Resources

Digital Skills Global. The Top Ten Digital Skills Tech Companies are Looking for Today. Retrieved January 18, 2024, from https://digitalskillsglobal.com/blog/the-top-10-digital-skills-tech-companies-are-looking-for-today?select_category=7

Future Learn. Gain the digital skills to take your career to the next level with free courses for everyone. Retrieved January 18, 2024, from https://www.futurelearn.com/career-advice/grow-your-digital-skills

Internet World Stats: Usage and Population Statistics. Retrieved January 18, 2024, from https://internetworldstats.com/stats.html

Khan Academy. Learn anything, anytime, with your AI-powered tutor. Retrieved January 18, 2024, from https://www.khanacademy.org/

White, S. K. (2020, June 5). 12 free online course sites for growing your tech skills. CIO. Retrieved from https://www.cio.com/article/3281388/8-free-online-course-sites-for-growing-your-tech-skills.html

References

Abril, P. S., Levin, A., & Riego, A. D. (2012). Blurred boundaries: Social media privacy and the twenty-first-century employee. *American Business Law Journal, 49*(1): 63-124. https://doi.org/10.32920/22227769

Arthur, K. 2012. Mind Maps: Improve Memory, Concentration, Communication, Organization, Creativity, and Time Management (Ebook). Book Stream Publishing.

Buzan, T. (1974). Use your head. London, UK: BBC Books.

CareerBuilder.com (2018). More than half of employers have found content on social media that caused them not to hire a candidate, according to recent CareerBuilder survey. Press Room | Career Builder. (n.d.-b). https://press.careerbuilder.com/2018-08-09-More-Than-Half-of-Employers-Have-Found-Content-on-Social-Media-That-Caused-Them-NOT-to-Hire-a-Candidate-According-to-Recent-CareerBuilder-Survey

Duchess Community College. (2007, November 7). *Technology Skill Assessment*. TLC - Technical Skills Self-assessment. https://www8.sunydutchess.edu/tlc_web/techskillsquiz.html

Fetzer, J. H (2004). "Disinformation: The use of false information." *Minds and Machines 14*(2): 231–40.

Fuller, R. B. (1982). Critical path. New York: St. Martin's Griffin, 1982.

Garner, B. (2019), Helping students become digital content curators: Fact or fiction? Newcastle upon Tyne. Cambridge Scholars Publishing.

Guinee, K., Eagleton, M. B., & Hall, T. E. (2003). Adolescents' internet search strategies: Drawing upon familiar cognitive paradigms when accessing electronic information sources. *Journal of Educational Computing Research, 29*(3), 363–374.

Hargittai, E. (2003). The digital divide and what to do about it. In D. C. Jones (ed.). *New economy handbook*, pp. 822–841. Academic Press.

Lewandowsky, S., Ecker, U. K. H., Seifert, C. S., Schwarz, N., & and Cook, J. (2012). Misinformation and its correction: Continued influence and successful debiasing." *Psychological Science in the Public Interest, 13*(3): 106–31. https://doi.org/10.1177/1529100612451018

Mitra, S. (2012, February 3). *The Hole in the Wall Project and the power of self-organized learning*. Edutopia. https://www.edutopia.org/blog/self-organized-learning-sugata-mitra

Prensky, M. (2001). Digital natives, Digital immigrants Part 2: Do they really think differently? *On the Horizon, 9*(6): 1–6. doi: 10.1108/10748120110424843

Tsinakos, A. A., & Balafoutis, T. (2009). A comparative study on mind mapping tools. *Turkish Online Journal of Distance Education, 10*(3), 55–72.

Wathen, C. N., & Burkell, J. (2002). Believe it or not: Factors influencing credibility on the web. *Journal of the American Society for Information Science and Technology, 53*(2):134–144. DOI: 10.1002/asi.10016

Wright, A. (2014). *Cataloging the world: Paul Otlet and the birth of the information age*. Oxford University Press.

Test Taking

1. Be ready.

The most important strategy for doing well on tests is to come prepared. Follow these tips:

- Go to class every day and complete homework assignments.
- Know the material and the question types to expect on the test.
- Develop and use an effective plan so you have time to study and review.
- Test yourself to practice answering questions. Use the same question formats and types that will be on the test.

2. Come physically prepared.

Get a good night's sleep before the test. Cramming for a test makes it harder to recall information. Eat something before the test so you aren't hungry. Bring water, coffee, or an energy drink to class, if your professor allows, to stay alert.

3. Arrive early.

If you arrive early, you can ask the instructor a last-minute question and ready your pens and pencils. Similarly, if you are taking an online test, assemble the tools you will need before logging onto the testing platform.

4. Pay attention to instructions.

Listen to or read instructions carefully. You may learn which questions are worth the most points. You may learn about acceptable answer format, bullet points or sentences, for example. You may also learn where you can choose questions, out of a set, to answer. Look out for multiple-choice questions that ask you to identify *false* answers.

5. Write down everything.

Start the test by writing down everything you are trying to remember on scrap paper or on the back of the exam. This information can include dates, names, theories, or equations. Writing down the material frees up your mind so you can focus on the test.

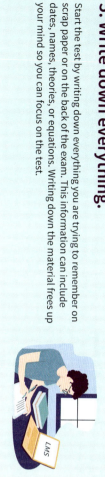

6. Plan.

Most tests are timed. Therefore, it's important to plan so you can answer all questions. Here are planning strategies:

- If possible, skim the test so you can decide where to start.
- If you can, answer the easiest questions first. Answering these questions can give you confidence.
- Pace yourself. Remember that some sections will take longer than others.
- Leave time to review your answers.

7. Stay positive and relax.

Starting with easier questions can help you keep a positive attitude throughout a test. If you run into a confusing or difficult question, skip it, and return to it later. Think of positive affirmations to calm and focus yourself. Remind yourself one test does not determine your college or career success.

8. Answer all questions.

With most tests, it's important to answer all questions. If you leave a question blank, you miss the opportunity to get the question correct or to receive partial credit. If you are unsure about an answer, cross out answers you can eliminate. Then, make your best guess and move on. Don't worry if you have similar answers, such as several *trues* or Cs, in a row. That pattern is probably a coincidence.

9. Trust first impressions.

Read each question slowly and carefully. In most cases, the first answer that pops into your mind is correct. Only change an answer if you read a question wrong or are confident your first answer was wrong.

10. Learn from experience.

After each test, think about what went well and how you could improve. On which questions do you perform well? On which ones do you struggle? Talk to your professor for suggestions. Remember that it takes time to develop effective study and test-taking skills.

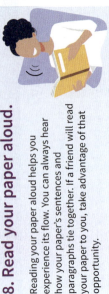

ℳriting

1. Understand the assignment.

Consider the following:

- The type of writing—essay, research, expository, technical— your instructor is requesting.
- Length, margins, and font size requirements; reference page format.
- Instructor's rubric for evaluating your writing.

2. Refine your topic.

Students often select topics that are too expansive to cover. Narrow down your topic so you can concisely cover it.

3. Plan before you write.

Create an outline of your paper, featuring the main point's sub-topics you will discuss. Then, fill in the blanks with facts, sources, evidence, quotes, and illustrations that will strengthen your message.

4. Open with style.

Grab your readers' attention. Convince your readers they need to continue reading to gather more information. You can open with a quotation, an illustration, or a statistic.

5. Organize and make good transitions.

When writing, consider how your paper will flow from one paragraph to the next. Identify where you will need to provide good transitions between sub-topics.

6. Use your own words, but cite experts.

Writing is a process of weaving your thoughts with experts' research, quotations, and insights. Experts' contributions can bolster your arguments. Most important, credit experts by using citations and references.

7. Use digital tools to enhance your writing.

Online tools can guide you in terms of spelling, grammar, formatting, and punctuation. Many of these tools are inexpensive or free. One or more of these tools may already be available through your learning management system (LMS).

8. Read your paper aloud.

Reading your paper aloud helps you experience its flow. You can always hear how your paper's sentences and paragraphs tie together. If a friend will read your paper to you, take advantage of that opportunity.

9. Ask for feedback.

Think about people who can give you feedback on your paper. Or visit your college's writing center. Here are questions a reviewer may consider:

- Does the paper make logical sense?
- Does the paper contain spelling, grammar, punctuation, or formatting errors?
- Does the paper provide support for its arguments?
- Does the paper include citations and references for experts' quotations and content?
- Does the paper address the assignment's specifications?
- Does the paper connect the introduction to the conclusion?

10. Revise and edit then edit again.

Revising and editing are important parts of the writing process. The time you spend reviewing and editing your paper is always valuable.

Presentations

1. IDENTIFY THE MOST IMPORTANT POINTS.

Begin by creating an outline of topics and sub-topics. Ask yourself, "What is the message I wish to communicate through this presentation?" Keep the message in mind as you craft your slideshow. Without this focus, you can easily add a detail or a Powerpoint slide that detracts from the message.

2. FOCUS ON THE STORY.

Often, after hearing someone speak or present, we remember the stories that person told. You can capitalize storytelling in two ways:

- Think of your presentation as a story with an introduction, a problem, a climax, a resolution, and a conclusion.
- Throughout your presentation, use stories and examples to illustrate your points.

3. HOOK THE AUDIENCE WITH A POWERFUL OPENER.

Tell a story, show a video, share a statistic, recount a quote. If you are presenting virtually, pose a question via the Chat feature or launch a poll. Do something memorable to pique audience interest in the content you will share.

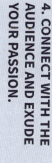

4. CONNECT WITH THE AUDIENCE AND EXUDE YOUR PASSION.

A presentation is a performance. Establish eye contact by looking at individual participants. Move around as if on stage. Use inflections and vary your pitch. Pause for silence. Convince the audience you are passionate about the topic and the information you are sharing.

5. BE CAUTIOUS WITH POWERPOINT.

Presenters commonly misuse presentation software, like Powerpoint. Consider these pointers:

- Visuals should supplement and reinforce your words, not replace them.
- Use large, clear, well-placed images that cover the slide whitespace.
- Use few words and bullet points.
- Rehearse so you can present without looking at the screen.
- Be careful when using transitions, animations, and sound effects.

Financial Wellness

01 Look for scholarships. More scholarship opportunities than you may imagine are available. Check with your college's Financial Aid Office for leads. Then, check the various online sites that provide resources for scholarship seekers. Remember: There is no harm in applying!

02 Take out college loans for value-added experiences. You may be tempted to apply for extra loans to cover perks, like eating out or booking a spring break trip. However, focus on opportunities for experiences that contribute to your learning and add value to your résumé. For example, imagine you have the opportunity to complete a two-week experience in another country. Your first response may be: "I can't afford that!" Consider, though, the benefit of including this experience on your résumé. You will demonstrate your ability to navigate and learn in a different culture.

03 Learn the details of your college loans. You cannot ask too many questions about your college loans, and no question about college loans can be stupid. Check out your loan provider's website for loan amounts, frequently asked questions, and contact information. Spending time up front may save you needless pain when you make payments on those loans.

04 Test out of courses. Thirty-three College-Level Examination Program (CLEP) exams are available in five areas of study: history and social sciences, science and math, composition and literature, world languages, and business. With a passing score on one CLEP exam, you could earn three or more college credits at over 2,900 U.S. colleges and universities. Ensure CLEP credits are acceptable at your college.

05 Explore an eText option. Most if not all traditional texts are available as eTexts. There are various online locations from where you can buy or order a subscription to access an eText. Plus, eTexts are a cheaper and better option than purchasing used textbooks that you may not want or need after you finish your course.

06 Consider online classes to accelerate your graduation date. To accelerate your coursework, you can take online courses that align with your schedule and obligations. First, check with your college about restrictions on taking online courses from your school, another school, or a private vendor.

07 Get a credit card and pay it off. Credit can be a good thing — and a dangerous thing. Although you should pay cash when possible, you may consider getting a credit card, making carefully chosen purchases within your budget, and paying off the credit card balance. This will provide you with a good credit rating now and in the future. Again, we emphasize: Be careful with your credit.

08 Set financial goals. Although you may not be able to control your salary, you can control how you spend that money. Remember that sacrifices you make now, during college, will benefit you later. Resist the temptation to make extravagant purchases. You may also consider saving income for unseen circumstances.

09 Establish a budget. Create a spreadsheet or use a phone app to list your expenses for the next several months. This way, you can pinpoint when you will have and lack funds. You can then decide where and when to save, to pay extra, or to set aside money.

10 Track your spending. Sometimes we walk around with money in our pockets, then notice that money is gone without knowing how we spent it. You can remedy this situation by tracking, for one month, where you spend every penny. This process helps you identify places where you can curb your spending to cushion your budget.

11 Plan for emergencies. Saving for emergencies requires discipline. When emergencies arise, you will be happy you have set aside money, over months. You can then pay for the car repair, the dental appointment, or the emergency room visit without disrupting your budget.

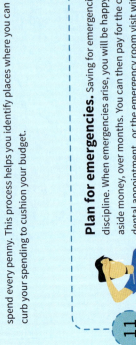

PART 3

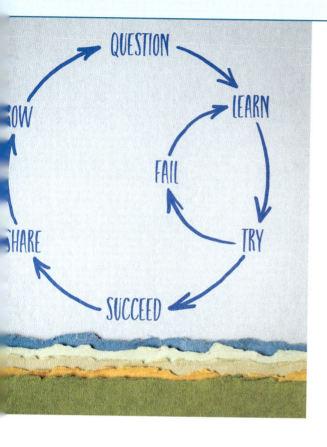

Persist

Rising Above the Challenges

The time you spend in college is an important part of preparing for the rest of your life's journey. Even the best test takers sometimes find an exam particularly challenging. The best writers or presenters sometimes don't connect with their audience the way they had hoped to. As we travel through life, there are often ups and downs. This reality allows us to celebrate success and also be ready to respond when things don't go well or when we experience unexpected setbacks. Those things happen to all of us. The difference maker is how we are prepared to respond and move forward. That ability to move forward requires practice identifying and taking advantage of opportunities, understanding what defines your own and others' identities and abilities, appreciating differences, and having a persistent focus on finding your happiness.

8   Take Advantage of Every Opportunity   **175**

9   Embrace Diversity, Equity, and Inclusion   **193**

10   Find Your Happiness   **227**

CHAPTER 8

GoodIdeas/Adobe stock

Take Advantage of Every Opportunity

VIDEO CONTENT
Author's Introduction

"Expect change. Analyze the landscape. Take the opportunities. Stop being the chess piece; become the player. It's your move."
—Tony Robbins

CHAPTER OUTLINE	LEARNING OBJECTIVES
Envision, Pursue, and Persist: Curtis Jackson/50 Cent	
Module 8.1 Looking to the Future *Think Deeper: Your Graduation Speech* The Nature of Employment in the 21st Century *Test Yourself: Skills That Employers Value* *Make It Personal: My Power Skills* What Do Graduate Schools Look for from College Graduates?	**LO 8.1** To understand how success in college can lead to success in a career and everyday life
Module 8.2 Opportunities to Build Your Skills and Employability Quotient Activities On and Off Campus *Think Deeper: Your Mission/Your Next Move* *Think Deeper: Examples of Your Readiness* Find a Mentor *Make It Personal: Prospective Mentors* Engage with Faculty in Research	**LO 8.2** To recognize and take advantage of campus activities and other experiences that can contribute to a marketable résumé
Module 8.3 Opportunities to Market Your Skills *Make It Personal: What Is My Marketing Plan?* Use Your LinkedIn Profile as a Networking Tool Keep Updating Your Résumé *Make It Personal: Your Résumé Template*	**LO 8.3** To leverage learning and networking opportunities for success during and after college
Take Some Action: Here and Now	
Chapter Summary Key Terms Resources References	

Envision, Pursue, and Persist | Curtis Jackson/50 Cent

Curtis Jackson was born in 1975 in Queens, New York City. When he was eight years old, his mother died in a mysterious house fire and his father left, leaving only his grandmother to help raise young Jackson. At the age of twelve, he began selling drugs. At nineteen, he was arrested for selling cocaine to an undercover officer, and then three weeks later, he was again arrested. The police found heroin, crack cocaine, and a starter pistol at his home. He was sentenced to three to nine years in prison but was able to spend six months in a boot camp program where he earned his GED. He adopted the name 50 Cent as a metaphor for change.

He began rapping and making recordings in a friend's basement. He was greatly influenced by Jam Master Jay of Run-DMC, who recorded his first album. With the help of Eminem and Dr. Dre, 50 Cent began a recording career that includes selling 30 million albums, a Grammy Award, thirteen Billboard Music Awards, six World Music Awards, three American Music Awards, and four BET Awards. His first studio album, *Get Rich or Die Tryin,'* went six times platinum in the United States. 50 Cent has become one of the world's most famous and best-selling rappers while also developing an active career in television and film.

The life career of 50 Cent represents an individual who started his life under highly adverse conditions. Additionally, he experienced many setbacks, including being shot nine times, sued for millions of dollars, and filing for bankruptcy. Despite those circumstances, he has persisted in his goals. He observed the following:

> Some people are born with very little; some are fortunate to have it all. When I grew up, we didn't have much. I had to hustle to get what I wanted...but I had that hunger for more. I didn't always make the right choices, but I learned from my mistakes.

Another aspect of his success is his ability to take full advantage of opportunities. Consider, for example, that he has collaborated with Dr. Dre, Eminem, and Jam Master Jay, among others. He has been able to use his talent, take the advice of others, move forward, and continually improve his craft.

As a college student, you have visualized your plan and future. Stay true to those dreams and goals. At the same time, take full advantage of the resources around you that can move you forward. This chapter will examine resources designed to enhance your success as a student.

Module 8.1 | Looking to the Future

LO 8.1.1 To understand what twenty-first-century employers are looking for in job candidates

LO 8.1.2 To understand what graduate schools are looking for in applicants

---

Throughout this text, we have encouraged you to focus on the here and now by attending class, completing assignments, taking care of yourself, remaining aware of your emotions, and building healthy relationships. All of these activities are critically important to your success as a student. We also recommend that you systematically begin building toward your future by taking advantage of the various opportunities available on your campus as a college student.

The day that you graduate from college will be memorable. You will celebrate with family and friends and take great pride in that accomplishment. Interestingly, you notice that the event designed by your college or university to award your diploma is entitled a **commencement** ceremony. Even though this event marks the end of your time in college, the term *commencement* means the beginning or start of something. So, although your college career is ending, you are beginning another new chapter of your life as a college graduate, entering the job market, and moving toward your goals and the future.

> **Think Deeper** | Your Graduation Speech  DOWNLOAD DOCUMENTS & TEMPLATES
>
> Let's turn the clock ahead a few years. You have just walked across the stage and received your diploma. You are now a college graduate! As part of that ceremony, imagine you have been asked to give a short speech reflecting on your college experience, those who helped you achieve this great accomplishment, and your plans for the future. Take a few minutes now and write the script for that speech. Then deliver the speech on video. That moment, your accomplishments, and your plans for the future can come true.

The Nature of Employment in the 21st Century VIDEO CONTENT

Consider these facts regarding the nature of employment in the twenty-first century:

- The Bureau of Labor Statistics has reported that the median number of years employees have been with their current employer is 4.6.
- For employees aged 25–34 years, the median length of employment is 3.2 years. It is also interesting to note that these numbers are declining over time. In other words, people tend to stay with their employer for shorter and shorter periods.
- The average person changes careers 5–7 times.
- The average person will have 10 different jobs before the age of 40 or 11.7 jobs between the ages of 18 and 48.
- Thirty percent of the workforce will change careers every 12 months.

All of this adds up to a very fluid workforce. And not only that! It has been speculated that many of the jobs that will be available in 2030 have not yet been invented. This remarkable trend is expected to continue and accelerate. This all can be great news for you, provided that you do three important things: (1) Consider yourself a lifelong learner, (2) constantly remain aware of new opportunities, and (3) always remain ready to take on new challenges.

What Do Employers Want from College Graduates?

A good starting point is to examine what employers value as they assess the potential applicants for available positions. According to the National Center for Educational Statistics, during the 2016–2017 school year, about 4.5 million college degrees were awarded, including 1.29 million associate degrees and 2.03 million bachelor's degrees. Consider these individuals as competition for potential jobs you may seek after graduation. That perspective requires you to consider how to elevate your profile to an impressive, factual, and highly competitive level.

It has become commonplace to routinely survey employers to determine the skills and competencies most valued when considering the employment of college graduates. In a recent survey published by the National Association of Colleges and Employers (2022), the following skills were identified:

Attributes Desired by Employers	Percent of Respondents
Critical thinking	95.6%
Problem-solving skills	94.4%
Ability to work on a team	92.3%
Professionalism	91.2%
Equity and inclusion	86.2%
Technology skills	74.0%
Self-development	68.0%
Leadership	54.1%

CHAPTER 8 Take Advantage of Every Opportunity

Mykyta/Adobe Stock

You might recognize some of these skills as things you will learn as part of your coursework (e.g., communication, problem-solving, ability to work on a team). Many of these have long been referred to as soft skills. An article in the business magazine *Forbes* (Agarwal, 2018) made the following observation about this term:

> **Many believe that the term "soft skills" is a misnomer. Critical thinking, persuasive writing, communications, and teamwork are not fluffy, nice-to-have value-adds. They're hard-won and rigorously maintained abilities that are better referred to as "power skills."**

These power skills are generally interpersonal and come into play in the workplace, where teamwork and effective collaboration are valued and required. For you as a future employee, it will be important not only to demonstrate the discipline-specific knowledge and skill that you acquired in your college courses but also to document that you can effectively work with others to achieve common goals. Although you may have an opportunity to build your verbal or written communication skills in specific courses, you may need to work independently to develop your skills in collaboration, tactfulness, problem-solving, and demonstrating a solid work ethic.

If you think of your college experience as a way of preparing for a chosen career, that preparation goes beyond what you will learn in your classes. That extension involves engaging with additional opportunities available to you on your campus.

Test Yourself | Skills That Employers Value

INTERACTIVE SELF-ASSESSMENTS

Rate yourself on a 1–10 scale concerning this list of skills employers often look for as they evaluate recent college graduates, where 1 is very weak and 10 is highly proficient.

Critical thinking	Flexibility/adaptability
Problem-solving skills	Organizational ability
Ability to work on a team	Tactfulness
Professionalism	Creativity
Equity and inclusion	Friendly/outgoing personality
Technology skills	Entrepreneurial skills/risk-taker
Leadership	Fluency in a foreign language
Detail oriented	

Make It Personal | My Power Skills

DOWNLOAD DOCUMENTS & TEMPLATES

What are some of the areas where you currently feel competent? What are some of the places where you may need to enhance your skills? List those here:

My top three power skills:

1. _____
2. _____
3. _____

Power skills that I may need to work on during my time in college:

1. _____
2. _____
3. _____

What Do Graduate Schools Look for from College Graduates?

After graduation, you may decide that a graduate degree will better position you to pursue a career in your chosen field or that a graduate degree may be an essential requirement for licensure or certification. As critical qualifications for attending graduate school, you will want to attain the highest possible grade point average, perform well on graduate school admission tests, and have strong letters of recommendation. Those are the basics that you will share with every other applicant. Additionally, however, when competitive decisions are made among applicants, the following factors may impact your acceptance as a graduate student at your preferred schools:

- The ability to think critically
- Passion for your chosen academic path and career
- Demonstrated activities beyond your classroom accomplishments
- The ability to articulate your purpose in pursuing a graduate degree
- A portfolio of activities and achievements during your undergraduate career
- Demonstrations of leadership

Review, Discuss, and Apply

Discussion Questions

1. Having identified some areas where you might need to develop additional skills beyond your classroom academic experiences, where do you plan to learn and practice these skills?
2. Who are people you know who exemplify some of the soft skills described above?

Module 8.2 Opportunities to Build Your Skills and Employability Quotient

LO 8.2.1 To explore on- and off-campus activities that build employable skills

LO 8.2.2 To identify the attributes of a mentor that will be important to you in finding a mentor

LO 8.2.3 To consider the possibilities of engaging in research alongside a faculty member in your academic discipline

---

One of the secrets of success is focusing on completing your coursework requirements while remaining aware of opportunities that can supplement that learning and move you closer to your dreams and goals. Let's review some of those opportunities.

Activities On and Off Campus

There is no doubt that you will be exposed to vast amounts of information in college that will prepare you for your future plans and pursuits. You should certainly work to gather all that

you can from those experiences. At the same time, you can supplement that classroom-based learning by selecting from the multitude of on- and off-campus learning opportunities.

Experience a Semester Abroad We live on a planet that is growing smaller every day. International travel and digital communications among the continents are increasingly common, seamlessly and effortlessly connecting people from different cultures and countries. These are extraordinary times to be on the planet Earth.

This process of globalization is also being experienced in virtually every aspect of business and industry. With the disruptive power of the internet, increasing numbers of companies rely on a global customer base. At the same time, the Association for Talent Development summarized the results of a study (Ellis, 2016) where 46 percent of human resource managers report having difficulty finding employees suitable for overseas deployment. Reported challenges include understanding a new culture (48 percent), culture shock (25 percent), and language or communication issues (16 percent). No doubt, functioning effectively in a culture different from your own requires a unique mindset and total commitment to learning. Gaining experience in another culture through a **semester abroad** will help you determine if that lifestyle suits you on a short-term or long-term basis.

The International Student website (internationalstudent.com) has identified ten potential benefits to pursuing a semester abroad:

1. See the world.
2. Experience different styles of education.
3. Engage with the distinctive features of another culture.
4. Increase your language skills in a real-world setting.
5. Enhance your career opportunities.
6. Experience the opportunity to develop new interests as you engage with a unique culture.
7. Make new friends who may be different from you in one or more ways.
8. Grow personally as you engage with new experiences.
9. Enhance your opportunities for graduate school admission eligibility.
10. Add a unique experience to your life's résumé.

Over the past decade, there has been a dramatic increase in the number of college students who decide to study abroad. Approximately 10.9 percent of all college students in the United States take advantage of this opportunity. The question that you must ask yourself is whether this investment is a worthwhile investment for you. It is an investment that will cost you financially and may also, depending on the course-related aspect of your semester abroad program, delay your graduation date.

Participate in Campus Clubs and Organizations Part of the extracurricular experience in college is the opportunity to participate in various organizations and activities. The website Top Universities has identified seven categories of student organizations that are common to colleges and universities:

1. **Academic and educational organizations**—Colleges and universities often sponsor organizations that are explicitly related to academic fields of study (e.g., STEM club, drama club) and honors organizations with specific membership criteria (Alpha Beta Gamma Business Honorary, Delta Tau Alpha Agriculture Honorary).

Membership in these organizations is a demonstration of your sincere interest in the field that you are studying.

2. **Community service organizations**—Various organizations designed to serve the greater community can be found on college campuses. These are generally organized around specific interests and community needs. Some examples include Breathe Hope, Empower Mentoring, and Fresh Start.

3. **Media and publication organizations**—Many campuses have a school newspaper or other publications primarily written by students. If you have skills or interests in this area, it is a great way to develop a portfolio documenting these accomplishments while also gaining practical experience.

4. **Political and multicultural organizations**—These include organizations that are focused around particular political orientations (e.g., College Democrats, College Republicans, American Civil Liberties Union) or global/ethnic/racial cultures (e.g., Black Law Student Association, Thai Student Association).

5. **Recreation and sports organizations**—There are always a variety of sports and recreation activities available to students, ranging from varsity athletic teams to intermural leagues. There are also organizations focusing on specific athletic pursuits (e.g., cycling club, karate club, Ultimate Frisbee club).

6. **Student government organizations**—Student government organizations are found on virtually every college and university campus. Representatives from each graduating class, are organized to speak about campus policies and the life of the institution

7. **Religious and spiritual organizations**—Examples include Jewish on Campus, Muslim Students Association, Fellowship of Catholic University Students, and Silver Circle.

As you can see, these organizations offer a wide range of options for you to consider. Depending on your interests, you can meet with like-minded classmates and gain practical experience. The variety available will vary depending on where you are attending school. Chances are, however, if you are motivated, you can find one or more clubs or organizations compatible with your interests and passions.

Grab an Internship or Externship

Many types of opportunities are available to college students to stretch their learning beyond the classroom. **Internships** are opportunities offered by employers to give students practical experiences beyond the college campus. These can be of varied lengths, paid or nonpaid, and may include a chance to earn college credit. They are typically sponsored in some fashion by the college or university. Internships generally relate directly to the student's field of study but may also be designed simply to sample hands-on experiences to facilitate career decisions.

Externships tend to be of shorter duration and do not include an option for college credit. The external aspect of these experiences relates to the fact that they are typically not directly affiliated with the college or university and are performed outside the typical school year. An example of an externship would be shadowing a professional in the student's chosen field.

In either event, it is beneficial for college students to consider including an internship or externship as part of their academic program. In an article in the *Advanced Management Journal* (2020), Malcolm Coco proposed that internships are a "try before you buy" arrangement. That can be a valuable asset for college students if they want to see and experience the day-to-day work performed in their chosen field of study. Coco made the following key observation:

> **In these uneven economic times, internships are becoming increasingly valuable to students and employers. Internship programs can reinforce technical competencies, improve analytical skills, and, most important, foster an awareness of the constant need for adaptability and creativity in a changing world. The right internship can be the key to a great job, because it gives the student a chance to take on real responsibilities while working side-by-side with seasoned professionals (p. 41).**

A research study by the Georgetown University Center on Education and the Workforce (2015) referred to internships as "Learning While Earning: The New Normal." Their research indicated that 63 percent of students who participated in an internship received a job offer, compared to 35 percent who did not participate in an internship. Additionally, the starting salaries of internship participants were 28 percent higher than their nonparticipating counterparts.

Consider talking with career development personnel at your college or university about possibly including an internship experience in your academic program.

Get Some Volunteer Experience   Remember our conversation in Chapter 1 about ikigai and the intersection of "what I love to do" and "what the world needs," also known as "mission"? **Volunteering** in your local community fits into that category. Engaging in volunteer work is a great way to help others and also gain some unique learning experiences. Over the past decade, it has become increasingly common for colleges and universities to organize volunteer opportunities for their students as a way of connecting with the local community. Being a volunteer in any capacity helps you to have a deeper appreciation for the privileges and opportunities in your own life, practice naturally using your skills, and serve others who may be disadvantaged. All of these ingredients are a win for everyone involved.

Think Deeper | Your Mission/Your Next Move  DOWNLOAD DOCUMENTS & TEMPLATES

Let's focus on mission for a moment. Look back at Chapter 1 and review what you identified as possible mission-related activities that combine what you love to do while meeting a need of the world.

Now, brainstorm some possible volunteer activities that you might pursue in the community where your college is located:

1. _____
2. _____
3. _____

Now, what is your next move?

xtock/Adobe Stock

Find a Mentor

VIDEO CONTENT

A **mentor** is someone with whom you have a longstanding relationship and who serves as a role model and a source of wisdom and advice. Often, mentors are individuals in the mentee's chosen career field. At the same time, however, mentors can teach us important life lessons beyond a career or field of study. The website Thrive Global identified five things to look for when seeking out a mentor:

1. **Where are you going?**—First, it is vital for students to visualize where they might be headed in the next five to ten years. Then they can begin to observe and think about individuals they know, or could know, who may potentially serve as mentors.

2. **Character before qualifications**—Beyond looking at a prospective mentor's résumé or accomplishments, finding a mentor who demonstrates solid and consistent character is essential.

3. **Isn't your boss or judge**—A mentor provides sound advice but doesn't attempt to control the mentee. The mentor's best advice can come after times when the mentee has made some bad decisions and would benefit from advice rather than judgment.
4. **Open, honest, and not ego driven**—Good mentors will quickly share stories demonstrating the fallibility and imperfection. They are not driven by a motivation to impress you with their accomplishments.
5. **A history of crediting others for success and a record of service**—It could be very easy for mentors to spend time with you recounting their many accomplishments. Isaac Newton once observed that good mentors recognize that they "stand on the shoulders of giants"; that is, they have benefited from the work and influence of others who have gone before and prepared the way. Related to this is the level at which potential mentors have been motivated by serving others during their career.

Thrive Global also shared an exciting story that captures the mentoring process from two perspectives: a student who reached out to a guest speaker in one of her classes to serve as her mentor and the perspective of that guest speaker (Gillespie, 2019). First, Leah Shin, a student at the University of Washington, Bothell, shared her story:

> Winter quarter, I enrolled in a 400-level college course entitled Women, Culture, and Development at the University of Washington Bothell (UWB). The readings, films, and discussions in this class were new to me, eye opening. Frequently, I would hurry home to tell my mom over dinner what we discussed—the gender roles society set for us and how they confine us, especially as women of color.
>
> Diane, an emerita professor from UWB, came into this class at the very end, as a guest speaker to discuss the amazing nonprofit Tostan (Tostan.org), which has empowered women and their communities across West Africa. I was immediately drawn to Tostan, her presentation, and especially the interactive discussions she facilitated. She asked us questions that led to self-reflection, for example, to think about a time when we felt our voices mattered. We then shared some of those times with classmates. This interaction engaged me not only with the reading but also with my classmates' ideas. Diane's explanation of empowerment, the interactive teaching style, and remembering when my voice mattered lit the flame inside me—I, too, can make a positive difference in our world. And then I had a bold thought: "Would Diane consider mentoring me?"
>
> I have had mentors. As a high school student, I had a mentor from the Young Executives of Color UW Foster School mentorship program named Jessica Oscoy, who taught me to uplift marginalized groups with the power of business, technology, and design. Then in college, I leaned on my T-Mobile managers, who later became my mentors. Della Conley and David Kubiak taught me the concept of selfless leadership in the corporate tech world. Lastly, I relied on my student government vice president and good friend, Shugla Kakar, who taught me to take risks.
>
> And I took a risk, a leap of faith, when I approached Diane and left her my contact information. After all, she didn't know much about me—except that I was exuberant after class as I talked with her. This year has been the most challenging for me as I was chosen to work at Microsoft, a company that aligns with my core values of fairness and equality. I am in a two-year full-time marketing rotational program. What may have seemed like a relief for many to secure full-time employment after graduation is actually more pressure for me as I have a sense of urgency to perform well on many fronts. I need guidance from someone who shares my values.
>
> It worked. Diane emailed. Over coffee, she willingly told me her life story. As I told her about myself, I thought that she might offer advice. She said that she would help me make decisions as I thought about my future, but more, having shared projects could help her be a better guide. She self-published a book called *Stories for Getting Back to Sleep*, a fundraiser for Tostan. Would I help her navigate the social media world? She also has an upcoming diversity workshop. Would I, could I, co-lead with her? Our beginning surprised me as I found myself opening to new opportunities that aligned with our shared commitment to women's empowerment.

Here is the response from Diane Gillespie, emerita professor, community psychology, School of Interdisciplinary Arts and Sciences School at the University of Washington, Bothell:

It's true. When Leah came up after class, I saw the light in her eyes and felt her exuberance about how Tostan's way of working in communities spoke to her. Over coffee, she asked me to tell my life story, which I did. And then she told me about her work as a Microsoft intern and her schooling and majors—interactive media design and business. She had become a leader in high school and had been thoughtful about her engagement. As we were talking, I realized that I wanted to have a relationship based on more than my stories and any advice that I might have for her. I wanted to be able to engage with her in meaningful endeavors that would allow us to reciprocate and build on each other's strengths.

Mentoring is a delicate dance. One danger of mentoring is projection—to see in the mentee what the mentor either aspired toward or accomplished and unconsciously impose that on the mentee as an invisible framework. The beauty of mentoring is releasing potential and newly discovered interests on the part of both.

Leah wanted mentoring in writing and leadership. I could work best by engaging in projects with her, including coauthoring this series for Thrive Global. She's also taking a leadership role in a diversity workshop with me. In turn, it was clear to me that she could mentor me. She is a master of the social media world. She could help me promote my book, *Stories for Getting Back to Sleep*. And she's already, within a short period of time, designed a plan that I could not have imagined myself.

So we're off, mentor and mentee and mentee and mentor, sometimes blurring the lines and sometimes drawing them. We'll be back with more reflections.

These beautiful and honest stories demonstrate the level at which a connection can be made between a student and a seasoned veteran. Leah took the risk of reaching out to Dr. Gillespie based on the level at which she admired her as a professional and person. Dr. Gillespie agreed to participate in that process. Both were somewhat uncertain about where this relationship would lead, and both see their collaborations as a work in progress, which Dr. Gillespie described as a "delicate dance."

Another perspective on mentoring is the idea of seeing a mentor as a hero at a distance. For your academic program, it is hoped that you connect with the ideas and proposals of thought leaders who inspire and challenge your thinking. When that occurs, consider the possibility of digging deeper into the career and contributions of those individuals to get a sense of how their thought patterns developed and how they assumed a role of leading innovation and change in your academic discipline. Although not mentoring in the strictest sense, these individuals, through their writing and videos, can provide motivation and direction to your learning.

Make It Personal | Prospective Mentors

DOWNLOAD DOCUMENTS & TEMPLATES

Based on our discussion of mentor qualities, think about some people you know who might serve well in your life as a mentor. Name three good candidates:

1. _____
2. _____
3. _____

Now think about some thought leaders in your academic discipline who motivate and inspire you through their writings and contributions to your field. Name them here:

1. _____
2. _____
3. _____

Engage with Faculty in Research

There has been growing recognition of the value derived from collaborative research involving faculty and students. Likely, the faculty who teach you in class are also actively engaged in research around topics in their academic discipline. They will often reference that research during classroom lectures or in conversation. If you find that their research interests you, volunteer to provide assistance like doing literature reviews, compiling data, conducting interviews, or gathering survey data. Ensuring you have the time for these activities in your schedule is important. Committing to assisting in a project or research effort and not following through is never good.

An occasional spinoff of doing research with faculty is an opportunity to collaborate on a conference presentation or poster session. Professional conferences often include provisions for student poster sessions as part of the program. Participating in these presentations is another way to grow your discipline and create additional content for your résumé.

> **Think Deeper** | **Examples of Your Readiness**
>
> It may seem like it's a long way off, but before you know it, you will be applying for jobs and engaging in interviews. That is an exciting scenario. Over the time you are in college, you will be building a case for why you would be a great hire and future employee. In the space provided below, consider the areas that are important to develop as a future job seeker, and identify the activities that you will undertake to build your résumé in preparation for upcoming job interviews:
>
> | Skills and Experiences of Interest to Employers | Activities I Can Undertake to Develop and Demonstrate These Skills and Experiences |
> |---|---|
> | Teamwork | |
> | Problem-solving | |
> | Initiative | |
> | Planning and organizing | |
> | Lifelong learning | |
> | Use of digital technology | |
> | Emotional intelligence | |
> | Conflict resolution | |
>
> Begin planning now how you will undertake your growth in these areas.

Review, Discuss, and Apply

Discussion Questions

1. As you think about your chosen academic major, what are some of the on- and off-campus opportunities that align with your goals and dreams?
2. What are some of the qualities that you would look for in a potential mentor?

Module 8.3 Opportunities to Market Your Skills

LO 8.3.1 To create an initial LinkedIn profile as a tool for marketing personal skills and experiences

LO 8.3.2 To create a draft résumé as a tool for marketing personal skills and experiences

186 CHAPTER 8 Take Advantage of Every Opportunity

bongkarn/Adobe Stock

As you move through college, you will gain new skills, competencies, and experiences in various subjects. It will be essential to catalog that learning to present a comprehensive picture of who you are and what you know to potential employers or graduate schools after graduation. The time to begin that process is now. This preemptive step provides a way to celebrate what you are learning and accomplishing while providing guidance on areas you wish to strengthen.

The process of how you market yourself to potential employers should not be uncomfortable or awkward. So, pick items from the list above that match your personality and skills. At the same time, don't be afraid to stretch yourself.

And always think of your résumé as an ongoing work in progress. In this way, you reflect your mindset of being a lifelong learner—always open to new opportunities and the possibility of making yourself more marketable as a potential employee or candidate for promotion within your business or organization.

Make It Personal | What Is My Marketing Plan?

DOWNLOAD DOCUMENTS & TEMPLATES

The website Indeed.com has offered some very specific strategies for marketing yourself to potential employers (https://www.indeed.com/career-advice/finding-a-job/market-yourself-to-potential-employers). Consider their ideas, and describe your approach in each of the identified areas:

Tips for Marketing Yourself	My Strategies:
Develop your personal brand: A professional photo	
Develop your personal brand: A logo or color combination	
Develop your personal brand: A personal branding statement	
Maintain a strong online presence: You can also market yourself by showcasing your work online. Building a website featuring previous projects helps employers see the quality of your past work.	
Meet people at networking events: Develop a list of potential companies you'd be interested in and determine what events they may attend.	
Develop an elevator speech (i.e., a thirty-second pitch sharing your strengths, talents, goals and dreams): Whether you're meeting with people at networking events or applying for interviews, a captivating elevator pitch will grab the attention of potential employers.	
Demonstrate how your skills will help your potential employer: Take a common skill and explain how you will use it to benefit their company.	
Conduct research of potential employers: This will help you grasp more of an understanding of who the company is, what they're passionate about, and what their overall goals are.	
Work to become a knowledgeable expert on your industry of choice: Along with researching your target company's brand and product, educate yourself on the industry.	
Act and dress with confidence: Your overall appearance can help you market yourself strongly. If you dress and present yourself professionally and confidently, employers will notice this and assume you will apply this confidence and professionalism to your future position.	

Use Your LinkedIn Profile as a Networking Tool

LinkedIn is currently the most popular social **networking** site. According to Omnicore, LinkedIn has over 300 million monthly active users, with 90 million senior-level influencers and 63 million in decision-making positions. Some of the other "fun facts" about LinkedIn include the following:

- Forty-one percent of millionaires use LinkedIn.
- Twenty-seven percent of U.S. adults say they use LinkedIn.
- Fifty thousand skills are listed on LinkedIn.
- *Motivated* was the most overused word on LinkedIn in 2014.
- Thirty million companies are now on LinkedIn.
- Fifty-nine percent of LinkedIn members have never worked at a company with more than 200 members.
- An average CEO has 930 connections on LinkedIn.

This information should lead you to believe LinkedIn could be a rich environment in which to network and make connections. On its website, LinkedIn offers advice on how to make the most of your profile while you are in college and beyond:

- **Add a photo**—Be sure to wear nice clothes and have a plain background (with you wearing a big smile).
- **Create a headline**—Advertise the things you want to accomplish in the future.
- **Include a summary**—Describe what motivates you, what you are good at doing, and where you want to go next.
- **Document your experience**—Describe the unique things that you have done to expand your understanding and readiness for the employment market.
- **List your skills and expertise**—Begin to document the skills that you have developed. This might include digital badges that you have earned as documentation of your learning.
- **Honors and awards**—Share information on any honors or awards that you have earned.
- **Courses**—Define the nature of your studies and what you have learned.
- **Projects**—Describe the various projects with which you have been involved and the things that you have learned and are practicing (e.g., teamwork, creativity, written and verbal communication, flexibility).
- **Recommendations**—Ask professors and supervisors to post recommendations focusing on your accomplishments and qualities.

Michael Hyatt, a *New York Times* best-selling author, observed, "Marketing is just really about sharing your passion." (Hyatt, 2012) How might you translate that statement into your current role as a college student, your future role as someone seeking employment, and on your LinkedIn profile? To begin, consider this proposal: your quest is to find a job and an employer that are a match for your skills and passion. LinkedIn can be an important part of that process. Consider, however, a word of caution. Be careful about what you choose to include in your LinkedIn profile. In engaging with this website, you are making a definitive effort to connect with possible future employers. With this in mind, carefully choose what you post and how you craft your profile.

Create a LinkedIn Profile Now is a great time to begin building your brand. By creating your LinkedIn profile, you are starting to post your experiences and accomplishments while networking with employers and thought leaders in your chosen profession. As you build your LinkedIn profile, remember that you are posting information to a primarily professional social media site. Proofread your entries and ensure they reflect the image you desire to portray.

Here are the steps for completing your LinkedIn profile:

1. Navigate to the LinkedIn website: https://www.linkedin.com/.
2. Select Sign Up.

3. Enter your email and create a password.
4. After completing the necessary security checks, begin entering the relevant information:
   a. **Introduction section**—The top section of your profile displays details of your current personal and professional status. This includes the following:
      i. **Name**
      ii. **Profile photo**
      iii. **Background photo**
      iv. **Headline**
      v. **Current position**
      vi. **Education**
      vii. **Location**
      viii. **Industry**
      ix. **Contact Info**
      x. **Summary**
      xi. **Open to** finding a new job, hiring, and **providing services**.
      xii. **Experience**—Professional positions and experience, including employment, volunteering, military, board of directors, nonprofit, or pro sports.
      xiii. **Education**—School and educational information.
      xiv. **Licenses & certifications**—Certifications, licenses, or clearances you've attained.
      xv. **Skills**—A relevant list of skills on your profile helps others to understand your strengths and improves your likelihood of being found in others' searches.
      xvi. **Recommendations**—You can request professional recommendations from your peers.
      xvii. **Courses**—Adding your body of coursework can help your education to stand out.
      xviii. **Honors & Awards**—Show off your hard-earned awards.
      xix. **Languages**—Languages you understand or speak.
      xx. **Organizations**—Show your involvement with communities that are important to you.
      xxi. **Patents**—Any patents you've applied for or received.
      xxii. **Publications**—Publications that have featured your work.
      xxiii. **Projects**—Showcase the projects you've worked on, along with team members.
      xxiv. **Test Scores**—List your scores on tests to highlight high achievement.
      xxv. **Volunteer experience**—Highlight your passions and how you have given back.

Your profile may be somewhat scant as you begin. This will change, however, as you engage with new experiences.

Keep Updating Your Résumé

We are always in the process of building our life stories. One way to document that process is to maintain a current *résumé*. Your résumé provides a brief description of your experiences, including the following:

- **Education**, including the schools you have attended, degrees received, and any honors, awards, or certifications that you have received
- **Relevant work experience**, including length of employment, titles, and duties
- **Extracurricular activities**, with an emphasis on activities and any roles that you played in leadership
- **Link** to your LinkedIn page (or personal website, as described below)
- **References** from professors, employers, and others who can and will affirm your skills and character

The balancecareers.com website recommends some key factors to make sure you have the best possible résumé:

- **Use action verbs**—The use of action verbs demonstrates your orientation toward achievement and accomplishment.
- **Quantify when possible**—This could include, for example, the number of hours you worked or volunteered per week, amounts associated with grants or scholarships, or the number of people you supervised.
- **Showcase your skills**—Identify your most important skills and a strategy for demonstrating your level of competence in performing those skills in real-world situations. Receiving an A in a leadership course is a great accomplishment. Better yet, however, is a description of your leadership role in an organization or a campus/community project.
- **Carefully edit and proofread**—Nothing kills a résumé faster than typographical errors. You simply cannot proofread enough when it comes to your résumé. Getting the eyes of others on your final draft is also very helpful.
- **Use a résumé example**—The internet offers access to many résumé websites with templates, advice, and resources. Take full advantage of what these tools have to offer.

It is important to remember that when you apply for a position, your perceived eligibility will often be based upon a quick review of your résumé. For this reason, it is critically important that this document be flawless. This includes visual organization on the page, consistent use of professional fonts, long enough to be informative but at a level that does not overwhelm the reader, and perfectly accurate content. Don't exaggerate. Provide a clear and precise picture of who you are.

As an additional consideration in the digital age, creating websites and electronic portfolios to illustrate your education, skills, and experiences has become increasingly common. These options open up the possibility of including videos and images that support the overall message and content. Again, as a caution, it is important to be selective about the number and types of video/audio/images selected for inclusion on a website or in a portfolio.

As a final suggestion, it is always a good idea to get multiple reviews of your résumé/website/portfolio. The reviewers can include friends and classmates, but it may also be helpful to get feedback from others (e.g., professors and career development professionals on campus) to ensure that your message is entirely favorable and helpful.

Make It Personal | Your Résumé Template

Your résumé should be viewed as a living document—always growing and changing. Use this template to begin filling in details about your life and who you are. Remember to check back periodically to make sure that your résumé is up to date.

DOWNLOAD DOCUMENTS & TEMPLATES

Review, Discuss, and Apply

INTERACTIVE SELF-SCORING QUIZZES

Discussion Questions

1. As you begin your college career, before you complete your degree and gain additional skills and qualifications, what are some of your best personal qualities that you could share with a potential employer?
2. As you begin building your LinkedIn profile and network with professionals in your chosen field, what are some of the criteria you will use to choose those potential connections?

Think Ahead | Career and Lifelong Applications

Abraham Lincoln once said, "Give me six hours to chop down a tree and I will spend the first four sharpening the axe." The time, effort, and energy that you are spending now are preparation for the future. Part of that preparation will be related to employment. But it is also important to consider the other, more personal, aspects of your life. These include relationships, where you hope to live, hobbies and personal interests, volunteer activities, and so forth. Begin visualizing the future that you want for yourself and take action steps to make it happen.

Colleges and universities were started for one primary purpose: to prepare students for their chosen future. With that in mind, all the resources and services on your college campus have been designed to help you accomplish that goal. How will you take advantage of these opportunities? Before jumping in with both feet, take an inventory of the available opportunities and match them with your goals and interests. Taking the time to do that will help you make the best choices that will pay the greatest benefits.

For an average job, employers will receive roughly 250 applications. To be competitive, and get the attention of people doing the hiring, you will need to effectively market your skills, preparation, and character. That may sound strange, but it is an important part of the job-seeking process. The skills, preparation, and character you have worked hard to develop can now be shared with the world through LinkedIn, your résumé, and the network of contacts that you have worked hard to develop. Believe in yourself and communicate that confidence as you move forward.

What Would You Do?

William needs advice on his résumé in this chapter, and Dewayne has some questions for you.

DEWAYNE

Dewayne feels like it's time to advance his career after working at the small record label where his boss has been a good mentor. He needs your advice on how to market himself.

Watch Dewayne's video: **Dream Prep**

WILLIAM

William is thinking about both graduate school and employment and wants your help polishing his résumé.

Watch William's video: **Building a Résumé;** download a copy of what he has so far.

How would you suggest William improve his résumé? (Here's a hint on where to start: It looks like he might have borrowed the résumé of one the other people to whom you gave advice in earlier chapters to use as a starting point for his own. Can you find evidence of that?) What would you tell Dewayne?

Take Some Action | Here and Now

We all have strengths and weaknesses when it comes to seeking opportunities or taking advantage of the opportunities that are presented to us. Awareness of those strengths and weaknesses is key to success in college, the workplace, and life.

Review your outcomes on the Test Yourself assessments and your responses to the Think Deeper questions throughout this chapter. Reflect on your results and reactions, and then answer these questions:

1. What are your strengths with respect to knowing how to seek out and take advantage of opportunities? How will you put those strengths to work for you toward succeeding? How will sharpening those strengths in college help you be successful in the workplace?
2. How do you want to improve your strengths when taking advantage of opportunities?
3. Review the suggested action steps in that area and choose two or three of those to commit to here and now, and for each, say how taking that action step will help you succeed in college and beyond.

Share and discuss your responses to these questions with a friend, classmate, or family member.

Chapter Summary

Chapter 8 Practice Quiz

Module 8.1 Looking to the Future

- The job market has become very fluid, and that trend is expected to continue. For example, it is expected that the average person will have 10 different jobs by the age of 40.
- To remain competitive in this job market, reflect on doing the following: (1) Consider yourself a lifelong learner, (2) constantly remain aware of new opportunities, and (3) always remain ready to take on new challenges.
- Employers and graduate schools are interested in your high grade point average and performance on standardized examinations. However, they also seek skills beyond these academic accomplishments—for example, critical-thinking and problem-solving skills and ability to work on a team.

Module 8.2 Opportunities to Build Your Skills and Employability Quotient

- Beyond your classes, your college or university offers a variety of experiences and opportunities that will extend your learning. Taking full advantage of these opportunities will allow you to engage further with classmates and faculty and build the elements of your résumé that will be attractive to future employers and graduate schools.
- Your college or university sponsors various clubs, organizations, and activities that will extend your learning. Many of these opportunities will provide evidence of your skills in areas that are of interest to potential employers (e.g., ability to work on a team, strong work ethic, communication skills, leadership).
- Consider participating in a semester abroad program, campus clubs and organizations, an internship or externship, or volunteer activities.
- Consider finding a mentor—an experienced person, such as a faculty member, who will supply information and advice related to your field of study, as well as other valuable life lessons.
- You may also be able to connect with faculty members by taking part in their research, which will provide another way to grow your discipline and build your credentials.

Module 8.3 Opportunities to Market Your Skills

- As you gain new skills, competencies, and experiences, it will be essential to document your activities in locations and formats that will interest potential employers and graduate schools.
- Creating a profile on LinkedIn, the popular networking site for business professionals, will give you access to many people in decision-making positions. Prepare your profile carefully, including your experience, skills, coursework, honors and awards, and so forth.
- Maintain an up-to-date résumé, including your education, experience, activities, recommendations, and other relevant information. Get reviews of your résumé from experts on campus, such as instructors and career development professionals.

Key Terms

Commencement Formal ceremony awarding undergraduate, graduate, and professional degrees.

Externships A short, unpaid, and informal experience where students primarily observe the experiences of working in a company aligned with their academic major. These opportunities are also often available for credit.

Internships A professional learning experience that offers practical experiences related to a student's field of study or career interest. In an internship, students are assigned actual tasks performed by employees. These opportunities are also often available for credit.

LinkedIn A business- and employment-oriented website that provides opportunities for networking and career development.

Mentor A professional relationship in which an experienced individual (e.g., faculty member) shares knowledge, expertise, and guidance.

Networking The processes of interacting and exchanging ideas with individuals with similar interests. These interactions are often mutually beneficial and lead to new opportunities and connections.

Résumé A document that summarizes an individual's qualifications, including training, credentials, and professional experiences. Résumés often accompany job applications or letters of interest for prospective employment.

Semester abroad Programs offered by colleges and universities that provide students with an immersive experience in another country or culture.

Volunteering When an individual provides free time, resources, and services to an organization.

Resources

How to Make a Comprehensive Résumé https://www.indeed.com/career-advice/resumes-cover-letters/how-to-make-a-resume-with-examples

The Right Mentor Can Change Your Career: Here's How to Find One https://www.npr.org/2019/10/25/773158390/how-to-find-a-mentor-and-make-it-work

15 Best Networking Strategies You're Not Using https://www.forbes.com/sites/forbescoachescouncil/2020/07/22/the-15-best-networking-strategies-youre-not-using/

Study Abroad Programs https://www.gooverseas.com/study-abroad

Find a Volunteer Opportunity https://www.indeed.com/career-advice/finding-a-job/how-to-find-a-volunteer-opportunity

References

Agarwal, A. (2018, October 3). Data reveals why the 'soft' In 'soft skills' is a significant misnomer. *Forbes*. https://www.forbes.com/sites/anantagarwal/2018/10/02/data-reveals-why-the-soft-in-soft-skills-is-a-major-misnomer/

Carnevale, A. P., Smith, N., Melton, M., & Price, E. W. (2015). *Learning While Earning: The New Normal*. Washington, DC: Georgetown University.

Coco, M. (2000). Internships: A try before you buy arrangement. *Advanced Management Journal, 65*(2), 41-43.

Ellis, R. K. (2016, August 5). Half of global companies struggle to find candidates with International Mindset | ATD. *Association for Talent Development*. https://www.td.org/insights/half-of-global-companies-struggle-to-find-candidates-with-international-mindset

Gillespie, D. (2019, April 29). Mentoring: How it Begins. *Thrive Global*. https://community.thriveglobal.com/mentoring-how-it-begins/

Hyatt, M. (2012). Platform: Get noticed in a noisy world. *Thomas Nelson*. p. 129

National Association of Colleges and Employers (October 2022). *Job Outlook 2023*. https://wwwcdn.ithaca.edu/file-download/download/public/63317

CHAPTER 9

Embrace Diversity, Equity, and Inclusion

VIDEO CONTENT
Author's Introduction

"I know there is strength in the differences between us. I know there is comfort, where we overlap."
—Ani DiFranco, American singer/songwriter

CHAPTER OUTLINE	LEARNING OBJECTIVES
Envision, Pursue, and Persist: Sarah McBride	
Module 9.1 Our Multiple Identities: The Many Ways That We Are Different	**LO 9.1** To understand the various identities that are part of our life experience
Ability	
Make It Personal: What Are My Top Five Strengths?	
Age	
Ethnicity	
Gender	
Race	
Religion	
Test Yourself: What Are Your Worldviews?	
Sexual Orientation	
Socioeconomic Status	
Module 9.2 The Types and Impacts of Identities	**LO 9.2** To assess our own biases in relation to the identities of others
Make It Personal: Who Are You?	
Privileged Identities	
Targeted Identities	
Test Yourself: My Comfort Levels	
Think Deeper: Privileged Identities, Targeted Identities, and Stereotypes	
Module 9.3 Diversity As a Weapon and a Tool	**LO 9.3** To identify strategies for engaging with people who have differing identities
Diversity As a Weapon	
Diversity As a Tool	
Test Yourself: Diversity/Cultural Competence Self-Assessment	
Make It Personal: My Experiences and Responses	
Think Ahead: Career and Lifelong Applications	
Take Some Action: Here and Now	
Chapter Summary	
Key Terms	
Resources	
References	

193

Envision, Pursue, and Persist | Sarah McBride

Tim McBride was born on April 9, 1990, to David and Sally McBride in Wilmington, Delaware. After graduating from high school, Tim put his ongoing interest in politics to work while volunteering for several election campaigns. The rest of the story is best told by the person who lived it, as shared in a TED Talk. Here is a description of that journey:

> I'm a movie buff, a policy nerd, a sister, and a daughter. It took me twenty-one years to muster up the courage to say those last words, sister and daughter. Today they are among my proudest identities, and tonight I'm able to walk out on this stage as the woman that I am. But I have to admit that it hasn't always been that way. I remember as a child lying in my bed at night praying that I would wake up the next day and be a girl. To be my authentic self and to just have my family be proud of me. I remember looking into the mirror struggling to say just two words, "I'm transgender." It was a fact that I thought about every single waking hour of every single day. With every penny thrown, with every birthday candle blown out, my wish was always the same....
>
> During my sophomore year at American University, I was elected president of the student body at the same time I was also struggling with my identity and whether or not to come out as transgender. In the end, though, I had to be true to myself. My life was passing by and I was done wasting it as someone I wasn't. I came out to my family on Christmas Day in 2011. There's really nothing to do once you open the presents. And I came out to my friends during the following weeks....Eventually, on my last day as president of the student body, I told the world that I was really Sarah McBride in an op-ed in the AU student newspaper
>
> I have to be honest that I was scared about the possible reaction from the university community, but all I got was support. At the same time though people oftentimes tried to express their support by saying, "I hope you're happy now." I hope you're happy now seems like such a small motivation for transitioning. For taking the steps that I felt like I needed to take to have my inner gender identity seen and respected. I didn't transition to be happy. I transitioned to be me. I didn't transition to create a positive but to remove a negative. To alleviate a nearly constant pain and incompleteness. Transitioning didn't bring me happiness. It allowed me to be free to feel every emotion, to think more clearly, to live more fully, to survive to be seen, to be me.

Sarah's story is unique and compelling. Her courageous act of revealing her transgender identity provided a path for her to move on to the remainder of her life in an authentic manner. That declaration, however, creates new challenges as she moves on to living the rest of her life as a woman.

After graduating from American University, Sarah McBride became the first transgender intern at the White House and the first transgender person to be a speaker at a major political party convention. In August 2014, Sarah married Andrew Cray. He had been diagnosed with terminal cancer and died four days after their wedding.

Sarah's activism and political savvy have made her a force in mobilizing support for the transgender community. In 2016, she developed a TED Talk on the topic of gender assignment at birth. She also worked on the presidential campaign of Hillary Clinton, supporting issues of concern for people who are transgender. As part of this experience, Sarah became the first transgender person to give a speech at the Democratic National Convention.

Her journey of advocacy and policy influence did not stop there. On November 3, 2020, Sarah was elected to the Delaware State Senate, making her the first transgender state senator in United States history. She is the chair of the Health and Social Services Committee, a member of the Corrections and Public Safety Committee, and a member of the Housing, Judiciary, and Veterans Affairs Committee.

On November 5, 2024, Sarah McBride was elected by the people of Delaware to be their representative in the United States Congress. It will be interesting to follow Sarah's career and achievements as she continues to break new ground on behalf of transgender people.

Each of us, just like Sarah McBride, has a story to share. In this chapter, we will examine some of the elements that contribute to making our individual stories totally unique. The elements that we will discuss are commonly described using the term **diversity**. This descriptor can evoke many different reactions. For some people, it may generate feelings associated with a painful personal experience. For others, the response might be "Not that again?" based on repeated exposure to required activities that focus on adjusting our **attitudes**. And for still others, the term *diversity* may have very little meaning or impact.

Regardless of how you may feel, the reality is that observed differences between us are part of our daily lives, and our history, and they continue today in the twenty-first century.

Over the past several years, issues surrounding diversity, **equity**, and **inclusion** have been widely discussed in the media. These discussions were prompted by the Black Lives Matter movement and prevailing issues of social justice. This chapter is intended to enhance your **awareness** of the many ways in which all of us are different. Further, it is hoped that you will reflect on the ways in which we all can improve our abilities to interact with people who are different from us in one or more ways.

Yevhenii/Adobe Stock

Module 9.1 — Our Multiple Identities: The Many Ways That We Are Different

LO 9.1.1 To articulate the ways in which our varied identities (which include ability, age, ethnicity, gender, religion, sexual orientation, and socioeconomic status) impact our lives and opportunities

LO 9.1.2 To reflect on how we interact with others who may be different from us in one or more ways

---

Looking around, you can easily observe our culture's increasing diversity. America has been known for religious and political freedom, but the population of the United States is consistently becoming older and more racially and ethnically diverse, with an increasing socioeconomic divide and a growing level of openness about sharing one's sexual orientation. In practical terms, this means that all of us will have friends, neighbors, coworkers, and family members who may be different from us in one or more ways. These differences can create tensions, but also opportunities for each of us to grow and adapt.

During your time in college, you will have opportunities to engage in and build relationships. Embrace these opportunities and learn from them! Think about college as a place where you can prepare for what lies ahead. Certainly, you will want to gain the knowledge, skills, and dispositions that are important to where you envision yourself working after graduation. In the context of an increasingly diverse world community, this will include the ability to easily engage with people who may be different from you in one or more ways. Consider that skill set as one more element of your ability to move into careers and spaces where you naturally engage and collaborate with others.

Suppose you are at one of the get-to-know-everyone social events during orientation on your campus and you are asked to introduce yourself to someone you had never met, what types of words would you use to describe who you are as a person? Your initial response might include references to your age and gender ("I'm a twenty-two-year-old female"). As the conversation continues, however, you might also share information about your racial and ethnic background ("I'm Black and Hispanic"), your socioeconomic status ("I am glad to be in college but uncertain about how I will pay off my loans"), your beliefs ("I have strong moral values, but consider myself to be agnostic"), and your relationships ("My partner and I are planning to be married next year"). As you share these pieces of information, some of which may be apparent while others are not, you are revealing your multiple **identities**. The composite of these identities, and the manner in which they interact with one another and the world, help to define the role of diversity in your life. As we will examine, understanding the nature and role of our own identities is an important aspect of self-understanding and impacts our relationships with others.

This conversation about our personal identities illustrates the manner in which sociologists explain the phenomenon of diversity. They have identified eight key identities that each of us carries with us throughout our lifetimes: ability, age, ethnicity, gender, race, religion, sexual orientation, and socioeconomic status. Within each of these identities, a variety of descriptors illustrate who we are as individuals

You may have given little thought to having specific identities, but sociologist Richard Jenkins has argued that identities help us to understand who we are as individuals and the nature of our relationship to the larger culture. He also asserts, however, that our identities do not necessarily dictate our behavior. As an illustration, consider the numbers of people in the world who, within the identity of religion, are part of groups representing the Jewish faith. Even though these individuals affiliate with Jewish religious groups, there is no reason to believe that all members sharing this identity will behave in the same way in all circumstances. There may be a variety of attitudes, beliefs, and behaviors that are common to these groups but also some that would be considered widely outside the group's norms.

Let's examine each of the identities. As you read, think about the following:

- The various descriptors that you might use to summarize who you are in relation to each identity
- People you know who may use vastly different descriptors in relation to each identity
- How your descriptors in relation to each identity have either favorably or negatively impacted you

Ability

Ability is defined as the means and skills to perform well in a particular area. As a culture, we often give value and celebrity status to individuals, such as professional athletes, television and movie actors, and musical performers, who demonstrate exceptional abilities in a particular area. On a more personal level, however, each of us may be able to make a list of "those things we're good at doing," or those things that our friends can do at a level above what is commonly observed.

As a way of thinking about the identity of ability, do the following:

1. Make a list of things that you are really good at doing. This is not an exercise in bragging or boasting, but rather an inventory of your assets.
2. Identify the ways in which your abilities in these areas have been affirmed to you, such as the comments of others, awards, and accomplishments.
3. Finally, think about what you are currently doing to continually improve on these identified abilities.

Whether looking at our own abilities, or those of our friends, we enter into a process of comparison. These comparisons, however, may not always be totally accurate. Consider, for example, the many YouTube videos that feature someone confidently walking onto the stage to perform for the judges of *The Voice* or similar talent-based programs. By all standards, many of these performances are absolutely painful to watch. Further, as the judges deliver their critical, and often caustic, evaluations, these contestants are

often shocked and surprised. Although their friends and family have convinced them that they have star-level talent, reality tells a different story. Ability, as we will see with each of the other identities, involves an element of self-awareness (willingness to make accurate assessments, willingness to accept feedback from others) and the objectivity of feedback received from those around us.

Comparing Abilities Thinking back to your time in high school, whether it was months ago or years ago, you could probably make a list of the people who were incredibly smart, or popular, or acclaimed as the best athletes (or you may have been one of those people). As you enter college, you now find yourself in the midst of a different group of individuals. All of them have qualified for college enrollment based upon their previous performance, so you may begin to feel that the playing field has been changed. The level of performance necessary to compete in college will probably be up a few notches from your high school experience. The reality of a need to up your game in relation to learning in college is important. At the same time, focusing on the competitive element of this process may not be so helpful. Focus on yourself, not the competition, emphasizing ways that you can improve your skills in relation to your chosen field of study. That commitment to continuous improvement, over the span of your life, will pay tremendous benefits.

Another perspective, one that goes beyond skills that we or our friends might have, comes from the field of **positive psychology**. Researchers in this field have proposed that each of us has a unique collection of individual **strengths**. Further, they suggest that each of us can achieve our highest potential in life by intentionally cultivating those identified areas of personal capability. Many of our previous conversations in this text in relation to having a growth mindset, exemplifying grit, and being resilient during life challenges are offshoots of this strengths-based perspective on living a successful and fulfilling life.

The Gallup organization, as a way of helping people understand their personal strengths, interviewed thousands of successful people across a variety of fields to determine the patterns of behavior that contributed most to their success. As a result of this process, these investigators identified thirty-four themes (listed in the following *Make It Personal* exercise) and created the **CliftonStrengths assessment** as a tool to help people identify their individually unique areas of strength. Once you have identified those strengths, according to positive psychology research, the best path to self-improvement is to focus on those identified areas rather than try to remediate areas of challenge or weakness. Martin Seligman, considered the leading voice of positive psychology, observed that the aim is "to catalyze a change in psychology from a preoccupation only with repairing the worst things in life to also building the best qualities in life." (Seligman, 2002)

Make It Personal | What Are My Top Five Strengths?

Here is a list of the thirty-four strengths identified by the Gallup Organization. Pick the strengths that you believe could be identified as your top five.

	Achiever—One with a constant drive for accomplishing tasks
	Activator—One who acts to start things in motion
	Adaptability—One who is especially adept at accommodating to changes in direction/plan
	Analytical—One who requires data and/or proof to make sense of their circumstances
	Arranger—One who enjoys orchestrating many tasks and variables to a successful outcome
	Belief—One who strives to find some ultimate meaning behind everything they do
	Command—One who steps up to positions of leadership without fear of confrontation
	Communication—One who uses words to inspire action and education
	Competition—One who thrives on comparison and competition to be successful
	Connectedness—One who seeks to unite others through commonality
	Consistency—One who believes in treating everyone the same to avoid unfair advantage

Context	One who is able to use the past to make better decisions in the present
Deliberative	One who proceeds with caution, seeking to always have a plan and know all of the details
Developer	One who sees the untapped potential in others
Discipline	One who seeks to make sense of the world by imposition of order
Empathy	One who is especially in tune with the emotions of others
Focus	One who requires a clear sense of direction to be successful
Futuristic	One who has a keen sense of using an eye toward the future to drive today's success
Harmony	One who seeks to avoid conflict and achieve success through consensus
Ideation	One who is adept at seeing underlying concepts that unite disparate ideas
Includer	One who instinctively works to include everyone
Individualization	One who draws upon the uniqueness of individuals to create successful teams
Input	One who is constantly collecting information or objects for future use
Intellection	One who enjoys thinking and thought-provoking conversation often for its own sake and who also can compress complex concepts into simplified models
Learner	One who must constantly be challenged and learning new things to feel successful
Maximizer	One who seeks to take people and projects from great to excellent
Positivity	One who has a knack for bringing the bright side to any situation
Relator	One who is most comfortable with fewer, deeper relationships
Responsibility	One who must follow through on commitments
Restorative	One who thrives on solving difficult problems
Self-Assurance	One who stays true to their beliefs and judgments and is confident
Significance	One who seeks to be seen as significant by others
Strategic	One who is able to see a clear direction through the complexity of a situation
Woo	One who is able to easily persuade (short for winning others over)

Adapted from Gallup, Inc. (2019, December 30). CliftonStrengths. Retrieved from https://www.gallup.com/cliftonstrengths/en/252137/home.aspx?utm_source=google&utm_medium=cpc&utm_campaign=Strengths_ECommerce_Brand_Search_US&utm_content=+cliftonstrengths&gclid=EAIaIQobChMIvOPqxpCk5wIVS73ACh2XxwZIEAAYASAAEgITtvD_BwE

It would also be interesting to ask a person who knows you well to go through the same process, identifying the strengths that you display on a consistent basic. This could lead to a conversation about the similarities and differences between the two lists (i.e., yours and theirs).

Improving on Your Abilities Think about the people you know who may demonstrate above-average skills in specific areas (learning, speaking, sports activities, performance arts). It is somewhat common to think about these abilities as being naturally endowed in the absence of additional effort and practice on the part of the individual. Malcolm Gladwell, in the book *Outliers*, has proposed, however, that to gain world-class proficiency in any field, it is necessary to engage in a minimum of 10,000 hours of **deliberate practice**. Those 10,000 hours are equivalent to investing 20 hours per week, in the activities of deliberate practice, over a 10-year period. Serious business, indeed. It is reasonable to speculate that people like Lebron James, Jay-Z, Natalie Portman, Serena Williams, Angela Merkel, and Ruth Bader Ginsburg, although born with more than ample amounts of unique abilities, also invested themselves (at a level of 10,000 hours or more) in enhancing those abilities to a level far beyond what is common for the rest of us. Their celebrity status is a validation of their strengths, their investments in excellence, and the manner in which the final results of their investments are valued by the rest of us.

In his blog and elsewhere, writer Nat Eliason (2017, 2018) has defined three levels of practice. At the lowest level is **naïve practice**. This involves simply repeating the skill over and over again without any expectation of improving performance (playing songs on a musical instrument that you already know, cooking with recipes that you have already used). One notch up is **purposeful practice**. Here, you are working to improve your performance to meet a specified goal. This could include making twenty basketball free throws in a row or reciting a poem without any errors or hesitations. Purposeful practice, unlike naïve practice, is focused, involves feedback, and moves you to a level beyond what you are currently able to accomplish. Finally, at the highest level, is deliberate practice, which we mentioned earlier. This level of practice often requires a teacher or mentor who can provide expert guidance on areas of needed improvement. People who engage in deliberate practice have a singular focus on being the best at what they are doing. That is a high mountain to climb and always comes with sacrifice.

In the *Make It Personal* above, you identified some things that you can do well, the affirmations that you have received for those abilities, and the level at which you are working to continuously improve in those areas. Now, as you begin your college career, you have some decisions to make about the way you will approach learning in your academic discipline. So, will your approach to college be naïve, purposeful, or deliberate? Eliason proposed that people who achieve their goal of being in the top 1 percent of their field choose the path of deliberate practice. During your time in college, you will have access to a variety of experts who can guide you as you pursue excellence. Take advantage of their counsel and take intentional steps to build connections with faculty.

As with any theory, research and public opinion have been generated to both support and debunk the validity of the 10,000-hour rule. One finding, that makes perfect sense, is the principle that additional deliberate practice will always provide a benefit—that is, additional deliberate practice will always make you better at what you are trying to learn or master. In understanding this belief, however, there are two important things to remember:

1. Deliberate practice means pushing yourself as much as possible to enhance and refine your skills (as opposed to going through the motions mindlessly and then saying you practiced).
2. The benefits of reaching the 10,000-hour mark of deliberate practice will have more benefit in some fields (music, sports) than others (education, professions). In any event, it is important for each of us to assess our natural abilities (speaking, writing, relationships, athletics) and work to make better what we were given at birth.

So, even if you have some level of ability in a particular area, to fully realize its potential, you must be committed and dedicated and engage in extended practice and refinement.

As you think about your own ability identity, consider the three following questions:

DOWNLOAD DOCUMENTS & TEMPLATES

1. What words would you use to describe yourself in relation to ability?
2. What types of comments have people made to you about areas in which you excel?
3. At what level are you engaging in deliberate practice as a means to continuously enhance your abilities?

Age

VIDEO CONTENT

Age refers to your chronological age. Quite often, our chronological age is linked to certain expectations that others may have of us. Young people may be told "Act your age," "Grow up," or "When I was your age," while older people may be told "Your memory isn't what it used to be." At the same time, there are privileges and opportunities that come with age such as voting, driving, going to college, consuming alcohol, getting a marriage license, or moving into your own apartment.

The work of Neil Strauss and William Howe, beginning with their book *Generations* (1991), reflects on the ways in which people born in a certain era generally share similar experiences and patterns of thinking. As they describe: "You and your peers share the same 'age location' in history and

your generation's collective mindset cannot help but influence you—whether you agree with it or spend a lifetime battling against it." As you think about the people you grew up with, you will probably realize that you share many defining experiences, including musical genres, television programs and movies, world-changing events, fashion trends, and slang terms. Those elements define your generation and have influenced your views of the world and your place in it. This reality will become clearer if, in future years, you decide to attend your high school reunion. Your first conversations with former classmates will undoubtedly move to topics related to music, television, movies, and fashion that you all shared when you were in high school. Oddly, as you have likely pursued different paths since graduation, the conversations will probably be a bit more challenging as you struggle to find common points of interest or overlap in the conversation.

Consider Figure 9.1 as a resource for a common language about identified generations. Observe the ways in which varied generations share, at some level, values, global events, icons, and communication mediums:

Howe and Strauss have described the positions and beliefs of various generations throughout history (boomers, Generation X, millennials). Interestingly, the idea of differing generations with unique personal qualities has become a very popular way of labeling people

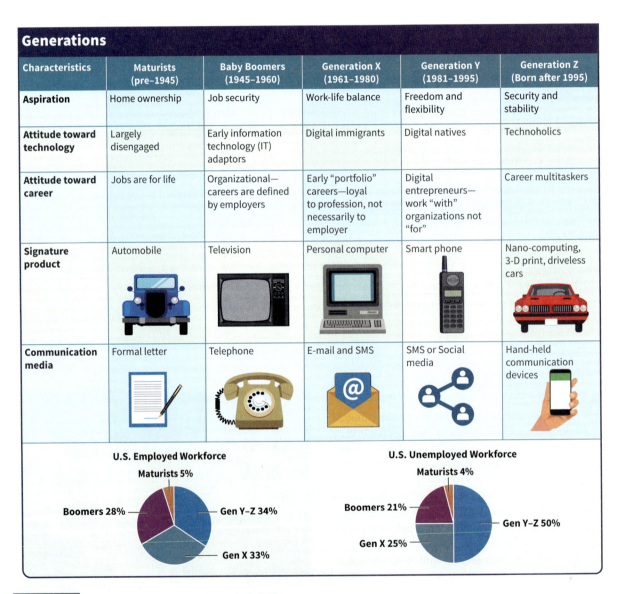

FIGURE 9.1 Generational characteristics and differences.

Source: Adapted from https://www.vecteezy.com/vector-art/98290-generations

from different age groups (e.g., younger boomers, older boomers, 9/11 Generation, Gen X, Gen Y, Gen Z, Gen Alpha) to the extent that it can be somewhat confusing. It is important to remember that although you are part of a generation, that designation does not define who you are as an individual.

Your previous experiences in education have largely placed you in classes, like Sophomore English or Senior Seminar, with other students of the same age and grade. In college, it is likely that you will be in classes that include a wider age range. Ultimately, as you leave college and enter the workplace, and for the remainder of your career, you will be working alongside individuals from an even greater age span. Think of this opportunity as a learning experience. As with all of the areas that comprise diversity, it is helpful to begin to consider your own thoughts about people who are younger or older than you and how you engage with them.

As you think about your own identity in relation to age, consider the two following questions:

1. What words would you use to describe your identity in relation to age?
2. Have there been times when others have applied certain stereotypes to you based on your age? Have you ever engaged in similar types of behavior?

Ethnicity

Imagine that your family immigrated to the United States from the mythical country of Ethnicia. You still have relatives in Ethnicia. Most of your relatives, however, who currently live in the United States, are fluent in Ethnician but also speak English. Ethnicians (people from Ethnicia) have characteristic skin, eye, and hair color, but do not have an overall appearance that would distinguish them from several other more familiar ethnicities. As part of your family heritage, you do, however, continue to celebrate Ethnician holidays with traditional songs, dances, and food in remembrance of your native ancestry—your **ethnicity**.

The people of Ethnician descent are often the subject of tasteless jokes, rude comments, and generalities ("Ethnicians are lazy and unmotivated," "Two Ethnicians" walked into a bar..."). These comments are often hurtful and difficult to hear. Although you are an American, you still have pride and respect for the people of Ethnicia and all that they have accomplished against great odds. Each of us has an ethnic identity. It may be strong, visible, and obvious, or it could be something that is given little consideration. Once again, we all see that we all are different in a variety of ways.

As an additional twist in discussing ethnicity, a variety of online services are now able to help determine an individual's ethnic heritage based on a DNA sample. Consider, for example, an individual who identifies as a white American male and his derived DNA results in **Figure 9.2**.

For this individual, finding out that he had ethnic heritage from Great Britain and Western Europe came as no surprise. What was surprising, however, was additional information indicating his ethnic connections with North Africa, Russia, and other regions of the world (including Asia). This example illustrates the level at which we are all, to some extent, a composite of many cultures and ethnicities.

What kind of answers do you think you would get if you stopped random students while walking to class tomorrow morning and asked them "What is your ethnic background?" Most students will answer with what they believe to be the nationality or country of origin of their ancestors. In 2015, the United States Census

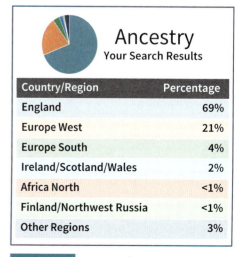

FIGURE 9.2 Ancestral roots.

Bureau conducted the "American Community Survey." Part of the data generated by this survey focused on the ancestry of American citizens. The top five recorded ethnic groups were German (14.7 percent), African American (12.3 percent), Mexican (10.9 percent), Irish (10.6 percent), and English (7.8 percent). Interestingly, 7.2 percent of the respondents identified themselves as American. This response could either be political in nature ("I am an American!") or simply an indication that the respondents were unsure of their ethnic ancestry. A related investigation by the Pew Research Center (2019) indicated that roughly 14 percent of United States residents were "foreign born" (compared with 4.8 percent in 1965). Current projections indicate that by 2065, this percentage will rise to 17.7. As time passes, the United States will continue to become increasingly diverse in relation to its ethnic background.

In conversations about diversity, there is often confusion regarding the distinctions among ethnicity, nationality, and race. As we explore identities, it is important to understand the distinctions among the terms:

- *Ethnicity* refers to a group of people who can identify with one another based on ancestry, nationality, language, society, culture, or country of origin. Examples of ethnicity would include people who identify as Italian, French, or Hispanic.
- *Race* (discussed in further detail below) refers to a group of people of common ancestry, distinguished from others by physical characteristics, such as hair type, eye color, and skin color. This would include individuals who are Caucasian, African American, or Asian.
- *Nationality* refers to the country in which a person was born (American, Canadian, Russian).

As an additional point of clarification, there is common confusion between the terms *Hispanic* and *Latino*. The term *Hispanic* refers to people, nations, and cultures that are historically connected to the Spanish language or the country of Spain. The term *Latino* or *Latina*, is used to refer to individuals from Latin America or with Latin American ancestry (Cuban, Mexican, Puerto Rican, Dominican, South or Central American). As you might guess, individuals who describe themselves as Hispanic or Latino/Latina) often do so with pride. For the rest of us to remain unaware of this and casually mix up these terms is disrespectful. Most recently, there has been controversy around the increased use of the term *Latinx* to refer to individuals of Latin American cultural or ethnic identity. The controversy is related to the elimination of gender identity as part of this reference (i.e., as opposed to Latina/Latino).

As a way of thinking about ethnicity, consider the high school you attended, the neighborhood in which you lived, and your collection of friends. How would you describe the level of diversity represented among the individuals in these places? The same question is relevant to your college campus. We all have different experiences in relation to the ethnic diversity among our friends, neighbors, and classmates. One thing to consider, regardless of how you answered these questions, is the recommendation that we all continue to grow in relation to our interactions with people who may be different from us in one or more ways. If you find that your history of relationships with people from varied ethnic backgrounds is limited, now would be a great time to open yourself to those opportunities.

As you think about your own identity in relation to ethnicity, consider the three following questions:

1. What words would you use to describe your identity in relation to ethnicity?
2. How familiar are you with the ethnicity of friends, neighbors, and classmates?
3. To what extent have differences in ethnicity ever made an impact on your relationships with those individuals?

Gender

Gender refers to the socially constructed attitudes, feelings, and behaviors that are associated with a person's assigned biological sex. In the past few years, the number of individuals who assert that their gender is different from their assigned biological sex has increased. This

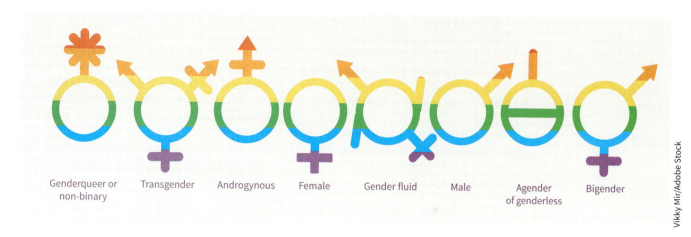

Genderqueer or non-binary | Transgender | Androgynous | Female | Gender fluid | Male | Agender of genderless | Bigender

reality has created a variety of reactions and has blurred conversations about gender. On a larger scale, it has resulted in a number of notable cultural shifts:

- The social media site Facebook offers seventy-one different gender options to its subscribers when they enroll (agender, gender fluid, neutrois, pangender, trans person, two-spirit).
- Princeton University offers prospective students seven options: cisgender, genderqueer, gender nonconforming, trans/transgender, man, woman, and other.
- The Law School Admission Test (LSAT) provides applicants with twelve different options for identifying their gender (including agender, demigender, questioning, unsure, queer, and gender fluid).
- Several locations around the country (Washington, Oregon, New York, Washington, DC) are offering residents the option of identifying themselves as X in relation to gender.
- Germany's high court has ruled that the country must provide a third gender option on the nation's birth registry. The third gender option is *divers*, which roughly translates to "miscellaneous." This trend is also noted in Nepal, Pakistan, Bangladesh, Australia, New Zealand, and Canada.

As we explore this component of identity, it may first be helpful to define some terms:

- **Sex** refers to the biological characteristics of an individual (chromosomes, internal and external sex organs, secondary sex characteristics).
- **Intersex** refers to individuals who are born with biological traits of both sexes.
- **Gender,** as mentioned above, is primarily a social construction that describes the attitudes, feelings, and behaviors associated with a person's assigned biological sex.
- **Nonbinary** refers to individuals who have gender identities that are not exclusively masculine or feminine.
- **Transgender** refers to individuals whose gender identity is different from their biological sex.
- **Transsexual** refers to individuals who have chosen medical procedures to change internal and external sex organs and secondary sex characteristics.
- **Gender pronoun(s)** are the pronouns with which an individual prefers others to address them based on their gender identity (he, she, per, ve, xe, ze, etc.).

It is common to confuse gender and sexual orientation (which is discussed below). Gender, in our current vernacular, refers to the manner in which individuals identify themselves and wish to be identified by others. Sexual orientation, on the other hand, typically refers to a pattern of recurring romantic or sexual attraction (e.g., heterosexual, lesbian, gay, bisexual).

Although there is some noticeable overlap between these identities, we will use these definitions to guide our discussions.

Gender has become a frequent topic of discussion. These conversations have focused on two key elements: First are issues related to men and women. This includes disparities in pay and opportunities that are unfavorable to women and the Me Too movement, which focuses on the ongoing, and often unreported, instances of sexual harassment and sexual assault that occur in a variety of venues. These are issues of respect and equality. Every person should be respected and treated with dignity without reference to their gender.

Second, in increasing numbers, individuals are publicly declaring a gender status that goes beyond the binary classifications of male and female. To put this in perspective, consider this analysis by the BBC in 2015:

> At Harvard University, . . . about half of the approximately 10,000 students registered in the Faculty of Arts and Sciences have specified preferred pronouns, and slightly more than 1% of those—about 50 out of 5,000—chose pronouns other than "she" or "he", according to registrar Mike Burke.
>
> At most other US universities, the growing use of "non-binary" pronouns remains less formalized but is often encouraged in various ways. Signs and badges found throughout campuses display slogans such as Pronouns Matter or Ask Me About My Pronouns. Professors may be invited to training sessions at the start of each year and are sometimes urged to include their pronouns in their email signature, for example, "John Smith (he/him/his)".

As you enter college, you may be able to observe the level at which your school is adapting to this new reality, including pronoun choices, gender options on admissions forms, transgender restrooms/locker rooms, and housing options.

On a more personal level, it is becoming increasingly important for each of us to reflect on our own personal experiences in this area. This may be realized in several ways. First, in the diverse culture of a college or university, you may find yourself engaging with classmates and friends who proclaim a variety of gender choices. As you build those relationships, and have conversations with these individuals, it is likely that you will begin to realize, or perhaps it will be affirmed, that each of us is more than what can be captured by a singular identity label. Each of us is a complex combination of multiple identities along with a diverse collection of experiences.

As you think about your own identity in relation to gender, consider the four following questions:

1. What words would you use to describe your identity in relation to gender?
2. Do you currently have friends, family members, or classmates who identify their gender in ways other than the traditional designations of male and female?
3. Have you had an opportunity to learn from them about this decision and the manner in which they have been affected by this choice?
4. Are there further questions that you have about gender identity? If so, there are people and resources on campus that can help you process these questions.

Race

Race is a social construct used to categorize people into groups based on combinations of shared physical characteristics and ancestry. In the United States, the Census Bureau officially recognizes six racial categories: (1) White, (2) Black or African American, (3) American Indian or Alaska Native, (4) Asian, (5) Native Hawaiian or Other Pacific Islander, or (6) Some Other Race/Two or more Races (write-in entry). The United States Census states that people of Hispanic or Latino origin can be of any race; therefore, the United States Census includes them in their applicable race categories (in the numbers below) rather than breaking out their numbers as their own race. The distribution of these groups in the 2020 Census was as follows:

- White (76.6 percent)
- Black or African American (13.4 percent)
- Asian (5.8 percent)

- Two or more races (2.7 percent)
- American Indian or Alaska Native (1.3 percent)
- Native Hawaiian or Other Pacific Islander (0.2 percent)

Note that in other reports, the Census Bureau does break out Hispanics and Latinos (18.1 percent) as a group and changes the White group to White alone, not including Hispanic or Latino (60.7 percent). As this juxtaposition of a term used to describe race (White) and a term more closely related to ethnicity (Hispanic/Latino), along with the use of specific geographic markers to categorize people's race like *Alaska* Native or Native *Hawaiian* show, the concepts of race and ethnicity are often intertwined and easily confused.

From a historical perspective, race has been a longstanding and divisive issue in the United States (e.g., slavery, inequalities, voting rights, discrimination, segregation, health care access, wealth distribution, justice system). It is sometimes easy to minimize these historical facts as cultural and institutional issues. That perspective can be a way of divesting ourselves of personal responsibility. It is true that there are complicated matters that will require ongoing efforts at the state and national levels. At the same time, however, as individuals, we can make a concerted effort to build relationships with people who are racially different from us. This can occur in college and throughout our lives. These relationships can lead to conversations about difficult topics and shared feelings about the state of race relations on a wider scale. These individual connections can be building blocks to change the local level (e.g., neighborhood, workplace, community) in spite of perceptions that progress toward change is slow on a wider scale.

According to the Brookings Institution, a research think tank, current projections are that the United States will demographically become a "minority white" nation by the year 2045. As the United States becomes more diverse, there will be a growing need for people to connect and build bridges through relationships. Many colleges and universities have embraced the inherent value of having racially diverse campus populations. The level at which this goal is being achieved, however, is widely varied. If you are attending a racially diverse college or university, take advantage of this opportunity to build new relationships. On the other hand, if your campus does not provide this experience, seek out off-campus events and opportunities to engage with individuals whose racial background is different from your own.

As you think about your own identity in relation to race, consider the three following questions:

1. What words would you use to describe your identity in relation to race?
2. To what extent do you currently have deep relationships with people who are racially different from you?
3. How might you begin to build connections and relationships with people who have a racial identity that differs from yours?

DOWNLOAD DOCUMENTS & TEMPLATES

Religion

 VIDEO CONTENT

Religion is any cultural system of designated behaviors and practices, worldviews, texts, sanctified places, ethics, or organizations that relate humanity to the supernatural or transcendental. It would be difficult to accurately estimate the number of religions that are practiced around the world. At the same time, however, it is possible to identify the most

widely practiced religions. These include, in order of the number of followers, the groups in the chart below:

Religious Groups	Number of Followers
Christianity	2.4 billion
Islam	1.9 billion
Hinduism	1.2 billion
Nonreligious (Secular/Agnostic/Atheist)	1.2 billion
Buddhism	521 million
Chinese traditional religion	394 million
Primal-Indigenous	300 million
African traditional and Diasporic	100 million
Sikhism	23 million
Judaism	14.5 million

Note that people might respond to a survey about their religious preferences without being fully devoted followers of their stated choice (not actively practicing the tenets of the religion, not affiliating in a public manner).

Of the major world religions, on a global basis, Islam is the fastest-growing religion. The Pew Research Center predicted a 70 percent increase in the number of Muslims between the years 2015 and 2060. During the same time period, they predicted a 34 percent increase in the number of Christians, a 27 percent increase in the number of Hindus, and a 15 percent increase in the number of Jews. Pew attributes the rapid growth of Islam to demographic

Test Yourself | What Are Your Worldviews?

INTERACTIVE SELF-ASSESSMENTS

In general, religious beliefs are an important component in defining one's view of the world. A study by Goplen and Plant (2015) posed some interesting questions to prompt thinking about worldviews and religious affiliations. Read each statement and indicate whether it is true (T) or false (F) for you.

	My religious scriptures (Bible, Torah) are a reliable source of knowledge.
	My morals come from my religion.
	The purpose of my life is to do God's work on earth.
	My religious leaders give me important information about the world.
	I try hard to live my life the way my religion tells me to live it.
	I believe science is the only way that one can obtain knowledge about the universe.
	When I am unsure whether an act is right or wrong, I often look to my religion to give me the answer.
	My purpose in life is not determined by my religion.
	There are some things about the way the world works that I can come to understand only through religion.
	My religion gives me a clear, stable set of morals.
	The meaning of life actually lies in what is beyond this life.
	My sense of right and wrong does not come from my religion.
	My religious beliefs will not influence the career I choose for myself.
	My religion has taught me how to lead a moral life.
	I often look to my religion for directions when making important life decisions.
	I believe my religion has a plan for my life.
	I believe that my religion holds the answers as to how the universe was created.
	If I were considering who to vote for in a political election, I would not look to my religion to help me decide.
	I believe my life is controlled by God.

What kind of summary statement could you create describing your belief system in relation to these statements?

Adapted from: Goplen, J., & Plant, E. A. (2015). A religious worldview: Protecting one's meaning system through religious prejudice. Personality and Social Psychology Bulletin, 41(11), 1474–1487. https://doi.org/10.1177/0146167215599761

factors including higher birth rates among members, the youngest median age, and predominance in Africa and the Middle East, areas that consistently have the highest population increases. It is predicted that by 2070, Islam will be the most widely practiced religion.

The statements in *Test Yourself: What Are Your Worldviews?* provide a thoughtful path for anyone, regardless of their religious affiliation, to think deeply about their worldview/belief system. Whether someone identifies these statements as true or false is not a clear path to identifying that person's religious affiliation (Christian, Muslim, agnostic). These statements may, in fact, provide overlapping results (Christians and Muslims may both answer T (true) to the statement "My morals come from my religion").

An individual's religion is a deeply personal choice. This includes those who publicly identify with a religious tradition, those who privately make those commitments, and those who deny and oppose the concept of formalized religions. You may have chosen your college for religious reasons. Is your school affiliated with a particular faith? Regardless of your choices in this area, it is also relevant to think about the moral principles that guide your decision making on a daily basis. These morals may be, and often are, affiliated with an individual's religious beliefs. At the same time, however, whether an individual is affiliated with a religion does not preclude the need to have a strong, definable sense of what is considered to be right and wrong.

As a final thought, religion, like each of the other identities, is often the focus of stereotypes. There has long been a tendency to assume that all members of a faith tradition act and believe in exactly the same way (e.g., "All Christians...", "Jews are...," "Muslims are..."). Fight against these generalizations by getting to know people of different faith traditions on a personal, relationship-oriented level.

As you think about your own identity in relation to religion, consider the following three questions:

DOWNLOAD DOCUMENTS & TEMPLATES

1. What words would you use to describe your identity in relation to religion?
2. Is this a private or public declaration in your life?
3. Have you engaged in conversations with friends, family, and classmates who may have a religious identity that is different from yours? What could you learn from those conversations?

Sexual Orientation

VIDEO CONTENT

Sexual orientation is an enduring pattern of romantic or sexual attraction (or a combination of these) to persons of the opposite sex or gender, the same sex or gender, or both sexes or more than one gender. These attractions are often described as heterosexuality (attraction to the opposite gender), homosexuality (attraction to the same gender), and bisexuality (attraction

arloo/Adobe Stock

to both genders). Since the early 1990s, it has been common to use the initials LGBTQ to refer to the community of individuals who are lesbian, gay, bisexual, transgender, or queer. The Pew Research Center (2023) estimated that 7 percent of the United States population identify as LGBTQ. There is probably an LGBTQ organization advocating for LGBTQ rights on your campus.

Words matter. Quite often, in our current culture, it is sadly common to hear people using derogatory comments that reflect on sexual orientation (e.g., "That's so gay," "He's a fag"). These are hurtful and unnecessary statements. So, as a starting point for this conversation about sexual orientation, we will define the elements of LGBTQ:

- **Lesbian** refers to women who have the capacity to be attracted romantically, erotically, and/or emotionally to other women.
- **Gay** refers to individuals who are primarily emotionally, physically, and/or sexually attracted to members of the same sex and/or gender. This term is also commonly used to refer to anyone who does not identify as heterosexual.
- **Bisexual** refers to a person who is emotionally, physically, and/or sexually attracted to men and women (their gender and another gender as well). There is no expectation that this attraction will be equally divided between the two genders.
- **Transgender** refers to someone who lives as a member of a gender other than that assigned at birth based on anatomical sex.
- **Queer** is often used as an umbrella term to describe people who don't identify as straight (*straight* is typically similar in meaning to heterosexual). Queer is also used to describe people who have a nonnormative gender identity, or as a political affiliation. Due to its historical use as a derogatory term, it is not embraced or used by all members of the LGBTQ community. The term *queer* can often be used interchangeably with LGBTQ (queer folks instead of LGBTQ folks).

In the past several years, sexual orientation has become a flashpoint for a variety of social issues. Foremost among these has been the level at which it is legal for people of the same gender to be legally married in the eyes of the government. In 2015, the Supreme Court held that the Fourteenth Amendment requires states to recognize same-sex marriage and recognize those marriages that were conducted in other states (*Obergefell v. Hodges*). Same-sex marriages are recognized in twenty-six countries. Adoption by same-sex couples is also legal (since a 2016 ruling by the Supreme Court) in all fifty states.

Opposition to LGBTQ lifestyles, marriages, and adoptions has been common among many religious groups based upon their belief that these practices violate their sacred teachings (Christians, Muslims, Hindus). It is always interesting to observe, however, the manner in which public attitudes on campus about a particular issue seem to ebb and flow over the span of time.

Varying reports demonstrate gains and losses in the level at which LGBTQ lifestyles are accepted by the general population. Part of this process has been impacted by the ways in which the personal stories that people share (family, friends, neighbors, coworkers) have tended to personalize this issue to a level that is more significant than "Do you agree or disagree?" In a similar manner, the results of a 2017 survey by the Pew Research Center reported an ongoing trend toward greater levels of approval for gay marriage, even among more conservative religious denominations, political groups, and racial groupings.

An interesting perspective on reactions to sexual orientation comes from writer and activist Dylan Marron. He hosts a podcast entitled *Conversations with People Who Hate Me* in which he engages in conversations with people who have participated in hateful commentary toward him on Facebook. He invites those individuals on the program to get better acquainted, talk about the hate speech, and begin to understand one another better as people. Marron coined the phrase "Empathy is not endorsement." This powerful statement calls on us to look beyond our differences (in situations where we might think that a person with a given label is engaged in immoral behavior) to get to know the person behind the label, and to show empathy for the person.

In today's world, it is probable that you have friends or acquaintances who have declared their sexual orientation as lesbian, gay, bisexual, transgender, or queer. Is that how you primarily think about them—that is, in relation to their sexual orientation? Probably not. It is likely that you think of them in relation to a variety of personal characteristics like being funny, thoughtful, opinionated, or faithful and trusted as a friend. That reality exemplifies the complexity of our individual identities and the manner in which they interact with one another. We will discuss this further in our conversation below about intersectionality.

As you think about your own identity in relation to sexual orientation, consider the three following questions:

1. What words would you use to describe your identity in relation to sexual orientation?
2. What is your level of exposure (friends, family, classmates) to individuals from the LGBTQ community?
3. How would you describe your values and attitudes in relation to this identity?

Socioeconomic Status

Socioeconomic status is the social standing or class of an individual or group. It is often measured as a combination of education, occupation, and income. These factors are clearly interrelated, as people with higher levels of education generally have better occupational choices and, therefore, earn higher salaries. These factors have also been shown to have an impact on home environment, health, literacy skills, verbal and nonverbal communication skills, and the nature of school and neighborhood environments. By enrolling in college, and then graduating, you have enhanced economic opportunities for your future and that of your family.

Sociologists often describe how these factors combine to form five to seven different class divisions. Here is one model based on a median household income of $74,580 in 2022 as reported by the U.S. Census Bureau:

- **Upper class:** greater than $153,000
- **Upper-middle class:** $94,001 to $153,000
- **Middle class:** $58,021 to $94,000
- **Lower-middle class:** $30,001 to $58,020
- **Lower class:** less than or equal to $30,000

If you do a Google search for these terms, you will find a variety of income levels listed for each category. In some ways, these delineations are rather subjective and are open to change

based upon the prevailing economic climate. These dollar figures, however, should give you a general idea of how the various groupings are defined.

As you reflect on socioeconomic status as an identity, consider the following questions:

1. Which of these socioeconomic class categories are compatible with what you know about your family background?
2. What did you notice about your family's income level and those of your friends?
3. Did your family's income level present any unique challenges for you?

Much of the conversation about socioeconomic identity in America has been focused on a different metric: the differences between groups identified as the *haves* and the *have-nots*. The haves are those individuals and families who have access to all of the resources they need to live the good life, and the have-nots are individuals and families who experience an ongoing struggle to meet their basic needs.

People often have a sense of their personal socioeconomic status based on their subjective experiences of having enough, more than enough, or not enough resources to get by. The individualistic culture of the United States tends to place the responsibility of financial success, or lack thereof, on the effort of the individual. This perspective does not take into account the enhanced resources and connections of the affluent and the lack of access to resources or connections of those who are in the working class or in poverty. Education is a path to upward mobility and increased economic stability. College graduates are more likely to vote, have health and life insurance, and enjoy other advantages.

It bears mentioning that the perspective of Americans on being a have or a have-not is distinctly different from what might be perceived in other, less fortunate, locations around the world. The United Nations, in a 1995 resolution, defined poverty in a more qualitative manner, distinguishing between "absolute" and "overall" poverty:

Absolute poverty A condition characterised by severe deprivation of basic human needs, including food, safe drinking water, sanitation facilities, health, shelter, education and information. It depends not only on income but also on access to services.

Overall poverty May include lack of income and productive resources to ensure sustainable livelihoods; hunger and malnutrition; ill health; limited or lack of access to education and other basic services; increased morbidity and mortality from illness; homelessness and inadequate housing; unsafe environments and social discrimination and exclusion. It is also characterised by lack of participation in decision making and in civil, social and cultural life. It occurs in all countries: as mass poverty in many developing countries, pockets of poverty amid wealth in developed countries, loss of livelihoods as a result of economic recession, sudden poverty as a result of disaster or conflict, the poverty of low-wage workers, and the utter destitution of people who fall outside family support systems, social institutions and safety nets.

These definitions emphasize the level at which poverty is a global issue. By-products of people living in poverty around the world include illness, limited access to educational opportunities, deprivation of basic human needs, inadequate housing, unsafe environments, and lack of participation in civil decision making.

Entering college, you can often observe the impact of socioeconomic status among your classmates. There are undoubtedly students in your classes whose parents are paying for their tuition, room and board, and expenses. They may have their own car to drive, become members of a fraternity or sorority, and take full advantage of extracurricular and academic opportunities such as studying abroad for a semester. Other students, however, may be scraping together their tuition and living expenses through a variety of part-time jobs, loans, and financial aid. Moving ahead from one semester to the next and paying tuition is, for them, a constant source of anxiety. The possibility of doing something extra or taking a spring break trip is totally out of the question. And to be fair, a majority of college students probably find themselves somewhere between these two extremes.

As you think about your own identity in relation to socioeconomic status, consider the following questions:

1. What words would you use to describe your identity in relation to socioeconomic status?
2. When you think about your childhood, how would you assess the socioeconomic status of your family? Is your current situation different from that of your family growing up?
3. What are your attitudes and beliefs about people living in poverty (provision of welfare, people in poverty seen as being different, the need to do more, level of social empathy)?

Review, Discuss, and Apply

INTERACTIVE SELF-SCORING QUIZZES

Discussion Questions

1. What surprised you about the major identities that we all carry with us as we interact with the world?
2. Do you find that you may have certain preconceptions about various identities?
3. At what level do you have friendships and relationships with people who are different from you in one or more ways?

Module 9.2 | The Types and Impacts of Identities

LO 9.2.1 To articulate observed examples of privileged identities

LO 9.2.2 To articulate observed examples of targeted identities

We define ourselves and interact with others based on our identities as described above. The concept of **intersectionality** is often used to describe how our identities merge and overlap. Think, for example, about the many different combinations of words that people could use to describe themselves in relation to ability, age, ethnicity, gender, race, religion, sexual orientation, and socioeconomic status. The possibilities are virtually endless—which speaks once again to the fact that all of us, and our stories, are incredibly unique. In a very real way, each of us lives at the intersection of our individual identities.

Make It Personal | Who Are You?

Before we proceed, take a few minutes to reflect on your learning in relation to your own identities. Identify some terms that you would use to describe yourself in relation to each of your identities:

Ability:	
Age:	
Ethnicity:	
Gender:	
Race:	
Religion:	
Sexual Orientation:	
Socioeconomic Status:	

The idea of intersectionality is more than a philosophical theory or an academic exercise. As individuals, we are looking at the world, and our relationships with others through a variety of lenses (Black, transgender, wealthy, woman, Muslim, Haitian). Some of those lenses may be more significant to us than others, perhaps on the basis of how much they help or hinder us as we move through our lives. We will now explore two subtle, yet powerful, aspects of intersectionality that impact our identities, our lives, and our interactions with one another: privileged identities and targeted identities.

Privileged Identities

Privileged identities tend to be associated with ease of access—that is, the more privileged identities a person holds, the more likely that person will be to obtain desired positions of employment, residence, opportunity, and power. Privilege can be observed at interpersonal, cultural, and institutional levels. In the United States, the following social identity groups are more likely to have privileged identities:

- White people
- Nondisabled people
- Heterosexuals
- Males
- Christians
- Middle- or upper-class people
- English speakers

Privileged identities do not guarantee success. They may, however, make the pathway to success less challenging and more achievable. Individuals with privileged identities commonly believe they have earned the privileges they enjoy, or that anyone who wishes to have these privileges could work to earn them if they chose to do so. In the words of former University of Oklahoma football coach Barry Switzer, "Some people are born on third base and go through life thinking they hit a triple."

Privileged identities do tend to provide a head start in progress toward framing and achieving life goals. It is worth noting, however, that many privileged people have no real awareness of the advantages they have. You might have encountered some people of privilege on your campus. They were born into privilege, like the way that their life is proceeding, and feel comfortable with their progress toward desired goals, but they are largely unaware that their privilege is contributing to their accomplishments in dramatic ways.

There is, of course, a need to balance the views of individuals with privileged identities. By definition, they did not earn those benefits. Any benefits that come from privileged identities come as a result of skin color, native language, native country, gender, and/or religious affiliation, and others that may be culture specific. Those born with privileged identities can exploit those circumstances and hold themselves to be above everyone who may be different from them in one or more ways. Alternatively, they can maintain a spirit of humility with a view that with their privilege comes an opportunity to be in relationships with others who may not have the same inherent level of opportunity.

Targeted Identities

Opposite privileged identities on the identity spectrum are **targeted identities**. Individuals with targeted identities usually come from typically marginalized, disenfranchised, and oppressed groups. Targeted identities are associated with obstacles that range from microaggressions (covered in the next section) to internalized oppression, to violence. Individuals with targeted identities are typically considered to be outside the "norm" of their culture or organization. For each of the identities that we have discussed, there are individuals who may be oppressed based on their group membership and identity (e.g., race–nonwhite, gender–women, sexual orientation–LGBTQ+). People with targeted identities can easily identify the privilege they have lived without.

Closely related to targeted identities are **stereotypes**. A stereotype is a widely held but fixed and oversimplified image or idea of a particular group or class of people. Stereotypical thinking can be found in relation to any of the features of diversity that we have discussed (ability, age, ethnicity, gender, race, religion, sexual orientation, socioeconomic status):

Ability
- People with physical disabilities are also intellectually challenged.
- People who are intellectually gifted have little in the way of personality.
- People who are excellent in their area of performance were just lucky to be born that way.

Age
- People over the age of 40 are less productive.
- Young people are irresponsible and lack direction in their lives.

Ethnicity
- Hispanics are all illegal aliens.
- All Arabs and Muslims are terrorists.
- All Americans are generally considered to be friendly, generous, and tolerant, but also arrogant, impatient, and domineering.

Gender
- Women are not as strong as men.
- Women are supposed to be submissive and do as they are told.
- Men are better at math than women.
- Men do not cook, sew, or do crafts.

Race
- White people don't have rhythm.
- African Americans are good at basketball.
- All Asians are mathematical geniuses.

Religion
- Christians are self-righteous and narrow-minded about social issues.
- Jews are greedy and business minded.
- Muslims are terrorists.

Sexual Orientation
- People who are gay have artistic abilities.
- Lesbians hate men.
- People who are transgender are just confused.

Socioeconomic Status
- People who are poor are unmotivated to improve their life circumstances.
- People who are rich don't care about others.

How many of the stereotypes you just read do you find offensive? How many of them reflect thoughts you have had yourself? None of us wants to be a victim of stereotypical thinking. At the same time, we all are reluctant to admit that we might hold certain stereotypes about certain groups. We all have **biases**, or preconceived ideas about people who are different from us, whether we are aware of those biases or not. The key is to come to grips with that thinking, identify its sources, and work to become a more accepting and inclusive individual.

Test Yourself | My Comfort Levels

Consider the elements of the identities we have discussed, and the range of diversities included in each. As part of that reflection, also think about the range of relationships that you currently have in your life. Do those relationships reflect your comfort with individual differences?

Identities	Very Uncomfortable	Uncomfortable	Neutral	Comfortable	Very Comfortable
My level of personal comfort around issues of ability in my interactions with others is:	☐	☐	☐	☐	☐
My level of personal comfort around issues of age in my interactions with others is:	☐	☐	☐	☐	☐
My level of personal comfort around issues of ethnicity in my interactions with others is:	☐	☐	☐	☐	☐
My level of personal comfort around issues of gender in my interactions with others is:	☐	☐	☐	☐	☐
My level of personal comfort around issues of race in my interactions with others is:	☐	☐	☐	☐	☐
My level of personal comfort around issues of religion in my interactions with others is:	☐	☐	☐	☐	☐
My level of personal comfort around issues of sexual orientation in my interactions with others is:	☐	☐	☐	☐	☐
My level of personal comfort around issues of socioeconomic status in my interactions with others is:	☐	☐	☐	☐	☐

What are some things you can do to expand the level of diversity reflected here and in your daily interactions and ongoing relationships?

> **Think Deeper** | Privileged Identities, Targeted Identities, and Stereotypes
>
> 1. How would you assess the level at which you have privileged or targeted identities?
> 2. Have you ever been the victim of a stereotype?
> 3. Do you currently hold stereotypes about certain people groups?

Review, Discuss, and Apply

Discussion Questions

1. What are some steps that we all can take to reduce the impact and influence of privileged and targeted identities?
2. Can you identify examples of privileged and targeted identities as portrayed in the media?

Module 9.3 | Diversity As a Weapon and a Tool

LO 9.3.1 To identify and describe situations in which diversity is used as a weapon

LO 9.3.2 To identify and describe situations in which diversity can be used as a tool

The fact that we live in an increasingly diverse world is indisputable. The question for each of us is how we respond to people who are different from us. We have a choice whether to use diversity as a weapon or a tool.

Diversity As a Weapon

When an individual, or a group, has identities that are viewed in a negative, limiting, critical, or hurtful manner, opportunities for success and self-fulfillment can be denied, and the people or groups can experience personal anguish. In this section, we will talk about four by-products of that type of thinking:

- Microaggressions
- Prejudice
- Discrimination
- Oppression

Microaggressions Microaggressions are everyday actions (verbal, interpersonal, environmental) that can be intentional or unintentional. Regardless of the circumstance, however, these actions communicate negative, insulting, derogatory, or prejudicial messages to an individual or a group. Although typically associated with racially motivated slights or snubs, microaggressions can

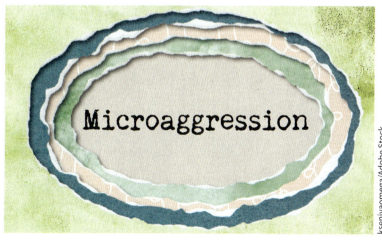

be directed toward a number of identities. An article in *Psychology Today* (Sue, 2010) cited the following examples:

Ethnicity

- When bargaining over the price of an item, a store owner says to a customer, "Don't try to Jew me down." (Hidden message: Jews are stingy and money-grubbing.)

Gender

- An assertive female manager is labeled a "bitch," while her male counterpart is described as a "forceful leader." (Hidden message: Women should be passive and allow men to be decision-makers.)
- A female physician wearing a stethoscope is mistaken for a nurse. (Hidden messages: Women should occupy nurturing and not decision-making roles. Women are less capable than men.)
- Men whistle or make catcalls as a woman walks down the street. (Hidden messages: Your body/appearance is for the enjoyment of men. You are a sex object.)

Racial

- A white man checks his wallet or a woman clutches her purse as a Black or Latino man approaches or passes them. (Hidden message: You and your group are criminals.)
- An Asian American, born and raised in the United States, is complimented for speaking "good English." (Hidden messages: You are not a true American. You are a perpetual foreigner in your own country.)
- A Black couple is seated at a table in the restaurant next to the kitchen despite there being other empty and more desirable tables located at the front. (Hidden message: Black people are treated differently in this restaurant.)

Sexual Orientation

- A young person uses the term *gay* to describe a movie that she didn't like. (Hidden message: Being gay is associated with negative and undesirable characteristics.)
- A lesbian client in therapy reluctantly discloses her sexual orientation to a straight therapist by stating she is "into women." The therapist indicates he is not shocked by the disclosure because he once had a client who was "into dogs." (Hidden message: Same-sex attraction is abnormal and deviant.)

Granted, microaggressions can be intentional or unintentional. For those who wish to hold themselves accountable in limiting the use of unintentional microaggressions, one strategy would be to build relationships with individuals from diverse identity groups.

Prejudice If you are aware of holding a negative belief about a person or a people group without reason to do so, that thought pattern is an example of **prejudice**. If one is unaware, the belief is unconscious. People are often conscious of some of their prejudicial beliefs and are able to regulate them (choose whether or not to disclose or act on them). Whether conscious or unconscious, however, these thoughts and feelings are still prejudicial. To identify examples, "Breaking the Prejudice Habit" (breakingprejudice.org) has developed the "Unconscious Prejudice Questionnaire," which the author states has no right or wrong answers but serves as a tool for self-reflection.[1]

---

[1] These examples have been adapted from the work of "Breaking the Prejudice Habit" and their "Unconscious Prejudice Questionnaire" and supplemented by the authors.

Ability
- A person with disabilities speaks to you in a local store. How do you respond?
- Your best friend is dating someone with Tourette Syndrome.
- A classmate who is obviously the smartest person in the room also has highly under-developed social skills.

Age
- You are assigned to work with a classmate on a project. The classmate is twenty-five years older than you.
- Your grandmother continually asks you for assistance with her computer.
- An elderly neighbor frequently calls you a name other than your own.

Ethnicity
- Your best friend begins dating a person from an ethnic group other than yours.
- You are Caucasian and go to a Japanese restaurant where all of the employees and patrons are Asian.
- Your newly assigned doctor is Indian and does not speak clear English.

Gender
- A married friend announces that he has decided to be a stay-at-home dad.
- You meet someone and cannot figure out their gender.
- You see a little boy playing with dolls.

Race
- You see an African American man wearing a hoodie, so you cross to the other side of the street.
- A Native American wears clothing compatible with his heritage.

Sexual Orientation
- You see two men holding hands and being affectionate with one another.
- A person of the same sex begins openly flirting with you.
- You go on a date with someone of the opposite sex who previously dated a person of their same sex.

Socioeconomic Status
- You are walking down the street and a homeless person asks you for money.
- Your neighbor tells you that a vacant lot near your neighborhood is going to be developed for public housing.

Discrimination

Discrimination can take many forms. When a member of a more powerful social group acts based on prejudice and directly impacts a member or members of a less powerful social group, discrimination has occurred. Discrimination may occur consciously, within the individual's awareness, or unconsciously, outside the individual's awareness.

Here are some examples to consider and discuss:

- Discrimination can occur on an individual level (choosing not to hire someone who is in a wheelchair because of unconscious prejudice) or on a societal level (an office does not have wheelchair access, which prevents people in wheelchairs from working there).
- One can discriminate along any domain of identity in which there is a power differential. A consistent pattern of individual and systemic discrimination occurring over time creates the phenomenon of oppression, discussed below.
- Until the early years of the twentieth century, women were not allowed to vote in the United States.
- The Holocaust happened partially because of prejudice toward Jews.
- Afghanistani women could not attend school and had to cover their faces when outside their home.
- In the United States, Black people could not sit in the front of buses or use the same water fountains as White people until the 1960s.
- Private clubs are often exclusive. For example, some don't allow members who are Black or Jewish.
- After 9/11, people who looked Middle Eastern often were viewed suspiciously and often were the victims of prejudice.
- Some landlords will not rent to a gay couple.
- After the bombing of Pearl Harbor, Japanese people who lived in the United States, including Japanese-American citizens, were arrested and held in internment camps.
- Apartheid in South Africa consisted of racial segregation where non-whites could not vote and had to live in communities separate from Whites.
- It is sometimes assumed that someone who is physically disabled is also mentally disabled.

Oppression Oppression occurs when a person or group that holds relative societal power, uses this power consciously or unconsciously, to deny opportunities, resources, or access to others because of their group membership. The system of oppression is maintained by social beliefs and practices. Here are some examples of oppression:

- A society in which women are the property of their fathers or husbands. Women are not permitted to wear clothing of their own choosing or to go anywhere without permission from a man. Women are being oppressed.
- A society in which people of a certain race are denied opportunities and equality under the law. People within the disfavored race are not permitted to learn to read or to attend

school. They have to live in certain designated areas and must do the jobs that they are told to do by leaders of the society. The people who are denied opportunities are being oppressed.

- A society in which people of a certain religion are considered inferior to people who accept a state religion. Those who practice their own religious beliefs can be punished or even jailed for their opinions and practices. In this society, the people who practice the forbidden religion are oppressed.
- A society that is under the thumb of a cruel dictator. Anyone who disagrees with the policies of the dictator can be killed for sharing their opinion and voicing their disagreement. The people who live under the dictator are oppressed.
- A society that is controlled by a small percentage of very wealthy people. The wealthy people deny opportunities to those who are poor. The poor work for almost no wages and struggle to achieve a basic human standard of living, such as having food and shelter. The poor are carefully controlled by the oppressors and prevented from organizing or resisting the will of the wealthy. In this society, the poor are oppressed.
- A society that carefully controls the freedom of speech of all people. The internet is not accessible to the public, certain books are banned, and the media work for the state and are permitted to report only the news that the state allows. This is an example of a society where the people under the control of the authority are oppressed.
- A society that allows migrants to enter its borders but will not grant them any rights. The migrants are not allowed to participate in the political process and are not protected by the laws that apply to citizens. The migrants can be forced to work for low wages and are denied basic services such as access to food and health care. In this situation, the migrants are oppressed by society.

Diversity As a Tool

On the flip side, diversity can serve as a powerful tool for bringing people together to accomplish great things on individual and societal levels. It is critically important that each of us examine any bias we have, our beliefs, and our personal experiences on an ongoing basis. This should be a never-ending process that helps us learn more about ourselves and others. In this way, we can continually enhance the ways in which we interact with people who may be different from us in one or more ways.

It is likely that readers of this chapter hold a variety of thoughts, opinions, and feelings about the content we have just explored. That is a great outcome! As we have described, each of us has multiple identities. Some of those identities may be sources of discomfort as we examine our own personal histories. Further, we may have thought patterns and beliefs upon which we have built a collection of biases about other identities and people groups. Ultimately, the choice to actively engage with diverse groups of people lies with you, and the level at which you wish to take on the lifelong journey of moving toward acceptance of others who may be different from you. On the bright side, you may find that connections and relationships with people who are different from us individually can be an opportunity for personal enrichment. We wish the best for you as you travel this path.

Test Yourself | Diversity/Cultural Competence Self-Assessment

As a summative activity, spend a few minutes reflecting on the experiences, attitudes, and beliefs that have contributed to your level of engagement with diversity, equity, and inclusion. The following topics for self-reflection come from the Central Vancouver Island Multicultural Society and are used by a number of organizations.

Awareness		Never	Sometimes/ Occasionally	Fairly Often/ Pretty Well	Always/ Very Well
Value diversity	I view human difference as positive and a cause for celebration.	☐	☐	☐	☐
Know myself	I have a clear sense of my own ethnic, cultural, and racial identity.	☐	☐	☐	☐
Share my culture	I am aware that in order to learn more about others, I need to understand and be prepared to share my own culture.	☐	☐	☐	☐
Be aware of areas of discomfort	I am aware of my discomfort when I encounter differences in race, color, religion, sexual orientation, language, and ethnicity.	☐	☐	☐	☐
Check my assumptions	I am aware of the assumptions that I hold about people of cultures different from my own.	☐	☐	☐	☐
Challenge my stereotypes	I am aware of my stereotypes as they arise and have developed personal strategies for reducing the harm they cause.	☐	☐	☐	☐
Reflect on how my culture informs my judgment	I am aware of how my cultural perspective influences my judgment about what are "appropriate," "normal," or "superior" behaviors, values, and communication styles.	☐	☐	☐	☐
Accept ambiguity	I accept that in cross-cultural situations, there can be uncertainty and that uncertainty can make me anxious. It can also mean that I do not respond quickly and take the time needed to get more information.	☐	☐	☐	☐
Be curious	I take any opportunity to put myself in places where I can learn about difference and create relationships.	☐	☐	☐	☐
Aware of my privilege if I am White	If I am a White person working with an Aboriginal or Person of Color, I understand that I will likely be perceived as a person with power and racial privilege, and that I may not be seen as "unbiased" or as an ally.	☐	☐	☐	☐
Aware of social justice issues	I'm aware of the impact of the social context on the lives of culturally diverse populations and how power, privilege, and social oppression influence their lives.	☐	☐	☐	☐
Gain from my mistakes	I will make mistakes and I will learn from them.	☐	☐	☐	☐
Assess the limits of my knowledge	I will recognize that my knowledge of certain cultural groups is limited and commit to creating opportunities to learn more.	☐	☐	☐	☐
Acknowledge the importance of difference	I know that differences in color, culture, ethnicity, etc. are important parts of an individual's identity that they value and so do I. I will not hide behind the claim of "color blindness."	☐	☐	☐	☐
Understand the influence culture can have	I recognize that cultures change over time and can vary from person to person, as does attachment to culture.	☐	☐	☐	☐

Awareness		Never	Sometimes/ Occasionally	Fairly Often/ Pretty Well	Always/ Very Well
Commit to lifelong learning	I recognize that achieving cultural competence involves a commitment to learning over a lifetime.	☐	☐	☐	☐
Understand the impact of racism, sexism, homophobia...	I recognize that stereotypical attitudes and discriminatory actions can dehumanize or even encourage violence against individuals because of their membership in groups which are different from myself.	☐	☐	☐	☐
Know my limitations	I continue to develop my capacity for assessing areas where there are gaps in my knowledge.	☐	☐	☐	☐
Awareness of multiple social identities	I recognize that people have intersecting multiple identities drawn from race, sex, religion, ethnicity, etc., and the importance of each of these identities varies from person to person.	☐	☐	☐	☐
Intercultural and intracultural differences	I acknowledge both intercultural and intracultural differences.	☐	☐	☐	☐
Point of reference to assess appropriate behavior	I'm aware that everyone has a culture and my own culture should not be regarded as a point of reference to assess which behavior is appropriate or inappropriate.	☐	☐	☐	☐
Adapt to different situations	I am developing ways to interact respectfully and effectively with individuals and groups.	☐	☐	☐	☐
Challenge discriminatory and/or racist behavior	I can effectively intervene when I observe others behaving in racist and/or discriminatory behavior.	☐	☐	☐	☐
Communicate across cultures	I am able to adapt my communication style to effectively communicate with people who communicate in ways that are different from my own.	☐	☐	☐	☐
Seek out situations to expand my skills	I seek out people who challenge me to maintain and increase the cross-cultural skills I have.	☐	☐	☐	☐
Become engaged	I am actively involved in initiatives, small or big, that promote understanding among members of diverse groups.	☐	☐	☐	☐
Act respectfully in cross-cultural situations	I can act in ways that demonstrate respect for the culture and beliefs of others.	☐	☐	☐	☐
Be flexible	I work hard to understand the perspectives of others and consult with my diverse colleagues about culturally respectful and appropriate courses of action.	☐	☐	☐	☐
Be adaptive	I know and use a variety of relationship-building skills to create connections with people who are different from me.	☐	☐	☐	☐
Recognize my own cultural biases	I can recognize my own cultural biases in a given situation and I'm aware not to act based on my biases.	☐	☐	☐	☐
Be aware of within-group differences	I'm aware of within-group differences and I would not generalize a specific behavior presented by an individual to the entire cultural community.	☐	☐	☐	☐

These prompts and your responses provide a great starting point for personal reflection and action. Consider the possibility of gathering with a diverse group of fellow students to discuss the results of your self-assessment and how these might lead to specific action steps. As part of that process, also consider how you might invite others to hold you accountable for your plan of action.

Adapted from: Central Vancouver Island Multicultural Society (2021). Cultural Competency Self-assessment Checklist. Retrieved from https://www.cvims.org/community/cultural-competency/.

222 CHAPTER 9 Embrace Diversity, Equity, and Inclusion

 DOWNLOAD DOCUMENTS & TEMPLATES

Make It Personal | My Experiences and Responses

We have all been in situations during which we observed another person being treated in a disrespectful manner because of a personal characteristic. It is also likely that we might look back on these experiences and think of what we might have done differently (e.g., intervened on behalf of the individual who was a focus of this maltreatment). In the space provided below, provide a summary of the incident, your response at the time, and what you might have done differently.

Description of the Incident	My Response at the Time	An Alternative Response

Review, Discuss, and Apply

 INTERACTIVE SELF-SCORING QUIZZES

Discussion Questions

1. In recent times, what are some examples of diversity being used as a weapon?
2. In our personal relationships, how might we more effectively use diversity as a tool?

Think Ahead | Career and Lifelong Applications

There is no denying that we live in a diverse world. This reality will continue to be more and more evident in the coming years. This will impact both your personal and professional life. Consider this data (Reiners, 2023):

- People groups who were formerly seen as minorities may be in the majority by 2045.
- Forty-eight percent of people in Gen Z are racial minorities.
- Millennials are 19 percent more diverse as a group than baby boomers.
- Women are more likely to experience discrimination and sexual harassment.
- Of U.S. employees, 40 percent feel their companies aren't doing enough to hire and support more members of the LGBTQ+ community.

Individuals who are comfortable with their own identities and embrace the opportunity to build relationships with people who are different from them in one or more ways will have greater opportunities to learn and grow through these interactions. Consider how diversity, equity, and inclusion will impact your personal and professional life.

Earlier, we chose words that describe each of our eight identities. As you think about your responses, also consider the groups of people with whom you have typically associated over the span of your life. This could include family, friends, neighbors, high school classmates, and fellow participants in church and community activities. What kinds of diversity would we find across these groups of people? There may be a great deal of diversity noted, or you may conclude, "These people are more like me than they are different." Regardless of your response, college is a great time to prepare for the future by consciously seeking out friendships and relationships with people who are different from you in one or more ways. That intentional effort will prepare you to better collaborate and interact with a wide range of people. That mindset and skill will be an advantage in the workplace and in your personal life.

GraphicPapa/Adobe Stock

Module 9.3 Diversity As a Weapon and a Tool

Another insight into who we are as individuals is our ability to examine the level at which we have been privileged or targeted in relation to our identities. Those experiences have helped to form our character and sense of personhood. Moving forward, it is important to think about what we might need to learn from our experiences of privilege or being targeted. In our personal and professional lives, these reflections can serve as a reminder not to flaunt privilege or engage in targeting language or behavior. That will make us better friends, neighbors, and coworkers to others.

We have all observed times when diversity has served as a weapon and as a tool. Clearly, we would all hope for a world in which diversity provides opportunities for learning, differing perspectives, dialogue, and the creation of community. Each of us has an opportunity to be an advocate for the safety and well-being of others who might be ridiculed or excluded solely of the basis of their personal identities. This mindset helps to build harmony and a collaborative spirit in our communities and places of employment.

What Would You Do?

In this chapter, Ang and Isabela need your advice.

 VIDEO CONTENT

ANG

Ang had a really bad experience at work the other day that left him feeling very uneasy. What should he do?

Watch Ang's video: **The Power of Words**

ISABELA

Isabela is getting annoyed that people seem to have preconceived ideas about her position on various issues just because she's Latina. What can she do about it?

Watch Isabela's video: **My Heritage**

What would you tell Ang? What would you tell Isabela?

Take Some Action | Here and Now

 DOWNLOAD DOCUMENTS & TEMPLATES

We all have strengths and weaknesses when it comes to understanding and accepting differences. Being aware of those strengths and weaknesses is key to success in college, in the workplace, and in life.

Review your outcomes on the *Test Yourself* assessments throughout this chapter and your responses to the *Think Deeper* questions. Reflect on your results and responses, and then answer these questions:

1. What are your strengths with respect to understanding people who aren't like you? How will you put those strengths to work for you toward succeeding in college? How will sharpening those strengths in college help you be successful in the workplace?

2. How do you want to improve your strengths when it comes to understanding differences?

3. Review the suggested action steps in that area and choose two or three of those steps to commit to here and now, and for each, say how taking that action step will help you succeed in college and beyond.

Share and discuss your responses to these questions with a friend, classmate, or family member.

Chapter 9 Practice Quiz

Chapter Summary

Module 9.1 Our Multiple Identities: The Many Ways That We Are Different

- Ability is defined as the means and skills to perform well in a particular area. Each of us has areas of ability and areas where we can improve our performance. This requires that we each seek to improve our own abilities, value the abilities of others, and respect our individual differences.
- Age refers to your chronological age. We all start as babies. From there we grow and develop into adulthood. Each developmental phase across the span of life includes new opportunities to grow and challenges to overcome.
- Ethnicity refers to a group of people who share a common cultural background or descent.
- Gender refers to the attitudes, feelings, and behaviors that are associated with a person's assigned biological sex.
- Race is a social construct used to categorize people into groups based on combinations of shared physical characteristics and ancestry.
- Religion is any cultural system of designated behaviors and practices, worldviews, texts, sanctified places, ethics, or organizations that relate humanity to the supernatural or transcendental.
- Sexual orientation is an enduring pattern of romantic or sexual attraction (or a combination of these) to persons of the opposite sex or gender, the same sex or gender, or both sexes or more than one gender.
- Socioeconomic status is the social standing or class of an individual or group. It is often measured as a combination of education, occupation, and income.

Module 9.2 The Types and Impacts of Identities

- Privileged identities tend to be associated with ease of access—that is, the more privileged identities one holds, the more likely that person will be to obtain desired positions of employment, residence, opportunity, and power. Privilege can be observed at interpersonal, cultural, and institutional levels.
- Targeted identities usually represent marginalized, disenfranchised, and oppressed groups. Targeted identities are associated with encountering obstacles that range from microaggressions, to internalized oppression, to violence.

Module 9.3 Diversity As a Weapon and a Tool

- Diversity can be used as a weapon. When an individual, or a group, has identities that are viewed in a negative, limiting, critical, or hurtful manner, opportunities for success and self-fulfillment can be denied, and people or groups can experience personal anguish in the form of microaggressions, prejudice, discrimination, and oppression.
- Diversity can serve as a powerful tool for bringing people together to accomplish great things on individual and societal levels. It is critically important that each of us examine our own biases, beliefs, and personal experiences on an ongoing basis. This should be a never-ending process that helps us learn more about ourselves and others.

Key Terms

Attitude The synthesis of emotions, beliefs, and behaviors toward a particular object, person, thing, or event

Awareness Knowledge or perception related to a situation or fact

Bias Prejudice in favor of or against a person or group compared with another, usually in a way considered to be unfair.

CliftonStrengths assessment A tool designed to help individuals identify their five core strengths

Deliberate practice Highest level of practice designed to improve performance, often with a teacher, coach, or mentor

Discrimination When a member of a more powerful social group acts on his or her prejudice and directly impacts a member or members of a less powerful social group

Diversity The range of different backgrounds and personal characteristics including ability, age, ethnicity, gender, race, religion, sexual orientation, and socioeconomic status

Ethnicity A common cultural background or descent shared by a group of people

Equity The fair and impartial treatment of all people, especially groups that have been historically denied fair treatment

Gender The attitudes, feelings, and behaviors that are associated with a person's assigned biological sex

Inclusion The provision of equal access, opportunities, and resources for people who might otherwise be excluded or marginalized based on their personal characteristics

Identities Constructs, including ability, age, ethnicity, gender, race, religion, sexual orientation, and socioeconomic status, that combine to characterize a particular individual

Intersectionality The complex combination of our overlapping identities and experiences

Microaggressions Verbal, nonverbal, and environmental brush-offs, rebukes, or insults, whether intentional or unintentional, that communicate negative messages to targeted individuals

Naïve practice Practice that involves going through the motions without any motivation to improve performance or reach a desired goal

Oppression Cruel and unjust treatment

Positive psychology A branch of psychological theory and practice that focuses on positive events and influences in life (e.g., happiness, joy, inspiration, gratitude, resilience, compassion, empathy)

Prejudice Preconceived opinion or judgement about a person or group not based on reason, fact, or actual experience

Privileged identities Personal identities associated with certain preferred groups that confer inherent advantages to those who hold them

Purposeful practice Practice that involves working to improve performance to meet a specified goal

Stereotypes Common but simplified ideas, images, and beliefs about a group or class of people

Strengths Our built-in capacities and abilities for particular ways of thinking, acting, feeling, and behaving

Targeted identities Personal identities associated with certain groups that lead to their being discriminated against, marginalized, excluded, oppressed, or exploited

Resources

Clifton StrengthsFinder: The Gallup Organization provides access to the Clifton StrengthsFinder. The results of this online survey will give you insight as to your top five areas of strength. You can find this assessment at https://www.gallup.com/cliftonstrengths/en/252137/home.aspx

Project Implicit Social Attitudes: As a way of assessing your own patterns of thought and belief, you may wish to complete one or more of the "Implicit Attitude Tests." This website, https://implicit.harvard.edu/implicit/selectatest.html, offers assessments on a variety of topics including Arab-Muslim, disability, gender-career, race, religion, native, skin tone, weight, gender science, sexuality, presidents, Asian, age, and weapons.

What is privilege? This video depicts an activity where people assess the level at which they have/have not experienced privilege in their lives. Retrieved from https://www.youtube.com/watch?v=hD5f8GuNuGQ

Your American Dream Score (https://movingupusa.com/calc/) is a survey that analyzes the level at which an individual has had experiences, systems, and services that have helped or hindered their opportunities in life.

References

Central Vancouver Island Multicultural Society (2021). Cultural Competency Self-assessment Checklist. Retrieved from https://www.cvims.org/community/cultural-competency/.

Chak, A. (2017, December 7). Beyond "he" and "she": The rise of non-binary pronouns. Retrieved from https://www.bbc.com/news/magazine-34901704

Connor, P., & Budiman, A. (2019, January 30). Immigrant share in U.S. nears record high but remains below that of many other countries. Retrieved from https://www.pewresearch.org/fact-tank/2019/01/30/immigrant-share-in-u-s-nears-record-high-but-remains-below-that-of-many-other-countries/

Eliason, N. (2018, July 7). 45 Deliberate practice examples for rapidly improving your skills. Retrieved from https://www.nateliason.com/blog/deliberate-practice-examples

Eliason, N. (2017, August 3). How to use deliberate practice to reach the top 1 percent of your field. Retrieved from https://observer.com/2017/08/how-to-use-deliberate-practice-to-reach-the-top-1-percent-malcolm-gladwell-anders-ericsson-habits-mastery/

Frey, W. H. (2018, September 10). The US will become "minority white" in 2045, Census projects. Retrieved from https://www.brookings.edu/blog/the-avenue/2018/03/14/the-us-will-become-minority-white-in-2045-census-projects/

Gallup, Inc. (2019, December 30). CliftonStrengths. Retrieved from https://www.gallup.com/cliftonstrengths/en/252137/home.aspx?utm_source=google&utm_medium=cpc&utm_campaign=Strengths_ECommerce_Brand_Search_US&utm_content=+cliftonstrengths&gclid=EAIaIQobChMIvOPqxpCk5wIVS73ACh2Xxw ZIEAAYASAAEgITtvD_BwE

Gladwell, M. (2008). *Outliers: Why some people succeed and some don't*. Little Brown & Co.

Goplen, J., & Plant, E. A. (2015). A Religious Worldview. *Personality and Social Psychology Bulletin, 41*(11), 1474–1487. doi: 10.1177/0146167215599761

Jenkins, R. (2014). *Social identity*. New York: Routledge.

Pew Research Center (2023). 5 key findings about LGBTQ+ Americans. Retrieved from https://www.pewresearch.org/short-reads/2023/06/23/5-key-findings-about-lgbtq-americans/#:~:text=Some%207%25%20of%20Americans%20are,of%20those%2065%20and%20older.

Pew Research Center (2017). Support for Same-Sex Marriage Grows, Even Among Groups That Had Been Skeptical. Retrieved from https://www.pewresearch.org/politics/2017/06/26/support-for-same-sex-marriage-grows-even-among-groups-that-had-been-skeptical/

Reiners, B. (2023, March 28). 50 diversity in the workplace statistics to know. *Built In*. https://builtin.com/diversity-inclusion/diversity-in-the-workplace-statistics

Seligman, M. E. P. (2002). Positive psychology, positive prevention, and positive therapy. In C. R.Snyder & S. J.Lopez (Eds.), *Handbook of positive psychology* (p. 3–9). Oxford University Press.

Strauss, W., & Howe, N. (1991). *Generations: The history of Americas future, 1584 to 2069*. William Morrow & Company, Inc.

Sue, D. W. (2010). Racial microaggressions in everyday life. *Psychology Today*. https://www.psychologytoday.com/us/blog/microaggressions-in-everyday-life/201010/racial-microaggressions-in-everyday-life

United Nations, Department of Public Information. (1995). *World Summit for Social Development: the Copenhagen Declaration and Programme of Action, 6–12 March 1995*. New York, NY.

U.S. Census Bureau. (2019, December 11). American Community Survey (ACS). Retrieved from https://www.census.gov/programs-surveys/acs/

CHAPTER 10

Find Your Happiness

Author's Introduction

"Don't wait around for other people to be happy for you. Any happiness you get you've got to make yourself."

—Alice Walker

CHAPTER OUTLINE	LEARNING OBJECTIVES
Envision, Pursue, and Persist: Tony Hsieh	
Module 10.1 Predicting Happiness Benefits of Happiness Understanding Happiness *Think Deeper: Understanding Cultural Differences in Happiness* Myths about Happiness *Test Yourself: Can You Find Benefits in Difficult Life Events?*	**LO 10.1** To understand the benefits and components of happiness
Module 10.2 Understanding Stress Sources and Types of Stress *Test Yourself: How Much Stress Are You Experiencing?* Effects of Stress Strategies for Managing Stress *Think Deeper: Coping with Stress*	**LO 10.2** To understand the causes of stress and identify strategies for managing it
Module 10.3 Increasing Happiness Change Your Thoughts *Test Yourself: How Optimistic Are You?* *Make It Personal: Feeling Gratitude* Change Your Behaviors *Think Deeper: Your Path to Happiness*	**LO 10.3** To develop strategies for increasing happiness
Think Ahead: Career and Lifelong Applications Take Some Action: Here and Now	
Chapter Summary Key Terms Resources References	

Envision, Pursue, and Persist | Tony Hsieh

Tony Hsieh grew up in the San Francisco area and was the son of two immigrant parents from Taiwan. Throughout his childhood, he was focused on starting different businesses. These included garage sales, lemonade stands, and even selling earthworms. This interest in developing a business eventually led him to selling custom buttons, which eventually earned hundreds of dollars a month. It also sparked his excitement for mail-order businesses and the joy of getting a package in the mail.

In 1999, Hsieh began investing in and advising a new company, Zappos.com, an online shoe company. He was eventually hired as the CEO. He is credited with the company's tremendous success. In his first ten years as CEO, Zappos grew substantially. It is now estimated to be worth more than a billion dollars.

Zappos is particularly well known for providing excellent customer service. How does this company create such a positive customer experience? It focuses on creating an employee culture that emphasizes happiness. Their core values speak to this as a priority. These values include "create fun," "build a positive team," and "pursue growth and learning." Their focus on a happy culture pays off. Why? Because companies with the best financial performance focus not only on profits, but also on passion and purpose.

Tony Hsieh described the advantages of creating a work culture focused on happiness in his book, appropriately titled *Delivering Happiness: A Path to Profits, Passion and Purpose*. As he writes, "There's three types of happiness and really happiness is about being able to combine pleasure, passion, and purpose in one's personal life. I think it's helpful and useful to actually think about all three in terms of how you can make customers happier, employees happier, and ultimately, investors happier."

This chapter examines how you can find greater happiness during your college years and beyond. First, you'll learn about the benefits and components of happiness as well as common myths we hold about finding happiness. The next section of the chapter describes the link between stress and physical and psychological well-being. It also describes different approaches you can use to manage stress. The final section provides specific strategies you can use to feel happier, no matter your natural tendency or life circumstances.

Module 10.1 Predicting Happiness

LO 10.1.1 To examine the benefits of happiness

LO 10.1.2 To describe the different components of happiness

LO 10.1.3 To review common myths about happiness

Most people use the term **happiness** regularly in daily life. You feel happy when you do well on a test, get a summer job you want, or have a fun evening with friends. As these examples illustrate, the term *happiness* refers to experiencing different kinds of positive emotions. These include joy, pride, and contentment.

Benefits of Happiness

Why is it so important to focus on happiness? Why have we chosen to devote an entire chapter in this textbook to this topic?

Research demonstrates that happiness is strongly linked to psychological and physical well-being. Here are some of the benefits of happiness:

- **Better cardiovascular health**—People who are happy have lower heart rates and blood pressure; they are also less likely to develop coronary heart disease (one of the leading causes of death in the United States).

- **Stronger immune system**—People who are happy are less likely to come down with the common cold, even when researchers have directly exposed them to a cold virus (with the study participants' permission); their bodies show a stronger immune response, meaning they are better able to fight off infection.

- **Fewer aches and pains**—People who are happy have fewer minor health complaints, such as muscle strain, dizziness, and heartburn; this link is even true for people who chronic diseases such as arthritis.
- **Fewer long-term health conditions**—People who are happy are less likely to develop long-term health conditions, such as chronic pain and frailty (meaning impaired strength, endurance, and balance); they are also less likely to have a stroke.

Most important, people who are happy actually live longer. In one study, researchers examined the types of emotions Catholic nuns expressed in their daily diaries. They measured expressions of positive emotions, such as amusement, contentment, gratitude, and love. Then they examined how old the nuns were when they died. Amazingly enough, they found that nuns who expressed more positive emotions in their diaries lived on average seven to ten years longer!

Now, a really important question to ask is the following: What explains the link between happiness and health? After all, perhaps better health leads to happiness, instead of the other way around. To test this question, researchers often examine people over time. They measure people's happiness at one point in time, and then assess their health symptoms later on. What do these studies tell us? Happy people are less likely to develop health symptoms over time, and sometimes even become healthier. In sum, being happy is indeed good for your health.

Understanding Happiness VIDEO CONTENT

We often think about happiness as a single dimension. We think about times in which we've felt happy. We can also think of times in which we've felt less happy. But happiness actually consists of three distinct components (see **Figure 10.1**).

Components of Happiness
One component of happiness is pleasure, meaning how much you enjoy daily life experiences. You might experience happiness from eating a great piece of cheesecake, seeing a beautiful sunset, or watching a funny movie. These experiences all lead to positive emotions, which make us feel happy.

But this component of happiness is the least important. Why? Because each of these experiences is fleeting. You might feel very happy while listening to a beautiful piece of music, but this feeling fades once the song is over. This is why things that may cause brief moments of pleasure, such as buying a new purse or drinking a delicious milkshake, don't lead to long-term happiness.

Another essential component of happiness is feeling engaged with your life. People who are engaged with their lives understand their strengths. They also find ways to use these talents in their daily lives.

Why is engagement such an important part of happiness? People who are fully engaged in an activity experience **flow**, a psychological state in which time seems to fly by. They are fully absorbed in what they are doing and are not aware of time passing. You might experience the state of flow when going for a run, listening to music, or participating in a favorite hobby.

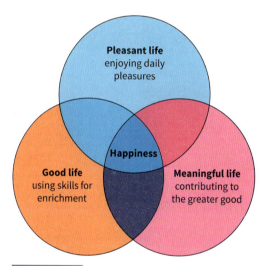

FIGURE 10.1 Three components of happiness.

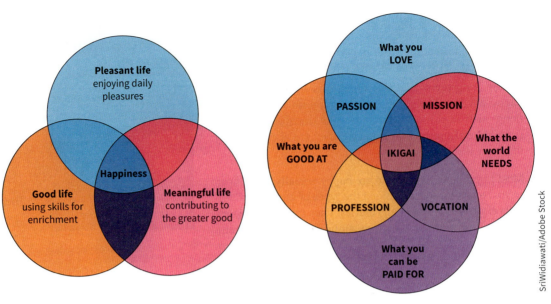

FIGURE 10.2 The concept of ikigai integrates all three components of happiness and connects your personal interests—passion, mission—with professional and vocational interests. In this way, ikigai is happiness plus a salary!

You can also find this type of deep engagement in academic classes. In fact, choosing classes, and a major, that you find fully engaging will help you feel happier. (You'll also tend to do better.)

One of the most important parts of happiness is feeling a deeper sense of meaning and purpose in life. Researchers describe **purpose** as "a stable and generalized intention to accomplish something that is at the same time meaningful to the self and consequential for the world beyond the self." For example, a person's sense of purpose could be a certain passion or desire to work for a cause. People who feel their lives are good, meaningful, and worthwhile experience the highest levels of happiness. This sense of purpose and meaning is similar to the concept of ikigai you learned about in Chapter 1, which is shown in **Figure 10.2**.

How can you find your purpose? Think about your strengths and talents and how you can use them to do something you find meaningful. Making a contribution to the world around us provides a deep sense of fulfillment. This is an essential component of long-term happiness.

Cultural Differences in Happiness

The concept of happiness has different meanings to people in different countries and cultures. In the United States, happiness is commonly associated with positive experiences and personal achievements. Happiness is often described in terms of intense emotions, such as excitement and enthusiasm.

In many Asian countries, such as Japan and China, happiness is more commonly associated with feelings of social harmony or getting along with others. People in these countries are more likely to describe happiness in terms of less intense emotions, such as relaxation and calmness.

Cultures also differ in how they think about what happiness really is. In Denmark, the term commonly used to mean happiness is *lykke*. This word describes small moments of well-being in everyday life, such as drinking a nice cup of coffee or eating a slice of bread with cheese. In other countries, such as Germany, France, Poland, and Russia, the terms used for happiness describe much less common experiences.

Still other cultures divide happiness into distinct components. In China, for example, three different words are used to describe happiness: *xingfu* (good life), *you yiyi* (meaning), and *kuaile* (good mood).

> **Think Deeper** | Understanding Cultural Differences in Happiness
>
> What factors do you think lead people in different countries to think about happiness in different ways? Are there other factors that could influence how people think about happiness—where they live in a given country, their spiritual beliefs, or their age or level of income? How does a culture's definitions of happiness impact how happy people feel?
>
> Now, think about your own life and values.
>
> 1. If you had to define the word *happiness* for yourself, what would your definition be?
> 2. How does this definition affect how happy you feel?
> 3. Are there things you could do in your own life to increase your happiness?

Myths about Happiness

Although most people want to be happy, we often make errors in thinking about what will or will not lead to happiness. For example, many people think happiness is determined by the events in their lives, such as being asked on a date, getting an A on a project, or receiving a promotion at work. But many of these beliefs aren't accurate. In this section, you'll learn about some of the most common myths we hold about the predictors of happiness.

Marriage or a Romantic Partner Many people believe that finding the perfect romantic partner is the key to happiness. It's certainly true that having close relationships increases happiness. But close relationships don't have to include marriage, or even a romantic partner.

Does marriage increase happiness? Yes, but only briefly. People who get married experience an increase in happiness, but that only lasts for about two years. They then adapt to the consistent presence of this relationship.

Fortunately, this adaptation process works both ways. When a relationship ends, we often believe that we will never feel happy again. But over time, we adjust to this new reality and can indeed find happiness (as well as a new romantic partner).

It also points to the importance of making good choices in our romantic lives. Staying in a bad relationship certainly leads to lower levels of happiness than being single. In fact, single people often show greater happiness in their close friendships than do married people. They also have more time to spend on hobbies, exercise, and other things that make them feel happy.

Age Have you ever heard that high school—or college—is supposedly the happiest time of your life? This belief that young people are happy, and that happiness then declines with age, is very common. It's also wrong.

In fact, older people—those in their sixties, seventies, and even eighties—tend to experience higher levels of happiness (as shown in **Figure 10.3**). They report feeling more positive emotions and fewer negative emotions. They are also more satisfied with their lives.

Why does happiness tend to increase with age? One explanation is that older people focus their time and energy on close relationships, more so than younger people. Placing a greater priority on relationships in turn leads to greater happiness. (You'll learn more about the benefits of close relationships later in this chapter.)

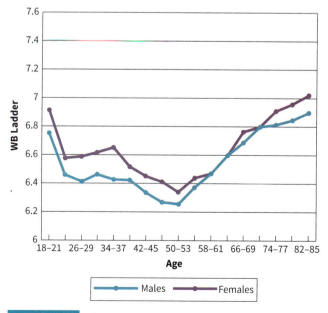

FIGURE 10.3 Changes in happiness across the lifespan.

Life Circumstances
Another common myth people hold is that life circumstances—both good and bad—determine how happy they can feel. You might expect that as soon as you graduate from college, or get a raise, or start a romantic relationship, then you will immediately feel happier.

This belief is partially right. Good events do initially make us feel happier. But here's the problem: as happens with marriage, we then adapt to these new circumstances and often revert back to our prior level of happiness. For example, you might be excited with your new job, but then you realize that you also have more responsibility or need to work more hours.

But here's the good news: This process of adaptation also explains why people can and do find happiness even when facing really difficult circumstances (as you learned in **Chapter 6**). In fact, some evidence even suggests that experiencing some adversity can help us feel better. How? Undergoing difficult life circumstances often forces us to think about ourselves and the world in new ways. For example, people who are diagnosed with cancer may report experiencing a change in life priorities, a richer spiritual life, and closer relationships with loved ones.

This type of change in thinking after struggling with a major life crisis is known as **post-traumatic growth**. If you've experienced some type of difficult life event, you can test your level of posttraumatic growth with the following *Test Yourself*.

Test Yourself | Can You Find Benefits in Difficult Life Events?

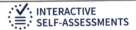

Think about difficult life events you have faced. Then, read the following statements and rate how much each of them is true for you using a 1–5 scale, where 1 = not at all and 5 = very much so.

1.	I changed my priorities about what is important in life.
2.	I have a greater appreciation for the value of my own life.
3.	I am able to do better things with my life.
4.	I have a better understanding of spiritual matters.
5.	I have a greater sense of closeness with others.
6.	I established a new path for my life.
7.	I now know that I can handle difficulties.
8.	I have a stronger religious faith.
9.	I discovered that I'm stronger than I thought I was.
10.	I learned a great deal about how wonderful people are.

Add up your scores on these ten items. Higher scores indicate a greater amount of overall posttraumatic growth. This scale assesses five distinct components of such growth: appreciation of life, relationships with others, new possibilities in life, personal strength, and spirituality. Each of these types of growth helps people cope with traumatic events in a positive way. As you might expect, people who are able to find some positive aspects in difficult situations experience better outcomes.

Cann, A., Calhoun, L. G., Tedeschi, R. G., Taku, K., Vishnevsky,T., Triplett, K. N., & Danhauer, S. C. (2010). A short form of the Posttraumatic Growth Inventory. *Anxiety, Stress & Coping*, 23(2), 127–137. https://doi.org/10.1080/10615800903094273

Review, Discuss, and Apply

Discussion Questions

1. When do you experience the state of flow? What can you learn from those experiences?
2. What explains the strong positive link between happiness and physical health?
3. Why do people often wrongly think that high school or college will be the happiest time of their lives?

Module 10.2 Understanding Stress

LO 10.2.1 To describe different types of stress

LO 10.2.2 To examine the effects of stress

LO 10.2.3 To review strategies for managing stress

Many different aspects of daily life can lead to stress, including academic tasks, work deadlines, and interpersonal conflict. These are all examples of **stressors**, meaning things that cause stress. The term **stress** describes our body's physical and psychological reaction to these challenges.

Sources and Types of Stress

VIDEO CONTENT

Job interviews, final exams, and public speaking are common sources of stresses for many people. But not all stresses are the same. Some stresses, such as a blind date, are very intense, but short-lived. Other stresses, such living in poverty, are less intense, but very long lasting.

Many college students experience stress caused by major life events. These events could include receiving a bad grade on a test or paper, breaking up with a romantic partner, or experiencing the death of a loved one. You can measure your own current stress level in the Test Yourself.

Although we often think about negative life events as causing stress, positive life events can also cause stress. For example, getting accepted to college is a positive event, but it also causes stress because you might have to move away from home, meet new friends, and manage more difficult academic work. All of those factors can create stress.

But major life events aren't the only, or most common, source of stress. Many stressors instead are relatively small daily life hassles. These could include having trouble finding parking, losing your keys, or running late to class. Since these daily hassles occur frequently, they can create more overall stress than major life events.

Stress can also be caused by cataclysmic events, meaning sudden events that happen to many people all at the same time. Natural disasters, such as hurricanes, fires, and floods, are common types of cataclysmic events. Sadly, mass shootings are an increasingly common type of cataclysmic event that causes considerable stress.

Common Causes of Stress during College
People sometimes describe college—at least in retrospect—as "the best time of their life." But the reality is that college students experience many distinct types of stress.

- **Academic stress**—College students often feel stress about their academic work. This can include writing papers, taking exams, and speaking in class. This stress is especially common in first-year students, who are not used to the pace and expectations of academic work in college.

- **Poor time management**—Another common source of stress for many college students is managing time. Students have to develop skills for balancing academic work with other demands, such as playing on an athletic team, working a part-time job, or participating in extracurricular activities. Many college students feel that they don't have enough time to do what they want to do each day. The feeling of having too much to do in too little time can create considerable stress.

- **Relationships**—We often think of personal relationships—with our friends, parents, and romantic partners—as making our lives easier, and they do. But relationships can also be a major source of stress. Sometimes people feel torn between spending time with different people. Maybe your parents want you to come home for the weekend to see them, but you'd rather spend time with your friends. Even good relationships can have conflicts that cause stress. Finally, the ending of a relationship can cause considerable stress.

- **Technology**—A relatively new type of stress—experienced by college students and others alike—is called **technostress**. This term describes a feeling of anxiety caused by the constant presence of technology. Many people can feel overwhelmed by various types of technology. This can include an overflowing email in-box, constant alerts of incoming texts, and pressure to stay active on social media platforms.
- **Internal pressure**—Pressure that you exert on yourself can also cause stress. Have you ever felt stress because you must make a difficult decision? Having to make choices, especially choices between two desirable options, can cause considerable stress. For example, many college students feel pressure to choose between different majors, summer internships, and career paths.

Test Yourself | How Much Stress Are You Experiencing?

Rate how frequently you feel distressed or anxious about each of the following parts of college life using the following scale:

| Never | Rarely | Sometimes | Often | Very Often |
| 1 | 2 | 3 | 4 | 5 |

1. Personal relationships
2. Family matters
3. Financial matters
4. Academic matters
5. Housing matters
6. Being away from home
7. Handling difficulties
8. Attaining your personal goals
9. Events not going as planned
10. Feeling a lack of control
11. Feeling overwhelmed by difficulties

Add up your scores on all 11 items. Higher scores indicate more frequent feelings of stress.

Feldt R. C. (2008). Development of a brief measure of college stress: the college student stress scale. *Psychological Reports, 102* (3), 855–860. https://doi.org/10.2466/pr0.102.3.855-860

Effects of Stress

Think about a time when you were about to do something very stressful, such as taking an exam, going on a job interview, or giving an oral presentation in a class. How did your body react in this situation? Even these relatively common types of everyday stressors can cause physical responses in the body, such as nausea, sweat, and headaches.

Physical Health
Your body reacts in particular ways when you encounter threatening situations. All types of stressors—from experiencing a breakup with a boyfriend or girlfriend, to giving an oral presentation, to having a job interview—can trigger the same physiological responses.

This physiological reaction to a threat is called the *fight-or-flight response*. According to this model of stress, when you are threatened, your body's immediate response is to either fight off the stressor or escape from it. To prepare for either fighting off or escaping from a predator, your body undergoes a number of changes, including increases in heart rate, blood flow, and muscle tension.

Module 10.2 Understanding Stress 235

The fight-or-flight response helps people respond to extreme, life-threatening stressors. The reaction was adaptive when our ancestors fought off predators such as lions and battled people from hostile groups. These physiological reactions may also help us during other high-pressure situations. During a job interview or athletic competition, it can be good to have some extra energy and arousal.

But the fight-or-flight response is often activated in daily life situations that are not life threatening. Over time, this type of ongoing physiological arousal can have negative health consequences (see **Figure 10.4**). It can lead to colds, eczema and hives, headaches, ulcers, and gastrointestinal disorders.

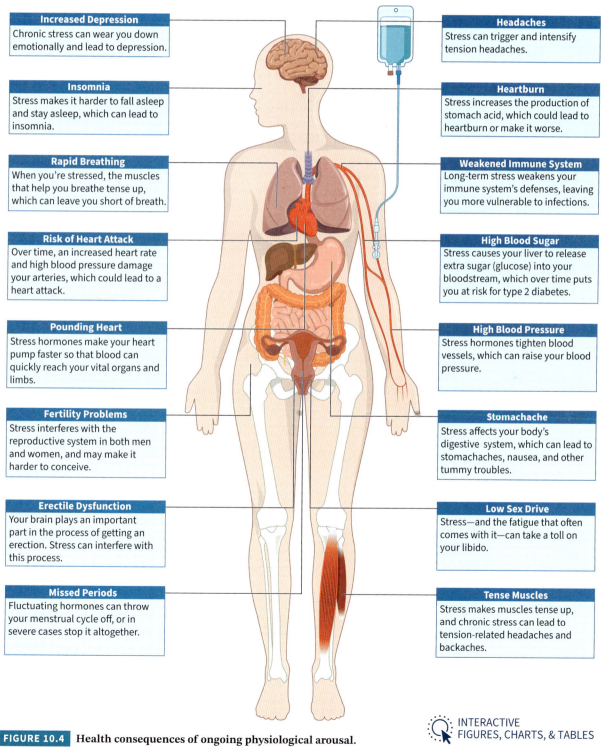

FIGURE 10.4 Health consequences of ongoing physiological arousal.

INTERACTIVE FIGURES, CHARTS, & TABLES

Cognitive Performance
Stress can also influence your cognitive abilities, meaning how you think and reason. It can even disrupt your ability to think clearly and remember information. Have you ever misread a question on a test and gotten the answer wrong, even though you knew the right answer?

People under stress are also more likely to think negative thoughts. For example, someone who is feeling stress during an audition for a starring role in a play may think, "The other people auditioning are probably much more talented than I am. I have no chance of getting this part." Not surprisingly, these types of thoughts would increase that person's level of stress and make it harder do well.

Stress can cause longer-term memory problems. During periods of high stress, hormones are released that interfere with normal brain functioning. These hormones impair the ability to create new memories or recall old memories.

Mental and Emotional Health
People facing stressful events often experience strong negative emotions, such as anxiety, frustration, and anger. Negative emotions caused by a stressful event can trigger hostile behavior toward others. These are common emotional responses to stress.

People's emotional reactions to stressful events vary depending on the type of stressor. If you've experienced the death of a beloved pet, you may remember your intense feelings in the days and even weeks following this loss. Obviously, these are different from the emotions you would experience in a stressful job interview. People who have had a major loss may feel disbelief, shock, and numbness. They may feel a sense of loss, sadness, loneliness, and isolation. These emotions can feel overwhelming, but they are a normal response to a major loss.

Major Depression and Suicide In some cases, people experience more severe and lasting mental health problems. People who feel intense loss and sadness for at least two weeks have **major depression**, a serious psychological disorder. Symptoms of major depression include the following:

- Very sad mood
- Decreased interest in activities that they previously enjoyed
- Gain or loss of weight
- Extreme tiredness
- Feelings of guilt
- Difficulty concentrating
- Irritability, anger, and hostility
- Recurrent thoughts of death

Major depression, if not treated, can have serious consequences.

The most serious consequence of major depression is suicide. According to the American College Health Association, suicide is now the second leading cause of death among college students. People who think about making a suicide attempt feel hopeless and believe that their lives are never going to get better.

Most people who are thinking about suicide show some warning signs about their intentions. This could include talking about the feeling that they have no reason to live or showing a preoccupation with death. They may share these thoughts, or hint at a plan to end their lives, with someone else in person, in email, or on social media. Other signs that someone may be at risk of making a suicide attempt include the following:

- Changes in eating and sleeping habits
- Withdrawal from friends, family, and regular activities
- Drug or alcohol use
- Searching for information on how to commit suicide in books or online
- Neglecting personal appearance
- Personality changes
- Difficulty concentrating
- Declines in the quality of academic work
- Giving away valued possessions
- Frequent complaints about physical symptoms, such as stomachaches, headaches, and tiredness
- Loss of interest in previously enjoyed activities

It is extremely important to seek help immediately if you, or someone you know, is contemplating suicide. All colleges and universities have a counseling center in which students can talk to a mental health professional. Help is also available through the 988 Suicide & Crisis Lifeline, which offers 24/7 support from trained counselors. You can call, text, or chat 988 if you are experiencing any type of mental health crisis. You can also use this lifeline if you are worried about a friend or loved one.

Post-Traumatic Stress Disorder (PTSD) Certain types of stress—such as chronic stress or extremely frightening events—can cause some people to develop emotional problems. People who experience chronic stress have a greater risk of developing depression.

jetcityimage/Adobe Stock

Post-traumatic stress disorder (PTSD) may develop following an extremely frightening and upsetting event. This could include a natural disaster, mass shooting, or sexual assault. Symptoms of PTSD include experiencing nightmares and recurring thoughts about the event, being startled easily, feeling irritable and angry, and having difficulty concentrating. If you, or someone you know, develops PTSD, it is important to get help. Talk to your campus counseling or health center.

Benefiting from Stress This section has focused on the negative consequences of stress. But experiencing stress can also have positive consequences. Moderate levels of stress can increase physiological arousal, which is a state of feeling especially excited. People experiencing such arousal have extra energy and concentration that can help them perform at their best. This helps explain why athletes may benefit from experiencing high arousal. Physiological arousal may also improve performance on other types of tasks, including performing on stage, interviewing for a job, and taking a test.

Perhaps most important, our interpretation of the meaning of a challenging event—and our ability to cope with it—is a better predictor of how stressful it is than the event itself. So, the next time you are feeling stress, try viewing the event as a learning experience that will push you to grow in new ways.

Strategies for Managing Stress

VIDEO CONTENT

Stress is unavoidable—during college and beyond. But we can all learn skills for managing stress that let us lead happier, healthier lives. Learning techniques for managing stress can help reduce the negative consequences of stress.

There are many strategies you can use to better cope with stress. But some strategies work better in certain situations than in others. Learning and practicing different types of strategies for managing stress will help you choose the strategies that work best for you in a particular situation.

Reducing or Avoiding Stress   One strategy for managing challenging situations is to directly confront and change the stressor. This strategy is called **problem-focused coping**. It is often used when you can do something to actually solve the problem or at least reduce its effects. For example, if you are feeling stress because you are doing poorly in a class, you could reduce this stress by talking to the professor about better ways to study the material, getting a tutor, or finding a study group.

- **Manage time well**—One of the best ways to decrease stress is to manage your time well. Many stressors—such as having too much to do at once—can be avoided with careful planning. Let's say you have a research paper due in a few weeks. Some students delay starting such a paper until a few days before it is due. They then experience considerable stress as they try to cram all of the necessary research and writing into a short period of time.

  Time management can be used not only to complete assignments for school, but also for getting other things done. For example, suppose you want a part-time job to earn extra money. You'll need to plan how to manage your other activities—athletic practice, play or music rehearsal, homework—so you also have time to hold a job. This is where planning is important in reducing stress.

- **Don't overcommit**—Another valuable problem-focused coping strategy is avoiding taking on too many things. In other words, try to "just say no." Sometimes college students underestimate how much time their academic work will take to complete. They then commit to numerous other activities, such as working a part-time job, volunteering, and/ or participating in an intensive extracurricular activity. Learning to set limits can help you avoid stress or at least reduce it.

Changing Thoughts about Stress   Problem-focused coping can be really helpful in cases in which there are practical steps you can take to reduce stress. But in some cases, the stress can't be eliminated. For example, if your parents are getting a divorce or your beloved cat dies, you can't really fix these problems.

In these cases, changing how you think about the stress can help reduce its negative effects. This strategy is called **emotion-focused coping** (see **Figure 10.5**). It involves changing how

FIGURE 10.5 Types of coping strategies.

you think about the problem, talking about the problem to others, and/or reducing the physical effects of stress on the body.

Some emotion-focused coping strategies include the following:

- **Distracting yourself**—Try to get your mind off the problem by watching a movie, going for a run, or reading a magazine. Laughing is a great way to distract yourself from stress. Consider watching a funny video or spending time with a friend who makes you laugh.
- **Sharing your feelings**—Talking to someone else about how you are feeling can help you think about the problem in a new way. You may even get useful advice for how to handle the problem you are facing, especially if the person with whom you are talking has had a similar experience.
- **Keeping a journal**—The simple act of writing about your problems in a journal can help you release stress. In fact, people who write about the stresses they experienced have fewer illnesses and minor health problems later on.

As you've learned, different types of problems require different types of coping strategies. For each of the following stressors you might face, first note whether you should use problem-focused coping or emotion-focused coping. Then describe what specific coping strategy you think would be most helpful.

	Problem-Focused or Emotion-Focused Coping?	Specific Coping Strategy
1. Receiving a C on a paper		
2. Feeling annoyed that your roommate plays video games while you are studying in the room		
3. Worrying because your grandfather is in the hospital		
4. Having a fight with your dating partner		

DOWNLOAD DOCUMENTS & TEMPLATES

Relax

Many of the harmful effects of stress are caused by its effects on our body. Learning how to relax your body and clear your mind when facing stress can therefore be really helpful. Here are some strategies that can change how your body reacts when facing stress:

- **Deep breathing**—Taking slow, deep breaths is a great way to help your brain and body calm down and relax. Breathing deeply lowers your heart rate, decreases your blood pressure, and reduces tension. All of these things help reduce the negative physical effects of stress.
- **Progressive muscle relaxation**—This technique involves tensing and then relaxing each part of your body until your entire body is relaxed. You focus on one body part at a time, starting with your toes and feet and moving up to your neck and head. You hold the tension in each body part for a short time before quickly releasing it. Taking deep breaths while relaxing each part of your body increases the effectiveness of this technique.
- **Yoga**—Yoga involves performing a series of postures and breathing exercises. Performing yoga poses involves balance, flexibility, and intense concentration. This requires both physical and mental discipline.
- **Imagery (visualization)**—The technique of imagery, or visualization, involves thinking about or imagining being in a pleasant environment. For example, you might imagine the sound of waves crashing, the warmth of the sun on your skin, and the feeling of sand beneath your toes. Putting yourself on the beach—at least in your mind—can help reduce the stress of daily life.

FIGURE 10.6 Mind Full, or Mindful?

- **Meditation**—The goal of meditation is to reduce negative or stressful thoughts that can lead your body to become tense. You focus on clearing your mind of all negative and stressful thoughts, such as the projects you need to complete or upcoming threatening events. You also concentrate on relaxing your body.
- **Mindfulness**—People who practice **mindfulness** pay concentrated attention to what is happening in the present moment. They avoid letting their mind focus on any other thoughts or concerns (see **Figure 10.6**). For example, while talking with a friend, you can focus intensely on this interaction, instead of thinking about what you will do later or how stressful your day has been.

Spend Time in Nature
One of the easiest ways to reduce stress is to simply spend time outside. In fact, spending time in nature leads to lower levels of depression, stress, and stress-related illnesses. It also leads to higher levels of energy and overall improved physical and mental well-being.

What is it about spending time in nature that leads to such dramatic benefits? Researchers believe that exposure to nature basically switches the body from the fight-or-flight response. This switch allows the body to divert resources toward the immune system, which in turn leads to important long-term health advantages.

Even brief periods of time outside reduce stress. For example, walking through a garden lowers stress and blood pressure. You can increase your happiness by hiking in the mountains, walking on a beach, or strolling through a park.

Exercise
Engaging in regular exercise is a great way to reduce stress. People who exercise regularly experience fewer of the negative physiological effects of stress. This is because exercise reduces the effect of stress on cardiovascular responses, including heart rate and blood pressure. Exercising also engages the muscles, which helps them relax instead of tense (a common reaction to stress). Activities such as jogging, hiking, or biking can also improve mood by distracting people from stressful experiences. They also help reduce levels of anxiety and depression.

Take Care of Yourself Many people fail to take care of themselves during times of stress. For example, college students may eat junk food while working on a paper, pull an all-nighter studying for an exam, or stop exercising when they feel too busy. Some people also use unhealthy strategies for managing stress, such as binge drinking or using drugs. Failing to take care of yourself during times of stress actually increases your risk for illness, which can contribute to further stress.

Seek Professional Help When Needed Recovery from major stressors—such as the death of a loved one, a physical assault, or a major natural disaster—can be really hard and take considerable time. People who experience symptoms of stress for more than a couple of weeks should talk to a mental health professional, such as a psychologist, therapist, or religious leader.

It is especially important to seek help from a professional if the symptoms of stress interfere with your ability to function in daily life, such as your ability to go to class, eat, or complete academic work. Most colleges and universities have a counseling center in which students can seek help, confidentially and at little or no cost.

Think Deeper | Coping with Stress  DOWNLOAD DOCUMENTS & TEMPLATES

Think about different stressors you've experienced in the last month—in your classes, social life, family, or job. Then consider the following questions:

1. What strategies did you use to cope?
2. Did these strategies help you reduce or manage these stressors? Or did they make them worse?
3. How could you have handled these stressors in a more effective way?

Reflecting on the strategies you've used to manage stress in the past can help you learn what works—and what doesn't work. This can help you manage stressors in a better way when they occur in the future.

Review, Discuss, and Apply  INTERACTIVE SELF-SCORING QUIZZES

Discussion Questions

1. Why is technology a source of stress?
2. Which of the findings about the impact of stress do you find most surprising?
3. Looking forward, what strategies will you use to manage stress?

Module 10.3 Increasing Happiness

LO 10.3.1 To examine strategies for changing thoughts to increase happiness

LO 10.3.2 To review strategies for changing behavior to increase happiness

We noted earlier that many people think happiness is a result of life circumstances, such as whether you have a romantic partner, how well you do in school, or even where you live. But these factors overall have a very small influence on happiness. Why? It's because of the power of adaptation, as you learned in the first section of this chapter.

What does predict happiness? One factor is your genes. Research shows that genetic make-up accounts for about half of a person's happiness. As a result, some people find it easier to be happy than do others.

Another factor is how much money you have. Perhaps not surprisingly, people who earn more money—up to $500,000 a year—are happier. More wealth probably leads to increased happiness by reducing some of the stressors in daily life. For example, if your car breaks down, that event is very stressful for someone with a limited income, but it is a minor inconvenience for someone with more savings.

But here's the most important finding from the research on positive psychology: no matter your genetic makeup or your income, many strategies for finding more happiness are entirely within your own control. In this final section, you'll learn strategies for changing your thoughts and your behavior to find more happiness.

Change Your Thoughts

We often think that our happiness depends on what happens to us. We feel happy when good things happen—we get a good grade on a test, have a fun evening with friends, or score the game-winning goal. But in reality, how we think about not-so-good events we experience has an even stronger influence.

When you feel disappointed or your day does not go the way you want, how do you react? Do you immediately become angry or frustrated? Do you withdraw and give up? Do you try to identify some positive aspect of the situation?

Some people get stuck in negative thought cycles. When bad events happen, they believe future events will go just as poorly. They also get stuck on negative thoughts and cannot seem to let them go and move on. For example, if their dating partner breaks up with them, they assume they will never find another person to date.

In contrast, people who adopt a positive mindset are better able to bounce back from negative experiences. They can take frustrations and disappointments in stride. They let go of negative emotions instead of replaying the event in their minds. Instead of giving up, they use coping strategies to help them feel better over time.

People who adopt a positive mindset are *optimistic*, meaning they are hopeful and confident about the future. You can measure your own tendency toward optimistic thinking in the following *Test Yourself*.

Test Yourself | How Optimistic Are You?

Rate your tendency to be optimistic by answering the following questions. Rate how much you agree with each statement on a 0–4 scale, where 0 = strongly disagree and 4 = strongly agree.

In uncertain times, I usually expect the best.
Overall, I expect more good things to happen to me than bad.
I'm always optimistic about my future.
I hardly ever expect things to go my way.
I rarely count on good things happening to me.
If something can go wrong for me, it will.

First, add up your scores on the first three items. Next, add up your scores on the next three items. Finally, subtract your score on the second set of items from your score on the first set of items to get your overall optimism score. Higher numbers indicate a greater tendency toward optimistic thinking.

Scheier, M. F., Carver, C. S., & Bridges, M. W. (1994). Distinguishing optimism from neuroticism (and trait anxiety, self-mastery, and self-esteem): A reevaluation of the Life Orientation Test. *Journal of Personality and Social Psychology, 67*, 1063–1078. http://dx.doi.org/10.1037/0022-3514.67.6.1063

Adopt a Positive Mindset Some people naturally adopt a positive mindset without much difficulty. But even if this does not come easily to you, there are strategies you can use to practice shifting your thoughts in a more positive direction. Over time, using these strategies will help you adopt a more positive mindset.

Here are some things to try:

- **Stop negative thoughts**—If you tend to have a negative outlook, try to stop negative thoughts as soon as they start. Then, replace the negative thoughts with more positive ones.

- **Reframe situations**—Try to shift the way you see or think about a situation. For example, try to think about a time in which your overly negative expectations were not accurate. This can help you develop a more realistic outlook. For example, maybe you remember a time you did poorly on a test in high school and thought you would never do better, but actually ended up understanding that material later. This type of positive reframing will take some practice, but it gets easier over time.

- **Find some good**—No matter the situation, try to find some positive aspects about it. For example, being stuck in a traffic jam may make you frustrated and anxious, especially if you focus on the minutes ticking by. You could remind yourself that this situation could be much worse. Although you are stuck in traffic, you are not the person in the car accident that caused the delays. You could also come up with productive ways of using the downtime, such as making a list of the things you'd like to do later.

Practice Positive Self-Talk Everyone has an inner voice that speaks to them regularly throughout the day. For example, you might think to yourself, "I really should go talk to my instructor about that paper I need to write" or "I think I'll try to go for a run after work tonight." These thoughts about yourself are known as **self-talk**.

The type of self-talk you engage in can have a major impact on how you feel. Some types of self-talk are positive and encouraging. For example, you might think about how well your upcoming job interview is going to go or how prepared you feel for your science test. These types of positive thoughts feel supportive and enhance your self-confidence.

Other types of self-talk are negative and can undermine confidence and motivation. For example, you might think, "I'm never going to be good at writing, no matter how hard I try" or "I bet no one at this party will want to talk to me." This type of self-defeating self-talk can make you feel worse. It can also lead these negative expectations to become reality. After all, it is hard to do well when you do not have confidence that a positive outcome is even possible.

Do you tend to engage in negative self-talk? If so, here are some strategies you can try to shift your thinking:

- **Pay attention to your thoughts**—The first step is to pay attention to your thoughts. By paying attention, you can recognize when you start running through pessimistic thoughts and stop the cycle faster.

- **Immediately stop negative self-talk**—For example, you could visualize a stop sign when you notice a negative thought. Some people find it helpful to wear rubber bands on their wrists and snap them when they recognize a negative thought. This type of immediate response can help remind you of the hazards of negative self-talk.

- **Replace negative thoughts with more positive ones**—Once you recognize your negative self-talk, you can replace these negative thoughts with more positive ones. For example, if you beat yourself up over getting any grade lower than an A, you might remind yourself that a B grade still shows a solid performance. If you feel hopeless as an athlete because you do not start the game, remind yourself of the accomplishment of making the team.

Focus on Gratitude It is perhaps human nature to focus often on what is bad in life instead of what is good. Focusing instead on **gratitude**, meaning an appreciation for what you have, can give you a more positive mindset. People who focus on gratitude pay attention to what they are thankful for in their lives. They show kindness and compassion to other people, including friends, family members, and even strangers. Practicing gratitude leads to more optimism, as well as increased energy, greater happiness, and better health. People also tend to notice more positive aspects of life when they focus on being grateful for those aspects.

Here are some easy strategies for practicing gratitude that you could try:

- **Keep a gratitude journal**—Before you go to sleep at night, write several reasons you are thankful in that moment.
- **Write a gratitude letter**—In your letter, thank someone for how that person has made your life better in some way. Then send that person the letter.
- **Fill a gratitude jar**—Every time you feel grateful, write why on a little piece of paper and put it in the jar. Then, if you are feeling down, go into the jar and remind yourself of what is good in your life.

Remember that you can feel grateful for even small moments throughout the day. You could feel grateful for eating a tasty meal, accomplishing a new weight-lifting goal, or going to a concert with friends. Take a minute at the end of the day and just reflect on feeling good about these experiences. Use the *Make It Personal* box to list five things you feel grateful for in your life right now.

Make It Personal | Feeling Gratitude   ⬇ DOWNLOAD DOCUMENTS & TEMPLATES

1. _____
2. _____
3. _____
4. _____
5. _____

Avoid Comparisons Many college students spend a lot of time comparing themselves to other people. This type of comparison can occur in almost any dimension, from how people look, to how many friends they have or how smart they are. Unfortunately, comparisons to other people often make us feel worse. After all, there is almost always going to be someone who is better than you in some area.

These comparisons may also not even be accurate. In one study, researchers asked college students how frequently they had experienced various negative and positive events. These negative events included receiving a low grade or being rejected by a potential romantic partner. The positive events included attending a fun party and going out with friends in the past two weeks. They were also asked to estimate how often other students had experienced these same events.

Can you predict their findings? For every single negative event, students believed they were experiencing these events more often than were their peers. For example, although 60 percent of students had received a bad grade in the past two weeks, they believed that only 44 percent of their peers had had this experience. On the other hand, students also believed that their peers were experiencing the positive events more frequently than they themselves were.

For example, although only 41 percent of students reported attending a fun party in the last two weeks, they believed that 62 percent of their peers had had this experience.

Sadly, feeling like you don't do as many positive things—and do more negative things—than other people has consequences. Students who underestimated how often their peers were experiencing negative events and overestimated how often their peers were experiencing positive events reported feeling lonelier and less satisfied with life.

These findings help explain why spending time on social media is linked with less happiness—and higher rates of anxiety, depression, and loneliness. Why? People on social media present the very best parts of their lives. Most college students post flattering, sometimes altered, photographs of themselves, talk about fun times with friends, and share impressive accomplishments. The constant stream of people looking great and having fun with friends can make you feel your own life does not measure up.

One of the best ways to feel happier is therefore to reduce the number of comparisons you make to other people. You should also keep in mind that what people outwardly present to others is almost never tells the true story of what they are experiencing. As the writer Anne Lamont says, "Never compare your insides to everyone else's outsides."

Change Your Behavior

Other strategies for increasing happiness focus not on changing your thoughts, but on changing your behavior. These strategies may not instantly make you feel happier, but over time, engaging in particular types of behavior will boost your mood. Here are a few behaviors you can try.

Perform Random Acts of Kindness
One of the best ways to find more happiness is to give to other people. In fact, giving to others increases people's happiness, improves their health, and may even extend their lives. Any type of giving counts, from volunteering in your community to donating gently used clothes or performing a random act of kindness.

Here are some other easy ways you can give to others:

- Volunteer in your community.
- Donate blood.
- Pay someone a compliment.
- Write someone an email or even a physical letter expressing your appreciation for them.

Build and Maintain Close Relationships
All people have different types of relationships in their lives, including relationships with family members, friends, romantic partners, and members of their communities. Having close and supportive relationships is an essential part of feeling happy. In fact, the single biggest predictor of life satisfaction is the quality of these relationships.

Close relationships have many benefits that contribute to happiness. For example, they provide opportunities for meaningful conversations and allow people to share positive experiences. They also help people cope with the daily stress of life.

There are steps you can take to develop and maintain close relationships with family members and friends. For example, you can join groups in which you can meet people with similar interests or do volunteer work. Chapter 4 describes how to build and maintain close relationships.

Spend Time with Positive People
Think about the people you spend time with regularly, including friends, family members, and even casual acquaintances. How do you feel when you are with these different people? If you are surrounded by people who are generally happy, spending time with them can make you feel better. In fact, happiness is contagious. When you spend time with people who are happy, the positive mood around you lifts you up. Whenever possible, choose to surround yourself with people who make you feel good.

Unfortunately, unhappiness is also contagious. If you have people in your life who are always negative and gloomy, you may want to limit how much time you spend with them. You can also try to assist these people in getting help. When you are with these people, plan to do an activity that lifts your mood after spending time with them. This will help protect you from adopting their negativity.

Think Deeper | Your Path to Happiness

Think about the different strategies described in this section that help people feel happier. Then consider the following questions:

1. Which of these strategies are you currently using in your own life?
2. Which of these strategies do you think might help you feel happier?
3. Can you make a plan to start using one or two of these strategies?

Reflecting on the types of things that make you happy is a good idea. This is the first step in changing your thoughts and behavior in a positive way. Feeling happy during college will also help you experience success in your classes and personal life.

Review, Discuss, and Apply

Discussion Questions

1. Why do many college students spend a lot of time comparing themselves to other people? What explains this finding?
2. Looking forward, in what situations can you use positive self-talk to feel better?
3. Which of the findings about strategies for increasing happiness do you find most surprising, and why?

Think Ahead | Career and Lifelong Applications

People who are generally happy experience many benefits in their personal and professional lives. As you've learned in this chapter, they have better physical health and better psychological well-being. They are also better able to manage stress. Here are some of the advantages:

Experience lower levels of stress—People who are happy take specific steps that reduce stress. They are good at managing their time. They start on projects early, so they can easily meet deadlines. They also avoid overcommitting to various projects and activities. This allows them to focus well on a smaller number of responsibilities.

Jadon Bester/peopleimages.com/Adobe Stock

Module 10.3 Increasing Happiness 247

Manage stress effectively—People who are happy manage stress in positive and productive ways. They get support from other people, which helps them feel better during difficult times. They also prioritize taking care of themselves, which gives them more strength to manage stressors.

Adopt a positive mindset—People who are happy can find some benefits in nearly any situation. When a work project doesn't go well, they focus on what they've learned from that situation. When their weekend plans fall through at the last minute, they focus on how they can use this time to finish a home improvement project. Their positive mindset lets them respond well to setbacks and disappointments in their personal and professional lives.

Perform random acts of kindness—People who are happy are kind to others. They volunteer in their community and donate to charitable causes. They compliment coworkers on their successes and express gratitude to their mentors. These small acts of kindness help them build close relationships with friends, family members, and colleagues.

As you can probably imagine, these skills help happy people succeed in all different types of environments. People who are happy experience less stress and, when they do experience stress, are better able to manage it. Their ability to adopt a positive mindset—no matter what—helps them cope with big and small challenges. Their kindness to others makes them feel good about themselves and helps them build close relationships with others. These skills all lead to lasting benefits for people's personal and professional lives.

What Would You Do?

In this chapter, Olivia and Dewayne need your advice.

VIDEO CONTENT

DEWAYNE

Dewayne feels like the stress of his deadline-driven job is spilling over into everyday life and wants your advice on what to do about it.

Watch Dewayne's video: **Stressed Out**

OLIVIA

Olivia is wondering how she could put some of her skills to use in doing volunteer work for the greater good and wants some ideas.

Watch Olivia's video: **Helping Others**

What would you tell Olivia? What would you tell Dewayne?

Take Some Action | Here and Now

DOWNLOAD DOCUMENTS & TEMPLATES

We all have strengths and weaknesses when it comes to pursuing happiness. Being aware of those strengths and weaknesses is key to success in college, in the workplace, and in life.

Review your outcomes on the *Test Yourself* assessments throughout this chapter and your responses to the *Think Deeper* questions. Reflect on your results and responses, and then answer these questions:

1. What are your strengths with respect to pursuing happiness? How will you put those strengths to work for you toward succeeding in college? How will sharpening those strengths in college help you be successful in the workplace?

2. In what aspects of pursuing happiness do you want to improve your strengths?

3. Review the suggested action steps in that area and choose two or three of those to commit to here and now. For each, say how taking that action step will help you succeed in college and beyond.

Share and discuss your responses to these questions with a friend, classmate, or family member.

Chapter Summary

INTERACTIVE SELF-SCORING QUIZZES
Chapter 10 Practice Quiz

Module 10.1 Predicting Happiness

- Happiness is strongly linked to psychological and physical well-being. People who are happier experience better cardiovascular health, stronger immune systems, fewer aches and pains, and fewer long-term health conditions. They also live longer.

- Happiness consists of three distinct components. One component of happiness is pleasure, meaning how much you enjoy daily life experiences. This component is the least important. Another component of happiness is feeling engaged with your life. People who are engaged with their lives understand their strengths and may experience flow, a psychological state in which time seems to fly by. The third component is feeling a deeper sense of meaning and purpose in life. People who feel their lives are good, meaningful, and worthwhile experience the highest levels of happiness. The concept of happiness has different meanings to people in different countries and cultures.

- People often make errors in thinking about what will or will not lead to happiness. Some of the most common myths people hold are that happiness depends on having a romantic partner, being a particular age, or having better life circumstances.

Module 10.2 Understanding Stress

- Many different aspects of daily life can lead to stress. These can include major life events, relatively small daily life hassles, or cataclysmic events. Common causes of stress during college include academic stress, time management, relationships, technology, and internal pressures.

- Stress can cause physical responses in the body. The physiological reaction to a threat is called the fight-or-flight response, which describes your body's immediate response to either fight off the stressor or escape from it. This type of ongoing physiological arousal can have negative health consequences, such as colds, eczema and hives, headaches, ulcers, and gastrointestinal disorders. Stress can also disrupt cognitive performance and cause problems with mental and emotional health. In some cases, stress can lead to major depression, suicide, and post-traumatic stress disorder (PTSD). However, moderate levels of stress can have beneficial effects, as can interpreting stress in a positive way.

- There are many strategies you can use to better cope with stress. These include reducing or avoiding stress (problem-focused coping), changing thoughts about stress (emotion-focused coping), relaxing, spending time in nature, exercising, and taking care of yourself. Learning and practicing different types of strategies for managing stress will help you choose the strategies that work best for you in a particular situation. People who experience symptoms of stress for more than a couple of weeks should talk to a mental health professional.

Module 10.3 Increasing Happiness

- Happiness is influenced in part by genes and in part by wealth. But many strategies for finding more happiness are entirely within your own control.

- How you think about yourself and the world has a strong influence on happiness. You can increase happiness by changing your thoughts, adopting a positive mindset (including stopping negative thoughts), reframing situations, and finding some good in all situations. Another strategy for changing your thoughts is practicing positive self-talk, including paying attention to your thoughts, stopping negative self-talk, and replacing negative thoughts with more positive ones. Other strategies include focusing on gratitude and avoiding comparisons.

- Additional strategies for increasing happiness involve engaging in particular types of behavior. This can include performing random acts of kindness, building and maintaining close relationships, and spending time with positive people.

Key Terms

Emotion-focused coping Changing how you think about a problem

Flow A psychological state in which you are fully absorbed in what you are doing and are not aware of time passing

Gratitude Having an appreciation for the good things in your life

Happiness Experiencing various kinds of positive emotions, such as joy, pride, and contentment

Major depression A severe psychological disorder in which people feel intense loss and sadness for at least two weeks

Mindfulness A state of concentrated, judgment-free awareness of what is happening in the present moment

Post-traumatic growth A change in thinking after struggling with a major life crisis

Post-traumatic stress disorder (PTSD) A psychological disorder that may develop following an extremely frightening and upsetting event. Symptoms can include experiencing nightmares and recurring thoughts about the event, being startled easily, feeling irritable and angry, and having difficulty concentrating.

Problem-focused coping A strategy for managing challenging situations by directly confronting and changing the stressor

Purpose An intention to accomplish something that is meaningful for yourself and the broader world

Self-talk Thoughts about yourself; an inner voice that speaks to you regularly throughout the day

Stress The body's physical and psychological reaction to daily life challenges

Stressors Things that cause stress

Technostress A feeling of anxiety caused by the constant presence of technology

Resources

Dunn, E., & Norton, M. (2013). *Happy money: The science of happier spending.* Simon & Schuster.

Gilbert, D. (2006). *Stumbling on happiness.* Alfred A. Knopf.

Kross, E. (2021). *Chatter: The voice in our head, why it matters, and how to harness it.* Crown.

McGonigal, K. (2015). *The upside of stress: Why stress is good for you, and how to get good at it.* Penguin Random House.

Sanderson, C. A. (2019). *The positive shift: Mastering mindset to improve happiness, health, and longevity.* BenBella Books.

Sapolsky, R. M. (1994). *Why zebras don't get ulcers: A guide to stress, stress-related diseases, and coping.* W. H. Freeman.

Vaillant, G. E. (2002). *Aging well: Surprising guideposts to a happier life from the landmark Harvard study of adult development.* Little, Brown.

Waldinger, R., & Schulz, M. (2023). *The good life: Lessons from the world's longest scientific study of happiness.* Simon & Schuster.

References

Cann, A., Calhoun, L. G., Tedeschi, R. G., Taku, K., Vishnevsky,T., Triplett, K. N., & Danhauer, S. C. (2010). A short form of the Posttraumatic Growth Inventory. *Anxiety, Stress & Coping, 23*(2), 127–137. https://doi.org/10.1080/10615800903094273

Danner, D. D., Snowdon, D. A., & Friesen, W. V. (2001). Positive emotions in early life and longevity: Findings from the nun study. *Journal of Personality and Social Psychology, 80*(5), 804–813. https://doi.org/10.1037/0022-3514.80.5.804

Dunn, E. W., Aknin, L. B., & Norton, M. I. (2008). Spending money on others promotes happiness. *Science, 319*(5870), 1687–1688. https://doi.org/10.1126/science.1150952

Emmons, R. A., & McCullough, M. E. (2003). Counting blessings versus burdens: An experimental investigation of gratitude and subjective well-being in daily life. *Journal of Personality and Social Psychology, 84*(2), 377–389. https://doi.org/10.1037/0022-3514.84.2.377

Feldt, R. C. (2008). Development of a brief measure of college stress: the college student stress scale. *Psychological Reports, 102*(3), 855–860. https://doi.org/10.2466/pr0.102.3.855-860

Folk, D., & Dunn, E. (2023). A systematic review of the strength of evidence for the most commonly recommended happiness strategies in mainstream media. *Nature Human Behaviour, 7*(10), 1697–1707. https://doi.org/10.1038/s41562-023-01651-4

Killingsworth, M. A., Kahneman, D., & Mellers, B. (2023). Income and emotional well-being: A conflict resolved. *Proceedings of the National Academy of Sciences of the United States of America, 120*(10), e2208661120. https://doi.org/10.1073/pnas.2208661120

Scheier, M. F., Carver, C. S., & Bridges, M. W. (1994). Distinguishing optimism from neuroticism (and trait anxiety, self-mastery, and self-esteem): A reevaluation of the Life Orientation Test. *Journal of Personality and Social Psychology, 67*, 1063–1078. http://dx.doi.org/10.1037/0022-3514.67.6.1063

Stone, A. A., Schwartz, J. E., Broderick, J. E., & Deaton, A. (2010). A snapshot of the age distribution of psychological well-being in the United States. *Proceedings of the National Academy of Sciences of the United States of America, 107*(22), 9985–9990. https://doi.org/10.1073/pnas.1003744107

Tedeschi, R. G., & Calhoun, L. G. (1996). The Posttraumatic Growth Inventory: Measuring the positive legacy of trauma. *Journal of Traumatic Stress, 9*(3), 455–472. https://doi.org/10.1002/jts.2490090305

Tice, D. M., & Baumeister, R. F. (1997). Longitudinal study of procrastination, performance, stress, and health: The costs and benefits of dawdling. *Psychological Science, 8*(6), 454–458. https://doi.org/10.1111/j.1467-9280.1997.tb00460.x

References

Abril, P. S., Levin, A., & Riego, A. D. (2012). Blurred boundaries: Social media privacy and the twenty-first-century employee. *American Business Law Journal, 49*(1): 63-124. https://doi.org/10.32920/22227769

Adams, R., & Biddle, B. (1970). *Realities of teaching*. Holt Rinehart & Winston.

Agarwal, A. (2018, October 3). Data reveals why the 'soft' In 'soft skills' is a significant misnomer. *Forbes*. https://www.forbes.com/sites/anantagarwal/2018/10/02/data-reveals-why-the-soft-in-soft-skills-is-a-major-misnomer/

Akhtar, M. (2017, April 8). What is self-efficacy? Bandura's four sources of efficacy beliefs. Retrieved from http://positivepsychology.org.uk/self-efficacy-definition bandura-meaning/

Arthur, K. 2012. Mind Maps: Improve Memory, Concentration, Communication, Organization, Creativity, and Time Management (Ebook). Book Stream Publishing.

Bandura, A. (1982). Self-efficacy mechanism in human agency. *American Psychologist, 37*(2), 122–147. doi:10.1037/0003-066X.37.2.122

Brackett, M. A., Rivers, S. E., & Salovey, P. (2011). Emotional intelligence: Implications for personal, social, academic, and workplace success. *Social and Personality Psychology Compass, 5*(1), 88–103. https://doi.org/10.1111/j.1751-9004.2010.00334.x

Brooks, D. (2016). *The road to character*. London: Penguin Books.

Buzan, T. (1974). Use your head. London, UK: BBC Books.

Cann, A., Calhoun, L. G., Tedeschi, R. G., Taku, K., Vishnevsky,T., Triplett, K. N., & Danhauer, S. C. (2010). A short form of the Posttraumatic Growth Inventory. *Anxiety, Stress & Coping, 23*(2), 127–137. https://doi.org/10.1080/10615800903094273

CareerBuilder.com (2018). More than half of employers have found content on social media that caused them not to hire a candidate, according to recent CareerBuilder survey. Press Room | Career Builder. (n.d.-b). https://press.careerbuilder.com/2018-08-09-More-Than-Half-of-Employers-Have-Found-Content-on-Social-Media-That-Caused-Them-NOT-to-Hire-a-Candidate-According-to-Recent-CareerBuilder-Survey

Carnevale, A. P., Smith, N., Melton, M., & Price, E. W. (2015). *Learning While Earning: The New Normal*. Washington, DC: Georgetown University.

Central Vancouver Island Multicultural Society (2021). Cultural Competency Self-assessment Checklist. Retrieved from https://www.cvims.org/community/cultural-competency/.

Chak, A. (2017, December 7). Beyond "he" and "she": The rise of non-binary pronouns. Retrieved from https://www.bbc.com/news/magazine-34901704

Coco, M. (2000). Internships: A try before you buy arrangement. *Advanced Management Journal, 65*(2), 41 -43.

Cohen, B.-Z. (1999). Measuring the willingness to seek help. *Journal of Social Service Research, 26*(1), 67–82. https://doi.org/10.1300/j079v26n01_04

Connor, P., & Budiman, A. (2019, January 30). Immigrant share in U.S. nears record high but remains below that of many other countries. Retrieved from https://www.pewresearch.org/fact-tank/2019/01/30/immigrant-share-in-u-s-nears-record-high-but-remains-below-that-of-many-other-countries/

Corry, P. (2018, November 15). *Focus is about past, present and future*. Medium. https://medium.com/serious-scrum/focus-is-about-past-present-and-future-d43583793012

Csikszentmihalyi, M. (2009). *Flow: the psychology of optimal experience*. Harper Row.

Danner, D. D., Snowdon, D. A., & Friesen, W. V. (2001). Positive emotions in early life and longevity: Findings from the nun study. *Journal of Personality and Social Psychology, 80*(5), 804–813. https://doi.org/10.1037/0022-3514.80.5.804

Davis, M. H. (1983). Measuring individual differences in empathy: Evidence for a multidimensional approach. *Journal of Personality and Social Psychology, 44*(1), 113–126. https://doi.org/10.1037/0022-3514.44.1.113

DePaulo, B. M., & Friedman, H. S. (1998). Nonverbal communication. In D. T.Gilbert, S. T.Fiske, & G.Lindzey (Eds.), *The handbook of social psychology* (3–40). McGraw-Hill.

Digital Badging in the MOOC Space. (n.d.). https://er.educause.edu/articles/2016/11/digital-badging-in-the-mooc-space Dispelling 7 myths about college tutoring. (2017, October 24). https://parent.wisc.edu/news/dispelling-7-myths-about-college-tutoring/

Duchess Community College. (2007, November 7). *Technology Skill Assessment*. TLC - Technical Skills Self-assessment. https://www8.sunydutchess.edu/tlc_web/techskillsquiz.html

Duckworth, A. L., & Quinn, P. D. (2009). Development and validation of the Short Grit Scale (GRIT–S). *Journal of Personality Assessment, 91*(2), 166–174. https://doi.org/10.1080/00223890802634290

Duckworth, A. L., Peterson, C., Matthews, M. D., & Kelly, D. R. (2007). Grit: Perseverance and passion for long-term goals. *Journal of Personality and Social Psychology, 92*(6), 1087–1101. https://doi.org/10.1037/0022-3514.92.6.1087

Duckworth, A. L., Quirk, A., Gallop, R., Hoyle, R. H., Kelly, D. R., & Matthews, M. D. (2019). Cognitive and noncognitive predictors of success. *Proceedings of the National Academy of Sciences of the United States of America, 116*(47), 23499–23504. https://doi.org/10.1073/pnas.1910510116

Dunn, E. W., Aknin, L. B., & Norton, M. I. (2008). Spending money on others promotes happiness. *Science, 319*(5870), 1687–1688. https://doi.org/10.1126/science.1150952

Dweck, C. (2006). Mindset: The new psychology of success. Random House.

Dweck, C. S., & Leggett, E. L. (1988). A social-cognitive approach to motivation and personality. *Psychological Review, 95*(2), 256–273. https://doi.org/10.1037/0033-295X.95.2.256

Dworkcn,A.(1985,February6).The three-circle test.*Washington Post*. https://www.washingtonpost.com/archive/lifestyle/wellness/1985/02/06/the-three-circle-test/e959299f-5640-4e17-bc0e-98e61ae18c2d/

Eliason, N. (2017, August 3). How to use deliberate practice to reach the top 1 percent of your field. Retrieved from https://observer.com/2017/08/how-to-use-deliberate-practice-to-reach-the-top-1-percent-malcolm-gladwell-anders-ericsson-habits-mastery/

Eliason, N. (2018, July 7). 45 Deliberate practice examples for rapidly improving your skills. Retrieved from https://www.nateliason.com/blog/deliberate-practice-examples

Ellis, R. K. (2016, August 5). Half of global companies struggle to find candidates with International Mindset | ATD. *Association for Talent Development*. https://www.td.org/insights/half-of-global-companies-struggle-to-find-candidates-with-international-mindset

Emmons, R. A., & McCullough, M. E. (2003). Counting blessings versus burdens: An experimental investigation of gratitude and subjective well-being in daily life. *Journal of Personality and Social Psychology, 84*(2), 377–389. https://doi.org/10.1037/0022-3514.84.2.377

Epstein, D. (2019). Range: *Why Generalists Triumph in a Specialized World*. New York: Riverhead Books.

Felder, F. M., & Soloman, B. A. (1991). Index of Learning Styles. North Carolina State University.

Felder, R. M., & Silverman, L. K. (1988). Learning and teaching styles in engineering education. *Engineering Education*, 78, 674–681.

Feldt, R. C. (2008). Development of a brief measure of college stress: the college student stress scale. *Psychological Reports*, 102(3), 855–860. https://doi.org/10.2466/pr0.102.3.855-860

Fetzer, J. H (2004). "Disinformation: The use of false information." *Minds and Machines* 14(2): 231–40.

Folk, D., & Dunn, E. (2023). A systematic review of the strength of evidence for the most commonly recommended happiness strategies in mainstream media. *Nature Human Behaviour*, 7(10), 1697–1707. https://doi.org/10.1038/s41562-023-01651-4

Framson, C., Kristal, A. R., Schenk, J. M., Littman, A. J., Zeliadt, S., & Benitez, D. (2009). Development and validation of the mindful eating questionnaire. *Journal of the American Dietetic Association*, 109(8), 1439–1444. https://doi.org/10.1016/j.jada.2009.05.006

Frey, W. H. (2018, September 10). The US will become "minority white" in 2045, Census projects. Retrieved from https://www.brookings.edu/blog/the-avenue/2018/03/14/the-us-will-become-minority-white-in-2045-census-projects/

Fuller, R. B. (1982). Critical path. New York: St. Martin's Griffin, 1982.

Gallup, Inc. (2019, December 30). CliftonStrengths. Retrieved from https://www.gallup.com/cliftonstrengths/en/252137/home.aspx?utm_source=google&utm_medium=cpc&utm_campaign=Strengths_ECommerce_Brand_Search_US&utm_content=+cliftonstrengths&gclid=EAIaIQobChMIvOPqxpCk5wIV-S73ACh2XxwZIEAAYASAAEgITtvD_BwE

Garcia, L., Pearce, M., Abbas, A., Mok, A., Strain, T., Ali, S., Crippa, A., Dempsey, P. C., Golubic, R., Kelly, P., Laird, Y., McNamara, E., Moore, S., de Sa, T. H., Smith, A. D., Wijndaele, K., Woodcock, J., & Brage, S. (2023). Non-occupational physical activity and risk of cardiovascular disease, cancer and mortality outcomes: A dose-response meta-analysis of large prospective studies. *British Journal of Sports Medicine*, bjsports-2022-105669. Advance online publication. https://doi.org/10.1136/bjsports-2022-105669

García, H., & Miralles, F. (2017). *Ikigai: The Japanese secret to a long and happy life*. Penguin Books.

Gardner, H. E. (2006). Multiple intelligences: *New horizons in theory and practice*. Basic Books.

Garner, B. (2019), Helping students become digital content curators: Fact or fiction? Newcastle upon Tyne. Cambridge Scholars Publishing.

Gaumer Erickson, A. S., Noonan, P. M., Monroe, K., & McCall, Z. (2016). Assertiveness Formative Questionnaire. In P. M. Noonan & A. S. Gaumer Erickson (2017), *The skills that matter: Teaching interpersonal and intrapersonal competencies in any classroom* (pp. 181–182). Corwin.

General education (2019, September 12). UNESCO Institute for Statistics. http://uis.unesco.org/en/glossary-term/general-education

Gillespie, D. (2019, April 29). Mentoring: How it Begins. *Thrive Global*. https://community.thriveglobal.com/mentoring-how-it-begins/

Gladwell, M. (2008). *Outliers: Why some people succeed and some don't*. Little Brown & Co.

Goplen, J., & Plant, E. A. (2015). A Religious Worldview. *Personality and Social Psychology Bulletin*, 41(11), 1474–1487. doi: 10.1177/0146167215599761

Guinee, K., Eagleton, M. B., & Hall, T. E. (2003). Adolescents' internet search strategies: Drawing upon familiar cognitive paradigms when accessing electronic information sources. *Journal of Educational Computing Research*, 29(3), 363–374.

Gunnell, K. E., Mosewich, A. D., McEwen, C. E., Eklund, R. C., & Crocker, P. R. E. (2017). Don't be so hard on yourself! Changes in self-compassion during the first year of university are associated with changes in well-being. *Personality and Individual Differences*, 107, 43–48. https://doi.org/10.1016/j.paid.2016.11.032

Hall, J. A., & Gunnery, S. D. (2013). Gender differences in nonverbal communication. In J. A. Hall & M. L. Knapp (Eds.), *Nonverbal communication* (639–669). De Gruyter Mouton. https://doi.org/10.1515/9783110238150.639

Hall-Ellis, S. D. (2016). Stackable micro-credentials – a framework for the future. *The Bottom Line: Managing Library Finances*, 29(4), 233–236. https://do1.org/10.1108/BL-02-2016-0006.

Hargittai, E. (2003). The digital divide and what to do about it. In D. C. Jones (ed.). *New economy handbook*, pp. 822–841. Academic Press.

Holmes, J. G., & Murray, S. L. (1996). Conflict in close relationships. In E. T. Higgins & A. W. Kruglanski (Eds.), *Social psychology: Handbook of basic principles* (622–654). Guilford Press.

Huff, C. (2022). A crisis of campus sexual assault. *Monitor on Psychology*, 53(3), p. 26.

Husmann, P. R., & O'Loughlin, V. D. (2019). Another nail in the coffin for learning styles? Disparities among undergraduate anatomy students' study strategies, class performance, and reported VARK learning styles. *Anatomical Sciences Education*, 12(1), 6–19. https://doi.org/10.1002/ase.1777

Hyatt, M. (2012). Platform: Get noticed in a noisy world. *Thomas Nelson*. p. 129

Jenkins, R. (2014). *Social identity*. New York: Routledge.

Johnson, N. L., Lipp, N. S., & Stone, H. K. (2023). Initial evaluation of a gender-inclusive version of the Illinois Rape Myth Acceptance Scale. *Psychology of Sexual Orientation and Gender Diversity*, 10(2), 206–216. https://doi.org/10.1037/sgd0000536

Kato, T. (2014). Development of the Sleep Quality Questionnaire in healthy adults. *Journal of Health Psychology*, 19(8), 977–986. https://doi.org/10.1177/1359105313482168

Killingsworth, M. A., Kahneman, D., & Mellers, B. (2023). Income and emotional well-being: A conflict resolved. *Proceedings of the National Academy of Sciences of the United States of America*, 120(10), e2208661120. https://doi.org/10.1073/pnas.2208661120

Kivlichan, A. E., Lowe, D. J. E., & George, T. P. (2022, May 25). Substance misuse in college students. *Psychiatric Times*, 39(5).

Koenig, F. (1979). Future orientation and external locus of control. *Psychological Reports*, 44(3), 957–958. https://doi.org/10.2466/pr0.1979.44.3.957

Krieger, H., Young, C. M., Anthenien, A. M., & Neighbors, C. (2018). The epidemiology of binge drinking among college-age individuals in the United States. *Alcohol Research: Current Reviews*, 39(1), 23–30.

LaMagna, M. (2017). Placing digital badges and microcredentials in context. *Journal of Electronic Resources Librarianship*, 29(4), 206–210. DOI: 10.1080/1941126X.2017.1378538

Levenson, R. W., & Gottman, J. M. (1983). Marital interaction: Physiological linkage and affective exchange. *Journal of Personality and Social Psychology*, 45(3), 587–597. https://doi.org/10.1037/0022-3514.45.3.587

Lewandowsky, S., Ecker, U. K. H., Seifert, C. S., Schwarz, N., & and Cook, J. (2012). Misinformation and its correction: Continued influence and successful debiasing." *Psychological Science in the Public Interest*, 13(3): 106–31. https://doi.org/10.1177/1529100612451018

MacCann, C., Jiang, Y., Brown, L. E. R., Double, K. S., Bucich, M., & Minbashian, A. (2020). Emotional intelligence predicts academic performance: A meta-analysis. *Psychological Bulletin*, 146(2), 150–186. https://doi.org/10.1037/bul0000219

Maddock, J. E., Laforge, R. G., Rossi, J. S., & O'Hare, T. (2001). The College Alcohol Problems Scale. *Addictive Behaviors*, *26*(3), 385–398. https://doi.org/10.1016/s0306-4603(00)00116-7

Martela, F., & Steger, M. F. (2016) The three meanings of meaning in life: Distinguishing coherence, purpose, and significance, *The Journal of Positive Psychology*, *11*(5), 531–545. DOI: 10.1080/17439760.2015.1137623

Mitra, S. (2012, February 3). *The Hole in the Wall Project and the power of self-organized learning*. Edutopia. https://www.edutopia.org/blog/self-organized-learning-sugata-mitra

Nancekivell, S. E., Shah, P., & Gelman, S. A. (2020). Maybe they're born with it, or maybe it's experience: Toward a deeper understanding of the learning style myth. *Journal of Educational Psychology*, *112*(2), 221–235. https://doi.org/10.1037/edu0000366

National Association of Colleges and Employers (October 2022). *Job Outlook 2023*. https://wwwcdn.ithaca.edu/file-download/download/public/63317

Neff, K. D. (2003). The development and validation of a scale to measure self-compassion. *Self and Identity*, *2*(3), 223–250. https://doi.org/10.1080/15298860309027

Neff, K. D., Hsieh, Y.-P., & Dejitterat, K. (2005). Self-compassion, achievement goals, and coping with academic failure. *Self and Identity*, *4*(3), 263–287. https://doi.org/10.1080/13576500444000317

Nevid, J. S. (2013). *An introduction to psychology*. Wadsworth, Cengage Learning.

Overall, N. C., & McNulty, J. K. (2017). What type of communication during conflict is beneficial for intimate relationships? *Current Opinion in Psychology*, *13*, 1–5. https://doi.org/10.1016/j.copsyc.2016.03.002

Pashler, H., McDaniel, M., Rohrer, D., & Bjork, R. (2008). Learning styles: Concepts and evidence. *Psychological Science in the Public Interest*, *9*(3), 105–119.

Petrone, P. (2019). The Skills Companies Need Most in 2019 – And How to Learn Them. https://learning.linkedin.com/blog/top-skills/the-skills-companies-need-most-in-2019—and-how-to-learn-them

Pew Research Center (2017). Support for Same-Sex Marriage Grows, Even Among Groups That Had Been Skeptical. Retrieved from https://www.pewresearch.org/politics/2017/06/26/support-for-same-sex-marriage-grows-even-among-groups-that-had-been-skeptical/

Pew Research Center (2023). 5 key findings about LGBTQ+ Americans. Retrieved from https://www.pewresearch.org/short-reads/2023/06/23/5-key-findings-about-lgbtq-americans/#:~:text=Some%207%25%20of%20Americans%20are,of%20those%2065%20and%20older.

Pittenger, D. J. (1993). The utility of the Myers-Briggs Type Indicator. *Review of Educational Research*, *63*(4), 467–488. https://doi.org/10.2307/1170497

Popomaronis, T. (2018, January 31). 3 Unforgettable life lessons learned from the iconic IKEA founder. https://www.inc.com/tom-popomaronis/3-unforgettable-life-lessons-learned-from-iconic-ikea-founder.html

Prather, A. A., Janicki-Deverts, D., Hall, M. H., & Cohen, S. (2015). Behaviorally assessed sleep and susceptibility to the common cold. *Sleep*, *38*(9), 1353–1359. https://doi.org/10.5665/sleep.4968

Prensky, M. (2001). Digital natives, Digital immigrants Part 2: Do they really think differently? *On the Horizon*, *9*(6): 1–6. doi: 10.1108/10748120110424843

Prentice, D. A., & Miller, D. T. (1993). Pluralistic ignorance and alcohol use on campus: Some consequences of misperceiving the social norm. *Journal of Personality and Social Psychology*, *64*(2), 243–256. https://doi.org/10.1037/0022-3514.64.2.243

R.Snyder & S. J.Lopez (Eds.), *Handbook of positive psychology* (p. 3–9). Oxford University Press.

Reiners, B. (2023, March 28). 50 diversity in the workplace statistics to know. *Built In*. https://builtin.com/diversity-inclusion/diversity-in-the-workplace-statistics

Rubin, B. J. (Director). (1993). *My Life* [Motion picture]. Columbia Pictures.

Rusbult, C. E., Martz, J. M., & Agnew, C. R. (1998). The Investment Model Scale: Measuring commitment level, satisfaction level, quality of alternatives, and investment size. *Personal Relationships*, *5*(4), 357–391. https://doi.org/10.1111/j.1475-6811.1998.tb00177.x

Russell, D., Peplau, L. A., & Cutrona, C. E. (1980). The revised UCLA Loneliness Scale: Concurrent and discriminant validity evidence. *Journal of Personality and Social Psychology*, *39*(3), 472–480. https://doi.org/10.1037/0022-3514.39.3.472

Russell, D. W. (1996). UCLA Loneliness Scale (Version 3): Reliability, validity, and factor structure. *Journal of Personality Assessment*, *66*(1), 20–40. https://doi.org/10.1207/s15327752jpa6601_2

Scheier, M. F., Carver, C. S., & Bridges, M. W. (1994). Distinguishing optimism from neuroticism (and trait anxiety, self-mastery, and self-esteem): A reevaluation of the Life Orientration Test. *Journal of Personality and Social Psychology*, *67*, 1063–1078. http://dx.doi.org/10.1037/0022-3514.67.6.1063

Schleider, J. L., & Weisz, J. R. (2016). Reducing risk for anxiety and depression in adolescents: Effects of a single-session intervention teaching that personality can change. *Behaviour Research and Therapy*, *87*, 170–181. https://doi.org/10.1016/j.brat.2016.09.011

Schutte, N. S., Malouff, J. M., Hall, L. E., Haggerty, D. J., Cooper, J. T., Golden, C. J., & Dornheim, L. (1998). Development and validation of a measure of emotional intelligence. *Personality and Individual Differences*, *25*(2), 167–177. https://doi.org/10.1016/S0191-8869(98)00001-4

Schwarzer, R., & Jerusalem, M. (1995). General Self-Efficacy Scale. In J. Weinman, S. Wright, & M. Johnston, *Measures in health psychology: A user's portfolio. Causal and control beliefs* (35–37). NFER-NELSON.

Seery, M. D., Holman, E. A., & Silver, R. C. (2010). Whatever does not kill us: Cumulative lifetime adversity, vulnerability, and resilience. *Journal of Personality and Social Psychology*, *99*(6), 1025–1041. https://doi.org/10.1037/a0021344

Seligman, M. E. P. (2002). Positive psychology, positive prevention, and positive therapy. In C.

Smith, B. W., Dalen, J., Wiggins, K., Tooley, E., Christopher, P., & Bernard, J. (2008). The brief resilience scale: Assessing the ability to bounce back. *International Journal of Behavioral Medicine*, *15*(3), 194–200. https://doi.org/10.1080/10705500802222972

Steger, M. F., Frazier, P., Oishi, S., & Kaler, M. (2006). The meaning in life questionnaire: Assessing the presence of and search for meaning in life. *Journal of Counseling Psychology*, *53*, 80–93.

Stone, A. A., Schwartz, J. E., Broderick, J. E., & Deaton, A. (2010). A snapshot of the age distribution of psychological well-being in the United States. *Proceedings of the National Academy of Sciences of the United States of America*, *107*(22), 9985–9990. https://doi.org/10.1073/pnas.1003744107

Strauss, W., & Howe, N. (1991). *Generations: The history of Americas future, 1584 to 2069*. William Morrow & Company, Inc.

Sue, D. W. (2010). Racial microaggressions in everyday life. *Psychology Today*. https://www.psychologytoday.com/us/blog/microaggressions-in-everyday-life/201010/racial-microaggressions-in-everyday-life

Tedeschi, R. G., & Calhoun, L. G. (1996). The Posttraumatic Growth Inventory: Measuring the positive legacy of trauma. *Journal of Traumatic Stress, 9*(3), 455–472. https://doi.org/10.1002/jts.2490090305

Tice, D. M., & Baumeister, R. F. (1997). Longitudinal study of procrastination, performance, stress, and health: The costs and benefits of dawdling. *Psychological Science, 8*(6), 454–458. https://doi.org/10.1111/j.1467-9280.1997.tb00460.x

Tsinakos, A. A., & Balafoutis, T. (2009). A comparative study on mind mapping tools. *Turkish Online Journal of Distance Education, 10*(3), 55–72.

Tugade, M. M., & Fredrickson, B. L. (2004). Resilient individuals use positive emotions to bounce back from negative emotional experiences. *Journal of Personality and Social Psychology, 86*(2), 320–333. https://doi.org/10.1037/0022-3514.86.2.320

U.S. Census Bureau. (2019, December 11). American Community Survey (ACS). Retrieved from https://www.census.gov/programs-surveys/acs/

United Nations, Department of Public Information. (1995). *World Summit for Social Development: the Copenhagen Declaration and Programme of Action, 6–12 March 1995*. New York, NY.

University of London, Centre for Higher Education Research and Scholarship. (n.d.). Educational self-efficacy scale. Imperial College London. https://www.imperial.ac.uk/education-research/evaluation/what-can-i-evaluate/self-efficacy/tools-for-assessing-self-efficacy/educational-self-efficacy-scale/

van Zyl, L. E., Klibert, J., Shankland, R., See-To, E. W., & Rothmann, S. (2022). The general academic self-efficacy scale: Psychometric properties, longitudinal invariance, and criterion validity. *Journal of Psychoeducational Assessment, 40*(6), 777–789. https://doi.org/10.1177/07342829221097174

Wathen, C. N., & Burkell, J. (2002). Believe it or not: Factors influencing credibility on the web. *Journal of the American Society for Information Science and Technology, 53*(2):134–144. DOI: 10.1002/asi.10016

Wilsnack, R. W., Wilsnack, S. C., Gmel, G., & Kantor, L. W. (2018). Gender differences in binge drinking: Prevalence, predictors, and consequences. *Alcohol Research: Current Reviews, 39*(1), 57–76.

Winerman, L. (2018). Making campuses safer. *APA Monitor, 49*(9), 45. https://www.apa.org/monitor/2018/10/campuses-safer

Wright, A. (2014). *Cataloging the world: Paul Otlet and the birth of the information age*. Oxford University Press.

Yeager, D. S., Johnson, R., Spitzer, B. J., Trzesniewski, K. H., Powers, J., & Dweck, C. S. (2014). The far-reaching effects of believing people can change: Implicit theories of personality shape stress, health, and achievement during adolescence. *Journal of Personality and Social Psychology, 106*(6), 867–884. https://doi.org/10.1037/a0036335

Subject Index

Note: Page numbers in *italics* indicate a figure and page numbers in **bold** indicate a table on the corresponding page.

A

ability, 196–199
   comparison, 197
   improvement, 198–199
absolute poverty, 210
abstinence, 71
academic advisors, 39
academic and educational organizations, 180–181
academic databases, 155
academic major, 29
academic minor, 29
academic resources, 38–40
   academic and student advising, 39
   academic support, 39–40
   tutoring resources, 39–40
   writing centers, 40
academic stress, 233
academic support, 39–40
action zone, 44
active listening, 90–91, *90*
active *vs.* reflective learners, 109
actual number of sex partners *vs.* perceived number of sex partners, *71*
addiction, 68
Advanced Management Journal (article), 181
advanced placement credits, 32
adversity, 137
affective perspective, 5
age, 199–201, 231
aggressive communication, 91
alcohol, 63–65
   abuse, risk for, 64
   and academic performance, *64*
   effects of, 65
   peer pressure, 70
   poisoning, 65, *66*
   usage, 64
Alison.com, 152
Alison courses, 153
AM Chicago (TV program), 126
American Business Law Journal, 166
American College Health Association, 236
American Community Survey, 202
American Psychological Association, 138
ancestral roots, *201*
anorexia nervosa, 58
assertive communication, 91–92
Association for Talent Development, 180
attitudes, 194
awareness, 195

B

balance, 16–19
balanced diet, 55
   recommendations, **55**
Baloney Detection Kit, 160
behavior
   acts of kindness, performing, 245
   close relationships, 245
   time with positive people, spending, 245–246
belief, 11–15
biases, 214

binge drinking, 65
binge eating disorder, 58
birth control pills, 71
bisexuality, 207–208
bodily-kinesthetic intelligence, 113
bulimia nervosa, 58
Bureau of Labor Statistics, 177

C

campus-and course-based resources
   campus library, 155, 157
   course-based resources, 157
   learning management system (LMS), 155
   password-protected web portals, 154–155
campus clubs, 180–181
campus internet resources, 154
campus library, 155, 157
career services, 41
Cataloguing the World: Paul Otlet and the Birth of the Information Age (book), 148
cervical cap, 72
chat tools, 155
chlamydia, **73**
chronological age. *See* age
classical conditioning, 105
CLEP. *See* College Level Exam Program (CLEP)
CliftonStrengths assessment, 197
cognitive performance, 236
cognitive perspective, 5
collaborative research, 185
college catalogs, 28–29
college credits, 31–35
   advanced placement credits, 32
   College Level Exam Program (CLEP), 34
   dual credits, 32
   micro-credentials, 34
   prior life experience credits, 32
   transfer credit hours, 34–35
college graduates, 210
   graduate schools, expectation from, 179
   skills, expected by employers, 177–178
College Level Exam Program (CLEP), 34
colleges, 27–28
   causes of stress, 233–234
   daily routines, for success, 44–45
   departments, 28
   faculty, 28
   schools, 28
commencement, 176
communication, 87–88. *See also* effective communication
   challenges, 89–90
   cultural differences, 89
   elements, *88*
   nonverbal, 88
   online communication, 89–90
   strategies, 90–93
   verbal, 88
communication styles, 91–92, *91*
   aggressive communication, 91
   assertive communication, 91–92

   passive-aggressive communication, 91
   passive communication, 91
community colleges, 27
community service organizations, 181
comparisons, avoiding, 244–245
complementary proteins pair, 57
condoms, 72
conflict, 93
   benefits, 94
   causes, 93–94
   management, 95
   resolving skills, 96–98
conflict resolving skills
   cause, identifying, 96–97
   with friend, 97
   solutions identification, 97–98
   solutions requesting from parties, 97
coping, 137
   emotion-focused, 238–239, *238*
   problem-focused, 238, *238*
counseling center, 41
course-based portfolio, *33*
course-based resources, 157
Crap Detection and Other Essential Network Skills, 160
Crap-Detection Mini-Course, 160
credibility, of internet content, 160
credit hour, 31–32
Crouching Tiger, Hidden Dragon (movie), 4
cultural competence self-assessment, 220–221
cultural differences, 230, 231
cultures, 89

D

date rape, 74
   drugs, 75
deep breathing, 239
degree requirements, 28–31
   academic major, 29
   academic minor, 29
   college catalogs, 28–29
   elective courses, 31
   general education, 30–31
deliberate practice, 198, 199
Delivering Happiness: A Path to Profits, Passion and Purpose (book), 228
desire, 11–15
details, attending to, 47
diaphragm, 72
Dietary Guidelines for Americans, 55
difficult life events
   benefits, 232
   responding to, 138
digital badges, 34
digital content curation, 157, 163
   search, 158–159
   select, 159–160
   share, 162
   specify, 157–158
   steward, 162–163
   survey, 158
   synthesize, 161–162

SI-1

SI-2 SUBJECT INDEX

digital divide, 152
digital footprint, 164, 166
   identity on social media, 165–166
   long-term impact, 164–165
   safety, 165
   security, 165
digital immigrant, 150
digital native, 150
digital technology
   in daily lives, 149–153
   digital footprint, 164–167
   in higher education, 154–163
digital tools and resources, 149
digital well-being, 164
discrimination, 217–218
disinformation, 159–160
diversity, 93, 194, 219
   discrimination, 217–218
   microaggressions, 215–216
   oppression, 218–219
   prejudice, 216–217
   self-assessment, 220–221
dot-com formula, 158
driving under the influence (DUI), 65
drug addiction, 68–70
   strategies to support people, 70
   substance use, 69
drugs, 67–68
   overdoses, 68, *68*
   types, *67*
dual credit courses, 32
DUI. *See* driving under the influence (DUI)
Dupli Checker program, 161

E

Eat Drink Man Woman (movie), 4
eating disorder, 58–59
effective communication, 88, 90–93
   active listening, 90–91, *90*
   diversity, valuing, 93
   I-statements usage, 92
   needs and preferences, communicating, 91
   nonverbal communication, 92–93
   pay attention, 90
   respect other people, 93
EI. *See* emotional intelligence (EI)
elective courses, 28, 31
emergency contraceptive pills, 72
emotional intelligence (EI), 126, 128
   advantages, 143
   components, 126–128, *127*
   empathy, 127, 128–129
   internal motivation, 127
   self-awareness, 127
   self-regulation, 127
   social skills, 127
   strategies, 130
emotional states, 12, 127
emotion-focused coping, 238–239
emotions management, 130
empathy, 127, 129, 130
   definition, 128
   role of, 128–129
employability quotient, 179–185
employers
   internships, 181
   skills, expected from college graduates, 177–178
   valuing, skills, 178
employment, in twenty-first century, 177

encouragement, 16
equity, 195
ER (television program), 30
ethnicity, 201–202
eulogy virtues, 18, 20
exercise, 59–60, 62
   benefits, *59*
   strategies, 59–60
externships, 181–182
extrinsic motivation, 15

F

Facebook, 148, 164
   gender options, 203
faculty and students, collaborative research, 185
family relationships, 85
fertility awareness, 72
fight-or-flight response, 234–235
financial aid, 37
fixed mindset, 117, 118, 120
flow, state of, 8, 229
Flow: The Psychology of Optimal Experience (book), 8
focus, 16–19
   future, 16
   live in moment, 16–17
   past, 16
Forbes (publication), 165, 178
freshman fifteen, 56
friendships, 84

G

gay, 208
gender, 202–204
   options, 203, 204
   pronoun(s), 203
general education, 30–31
   courses, 28
   definition, 30
   fields of study, *31*
generations, 201
   characteristics and differences, *200*
Generations (book), 199
genital herpes, **73**
genital warts, **73**
Georgetown University Center on Education and the Workforce, 182
Get Rich or Die Tryin (album), 176
goals
   achievement, 134
   learning, 119–120
   and mindsets, 119
   performance, 119
gonorrhea, **73**
good life, 4–5
   meaning in life, 5
   meaning of life, 5
GPA. *See* grade point average (GPA)
grade point average (GPA), 35
graduate schools, 186
   expectations, from college graduates, 179
gratitude, 244
grit, 131, 134
   components, 132–133, *132*
   examples, *132*
   strategies, 134–135
   success prediction, 133–134
growth mindset, 117, 118, 135
   advantages, 118–119

   developing, steps for, 120
   vs. fixed mindset, *117*

H

happiness, 228
   benefits, 228–229
   components, 229–230
   cultural differences, 230, 231
   myths, 231–232
   predicting, factors of, 242
have-nots group, 210
haves group, 210
health center, 40
healthy behaviors, 54–63
   components, 54–59
   exercise, 59–60
   healthy foods importance, 55
   sleep, 60–63
healthy diet, 55
healthy food options, strategies for, 56–58
hepatitis A, **73**
hepatitis B, **73**
heterosexuality, 207
higher education, 27–36, 46
   college credits, 31–35
   colleges, 27–28
   degree requirements, 28–31
   grade point average (GPA), 31–35
   universities, 27–28
Hispanic, 202, 205
HIV/AIDS, **73**
Hole in the Wall, 153
homosexuality, 207

I

IBM, 34
identities, 196
   ability, 196–199
   age, 199–201
   ethnicity, 201–202
   gender, 202–204
   impacts of, 211–215
   privileged identities, 212
   race, 204–205
   religion, 205–207
   sexual orientation, 207–209
   socioeconomic status, 209–211
   stereotypes, 213–214
   targeted identities, 213–214
   types, 211–215
IKEA, 24
ikigai, 7–10, 230
   aspects, 8
   elements, 7–8, *7*
   mission, 9
   passion, 8–9
   profession, 9–10
   vocation, 10–11
Ikigai: The Japanese Secret to a Long and Happy Life (book), 7
ILS. *See* Index of Learning Styles (ILS) model
imagery, 239
imaginal experiences, 12
implant, 72
Inc. (magazine), 24
inclusion, 195
Index of Learning Styles (ILS) model, *109*
injection, 72
Institut International de Bibliographie, 148
intelligence, *113*

bodily-kinesthetic, 113
interpersonal, 114
intrapersonal, 114
linguistic-verbal, 113
logical-mathematical, 113
musical, 113
naturalistic, 114
strengths, 114–115
visual-spatial, 113
intense emotions, 230
intense feelings, 97, 236
internal motivation, 127, 130
internal pressure, 234
internet access, around world, 152, **152**
internships, 181–182
interpersonal conflicts, 93, 94
interpersonal intelligence, 114
intersectionality, 211–212
intersex, 203
intrapersonal intelligence, 114
intrauterine device (IUD), 72
intrinsic motivation, 15
island of Okinawa, 7
I-statements, 92
IUD. *See* intrauterine device (IUD)

J
Jurassic Park (novel), 30

L
Latino/Latina, 202
Latinx, 202
Law School Admission Test (LSAT), 203
learning goals, 119, 120
learning in high school *vs.* learning in college, 43
learning management system (LMS), 155
learning models, 104
  classical conditioning, 105
  observational learning, 106
  operant conditioning, 105
Learning Style Inventory (LSI), 106, *107*
learning styles, 106–112
  evaluation of models, 108–111
  matching, to material, 112
  models, 106–107
  visual models, 111–112
lesbian, 208
Lesbian, Gay, Bisexual, Transgender, Queer (LGBTQ), 208
liberal arts colleges, 27
library resources, 38
life circumstances, 232
life map, 25–26
Life of Pi, The (movie), 4
linguistic-verbal intelligence, 113
LinkedIn, 149, 187
  as networking tool, 187–188
  profile, creating, 187–188
LMS. *See* learning management system (LMS)
logical-mathematical intelligence, 113
loneliness, 85, 86
long-distance relationships, strategies for, 85
LSAT. *See* Law School Admission Test (LSAT)
LSI. *See* Learning Style Inventory (LSI)
lykke, 230

M
magic ratio of five to one, 94
major depression, 236–237

marketing plan, 186
marriage, 231
massive open online courses (MOOCs), 34
mastery experiences, 12
material resources, 37–38
  financial aid, 37
  library resources, 38
  online resources on school's website, 38
meaning in life, 4–7, 19
  affective perspective, 5
  cognitive perspective, 5
  motivational perspective, 5
  visualization, 7–10
Meaning in Life Questionnaire (MLQ), 6
  presence score, 6
  results interpretation, 6
  search score, 6
meaning of life, 5
media and publication organizations, 181
meditation, 240
mental and emotional health, 236
  major depression, 236–237
  suicide, 236–237
Mental Floss (website), 165
mentor, 182–184
microaggressions, 215–216
  ethnicity, 216
  gender, 216
  racial, 216
  sexual orientation, 216
micro-credentials, 34
mindful eating, 57
mindfulness, 240
mind map, 161
  creation process, 161
mindsets, 116–121
  fixed mindset, 117
  and goals, 119
  growth mindset, 117
  shifting to growth mindset, 120
  types, 117–118
Minnesota Multiphasic Personality Inventory (MMPI), 107
misinformation, 159–160
mission, 9, 182
MLQ. *See* Meaning in Life Questionnaire (MLQ)
MMPI. *See* Minnesota Multiphasic Personality Inventory (MMPI)
MOOCs. *See* Massive open online courses (MOOCs)
motivation, 11–15, 131
  definition, 15
  elements, 15
  extrinsic motivation, 15
  intrinsic motivation, 15
motivational perspective, 5
multiple identities, 195–211
multiple intelligences, 112–116
musical intelligence, 113
Myers-Briggs test, 107
Myers-Briggs Type Indicator, 107, *108*
My Life (movie), 18
MyPlate, 56
myths, about happiness
  age, 231
  life circumstances, 232
  marriage/romantic partner, 231

N
naïve practice, 198
napping, 62
National Association of Colleges and Employers, 177
National Basketball Association (NBA), 54
National Center for Educational Statistics, 27, 177
nationality, 202
natural family planning, 72
naturalistic intelligence, 114
NBA. *See* National Basketball Association (NBA)
need of the world, 9
negative emotions, 236
negative event, 137
negative interactions, 94
negative self-talk, 243
negative thought cycles, 242
negotiation, 96
networking, 187
  LinkedIn profile as, 187–188
non-binary, 203, 204
nonverbal communication, 88, 92–93

O
observational learning, 106
on- and off-campus activities, 179–180
  campus clubs and organizations, participating, 180–181
  externships, 181–182
  internships, 181–182
  mentor, 182–184
  semester abroad, 180
  volunteering, 182
online communication, 89–90
online resources, on school's website, 38
operant conditioning, 105
opportunities
  to build employability quotient, 179–185
  to build skills, 179–185
  internships, 181
oppression, 218–219
Oprah Winfrey Show, The (TV program), 126
optimistic, 242
Outliers (book), 198
overall poverty, 210

P
passions, 8, 130, 132
passive-aggressive communication, 91
passive communication, 91
password-protected web portals, 154–155
patch, 72
pattern of thinking, 5
performance goals, 119
perseverance, 132, 133
personal relationships, 233
Pew Research Center, 202, 206
physical health, 234–235
physiological arousal, health consequences of, *235*
physiological state, 12
plagiarism, 161
Plagiarisma program, 161
political and multicultural organizations, 181
poor time management, 233
portfolio-based credit, 32, *33*
positive interactions, 94
positive mindset, 243

positive psychology, 197
post-traumatic growth, 232
   benefits, *138*
post-traumatic stress disorder (PTSD), 75, 237
power skills, 178
practice levels
   deliberate practice, 199
   naïve practice, 198
   purposeful practice, 198–199
prejudice, 216–217
   ability, 217
   age, 217
   ethnicity, 217
   gender, 217
   race, 217
   sexual orientation, 217
   socioeconomic status, 217
Presence: Bringing Your Boldest Self to Your Biggest Challenges (book), 104
Princeton University, 203
prior life experience credits, 32
privileged identities, 212
problem-focused coping, 238
profession, 9–10
progressive muscle relaxation, 239
Psychology Today (article), 216
PTSD. *See* post-traumatic stress disorder (PTSD)
purging, 58
purpose, 230
purposeful practice, 198–199

Q
queer, 208

R
race, 202, 204–205
   categories, 204
Range: Why Generalists Triumph in a Specialized World (book), 30
readiness, examples of, 185
recreation and sports organizations, 181
relationships
   building, 85–87
   communication, 87–93
   conflict management, 93–98
   extracurricular activities, participating in, 86–87
   maintaining, 82–87
   management, 82–85
   new people, meeting, 86
   shared activity, 87
   time in common spaces, spending, 86
religion, 205–207
religious and spiritual organizations, 181
religious resources, 41
resilience, 136, 137
   adversity, role of, 137
   change, acceptance, 139
   characteristics, 136
   crises, reframing, 139
   decisive actions, 140
   optimistic outlook, 141
   relationships development, 138–139
   self-compassion, 140–141
   self-discovery, 140
   strategies, 138–142, *142*
   taking care of yourself, 141
   value of, 136
   working toward goals, 139
response to failure, 119
résumé, 188
   key factors, 189
   template, 189
   virtues, 18, 20
ring, 72
Road to Character, The (book), 18
romantic partners, 84–85, 231
roommates, 83
   contract, *83*
   relationship strategies, 83–84

S
same-sex marriage, 208
search, 158–159
second-level digital divide, 153
select, 159–160
self-awareness, 127, 130
self-compassion, 140–141
self-discovery, 140
self-efficacy, 11–14
   activities consideration, 14
   assessment, 13
   definition, 11
   emotional and physiological states, 12
   evidence, 12
   imaginal experiences, 12
   mastery experiences, 12
   social persuasion, 12
   vicarious experiences, 12
self-regulation, 127
self-talk, 243
semester abroad, 180
   benefits, 180
Sense and Sensibility (movie), 4
sensing *vs.* intuitive learners, 109
sequential *vs.* global learners, 109
sex, 203
sextortion, 74
sexual assault, 74–76
   consequences, 75
   preventing, strategies for, 75–76
   treating, strategies for, 75–76
sexual decisions, 74
sexual health management, 71–76
   abstinence, 71
   sexual assault, 74–76
   sexually transmitted infections (STIs), 72–73, *73*
   unwanted pregnancy prevention, 71–72
sexually transmitted infections (STIs), 72–73, *73*
sexual orientation, 203, 207–209
share, 162
shopping mall approach, 158
skills, 149. *See also* soft skills
   building, opportunities for, 179–185
   employers, valuing, 178
   marketing, opportunities for, 185–189
   for resolving conflicts, 96–98
sleep, 60–63
   deprivation, 54, 61, *61*
   poor sleep consequences, 62
   strategies, 62–63
sleep–wake schedule, 62
social media, 165
   audit, 167
   identity protection, 165–166
social persuasion, 12
social responsibility, 130
social skills, 127
socioeconomic status, 209–211
soft skills, 178
specify, 157–158
spiritual resources, 41
state of flow, 8
stereotypes, 213
   ability, 213
   age, 213
   ethnicity, 213
   gender, 213
   race, 213
   religion, 214
   sexual orientation, 214
   socioeconomic status, 214
steward, 162–163
stimulants, 62
Stories for Getting Back to Sleep (book), 183, 184
strengths, 197–198
stress, 233
   benefits, 237
   cognitive performance, 236
   effects of, 234–237
   managing, strategies for, 237–241
   mental and emotional health, 236–237
   physical health, 234–235
   sources, 233–234
   types, 233–234
stress management, 237–238
   changing thoughts about stress, 238–239
   exercise, 240
   professional help, obtaining, 241
   reducing or avoiding stress, 238
   relaxing, 239–240
   taking care of yourself, 241
   time in nature, spending, 240
stressors, 233
student government organizations, 181
subscription services, 155
substance abuse, 63–70
substance use, 69
suicide, 236–237
survey, 158
synthesize, 161–162

T
targeted identities, 213–214
technical skills, 156
technology, 149–151, 234
   engagement, 152
   in higher education, 154–163
technophile, 150, 151
technophobe, 150, 151
technostress, 234
TED Talk, 194
thinking, pattern of, 5
Three Circles test, 17
Thrive Global, 182, 183
time management, 238
tobacco, 66
tolerance, 69
transfer credit hours, 34–35
transgender, 203, 208
   identity, 194
transsexual, 203

tutoring resources, 39–40
T-zone of learning, 44, *44*

U

unique stories, 24–26, 46
   personal characteristics, 24
United Nations Educational, Scientific and Cultural Organization (UNESCO), 30
United States Census Bureau, 201–202, 204
universities, 27–28
   departments, 28
   faculty, 28
   schools, 28
University of Washington Bothell (UWB), 183

unwanted pregnancy prevention, 71–72
UWB. *See* University of Washington Bothell (UWB)

V

VARK model, 106, *106*
verbal communication, 88
vicarious experiences, 12
Viper program, 161
Virgin Spring, The (movie), 4
visualization, 239
visual-spatial intelligence, 113
visual *vs.* verbal learners, 109
vocation, 10–11
volunteering, 182

W

Wedding Banquet, The (movie), 4
well-being resources, 40–41
   career services, 41
   counseling center, 41
   health center, 40
   religious resources, 41
   spiritual resources, 41
West Point Military Academy, 133
withdrawal, 69, 72
writing centers, 40

Y

yoga, 239